Instructor's Resource Manual

for

Siegel's

Criminology

Ninth Edition

Janet K. Wilson
University of Central Arkansas

THOMSON

WADSWORTH

Australia • Canada • Mexico • Singapore • Spain • United Kingdom • United States

Printed in the United States of America
1 2 3 4 5 6 7   09 08 07 06 05

Printer: Thomson West

ISBN 0-495-00096-5

For more information about our products, contact us at:
Thomson Learning Academic Resource Center
1-800-423-0563

For permission to use material from this text or product, submit a request online at
http://www.thomsonrights.com.
Any additional questions about permissions can be submitted by email to **thomsonrights@thomson.com.**

Thomson Higher Education
10 Davis Drive
Belmont, CA 94002-3098
USA

Asia (including India)
Thomson Learning
5 Shenton Way
#01-01 UIC Building
Singapore 068808

Australia/New Zealand
Thomson Learning Australia
102 Dodds Street
Southbank, Victoria 3006
Australia

Canada
Thomson Nelson
1120 Birchmount Road
Toronto, Ontario M1K 5G4
Canada

UK/Europe/Middle East/Africa
Thomson Learning
High Holborn House
50–51 Bedford Road
London WC1R 4LR
United Kingdom

Latin America
Thomson Learning
Seneca, 53
Colonia Polanco
11560 Mexico
D.F. Mexico

Spain (including Portugal)
Thomson Paraninfo
Calle Magallanes, 25
28015 Madrid, Spain

TABLE OF CONTENTS

Chapter One

Crime, Criminology, and the Criminal Law

Summary

Chapter One provides an overview of criminology. The development of the field is traced from its conception to today. Various sub-areas of criminology are presented with a discussion of the three perspectives of crime. A distinction is made between common law and contemporary criminal law. The chapter concludes by presenting a number of ethical issues in criminology.

Chapter Objectives

After reading this chapter students should be able to:

- Understand what is meant by the field of criminology
- Know the historical context of criminology
- Recognize the differences among the various schools of criminological thought
- Be familiar with the various elements of the criminological enterprise
- Be able to discuss how criminologists define crime
- Recognize the concepts of criminal law
- Know the difference between evil acts and evil intent
- Describe the various defenses to crime
- Show how the criminal law is undergoing change
- Be able to discuss ethical issues in criminology

Chapter Overview

Introduction
What Is Criminology?
      Criminology and Criminal Justice
      Criminology and Deviance
A Brief History of Criminology
      Classical Criminology
      Nineteenth-Century Positivism
      Foundations of Sociological Criminology
      The Chicago School and Beyond
      Conflict Criminology
      Contemporary Criminology

What Criminologists Do: The Criminological Enterprise
>Criminal Statistics
>Sociology of Law
>The Nature of Theory and Theory Development
>Criminal Behavior Systems
>Penology
>Victimology

How Criminologists View Crime
>The Consensus View of Crime
>The Conflict View of Crime
>The Interactionist View of Crime
>Defining Crime

Crime and the Criminal Law
>Common Law
>Contemporary Criminal Law

The Criminological Enterprise: The Elements of Criminal Law
>The Evolution of Criminal Law

Ethical Issues in Criminology
Summary

<u>Chapter Outline</u>

I. Introduction
>A. Concern about crime led to the development of criminology as an academic discipline.
>B. Criminologists use scientific methods to study the nature, extent, cause, and control of criminal behavior.

II. What is Criminology?
>A. Criminology is the scientific approach to studying criminal behavior.
>>1. Sutherland and Cressey define the important areas of interest to criminologists:
>>>a. the development of criminal law and its use to define crime.
>>>b. the cause of law violation.
>>>c. the methods used to control criminal behavior.
>B. An interdisciplinary science - criminologists have been trained in other fields, most commonly sociology.
>C. Criminology and criminal justice - there are key differences and areas of overlap.
>>1. Key differences between the fields of study:
>>>a. criminology explains the etiology, extent, and nature of crime, whereas criminal justice refers to agencies of social control.
>>>b. criminologists identify the nature, extent, and cause of crime, while criminal justice scholars describe, analyze, and explain the behavior of agencies of justice and effective methods of crime control.

2. Areas of overlap between the fields of study:
    a. criminologists must understand how agencies of justice operate and how they influence crime and criminals.
    b. before designing programs, criminal justice experts must understand the nature of crime.
D. Criminology and Deviance - a distinction can be made between the terms.
  1. Not all crimes are deviant or unusual acts and not all deviant acts are illegal or criminal.
    a. using marijuana may be illegal, but is it deviant considering a significant percentage of youth have used drugs?
    b. failing to assist a drowning person may not be illegal, but the public might condemn the person who did not act.
  2. Campaigns by individuals, institutions, or government agencies aim to convince the public and lawmakers to either criminalize a deviant act making it illegal or decriminalize an illegal act making it legal.

III. A Brief History of Criminology

A. Prior to the 18ᵗʰ century - punishment was cruel, including torture, and many were burned, whipped, branded, maimed, and executed.
B. Classical Criminology - mid 18ᵗʰ century social philosophers rethought the punishment approach.
  1. Punishment should be fair and balanced and related to the crime.
  2. Utilitarianism - behavior occurs when one considers it useful, purposeful, and reasonable.
  3. Cesare Beccaria (1738-1794) believed that people want to achieve pleasure and avoid pain.
    a. crimes provide some pleasure for the criminal.
    b. to deter crime, pain should counterbalance the pleasure.
    c. punishment should be public, prompt, necessary, proportionate to the crime, and dictated by the laws.
  4. Classical criminology
    a. people have free will to choose crime.
    b. crime may be more attractive if they get a greater payoff for less work.
    c. crime choices may be controlled by fear of punishment.
    d. the more severe, swift, and certain the punishment, the better able to control criminal behavior.
C. Nineteenth-Century Positivism
  1. August Comte (1798-1857), the founder of sociology, applied scientific methods to the study of society.
    a. positivists - people who embrace a rational, scientific view of the world.
    b. positivism
      i. human behavior is a function of internal and external forces beyond a person's control.
      ii. the use of the scientific method to solve problems.

2. Positivist Criminology - early scientific studies examining human behavior were biologically oriented.
    a. physiognomists - studied facial features of criminals to determine whether the shape of ears, nose, and eyes and their distance apart were associated with antisocial behavior.
    b. phrenologists - studied the shape of the skull and bumps on the head to see if these physical traits were linked to criminal behavior.
    c. Phillipe Pinel (1745-1826) - coined the term psychopathic personality.
    d. Henry Maudsley (1835-1918) - believed that insanity and criminal behavior were strongly linked.
3. Biological Determinism
    a. Cesare Lombroso (1835-1909) studied cadavers of executed criminals to see how they were physically different than noncriminals.
        i. known as the Father of Criminology.
        ii. viewed offenders as "born criminals" that inherited physical problems that impelled them into a life of crime - criminal anthropology.
        iii. held that born criminals suffer from atavistic anomalies - physically, they are throwbacks to more primitive times when people were savages.
    b. biological determinism is not taken seriously today. Rather, biosocial theory which reflects the assumed link between physical and mental traits, the social environment, and behavior.
D. Foundations of Sociological Criminology can be traced to:
1. L. A. J. (Adolphe) Quetelet (1796-1874) instigated the use of data and statistics in performing criminological research.
2. Emile Durkheim (1858-1917) defined crime as a normal and necessary social event. Further argued that crime can be useful and even healthy for society. Without crime, everyone would act the same.
    a. wrote *The Division of Labor in Society*, which discussed the shift from a small, rural society to the modern large urban population with division of labor and personal isolation.
    b. from this shift flowed anomie, or norm confusion.
E. The Chicago School and Beyond
1. Research began at the Sociology Department at the University of Chicago by Robert Ezra Park (1864-1944), Ernest W. Burgess (1886-1966), Louis Wirth (1897-1952) and their colleagues.
    a. they pioneered research on the social ecology of the city.
    b. they concluded that social forces operating in urban areas create criminal interactions; some neighborhoods become "natural areas" for crime.

2. In the 1930's and 1940's, sociologists linked social-psychology to criminality.
    a. renowned criminologist Edwin Sutherland proposed that people learn criminal attitudes from older, more experienced law violators.
    b. these views linked criminality to the failure of socialization.
3. By 1950's, most criminologists embraced either the ecological view or the socialization view of crime.

F. Conflict Criminology - Marx proposed that the character of every civilization is determined by its mode of production (the way its people develop and produce material goods).
  1. Capitalists - bourgeoisie.
  2. People who do the labor - proletariat.

G. Contemporary Criminology
  1. All of the original theories have continued to evolve.
  2. Classical theory has evolved into rational choice and deterrence.

IV. What Criminologists Do: The Criminological Enterprise

A. Primarily studying crime and criminal behavior.

B. The Criminological Enterprise - subareas of criminology:
  1. Criminal Statistics - gathering valid crime data.
  2. Sociology of Law - determining the origin of law.
  3. The Nature of Theory and Theory Development - predicting individual behavior.
  4. Criminal Behavior Systems - determining the nature and cause of specific crime patterns.
    a. Crime Typology - the study of criminal behavior involving research on the links between different types of crime and criminals.
  5. Penology - studying the correction and control of criminal behavior.
  6. Victimology - studying the nature and cause of victimization.

V. How Criminologists View Crime

A. The Consensus View of Crime - crimes are behaviors believed to be repugnant to all elements of society.
  1. Substantive criminal law - the written code that defines crimes and their punishments; reflects the values, beliefs, and opinions of society's mainstream.
  2. Social harm - that which sets deviant behavior apart from criminal behavior.

B. The Conflict View of Crime - depicts society as a collection of diverse groups - owners, workers, professionals, and students - who are in constant and continuing conflict.
  1. The definition of crime is controlled by wealth, power, and position and not by moral consensus or the fear of social disruption.
  2. Crime is a political concept designed to protect the power and position of the upper classes at the expense of the poor.

C. The Interactionist View of Crime

1. People act according to their own interpretations of reality, through which they assign meaning to things.
2. They learn the meaning of a thing from the way others react to it, either positively or negatively.
3. They reevaluate and interpret their own behavior according to the meaning and symbols they have learned from others.
4. They see the law as conforming to the beliefs of "moral crusaders" or moral entrepreneurs, who use their influence to shape the legal process in the way they see fit.

D. Defining Crime
1. Crime is a violation of societal rules of behavior as interpreted and expressed by a criminal legal code created by people holding social and political power.
2. Individuals who violate these rules are subject to sanctions by state authority, social stigma, and loss of status.

VI. Crime and the Criminal Law

A. The Origin of Law
1. Code of Hammurabi - King Hammurabi (1792-1750 BCE) of Babylon created the first known written laws based on physical retaliation ("an eye for an eye").
2. Mosaic Code of the Israelites (1200 BCE) - the 613 laws of the Old Testament, including the Ten Commandments; the foundation of Judeo-Christian moral teachings and the basis for the US legal system.
3. Dark Ages - formal legal codes were lost, but systems featuring monetary compensation were developed.
   a. Guilt determined by various methods:
      i. compurgation - having the accused swear to an oath of innocence while being backed by a group of "oathhelpers" who would attest to character and innocence.
      ii. trial by ordeal - based on divine intervention; the accused would, for example, place their hand in boiling water and then it would be seen if God intervened and healed the wounds.
      iii. trial by combat - one would challenge an accuser to a duel with the outcome determining the legitimacy of the accusation.

B. Common Law
1. Developed after the Norman Conquest of England in 1066; helped standardize law and justice.
2. Royal judges would travel to counties, summon citizens to tell of breaches of peace, then, using local customs as a guide, hand down a legal decision.
3. Present English system of law developed during King Henry II (1154-1189).

          a. royal judges published decisions in legal cases, leading to a fixed body of rules.

          b. when a rule was applied in a number of cases, a precedent was set.

          c. precedents would be applied in all similar cases, hence the term common law.

      4. Crime definitions

          a. m*ala in se* - inherently evil and depraved crimes initially defined by judges (e.g., murder, burglary, arson, and rape).

          b. *mala prohibitum* - or statutory crimes, crimes defined by Parliament reflecting existing social conditions.

  C. Contemporary Criminal Law

      1. Crime definitions

          a. felony - a serious offense such as murder, rape, and burglary punished with a long prison sentence or even death.

          b. misdemeanor - a minor or petty crime such as unarmed assault and battery, petty larceny, and disturbing the peace punished with a fine or a period of incarceration in a jail.

      2. Governmental goals achieved by outlawing behaviors:

          a. enforce social control - prohibit behaviors that threaten societal well-being or challenge those in positions of authority.

          b. discourage revenge - law shifts the burden of revenge from the individual to the state.

          c. express public opinion and morality - criminal law reflects change in public opinions and moral values.

          d. deter criminal behavior - criminal law has a social control function to control, restrain, and direct human behavior through its ability to punish and correct.

          e. punish wrongdoing - the deterrent power of law whereby violators are subject to physical coercion and punishment.

          f. maintain social order - the legal system supports and maintains the boundaries of the social system (the capitalist system in the US).

  D. The Criminological Enterprise: The Elements of Criminal Law

      1. Legal Definitions of a Crime

          a. a*ctus reus* - a guilty act.

             i. guilty actions must be voluntary; it is not a crime if done by accident or involuntarily.

            ii. failure to act is a crime when a legally required duty based on relationship or status (parents taking care of children), imposition by statute (stop and help those in traffic accident), or a contractual relationship (lifeguards saving swimmers).

          b. m*ens rea* - the intent to commit an act.

c. strict liability - some crimes do not require *mens rea*. Strict liability crimes are when one simply does what the statute prohibits, such as traffic laws.

d. criminal defenses - when people refute one or more elements of the crime of which they have been accused.

    1. deny *actus reus* - falsely accused, someone else did it.

    2. lacked *mens rea* - although they may have engaged in the criminal act, they lacked the intent needed to be found guilty.

    3. justification - admits committing the criminal act, but maintains that the act was justified and should not be held liable. The justifiable defenses include necessity, duress, self-defense, and entrapment.

E. The Evolution of Criminal Law

    1. Criminal law is constantly evolving to reflect social and economic conditions.

        a. highly publicized cases like the fatal shooting of actress Rebecca Schaefer led to stalking statutes.

        b. the murder of 7-year-old Megan Kanka led to legislation for public notification of local pedophiles (sexual offenders who target children).

        c. California's sexual predator law allows people convicted of 2 or more victims to be committed to a mental institution after their prison term.

    2. Criminal law may change to reflect a newfound tolerance for a behavior.

        a. *Lawrence v. Texas* (2003), the Supreme Court declared sodomy laws unconstitutional because they violated due process rights based on sexual orientation.

        b. it is possible laws will change in the future in relation to recreational drug use and changing technology.

VII. Ethical Issues in Criminology

A. What is to be studied?

B. Who is to be studied?

C. How studies are to be conducted?

D. Potential conflicts include:

    1. When the institution funding research is one of the principal subjects of the project.

    2. Who will be the subject? Criminologists tend to focus on one group while ignoring others.

    3. Subjects who are mislead about research purpose.

VIII. Summary

Key Terms

Actus Reus - An illegal act. The *actus reus* can be an affirmative act, such as taking money or shooting someone, or a failure to act, such as failing to take proper precautions while driving a car.

Anomie - A condition produced by normlessness. Because of rapidly shifting moral values, the individual has few guides to what is socially acceptable. According to Merton, anomie is a condition that occurs when personal goals cannot be achieved by available means. In Agnew's revision anomie can occur when positive or valued stimuli are removed or negative or painful ones applied.

Appellate Court - Courts that reconsider a case that has already been tried to determine whether the measures used complied with accepted rules of criminal procedure and were in line with constitutional doctrines.

Arson - The intentional or negligent burning of a home, structure, or vehicle for criminal purposes such as profit, revenge, fraud, or crime concealment.

Assault - An attack that may not involve physical contact; includes attempted battery or intentionally frightening the victim by word or deed.

Atavistic Anomalies - According to Lombroso, the physical characteristics that distinguish born criminals from the general population and are throwbacks to animals or primitive people.

Battery - A physical attack that includes hitting, punching, slapping, or other offensive touching of a victim.

Biological Determinism - A belief that crimogenic traits can be acquired through indirect heredity from a degenerate family whose members suffered from such ills as insanity, syphilis, and alcoholism, or through direct heredity - being related to a family of criminals.

Biosocial Theory - An approach to criminology that focuses on the interaction between biological and social factors as they relate to crime.

Bourgeoisie - In Marxist theory, the owners of the means of production; the capitalist ruling class.

Burglary - Breaking into and entering a home or structure for the purposes of committing a felony.

Cartographic School of Criminology - An approach developed in Europe in the early nineteenth century making use of social statistics to provide important demographic information on the population, including density, gender, religious affiliations, and wealth. Many of the relationships between crime and social phenomena identified then still serve as a basis for criminology today.

Chicago School - Group of urban sociologists who studied the relationship between environmental conditions and crime.

Classical Criminology - The theoretical perspective suggesting that (1) people have free will to choose criminal or conventional behaviors; (2) people choose to commit crime for reasons of greed or personal need; and (3) crime can be controlled only by the fear of criminal sanctions.

Code of Hammurabi - The first written criminal code developed in Babylonia around 4,000 years ago.

Common Law - Early English law, developed by judges, that incorporated Anglo-Saxon tribal custom, feudal rules and practices, and the everyday rules of behavior of local villages. Common law became the standardized law of the land in England and eventually formed the basis of the criminal law in the United States.

Compurgation - In early English law, a process whereby an accused person swore an oath of innocence while being backed up by a group of twelve to twenty-five "oathhelpers," who would attest to his character and claims of innocence.

Conflict View - The view that human behavior is shaped by interpersonal conflict and that those who maintain social power will use it to further their own needs.

Consensus View - The belief that the majority of citizens in a society share common ideals and work toward a common good and that crimes are acts that are outlawed because they conflict with the rules of the majority and are harmful to society.

Crime - A violation of societal rules of behavior as interpreted and expressed by a criminal legal code created by people holding social and political power. Individuals who violate these rules are subject to sanctions by state authority, social stigma, and loss of status.

Crime Typology - The study of criminal behavior involving research on the links between different types of crime and criminals. Because people often disagree about types of crimes and criminal motivation, no standard exists within the field. Some typologies focus on the criminal, suggesting the existence of offender groups, such as professional criminals, psychotic criminals, occasional criminals, and so on. Others focus on the crimes, clustering them into categories such as property crimes, sex crimes, and so on.

Criminal Anthropology - Early efforts to discover a biological basis of crime through measurement of physical and mental processes.

Criminological Enterprise - The areas of study and research that taken together make up the field of criminology. Criminologists typically specialize in one of the subareas of criminology, such as victimology or the sociology of law.

Criminologists - Researchers who use scientific methods to study the nature, extent, cause, and control of criminal behavior.

Criminology - The scientific study of the nature, extent, cause, and control of criminal behavior.

Decriminalized - Reducing the penalty for a criminal act but not actually legalizing it.

Deviant Behavior - Behavior that departs from the social norm.

Ecological View - A belief that social forces operating in urban areas create criminal interactions; social neighborhoods become "natural areas" for crime.

***Ex Post Facto* Laws** - Those laws that are made to punish actions committed before the existence of such laws and that had not been declared crimes by preceding laws.

Felony - A serious offense that carries a penalty of incarceration in a state prison, usually for one year or more. People convicted of felony offenses lose the right to vote, hold elective office, or maintain certain licenses.

First-Degree Murder - The killing of another person after premeditation and deliberation.

Inchoate Offenses - Incomplete or contemplated crimes such as criminal solicitation or criminal attempts.

Interactionist View - The view that one's perception of reality is significantly influenced by one's interpretation of the reactions of others to similar events and stimuli.

Interdisciplinary Science - Involving two or more academic fields.

Justification - A defense to a criminal charge in which the accused maintains that his or her actions were justified by the circumstances and therefore he or she should not be held criminally liable.

Larceny - Taking for one's own use the property of another, by means other than force or threats on the victim or forcibly breaking into a person's home or workplace; theft.

Legal Code - The specific laws that fall within the scope of criminal law.

Mala In Se - Acts that are outlawed because they violate basic moral values, such as rape, murder, assault, and robbery.

Mala Prohibitum - Acts that are outlawed because they clash with current norms and public opinion, such as tax, traffic, and drug laws.

Mens Rea - "Guilty mind." The mental element of a crime or the intent to commit a criminal act.

Moral Entrepreneurs - Interest groups that attempt to control social life and the legal order in such a way as to promote their own personal set of moral values. People who use their influence to shape the legal process in ways they see fit.

Mosaic Code - The laws of the ancient Israelites, found in the Old Testament of the Judeo-Christian Bible.

Ordeal - Based on the principle of divine intervention and the then-prevalent belief that divine forces would not allow an innocent person to be harmed, this was a way of determining guilt involving such measures as having the accused place his or her hand in boiling water or hold a hot iron to see if God would intervene and heal the wounds. If the wound healed, the person was found not guilty; conversely, if the wound did not heal, the accused was deemed guilty of the crime for which he or she was being punished.

Pedophiles - Sexual offenders who target children.

Penology - An aspect of criminology that overlaps with criminal justice; penology involves the correction and control of known criminal offenders.

Phrenologist - A scientist who studied the shape of the skull and bumps on the head to determine whether these physical attributes were linked to criminal behavior; phrenologists believed that external cranial characteristics dictate which areas of the brain control physical activity.

Physiognomist - A scientist who studied the facial features of criminals to determine whether the shape of ears, nose, and eyes and the distance between them are associated with antisocial behavior.

Positivism - The branch of social science that uses the scientific method of the natural sciences and suggests that human behavior is a product of social, biological, psychological, or economic forces.

Proletariat - A term used by Marx to refer to the working class members of society who produce goods and services but who do not own the means of production.

Psychopathic Personality - A personality characterized by a lack of warmth and feeling, inappropriate behavior responses, and an inability to learn from experience.

Some psychologists view psychopathy as a result of childhood trauma; others see it as a result of biological abnormality.

Rape - Unlawful sexual intercourse with a female without her consent.

Robbery - Taking or attempting to take something of value by force or threat of force and/or by putting the victim in fear.

Sexual Predator Law - Law that allows authorities to keep some criminals convicted of sexually violent crimes in custody even after their sentences are served.

Social Control Function - The ability of society and its institutions to control, manage, restrain, or direct human behavior.

Social Ecology - Environmental forces that have a direct influence on human behavior.

Social Harm - A view that behaviors harmful to other people and society in general must be controlled. These acts are usually outlawed, but some acts that cause enormous amounts of social harm are perfectly legal, such as the consumption of tobacco and alcohol.

Socialization - Process of human development and enculturation. Socialization is influenced by key social processes and institutions.

Socialization View - One view is that people learn criminal attitudes from older, more experienced law violators. Another view is that crime occurs when children develop an inadequate self-image, which renders them incapable of controlling their own misbehavior. Both of these views link criminality to the failure of socialization, the interactions people have with the various individuals, organizations, institutions, and processes of society that help them mature and develop.

Stalking - A pattern of behavior directed at a specific person that includes repeated physical or visual proximity, unwanted communications, and/or threats sufficient to cause fear in a reasonable person.

Statutory Crimes - Crimes defined by legislative bodies in response to changing social conditions, public opinion, and custom.

Strict Liability Crimes - Illegal acts whose elements do not contain the need for intent, or *mens rea*; they are usually acts that endanger the public welfare, such as illegal dumping of toxic wastes.

Substantive Criminal Law - A body of specific rules that declare what conduct is criminal and prescribe the punishment to be imposed for such conduct.

Utilitarianism - The view that people's behavior is motivated by the pursuit of pleasure and the avoidance of pain.

Voluntary Manslaughter - A homicide committed in the heat of passion or during a sudden quarrel; although intent may be present, malice is not.

White-Collar Crime - Illegal acts that capitalize on a person's status in the marketplace. White-collar crimes can involve theft, embezzlement, fraud, market manipulation, restraint of trade, and false advertising.

Discussion Exercises

1. Discuss the case of Dr. Jack Kevorkian of Michigan. Dr. Kevorkian has voluntarily participated in several physician-assisted suicides. The State of Michigan has contended that Dr. Kevorkian has murdered these individuals and subsequently convicted him of murder. Debate the issue of physician-assisted suicide or murder.

2. Siegel states that "criminologists study both the process by which deviant acts are criminalized and become crimes and, conversely, how criminal acts are decriminalized." Have students identify and explain which currently illegal behaviors they would like to see decriminalized.

3. Select a recent crime from a local newspaper. Ask students to identify how three different criminologists working from either the consensus view of crime, conflict view of crime, or interactionist view of crime might go about explaining the occurrence of that particular criminal incident and society's response to it.

InfoTrac Assignment

This text may come bundled with InfoTrac. This will allow students online access to journal articles. This service is updated daily and provides excellent resources for you and your students.

InfoTrac is very easy to navigate. Have students log on to the web site with their password. Assign various key words from the area to be studied. You will find InfoTrac to be a wonderful resource for discussion and research assignments.

GETTING STARTED: Search term words for subject guide: Law, Common Law, Statutory Law, Felony, Revenge, Criminal Defenses.

CRITICAL THINKING PROJECT: Using the search term "Criminal Defenses," find articles that discuss the various legal criminal defenses offered by defendants.

Here are three articles:

Allen, Ronald J., Melissa Luttrell, and Anne Kreeger. "Clarifying Entrapment." *Journal of Criminal Law and Criminology.*

Morse, Stephen J. "The 'New Syndrome Excuse Syndrome.'" *Criminal Justice Ethics.*

Shain, Martin and Gillian Higgins. "The Intoxication Defense and Theories of Criminal Liability: A praxeological approach." *Contemporary Drug Problems.*

Test Bank

Fill in the Blank

1. **Criminology** is devoted to the development of valid and reliable information that addresses the causes of crimes as well as crime patterns and trends.
    (page number 4)

2. Criminologists who study the facial features of criminals to determine whether the shape of ears, nose, and eyes and the distance between them are associated with antisocial behavior are known as **Physiognomists**.
    (page number 8)

3. Lombroso held that criminals suffer from **atavistic anomalies**.
    (page number 8)

4. According to **Durkheim**, crime is part of human nature because it has existed during periods of poverty and prosperity.
    (page number 9)

5. Interactions people have with various individuals, organizations, institutions, and processes of society which help them mature and develop are known as **socialization**.
    (page number 10)

6. The most important relationship in industrial culture is between the owners of the means of production, the capitalist **bourgeoisie**, and the people who do the actual labor, the **proletariat**.
    (page number 10)

7. Studying the correction and control of criminal behavior is known as **penology**.
    (page number 11)

8. **Victimology** is the study of the nature and cause of victimization.
    (page number 11)

9. According to the **consensus view**, crimes are behaviors believed to be repugnant to all elements of society.
    (page number 14)

10. The consensus view of crime links illegal behavior to the concept of **social harm**.
    (page number 15)

11. The **interactionist view** of crime is similar to the conflict perspective because they both suggest that behavior is outlawed when it offends people who maintain the social, economic, and political power necessary to have the law conform to their interests or needs.
　　　　(page number 16)

12. After the Norman conquest of England, in 1066, a **common law** developed, which helped standardize law and justice.
　　　　(page number 18)

13. A **felony** is a serious offense punishable by death or imprisonment for more than one year in a state prison.
　　　　(page number 19)

14. A **misdemeanor** is a less serious offense punishable in the community or in a local facility for less than one year.
　　　　(page number 19)

15. The **actus reus** is an aggressive act, such as taking someone's money, burning a building, or shooting someone.
　　　　(page number 20)

Multiple Choice

1. _____ use scientific methods to study the nature, extent, cause, and control of criminal behavior.
　　　a. Psychologists
　　　b. Criminologists
　　　c. Physiologists
　　　d. Biologists
　　　(Answer = b, page number 4)

2. _____ is the scientific approach to studying criminal behavior.
　　　a. Criminology
　　　b. Police science
　　　c. Political science
　　　d. Psychology
　　　(Answer = a, page number 4)

3. The writings of Beccaria and his followers form the core of what today is referred to as:
   a. survey research
   b. classical criminology
   c. criminal statistics
   d. sociology of law
   (Answer = b, page number 7)

4. The theory which believes that people have free will to choose criminal or unlawful solutions to meet their needs or settle their problems is:
   a. classical criminology
   b. the conflict theory
   c. the conflict view
   d. the consensus view
   (Answer = a, page number 7)

5. Those who follow the writings of Auguste Comte are known as:
   a. theorists
   b. positivists
   c. negativists
   d. victimologists
   (Answer = b, page numbers 7-8)

6. Individuals who pioneered the notion that the source of different mental functions is located in different parts of the brain are known as:
   a. phrenologists
   b. physiognomists
   c. psychologists
   d. sociologists
   (Answer = a, page number 8)

7. When people behave abnormally even without being mentally ill, they:
   a. are criminal
   b. are psychotic
   c. have a psychopathic personality
   d. are anomic
   (Answer = c, page number 8)

8. The founder of sociology is:
   a. Sigmund Freud
   b. Cesare Beccaria
   c. Edwin Sutherland
   d. Auguste Comte
   (Answer = d, page number 8)

9. The father of criminology is:
    a. Sigmund Freud
    b. Cesare Lombroso
    c. Edwin Sutherland
    d. Phillipe Pinel
    (Answer = b, page number 8)

10. The theory that reflects the assumed link between physical and mental traits, the social environment, and behavior, is:
    a. biosocial theory
    b. the consensus view of crime
    c. the conflict view of crime
    d. the interactionist view of crime
    (Answer = a, page number 8)

11. Which theorist felt that crime is normal because it is virtually impossible to imagine a society in which criminal behavior is totally absent?
    a. Cesare Becarria
    b. Phillipe Pinel
    c. Emile Durkheim
    d. Auguste Comte
    (Answer = c, page number 9)

12. The Chicago School was developed by a group of Sociologists at:
    a. the University of North Carolina
    b. Fayetteville State University
    c. Harvard University
    d. the University of Chicago
    (Answer = d, page number 9)

13. The sociologist who said that people learn criminal attitudes from older, more experienced law violators is:
    a. Edwin Sutherland
    b. Charles Darwin
    c. Cesare Lombroso
    d. Reggio Emilia
    (Answer = a, page number 10)

14. Interactions people have with various individuals, organizations, institutions, and processes of society which help them mature and develop are known as:
    a. socialization
    b. criminalization
    c. conflict
    d. consensus
    (Answer = a, page number 10)

15. The theorist who observed that the character of every civilization is determined by its mode of production is:
    a. Edwin Sutherland
    b. Karl Marx
    c. Cesare Lombroso
    d. Emile Durkheim
    (Answer = b, page number 10)

16. The capitalists or the owners of the means of production are known as:
    a. proletariat
    b. bourgeoisie
    c. interactionists
    d. positivists
    (Answer = b, page number 10)

17. The major perspectives of criminology focus on:
    a. Classical/Choice Perspective
    b. Biological/Psychological Perspective
    c. Structural Perspective
    d. all of the above
    (Answer = d, page number 11)

18. Several subareas of criminology exist within the broader areas of criminology. These subareas are called the:
    a. criminological enterprise
    b. criminal statistics
    c. sociology of law
    d. victimology
    (Answer = a, page number 11)

19. Studying the correction and control of criminal behavior is:
    a. criminal statistics
    b. sociology of law
    c. theory construction
    d. penology
    (Answer = d, page number 11)

20. The subarea of criminology concerned with the role social forces play in shaping criminal law and the role of criminal law plays in shaping society is known as:
    a. cohort research
    b. aggregate data research
    c. experimental research
    d. the sociology of law
    (Answer = d, page number 11)

21. Business-related offenses are known as:
    a. crimes of opportunity
    b. white-collar crime
    c. penology
    d. positivism
    (Answer = b, page number 14)

22. Research on the links between different types of crime and criminals is known as:
    a. crime typology
    b. penology
    c. victimology
    d. sociology
    (Answer = a, page number 14)

23. Victimology involves the study of:
    a. services for the victims of crime
    b. victim culpability
    c. probabilities of victimization risk
    d. all of the above
    (Answer = d, page number 14)

24. The written code that defines crimes and their punishments is:
    a. substantive criminal law
    b. procedural criminal law
    c. civil law
    d. tort law
    (Answer = a, page number 14)

25. The consensus view of crime links illegal behavior to the concept of:
    a. victimology
    b. sociology
    c. social harm
    d. theory construction
    (Answer = c, page number 15)

26. The _____ sees society as a collection of diverse groups who are in constant and continuing turmoil.
    a. consensus view
    b. conflict view
    c. interactionist view
    d. all of the above
    (Answer = b, page number 15)

27. The perspective which sees crime as the reflection of the preferences and opinions of people who hold social power in a particular legal jurisdiction is the:
    a. consensus view
    b. conflict view
    c. interactionist view
    d. all of the above
    (Answer = c, page number 16)

28. Statutory crimes are referred to as:
    a. *mala in se*
    b. *mala prohibitum*
    c. *actus reus*
    d. *mens rea*
    (Answer = b, page number 18)

29. Examples of crimes against property include:
    a. burglary
    b. arson
    c. larceny
    d. all of the above
    (Answer = d, page number 19)

30. A crime punishable by death or imprisonment for more than one year in a state prison is a(n):
    a. ordinance
    b. misdemeanor
    c. felony
    d. all of the above
    (Answer = c, page number 19)

31. An institution where felony defendants are held after sentencing is called a:
    a. jail
    b. juvenile detention center
    c. state prison
    d. house of correction
    (Answer = c, page number 19)

32. Which of the following is a function of the criminal law?
    a. social control
    b. deterrence
    c. discouraging revenge
    d. all of the above
    (Answer = d, page number 19)

33. _____ is the ability to control, restrain, and direct human behavior through punishing and correcting law violators.
   a. Social control function
   b. Deterrence
   c. Discouraging revenge
   d. all of the above
   (Answer = a, page number 19)

34. The aggressive act of the crime is the:
   a. *mens rea*
   b. *actus reus*
   c. strict liability
   d. concurrence
   (Answer = b, page number 20)

35. The intent to commit the criminal act is known as:
   a. *mens rea*
   b. *actus reus*
   c. strict liability
   d. concurrence
   (Answer = a, page number 20)

36. Failure to act can be considered a crime under which of the following circumstances?
   a. failure to perform a legally required duty based on relation or status
   b. imposition by statute
   c. a contractual relationship
   d. all of the above
   (Answer = d, page number 20)

37. The willful, malicious, and repeated following and harassing of another person is known as:
   a. murder
   b. stalking
   c. carjacking
   d. larceny
   (Answer = b, page number 20)

38. Public-welfare offenses are known as:
   a. limited liability crimes
   b. strict liability crimes
   c. unlimited liability crimes
   d. none of the above
   (Answer = b, page number 21)

39. When the individual admits committing the criminal act, but maintains that the act was justified and that he or she, therefore, should not be held criminally liable, it is known as:
   a. unjustification
   b. no justification
   c. justification
   d. none of the above
   (Answer = c, page number 21)

40. Sexual offenders who target children are known as:
   a. terrorists
   b. stalkers
   c. pedophiles
   d. none of the above
   (Answer = c, page number 21)

True/False

1. Criminologists use scientific methods to study the nature, extent, cause, and control of criminal behavior.
   (Answer = true, page number 4)

2. Criminology is a strict disciplined science; therefore criminologists have been trained only in criminology.
   (Answer = false, page number 4)

3. During the Middle Ages, people who violated social norms or religious practices were believed to be witches or possessed by demons.
   (Answer = true, page number 6)

4. Utilitarianism emphasized that behavior occurs when the actor considers it useful, purposeful, and reasonable.
   (Answer = true, page numbers 6-7)

5. Physiognomists studied the facial features of criminals to determine whether the shape of ears, nose, and eyes and the distance between them were associated with antisocial behavior.
   (Answer = true, page number 8)

6. Phrenologists studied the intellect of criminals and administered IQ tests.
   (answer = false, page number 8)

7. The chaos and disarray accompanying the loss of traditional values in modern society is known as anomie.
   (Answer = true, page number 9)

8. Marx felt that the most important relationship in industrial cultures is between the owners of the means of production and other owners.
   (Answer = false, page number 10)

9. According to the consensus view of crime, crimes are behaviors believed to be repugnant to all elements of society.
   (Answer = true, page number 14)

10. According to the conflict view of crime, "real" crimes would include unsafe working conditions, police brutality, and violations of human dignity.
    (Answer = true, page number 16)

11. Interactionists see the criminal law as conforming to the beliefs of moral crusaders who use their influence to shape the legal process in the way they see fit.
    (Answer = true, page number 16)

12. The Ten Commandments were the original written code of laws.
    (Answer = false, page number 17)

13. "Ordeal" is when an accused person swears an oath of innocence with the backing of 12-25 "oath-helpers."
    (Answer = false, page number 18)

14. Most U.S. jurisdictions have enacted some form of criminal attempt law, also known as inchoate crimes.
    (Answer = true, page number 18)

15. Contemporary criminal laws are now divided into felonies and misdemeanors.
    (Answer = true, page number 19)

Essay Questions

1. Describe the difference between criminology and criminal justice. What is the difference between criminology and deviance?
   (page numbers 4-5)

2. List and explain the major perspectives of the criminological enterprise.
   (page numbers 11-13)

3. Define the consensus view of crime, the conflict view of crime, and the interactionist view of crime. Compare and contrast these three theories.
   (page numbers 14-17)

4. Trace the history of the common law in America. Explain what contemporary criminal law looks like.
   (page numbers 18-22)

5. What is the difference between a misdemeanor and a felony? Identify the specific elements of a crime. Discuss the elements and whether they must be present or not for a crime to have occurred.
   (page numbers 19-20)

Chapter Two

The Nature and Extent of Crime

Summary

Chapter Two introduces the methods of measuring crime in our society. Crime data are collected from official crime data, victim surveys, and self-report surveys. The chapter looks at the various trends in crime and what the future holds. Chapter Two concludes with a thorough analysis of crime patterns.

Chapter Objectives

After reading this chapter the student should be able to:

- Be familiar with various forms of crime data
- Know the problems associated with collecting valid crime data
- Be able to discuss recent trends in the crime rate
- Be familiar with the factors that influence crime rates
- Be able to discuss patterns in the crime rate
- Recognize age, gender, and racial patterns in crime
- Be able to discuss the association between social class and crime
- Describe the various positions on gun control
- Be familiar with Wolfgang's pioneering research on chronic offending
- Be able to discuss the influence of the chronic offender on criminology

Chapter Overview

Introduction
How Criminologists Study Crime
    Survey Research
    Cohort Research: Longitudinal and Retrospective
    Official Record Research
    Experimental Research
    Observational and Interview Research
    Meta-Analysis and Systematic Review
Measuring Crime Trends and Rates
    Official Data: The Uniform Crime Report
    Victim Surveys: The National Crime Victimization Survey
    Self-Report Surveys
    Evaluating Crime Data Sources

Crime Trends
The Criminological Enterprise: Explaining Crime Trends
      Trends in Violent Crime
      Trends in Property Crime
      Trends in Victimization Data (NCVS Findings)
      Self-Report Findings
What the Future Holds
Comparative Criminology: International Crime Trends
Crime Patterns
      The Ecology of Crime
      Use of Firearms
Policy and Practice in Criminology: Should Guns be Controlled?
      Social Class and Crime
      Age and Crime
      Gender and Crime
Race, Culture, Gender, and Criminology: Gender Differences in Crime
      Race and Crime
      Criminal Careers
Summary

Chapter Outline

I. Introduction

II. How Criminologists Study Crime

    A. Survey Research

        1. Self-report surveys ask participants to describe their criminal activity.

        2. Victimization surveys ask people to describe their criminal victimizations.

        3. Surveys involve sampling, which is the process of selecting subjects sharing similar characteristics, called the population.

        4. A common type of survey is cross-sectional research - simultaneously questioning a diverse sample of subjects who are representative of all members of society.

        5. Strengths of survey research:

            a. cost-effective when measuring characteristics of large numbers of people.

            b. standardized questions and methods decreases researcher bias.

            c. carefully drawn samples allow for generalizability.

            d. surveys can measure current and past behaviors, and future goals and aspirations.

    B. Cohort Research

        1. Longitudinal - involves observing a group of people who share a like characteristic (cohort) over time.

2. Retrospective cohort study - take an intact cohort of known offenders and look back into their early life by checking their education, family, police, and hospital records.
  C. Official Record Research
    1. Uniform Crime Report (UCR)
      a. most important crime record data compiled by the Federal Bureau of Investigation.
      b. published yearly and includes crimes reported to local law enforcement and the number of arrests made by police.
    2. Official record data can be used to focus on social forces affecting crime.
  D. Experimental Research
    1. Criminologists manipulate or intervene in the lives of their subjects to see the outcome or effect of the intervention.
    2. True experiments have three elements:
      a. random selection of subjects.
      b. a control or comparison group.
      c. an experimental condition.
    3. Quasi-experimental design - when it is impossible to randomly select subjects or manipulate conditions.
    4. Criminological experiments are rare:
      a. difficult and expensive to conduct.
      b. manipulating subjects can involve ethical and legal problems.
      c. requires long follow-up periods.
  E. Observational and Interview Research
    1. Focusing on few subjects and interviewing them or observing them gives in-depth data absent in large-scale surveys.
    2. Some researchers may go into the field and participate in group activities, while others will remain in the background and just observe.
  F. Meta-Analysis and Systematic Review
    1. Meta-analysis involves gathering data from a number of previous studies to serve as an indicator of relationships between data.
    2. A systematic review involves collecting findings from previously conducted studies as an evaluation of the effectiveness of public policy interventions.

III. Measuring Crime
  A. Official Data: The Uniform Crime Report - best known, most widely cited source of official criminal statistics, generated by the FBI.
    1. Index crimes or Part I crimes: murder and nonnegligent manslaughter, forcible rape, robbery, aggravated assault, burglary, larceny, arson, and motor vehicle theft.
    2. Compiling the Uniform Crime Report
      a. law enforcement agencies report the number of index crimes known to the FBI.
      b. law enforcement agencies also report crimes cleared:

     i. by at least one person being arrested.

     ii. by exceptional means, such as offender leaving area.

   c. slightly more than 20% of all reported index crimes are cleared by arrest each year.

  3. Validity of the Uniform Crime Report - suspect, at least.

   a. reporting practices - many victims do not report victimization to police (less than 40% of all incidents are reported).

   b. law enforcement practices - method used by police to record crime are not always accurate.

   c. methodological problems:

     i. no federal crimes are reported.

     ii. reports are voluntary and vary in accuracy.

     iii. not all police departments submit reports.

     iv. the FBI uses estimates in its total crime projections.

     v. if offender commits multiple crimes, only most serious is recorded.

     vi. each act is listed as single offense for some crimes, but not others.

     vii. incomplete acts are lumped together with completed ones.

     viii. differences between FBI's definition of crimes and those of states.

  4. NIBRS: The future of the Uniform Crime Report

   a. a more comprehensive data collection process that requires police agencies to provide a brief account of each arrest, including information on the incident, victim, and offender.

   b. crime categories are expanded.

   c. currently 22 states have the NIBRS program and 12 are in the process.

B. Victim Surveys: The National Crime Victimization Survey (NCVS)

  1. To address the nonreporting issue, surveys ask crime victims about their encounters with criminals.

   a. in 2003, more than 83,000 households with more than 149,000 people age 12 or older were interviewed.

  2. Considered a relatively unbiased, valid estimate of all victimizations.

  3. Victims seem to report to the police only crimes that involve considerable loss or injury.

  4. Validity of the NCVS:

   a. overreporting due to misinterpretation of events.

   b. underreporting due to embarrassment, forgetting, etc.

   c. inability to record the personal criminal activity of those interviewed.

   d. sampling errors.

   e. inadequate question format that invalidates responses.

C. Self-Report Surveys

1. Like NCVS, uncovers the "dark figures of crime;" the figures missed by the UCR.
2. Most self-report studies have focused on juvenile delinquency and youth crime (e.g., Monitoring the Future):
   a. ease of access through schools.
   b. they have the highest crime rates.
3. Validity of Self-Reports
   a. the "known group" method compares known offenders with those who are not to see if the former report more delinquency; they do.
   b. critics suggest people won't admit illegal acts; people will exaggerate, forget, or be confused; surveys contain too many trivial offenses; and comparisons between groups can be misleading.
   c. the most serious chronic offenders may be absent from school when the survey is administered, less willing to participate, be institutionalized so unavailable.
   d. reporting accuracy differs by race, ethnicity, and gender.
   D. Evaluating Crime Data Sources
1. UCR - omits many crimes victims don't report to the police and is subject to reporting practices of police departments.
2. NCVS - includes unreported crime, but consists of a limited sample.
3. Self-report surveys - provide demographics of offenders, but accuracy is questionable.

IV. Crime Trends
   A. Short Timeline:
1. 1830-1860 - a gradual increase in the crime rate, especially in violent crime.
2. 1880 - First World War - reported crimes decreased.
3. 1930's - 1960's - crimes rates increased.
4. 1981 - index crimes peaked at 13.4 million.
5. 1991 - index crimes peaked again at 14.6 million.
6. 2003 - rates of crime have declined to about 11.8 million.
   B. Trends in Violent Crime - murder, rape, assault, and robbery.
1. Violent crimes have decreased; in 2003, 1.4 million violent crimes reported to police at a rate of 500 per 100,000 Americans.
   C. Trends in Property Crime - larceny, motor vehicle theft, and arson.
1. Property crimes have declined somewhat; in 2003, 10 million property crimes reported to police at a rate of 3,650 per 100,000 Americans.
   D. Trends in Victimization Data (NCVS Findings) - supports UCR's view of a declining crime rate.
1. In 2003, citizens 12 or older experienced about 24 million violent and property victimizations.
   E. Self-Report Findings - more stable than UCR results.
1. While use of drugs and alcohol has declined since 1997, theft, violence and damage-related crimes have been more stable.

V. What the Future Holds
  A. Criminologist James A. Fox predicts increased teen violence, in part because the number of pre-teen youth in our society has increased.
    1. Steven Levitt challenges this prediction with the aging population offsetting any crime rate increase.
  B. Criminologists Darrell Steffensmeier and Miles Harer predict a more moderate increase in crime.
    1. While the age structure of society is important, the economy, technology, and other social factors will offset any increases.
VI. Crime Patterns - criminologists look for stable crime rate patterns to gain insight into the nature of crime.
  A. The Ecology of Crime - patterns in the crime rate seem to be linked to temporal and ecological factors.
    1. Day, season and climate - most reported crimes occur during the warm months of July and August. Crime rates are higher on the first day of the month when government checks arrive.
    2. Temperature - crime rates increase with rising temperatures and then decline at some point (85 degrees) when it may be too hot for physical exertion.
    3. Regional differences
        a. large urban areas have higher rates of violence.
        b. southern states consistently have higher rates of crime.
  B. Use of Firearms - firearms are involved in 20% of robberies, 10% of assaults, 5% of rapes, and about two-thirds of murders.
  C. Social Class and Crime - lower class people have the greatest incentive to commit crime.
    1. Instrumental crimes - resorting to theft and other illegal activities to obtain desired goods and services.
    2. Expressive crimes - expressing rage and frustration through such crimes as rape and assault.
    3. Class and self-reports - self-reports do not show a direct relationship between crime and class.
        a. James Short and F. Ivan Nye found socioeconomic class was related to official processing through the criminal justice system, but not to the actual commission of crimes.
        b. Charles Tittle and associates argue official statistics reflect class bias in processing lower-class offenders.
        c. supporters of a class-crime relationship argue that when serious offenses only are examined, a significant relationship can be observed.
    4. The Class-Crime Controversy
        a. if class is related to crime, then economic and social factors, such as poverty and neighborhood disorganization, cause criminal behavior.
        b. association between class and crime is more complex than a simple linear relationship.

5. Does Class Matter?
   a. recent evidence suggests that serious, official crime is more prevalent among the lower classes, whereas less serious self-reported crime spread throughout the social structure.

D. Age and Crime - general agreement that age is related to crime; youth commit more of the crime.
   1. Aging out of crime
      a. all people commit less crime as they age; crime peaks in adolescence and declines rapidly thereafter.
      b. adults develop the ability to delay gratification and forgo the immediate gains that law violations bring.

E. Gender and Crime - male crime rates are higher than females.
   1. Explaining gender differences: Traits and temperament
      a. early criminologists pointed to emotional, physical and psychological differences between males and females.
      b. Cesare Lombroso's theory, the masculinity hypothesis, argues that a few "masculine" females are responsible for the few crimes women commit.
      c. the chivalry hypothesis states that much female criminality is hidden because our culture's generally protective and benevolent attitudes toward women.
      d. today, hormonal differences are linked to the gender gap in crime.
   2. Explaining gender differences: Socialization and development
      a. girls - socialized to be less aggressive; to respond to provocation by feeling anxious and depressed.
      b. boys - encouraged to retaliate with aggression.
   3. Explaining gender differences: Feminist views
      a. Liberal Feminist Theory - the traditionally lower crime rate for women could be explained by women's second-class economic and social position.
   4. Is convergence likely? - some do not think that female criminality will rise despite the emancipation of women; while others feel differently.

F. Race and Crime - official crime data indicates that minority group members are involved in a disproportionate share of criminal activity (African Americans comprise 12% of the population and account for 38% of the Part I violent crime arrests and 30% of property crime arrests).
   1. Racism and discrimination - some criminologists view black crime as a function of socialization in a society where black families were torn apart and black cultured destroyed due to slavery.
   2. Institutional racism - an element of daily life in the African American community.
      a. some jurisdictions treat young African American males more harshly.

      b. unemployed or indigent African Americans receive longer prison sentences than whites.

      c. African American victims receive less public concern and media attention then white victims.

   3. Economic and social disparity - blacks and whites face different economic and social realities.

      a. African Americans have higher unemployment rates and lower incomes than whites.

      b. African Americans face a higher degree of social isolation and economic deprivation.

   4. Family dissolution - tied to low employment rates among African American males, which places a strain on marriages.

   5. Is convergence possible? - although there is little difference in self-reported crime rates, African Americans are more likely to be arrested for violent crimes.

G. Criminal Careers - most offenders commit a single criminal act and upon arrest, discontinue their antisocial activity; a small group of criminal offenders account for a majority of all criminal offenders.

   1. Chronic offenders or career criminals ("the chronic 6 percent") - research by Schumacher and Kurt found certain traits may characterize the chronic offender:

      a. problems in the home.

      b. problems at school.

      c. substance abuse problems.

      d. delinquency factor.

   2. Persistence: The continuity of crime - persistent juvenile offenders are the ones most likely to continue their criminal careers into adulthood.

   3. Implications of the chronic offender concept - since few become chronic offenders then there is a common trait, but what is it?

      a. policy outcomes spurred by the chronic offender are mandatory sentences for violent and drug-related crimes and "three strikes and you're out" policies.

VII. Summary

Key Terms

Aging Out - The process by which individuals reduce the frequency of their offending behavior as they age. It is also known as spontaneous remission, because people are believed to spontaneously reduce the rate of their criminal behavior as they mature. Aging out is thought to occur among all groups of offenders.

Career Criminal - A person who repeatedly violates the law and organizes his or her lifestyle around criminality.

Chivalry Hypothesis - The idea that low female crime and delinquency rates are a reflection of the leniency with which police treat female offenders.

Chronic Offender - According to Wolfgang, a delinquent offender who is arrested five or more times before he or she is 18 and who stands a good chance of becoming an adult criminal; such offenders are responsible for more than half of all serious crimes.

Cleared Crimes - Crimes are cleared in two ways: when at least one person is arrested, charged, and turned over to the court for prosecution; or by exceptional means, when some element beyond police control precludes the physical arrest of an offender (for example, the offender leaves the country).

Cohort - A sample of subjects whose behavior is followed over a period of time.

Continuity of Crime - The view that crime begins early in life and continues throughout the life course. Thus, the best predictor of future criminality is past criminality.

Cross-Sectional Survey - Uses survey data derived from all age, race, gender, and income segments of the population measured simultaneously. Because people from every age group are represented, age-specific crime rates can be determined. Proponents believe this is a sufficient substitute for the more expensive longitudinal approach that follows a group of subjects over time to measure crime rate changes.

Expressive Crimes - Crimes that have no purpose except to accomplish the behavior at hand, such as shooting someone.

Index Crimes - The eight crimes that, because of their seriousness and frequency, the FBI reports the incidence of in the annual Uniform Crime Report. Index crimes include murder, rape, assault, robbery, burglary, arson, larceny, and motor vehicle theft.

Instrumental Crimes - Offenses designed to improve the financial or social position of the criminal.

Liberal Feminist Theory - Theory suggesting that the traditionally lower crime rate for women can be explained by their second class economic and social position. As women's social roles have changed and their lifestyles have become more like those of men, it is believed that their crime rates will converge.

Masculinity Hypothesis - The view that women who commit crimes have biological and psychological traits similar to those of men.

Meta-Analysis - A research technique that uses the grouped data from several different studies.

National Crime Victimization Survey (NCVS) - The ongoing victimization study conducted jointly by the Justice Department and the U.S. Census Bureau that surveys victims about their experiences with law violation.

National Incident-Based Reporting System (NIBRS) - A relatively new program that requires local police agencies to provide a brief account of each incident and arrest within twenty-two crime patterns, including incident, victim, and offender information.

Part I Crimes - Another term for index crimes; eight categories of serious, frequent crimes.

Part II Crimes - All crimes other than index and minor traffic offenses. The FBI records annual arrest information for Part II offenses.

Persistence - The idea that those who started their delinquent careers early and who committed serious violent crimes throughout adolescence were the most likely to persist as adults.

Population - All people who share a particular characteristic, such as all high school students or all police officers.

Retrospective Cohort Study - A study that uses an intact cohort of known offenders and looks back into their early life experiences by checking their educational, family, police, and hospital records.

Sampling - Selecting a limited number of people for study as representative of a larger group.

Self-Report Survey - A research approach that requires subjects to reveal their own participation in delinquent or criminal acts.

Systematic Review - A research technique that involves collecting the findings from previously conducted studies, appraising and synthesizing the evidence, and using the collective evidence to address a particular scientific question.

Three Strikes and You're Out - Policies whereby people convicted of three felony offenses receive a mandatory life sentence.

Uniform Crime Report (UCR) - Large database, compiled by the Federal Bureau of Investigation, of crimes reported and arrests made each year throughout the United States.

Victimization Survey - A statistical survey (such as the NCVS) that measures the amount, nature, and patterns of victimization in the population.

Discussion Exercises

1. Gun Control is a hot topic in the United States. Poll the class as to their views on gun control. Divide the class into two groups. One group will be pro gun control and the second group will be anti-gun control. Have each group prepare a presentation for their side. Poll the class again to see if the results changed after the presentations.

2. Break students into groups and have them construct a short self-report survey on underage drinking at their school. What questions should be included? How easy or difficult is it to construct a proper survey? How might they sample their fellow students? How might different sampling procedures lead to different results? What problems may arise like, for example, memory problems, lying, and revelations of illegal behaviors?

3. This chapter examines differences between females and males in their levels of criminal involvement. Find, or develop, a list of about 50 delinquent acts including alcohol and drug use, minor criminal acts, and more serious criminal acts. Hand this form out to the students. They are to mark on the form whether they are female or male and each item they committed prior to the age of 18. Have them turn these forms in and then redistribute them to the class. On the board, write two sets of 1 - 50 (one for male sheets and one for female sheets). Have the students place on the board a check mark next to the items that are marked on their sheet. Taking into account the gender

distribution within your class, discuss those items where females and males report similar levels of offending and those items where there is a clear disparity.

InfoTrac Assignment

GETTING STARTED: Search term words for subject guide: Uniform Crime Report, National Crime Victimization Survey, Self-Report Survey, Violent Crime, Crime Patterns.

CRITICAL THINKING PROJECT: Using the search term "National Crime Victimization Survey," find articles that examine the reporting behavior of rape victims. Discuss the differences in the National Crime Victimization Survey and the Uniform Crime Report's data on the crime of rape.

Here are three articles:

Bachman, Ronet. "The Factors Related to Rape Reporting Behavior and Arrest: New evidence from the National Crime Victimization Survey." *Criminal Justice and Behavior*.

Transcript. "Statement on the National Crime Victimization Survey." *Weekly Compilation of Presidential Documents*.

Bachman, Ronet and Raymond Paternoster. "A Contemporary Look at the Effects of Rape Law Reform: How far have we really come." *Journal of Criminal Law and Criminology*.

Test Bank

Fill in the Blank

1. **Sampling** refers to the process of selecting for study a limited number of subjects who are representative of entire groups sharing similar characteristics.
    (page number 30)

2. **Self-report surveys** ask participants to describe their recent and lifetime criminal activities.
    (page number 30)

3. **Longitudinal research** involves observing over time a group of people who share a like characteristic.
    (page number 30)

4. The Federal Bureau of Investigation's **Uniform Crime Report** is the best known and most widely cited source of official criminal statistics.
    (page number 33)

5. The most important and widely used victim survey is the **National Crime Victimization Survey**.
    (page number 36)

6. The **dark figures of crime** are those crime incidents missed by the UCR.
    (page number 36)

7. Property crimes rates may be **stabilizing**.
    (page number 39)

8. **Urban** areas have by far the highest violence rates.
    (page number 46)

9. **Southern** states have had consistently high crime rates in almost all crime categories.
    (page number 47)

10. **Aging out** is the process by which individuals reduce the frequency of their offending behavior as they age.
    (page number 53)

11. The view that women who commit crimes have biological and psychological traits similar to men is known as the **masculinity hypothesis**.
    (page number 54)

12. Female's criminality is often masked because criminal justice authorities are reluctant to take action against a woman is known as the **chivalry hypothesis**.
   (page number 54)

13. Persistent offenders are referred to as **career criminals (or chronic offenders)**.
   (page number 60)

14. **Continuity of crime** states crime begins early and continues throughout one's life.
   (page number 60)

15. The policy of giving people convicted of three violent offenses a mandatory life term without parole is known as the **Three Strikes** policy.
   (page number 61)

Multiple Choice

1. Criminologists conduct research to:
      a. measure the nature and extent of criminal behavior
      b. meet other criminologists
      c. gain recognition as criminologists
      d. have easy, well-paying positions
   (Answer = a, page number 30)

2. Simultaneously interviewing or questioning a diverse sample of subjects who represent the members of a community is known as:
      a. sampling
      b. cross-sectional research
      c. aggregate data research
      d. experimental research
   (Answer = b, page number 30)

3. Asking participants to describe their recent and lifetime criminal activity is:
      a. sampling
      b. cross-sectional research
      c. self-report surveys
      d. experimental research
   (Answer = c, page number 30)

4. Self-report studies can include offender information that includes:
      a. attitudes
      b. values
      c. beliefs
      d. all of the above
   (Answer = d, page number 30)

5. A like characteristic is associated with a(n):
   a. cohort
   b. anomie
   c. process perspective
   d. integrated perspective
   (Answer = a, page number 30)

6. Observing a group of people who share a like characteristic over time is(are):
   a. sampling
   b. cross-sectional research
   c. self-report surveys
   d. longitudinal research
   (Answer = d, page number 30)

7. When criminologists want to see the direct effect of one factor on another, they conduct:
   a. experimental research
   b. aggregate data research
   c. cohort research
   d. survey research
   (Answer = a, page number 31)

8. The Uniform Crime Report is collected by the:
   a. Federal Bureau of Investigation
   b. U.S. Congress
   c. state agencies
   d. local victim organizations
   (Answer = a, page number 33)

9. The number of crimes reported by citizens to local police departments and the number of arrests made by police agencies in a given year is compiled into the:
   a. Self-Report Study
   b. Youth Survey
   c. National Crime Victimization Survey
   d. Uniform Crime Report
   (Answer = d, page number 33)

10. The best known and most widely cited source of official criminal statistics is(are):
    a. the Uniform Crime Report
    b. the National Crime Victimization Survey
    c. Self-Report Studies
    d. none of the above
    (Answer = a, page number 33)

11. What is another name for index crimes?
   a. instrumental
   b. inchoate
   c. Part II
   d. Part I
   (Answer = d, page number 33)

12. The taking or attempting to take anything of value from the care, custody, or control of a person by force or threat of force or violence is known as:
   a. murder
   b. forcible rape
   c. robbery
   d. arson
   (Answer = c, page number 33)

13. An unlawful attack by one person upon another for the purpose of inflicting severe or aggravated bodily injury is called:
   a. murder
   b. forcible rape
   c. robbery
   d. aggravated assault
   (Answer = d, page number 33)

14. The unlawful entry of a structure to commit a felony or a theft is called:
   a. murder
   b. burglary
   c. forcible rape
   d. robbery
   (Answer = b, page number 33)

15. The unlawful taking, carrying, leading, or riding away of property from the possession or constructive possession of another is called:
   a. murder
   b. burglary
   c. larceny
   d. robbery
   (Answer = c, page number 33)

16. The theft or attempted theft of a motor vehicle is called:
   a. murder
   b. burglary
   c. larceny
   d. motor vehicle theft
   (Answer = d, page number 33)

17. Any willful or malicious burning or attempt to burn, with or without intent to defraud, a dwelling house, public building, motor vehicle or aircraft, personal property of another or the like, is called:
    a. murder
    b. theft
    c. larceny
    d. arson
    (Answer = d, page number 33)

18. Crimes are cleared by law enforcement officers:
    a. when at least one person is arrested
    b. by exceptional means when it is impossible to take the person into custody
    c. all of the above
    d. none of the above
    (Answer = c, page number 33)

19. Which crimes are more likely to be solved by the police?
    a. violent crimes
    b. property crimes
    c. larceny crimes
    d. theft crimes
    (Answer = a, page number 33)

20. Slightly more than _____ percent of all reported index crimes are cleared by arrest each year:
    a. 20
    b. 40
    c. 50
    d. 75
    (Answer = a, page number 33)

21. Which of the following methods does the UCR use to express crime data?
    a. number of crimes reported to the police and arrests made
    b. crime rates per 100,000 people
    c. changes in the number and rate of crime over time
    d. all of the above
    (Answer = d, page number 34)

22. A problem with the Uniform Crime Report includes:
    a. reporting practices
    b. law enforcement practices
    c. methodological problems
    d. all of the above
    (Answer = d, page numbers 34-35)

23. Which of the following is considered to be a methodological problem for the UCR?
    a. no federal crimes are reported
    b. police reports are involuntary
    c. all of the above
    d. none of the above
    (Answer = a, page number 35)

24. Embarrassment of reporting crime victimizations to NCVS interviewers may be a reason for:
    a. sampling error
    b. overreporting of victimizations
    c. underreporting of victimizations
    d. none of the above
    (Answer = c, page number 36)

25. The NCVS has been cited with which of the following problems?
    a. overreporting of victimizations
    b. underreporting of victimizations
    c. sampling errors
    d. all of the above
    (Answer = d, page number 36)

26. Crimes that the police do not know about are considered:
    a. the dark figures of crime
    b. missing data
    c. unfounded data
    d. none of the above
    (Answer = a, page number 36)

27. A research approach that requires subjects to reveal their own participation in delinquent or criminal acts is known as:
    a. the Uniform Crime Report
    b. Self-Report Surveys
    c. NCVS
    d. FBI
    (Answer = b, page number 36)

28. In the year 2003 there were an estimated _____ victimizations recorded in the US.
    a. 24 million
    b. 76 million
    c. 100 million
    d. 125 million
    (Answer = a, page number 42)

29. Most reported crimes occur during the:
    a. summer
    b. winter
    c. fall
    d. spring
    (Answer = a, page number 46)

30. The highest violence rates occur in:
    a. rural areas
    b. scenic areas
    c. urban areas
    d. Disney World
    (Answer = c, page number 46)

31. The highest crime rate is found in which region of the country?
    a. north
    b. south
    c. east
    d. west
    (Answer = b, page number 46)

32. Traditionally, crime has been thought of as a(n) _____-class phenomenon.
    a. upper
    b. middle
    c. upper-middle
    d. lower
    (Answer = d, page number 48)

33. Those unable to obtain desired goods and services through conventional means may consequently resort to theft and other illegal activities. These activities are known as:
    a. instrumental crimes
    b. expressive crimes
    c. index crimes
    d. crimes of passion
    (Answer = a, page number 48)

34. _____ are associated with those living in poverty who engage in disproportionate amounts of rape and assault as a means of expressing their rage, frustration, and anger against society.
    a. Instrumental crimes
    b. Expressive crimes
    c. Index crimes
    d. Crimes of passion
    (Answer = b, page number 48)

35. The process by which individuals reduce the frequency of their offending behavior as they age is known as:
    a. the continuity of crime
    b. aging out
    c. the chronic offender
    d. the career criminal
    (Answer = b, page number 53)

36. A repeat offender is also known as a:
    a. chronic offender
    b. career criminal
    c. all of the above
    d. none of the above
    (Answer = c, page number 60)

37. Chronic offenders begin their criminal careers:
    a. early in life
    b. late in life
    c. in their 30's
    d. in their 40's
    (Answer = a, page number 60)

38. Characteristics which predict chronic offending are:
    a. school behaviors
    b. family problems
    c. delinquency factors
    d. all of the above
    (Answer = d, page number 60)

39. Chronic offenders are known as the "chronic _____ percent."
    a. 6
    b. 12
    c. 15
    d. 21
    (Answer = a, page number 60)

40. The continuity of crime is also known as:
    a. desistance
    b. persistence
    c. resistance
    d. none of the above
    (Answer = b, page number 60)

True/False

1. Self-report surveys are administered to groups of subjects through a mass distribution of questionnaires.
    (Answer = true, page number 30)

2. Self-report surveys can provide information on the personal characteristics of offenders, such as their attitudes, values, beliefs, and psychological profiles.
    (Answer = true, page number 30)

3. Longitudinal research involves observing over a period of time a group of people who share like characteristics.
    (Answer = true, page number 30)

4. The Uniform Crime Report is an annual survey of crime victims.
    (Answer = false, page number 33)

5. The Bureau of Justice Statistics compiles the Uniform Crime Report.
    (Answer = false, page number 33)

6. Today, there are three significant methods used to measure the nature and extent of crime: official data, victim data, and self-report data.
    (Answer = true, page numbers 33-37)

7. Self-report surveys have most often been used with juveniles.
    (Answer = true, page number 36)

8. Studies have indicated that a gradual increase in the crime rate, especially in violent crime, occurred from 1830 to 1860.
    (Answer = true, page number 38)

9. Firearms play a dominant role in criminal activity.
    (Answer = true, page number 41)

10. Most reported crimes occur during the warm summer months of July and August.
    (Answer = true, page number 46)

11. Large urban areas have by far the highest violence rates.
    (Answer = true, page number 46)

12. For many years, northern states have had consistently high crime rates in almost all crime categories.
    (Answer = false, page number 47)

13. Instrumental crimes are committed by those who are unable to obtain desired goods and services through conventional means.
	(Answer = true, page number 48)

14. In the 1970's, liberal feminist theory focused attention on the social and economic role of women in society and its relationship to female crime rates.
	(Answer = true, page number 54)

15. Official crime data indicate that minority group members are involved in a disproportionate share of serious criminal activity.
	(Answer = true, page number 56)

Essay Questions

1. Describe the accepted methods of studying crime in the United States. What are the positive and negative aspects of each method?
	(page numbers 30-32)

2. What is the Uniform Crime Report? How is it complied? What are the pros and cons of this method of data collection? Describe the predicted future of the Uniform Crime Report.
	(page numbers 33-35)

3. What is self-report data? Is it useful and is it accurate. Discuss the pros and cons of self-report data.
	(page numbers 36-37)

4. Discuss the crime trends in the United States. Which areas of crime are on the decline and which areas are on the rise?
	(page numbers 38-44)

5. What are the patterns of crime in the United States? Do certain aspects of society or individuals predispose one to antisocial behavior?
	(page numbers 45-60)

Chapter Three

Victims and Victimization

Summary

Chapter Three begins with a discussion of the problems that victims face after the crime has occurred. The chapter then focuses on the nature of victimization. This discussion introduces the various demographics which may predispose one to victimization. Theories of victimization are defined and explained with a conclusion of how society should care for the victim.

Chapter Objectives

After reading this chapter the student should be able to:

- Be familiar with the concept of victimization
- Be familiar with the costs of victimization
- Be able to discuss the problems of crime victims
- Know the nature of victimization
- Recognize the age, gender, and racial patterns in victimization data
- Be able to discuss the association between lifestyle and victimization
- Be familiar with the term *victim precipitation*
- List the routine activities associated with victimization risk
- Be able to discuss the various victim assistance programs

Chapter Overview

Introduction
Problems of Crime Victims
     Economic Loss
     System Abuse
     Long-Term Stress
The Criminological Enterprise: Adolescent Victims of Violence
     Fear
     Antisocial Behavior
The Nature of Victimization
     The Social Ecology of Victimization
     The Victim's Household
     Victim Characteristics
     Victims and Their Criminals

Theories of Victimization
     Victim Precipitation Theory
     Lifestyle Theory
The Criminological Enterprise: Rape on Campus: Lifestyle and Risk
     Deviant Place Theory
     Routine Activities Theory
The Criminological Enterprise: Crime and Everyday Life
Caring for the Victim
     The Government's Response
     Victim Service Programs
     Victims' Rights
Comparative Criminology: Victims' Rights in Europe
     Victim Advocacy
     Self-Protection
     Community Organization
Summary

Chapter Outline

I. Introduction
     A. Victimologists - criminologists who focus their attention on crime victims.
II. Problems of Crime Victims
     A. The National Crime Victimization Survey (NCVS) estimates 24 million victimizations in the U.S. annually.
     B. Economic Loss
          1. Taken together, property and productivity losses run in the hundreds of billions of dollars.
          2. System costs - adding together the cost of the justice system, legal costs, treatment costs, etc., the total loss due to crime is about $450 billion annually, or about $1,800 per U.S. citizen.
          3. Individual costs - victims may suffer losses in earnings and occupational attainment.
               a. Macmillan estimates an $82,000 loss in earnings over the lifetime for American adolescent victims of violent crime; $237,000 loss for Canadian victims.
               b. the psychological and physical problems resulting from the victimization lead to delayed educational achievement and professional success.
     C. System Abuse
          1. Representatives of the justice system (police, counselors, prosecutors) may revictimize them with a calloused attitude or innuendos concerning blame.
     D. Long-Term Stress
          1. Victims may suffer stress and anxiety long after the incident.

        a. adolescent victims may report lower self-esteem, more suicidal, higher risk of being abused again, more likely to run away from home, eating disorders, homelessness, etc.

    2. Spousal abuse victims often are psychologically abused in addition to the physical abuse.

        a. they report higher levels of depression, posttraumatic stress disorder, anxiety disorder, and obsessive-compulsive disorder.

    3. Some victims have to deal with a resulting physical disability (including spinal cord injuries).

  E. Fear

    1. Fundamental life change - view world more suspiciously.

    2. Rather than forgetting past, some have found confronting it therapeutic.

  F. Antisocial Behavior

    1. Strong evidences that people who are crime victims seem more likely to commit crime themselves.

    2. Cycle of Violence

        a. abuse-crime phenomenon - boys and girls more likely to engage in violent behavior if they were:

           i. the target of physical abuse.

           ii. exposed to violent behavior among the adults they knew or lived with; and/or exposed to weapons.

III. The Nature of Victimization

  A. The Social Ecology of Victimization

    1. Violent crimes are more likely to take place in open, public areas, or at a commercial establishment during the daytime or early evening.

    2. More serious crimes (e.g., rape) usually take place after 6 p.m., while less serious (e.g., larceny) take place during the day.

  B. The Victim's Household

    1. Larger, African American, western, and urban homes are most vulnerable to crime, while rural, white, and northeastern homes are less likely to contain crime victims.

    2. People who own their home are less vulnerable than renters.

    3. Recent declines in household victimization rates may be due to an increase in smaller households in less populated areas.

  C. Victim Characteristics

    1. Gender:

        a. except for rape and sexual assault, males are more often victims.

        b. females more often are victimized by someone they know, while males more often are victimized by strangers.

    2. Age:

        a. young people face a greater victimization risk.

        b. the elderly are more susceptible to frauds and scams.

    3. Social status:

        a. lower income individuals are more likely to be victims.

            b. the wealthy are at highest risk for personal theft crimes.
        4. Martial status:
            a. never-married are victimized more than married people.
            b. widowed people are at lowest risk of victimization.

        5. Race and ethnicity:
            a. African Americans are more likely to be victims violent crime.
        6. Repeat victimization:
            a. prior victims have a higher chance of future victimization than nonvictims.
            b. victims of chronic or repeat victimizations
                i. target vulnerability - physical or psychological weakness makes them easy targets.
                ii. target gratifiability - having attractive possessions the offender wants
                iii. target antagonism - having characteristics that make the offender angry or jealous
    D. Victims and Their Criminals
        1. Most crimes are committed by a single offender over age 20.
        2. Crime tends to be intraracial.
        3. Substance abuse is involved in about 1/3 of violent crime.
        4. Relatives or acquaintances commit about 40% of violent crimes.
        5. Victimization is common among family (e.g., sibling homicide or siblicide).

IV. Theories of Victimization
    A. Victim Precipitation Theory - some people may actually initiate the confrontation that eventually leads to their injury or death.
        1. Active precipitation - occurs when victims act provocatively, use threats or fighting words, or even attack first.
        2. Passive precipitation - occurs when the victim exhibits some personal characteristic that unknowingly either threatens or encourages the attacker.
    B. Lifestyle Theory - people may become crime victims because their lifestyle increases their exposure to criminal offenders.
        1. High-risk lifestyles - drinking, taking drugs, getting involved in crime, runaways.
        2. Victims and criminals - a career as a criminal may predispose one to be victimized.
    C. Deviant Place Theory - victims do not encourage crime, but are victim prone because they reside in socially disorganized high-crime areas.
        1. Deviant places are poor, densely populated, highly transient neighborhoods
        2. Residents have to try harder to protect themselves because they live with many motivated offenders, or move out if possible.
    D. Routine Activities Theory - articulated by Lawrence Cohen and Marcus Felson, the volume and distribution of predatory crime are closely related

to the interaction of three variables that reflect the routine activities of the typical American lifestyle.

1. Three variables:
    a. the availability of suitable targets - homes with salable goods.
    b. the absence of capable guardians - police, homeowners.
    c. the presence of motivated offenders - such as a large number of unemployed teens.
2. Hot spots - a place where potentially motivated criminals congregate and elevate the chances of a victimization.
3. Moral guardianship - moral beliefs and socialization may influence the routine activities that produce crime.
4. Lifestyle, opportunity and routine activities
    a. a person's living arrangement can affect their risk; those who live in unguarded areas are at the mercy of motivated offenders.
    b. lifestyle effects the opportunity for crime because it controls a persons proximity to criminals, time of exposure to criminals, attractiveness as a target, and ability to be protected.
5. Empirical support
    a. Cohen and Felson argue that crime increased between 1960 and 1980 due to fewer guardians in the home (women in the workforce).
    b. skyrocketing drug use in the 1980's created motivated offenders.

V. Caring for the Victim
A. The Government's Response
    1. President Reagan created Task Force on Victims of Crime in 1982.
        a. suggested balancing victim's rights with defendant's due process.
        b. recommended protection from intimidation, requiring restitution, and expanding compensation programs.
    2. Omnibus Victim and Witness Protection Act
        a. required the use of victim impact statements at federal criminal case sentencing, protection for witnesses, stringent bail laws, and restitution.
    3. Comprehensive Crime Control Act and Victims of Crime Act (1984)
        a. authorized federal funding for state victim compensation and assistance projects.
B. Victim Service Programs - estimated 2,000 victim-witness assistance programs have developed in U.S.
    1. Victim compensation - victim may receive compensation from the state for losses incurred during the crime.
        a. most states have a lack of funding.
        b. compensation made for medical bills, loss of wages, loss of future earning, and counseling.

2. Court services - to help deal with the criminal justice system.
   a. explain how to be a witness, how bail works, what to do if the defendant makes a threat, provide transportation to and from court, and provide escort to court.
3. Public education - familiarize the public with their services and with other victim agencies.
   a. teach methods of dealing with conflict.
4. Crisis intervention - refer clients to area agencies to aid in dealing with their ordeal.
5. Victim-Offender Reconciliation Programs (VORP) - mediators to facilitate face-to-face encounters between victims and their attackers.
   a. goal - to agree on restitution and possibly reconciliation.
6. Victim impact statements - victims are able to make an impact statement before the sentencing judge.
   a. some debate as to impact on rate of incarceration.

C. Victims' Rights - more than 20 years ago, Frank Carrington suggests that crime victims have legal rights that should allow them basic rights from the government.
   1. Every state now has some form of legal rights for victims; often called a victims' Bill of Rights.

D. Victim Advocacy - those wanting to lobby for victims.

E. Self-Protection - many have invoked self-protection by taking matters into their own hands, building fences, surveillance cameras, and many more.
   1. Target hardening - making one's home or business crime proof through locks, alarms, etc.
   2. Fighting back - some victims fight back their assailant or get others around to help.
      a. may cause assailant to flee.
      b. may cause assailant to attack in a more violent way.

F. Community Organization - communities organizing on the neighborhood level against crime
   1. For example, block watches and neighborhood patrols.
   2. Little evidence they affect the crime rate.

VI. Summary

Key Terms

Active Precipitation - The view that the source of many criminal incidents is the aggressive or provocative behavior of victims.

Capable Guardians - Effective deterrents to crime, such as police or watchful neighbors.

Chronic Victimization - Those who have been crime victims maintain a significantly higher chance of future victimizations than people who have remained nonvictims. Most repeat victimizations occur soon after a previous crime has occurred, suggesting that repeat victims share some personal characteristic that makes them a magnet for predators.

Crisis Intervention - Emergency counseling for crime victims.

Cycle of Violence - The idea that victims of crime, especially childhood abuse, are more likely to commit crimes themselves.

Date Rape - Forcible sex during a courting relationship.

Deviant Place Theory - People become victims because they reside in socially disorganized, high-crime areas where they have the greatest risk of coming into contact with criminal offenders.

Elder Abuse - A disturbing form of domestic violence by children and other relatives with whom elderly people live.

Lifestyle Theory - People may become crime victims because their lifestyle increases their exposure to criminal offenders.

Motivated Offenders - The potential offenders in a population. According to rational choice theory, crime rates will vary according to the number of motivated offenders.

Obsessive-Compulsive Disorder - An extreme preoccupation with certain thoughts and compulsive performance of certain behaviors.

Passive Precipitation - The view that some people become victims because of personal and social characteristics that make them attractive targets for predatory criminals.

Posttraumatic Stress Disorder (PTSD) - Psychological reaction to a highly stressful event; symptoms may include depression, anxiety, flashbacks, and recurring nightmares.

Restitution Agreements - A condition of probation in which the offender repays society or the victim of crime for the trouble the offender caused. Monetary restitution involves a direct payment to the victim as a form of compensation. Community service restitution may be used in victimless crimes and involves work in the community in lieu of more severe criminal penalties.

Routine Activities Theory - The view that the volume and distribution of predatory crime is closely related to the interaction of suitable targets, motivated offenders, and capable guardians.

Siblicide - Sibling homicide. The median age of sibling homicide offenders is 23, and the median age of their victims is 25. The vast majority of sibling homicide offenders are males (87 percent), and they are most likely to kill their brothers. When lethal violence by brothers against their sisters occurs, it is more likely in juvenile sibling relationships rather than adult sibling relationships (31 percent versus 14 percent). Sisters killing their brothers or sisters are relatively rare events.

Suitable Target - According to routine activities theory, a target for crime that is relatively valuable, easily transportable, and not capably guarded.

Target Hardening - Making one's home or business crime proof through the use of locks, bars, alarms, and other devices.

Victim Compensation - The victim ordinarily receives compensation from the state to pay for damages associated with the crime. Rarely are two compensation schemes alike, however, and many state programs suffer from lack of both adequate funding and proper organization within the criminal justice system. Compensation may be made for medical bills, loss of wages, loss of future earnings, and counseling. In the case of death, the victim's survivors can receive burial expenses and aid for loss of support.

Victim Precipitation Theory - The idea that the victim's behavior was the spark that ignited the subsequent offense, as when the victim abused the offender verbally or physically.

Victimologist - A person who studies the victim's role in criminal transactions.

Victim-Witness Assistance Programs - Government programs that help crime victims and witnesses; may include compensation, court services, and/or crisis intervention.

Discussion Exercises

1. There are four main theories as to why individuals are victimized. Divide the class into four groups and have each discuss one of the theories: victim precipitation theory, lifestyle theory, deviant place theory, and routine activities theory. Have each group explain the theory to the class and cite examples of known cases.

2. Not every person in the United States is at equal risk of victimization. Using National Crime Victimization Survey information, have students develop a composite for that individual at highest risk and that individual at lowest risk.

3. Although most jurisdictions allow for victim/witness impact statements to be offered at the sentencing phase, much debate continues to surround this practice. Have students identify the pros and cons for the victim, offender, and criminal justice system as a whole.

InfoTrac Assignment

GETTING STARTED: Search term words for subject guide: Crime Victims, Loss, Fear.

CRITICAL THINKING PROJECT: Using the search term "Fear," find articles that discuss the fear of crime that is being generated in our society.

Here are three articles:

Perkins, Douglas D. and Ralph B. Taylor. "Ecological Assessments of Community Disorder: Their relationship to fear of crime and theoretical implications." *American Journal of Community Psychology*.

Schmidt, Brad and Jeffrey Winters. "Fear Not: Americans have been very jittery lately. As we cautiously open our mail, terror is ever present. Here, we take a look at fear itself." *Psychology Today*.

Warr, Mark and Christopher G. Ellison. "Rethinking Social Reactions to Crime: Personal and altruistic fear in family households." *The American Journal of Sociology*.

Fill in the Blank

1. Criminologists who focus their attention on crime victims refer to themselves as **Victimologists**.
    (page number 70)

2. The abuse-crime phenomenon is referred to as the **cycle of violence**.
    (page number 73)

3. Except for the crime of **rape or sexual assault**, males are more likely than females to be victims of crime.
    (page number 74)

4. The **elderly** are more likely to be victims of frauds and scams.
    (page number 75)

5. Individuals who are repeatedly crime victims are known as **chronic or repeat** victims.
    (page number 76)

6. **Victim precipitation** is the view that some people may actually initiate the confrontation that eventually leads to their injury or death.
    (page number 77)

7. Concerning Routine Activities Theory, police and homeowners would be considered **capable guardians**.
    (page number 80)

8. As defined in the Routine Activities Theory, an example of **suitable targets** would be a home that contained easily salable goods.
    (page number 80)

9. As defined by Routine Activities Theory, a large number of teenagers would be classified as **motivated offenders**.
    (page number 80)

10. In **Routine Activities Theory**, Cohen and Felson concluded that the volume and distribution of predatory crime are closely related to the interaction of three variables that reflect the routine activities of the typical American lifestyle: the availability of suitable targets, the absence of capable guardians, and the presence of motivated offenders.
    (page number 80)

11. Areas with elevated chances of victimization due to higher concentrations of motivated offenders are known as **hot spots**.
   (page number 80)

12. According to Felson, crime and delinquency rates **increased** between 1960 and 1990 because of structural changes like the growth of suburbs and the proliferation of convenience items like the microwave oven.
   (page number 82)

13. Surveys show that more than **75** percent of the general public has been victimized by crime at least once in their life.
   (page number 83)

14. **Victim compensation** is money paid to the victim, usually from a state victim compensation program.
   (page number 84)

15. Local programs designed to assist victims/witnesses with medical bills, transportation, loss of wages, counseling, and other needs caused by the crime are called **victim-witness assistance programs**.
   (page number 84)

Multiple Choice

1. Criminologists who focus their attention on crime victims refer to themselves as:
   a. Victimologists
   b. Sociologists
   c. Psychologists
   d. none of the above
   (Answer = a, page number 70)

2. The total cost of victimizations is estimated to be over _____ annually.
   a. $10,000
   b. $100,000
   c. $1 million
   d. $100 billion
   (Answer = d, page number 70)

3. Each heroin addict is estimated to cost society about _____ per year.
   a. $135
   b. $1,350
   c. $13,500
   d. $135,000
   (Answer = d, page number 70)

4. Victims of crime suffer which of the following:
   a. economic loss
   b. long-term stress
   c. fear
   d. all of the above
   (Answer = d, page numbers 70-72)

5. The abuse-crime phenomenon is referred to as:
   a. self-protection
   b. the cycle of violence
   c. antisocial behavior
   d. all of the above
   (Answer = b, page number 73)

6. The current leading source of information about the nature and extent of victimization is the:
   a. Uniform Crime Report
   b. Self-Report Surveys
   c. Youth Surveys
   d. National Crime Victimization Survey
   (Answer = d, page number 73)

7. Which age group has more violent crime committed against them?
   a. 65+
   b. 35-49
   c. 25-35
   d. 16-19
   (Answer = d, page number 74)

8. The group most vulnerable to crime is:
   a. low-income, African-American, western, and urban
   b. affluent, rural, white, and northeastern
   c. all of the above
   d. none of the above
   (Answer = a, page numbers 74-76)

9. Which income level has more violent crime committed against them?
   a. $75,000 or more
   b. $2,500-$34,000
   c. less than $7,500
   d. none of the above
   (Answer = c, page number 75)

10. Which of the following are less likely to become a crime victim?
   a. those who are married
   b. those who have never married
   c. those who are divorced
   d. none of the above
   (Answer = a, page number 75)

11. Which ethnic group members report the highest rate of victimization?
   a. African Americans
   b. Whites
   c. Hispanics
   d. Asians
   (Answer = a, page number 76)

12. Individuals who are repeatedly crime victims are called:
   a. motivated offenders
   b. capable guardians
   c. chronic victims
   d. none of the above
   (Answer = c, page number 76)

13. Some characteristics increase victimization risk because they arouse anger, jealousy, or destructive impulses in potential offenders. This is known as:
   a. target vulnerability
   b. target characterization
   c. target victims
   d. target antagonism
   (Answer = d, page number 76)

14. Sibling homicide is known as:
   a. siblicide
   b. genocide
   c. brothericide
   d. sistercide
   (Answer = a, page number 76)

15. Some people may actually initiate the confrontation that eventually leads to their injury or death. This is part of the:
   a. Lifestyle Theory
   b. High-Risk Lifestyle
   c. Deviant Place Theory
   d. Victim Precipitation Theory
   (Answer = d, page number 77)

16. When victims act provocatively, use threats or fighting words, or even attack first, it is known as:
   a. passive precipitation
   b. active precipitation
   c. Deviant Place Theory
   d. Lifestyle Theory
   (Answer = b, page number 77)

17. When the victim exhibits some personal characteristic that unknowingly either threatens or encourages the attacker it is known as:
   a. passive precipitation
   b. active precipitation
   c. Deviant Place Theory
   d. Lifestyle Theory
   (Answer = a, page number 77)

18. One's chances of victimization are reduced by:
   a. staying single
   b. staying out of public places
   c. moving to the city
   d. being out after 10 pm
   (Answer = b, page number 77)

19. Victim precipitation is:
   a. active
   b. passive
   c. all of the above
   d. none of the above
   (Answer = c, page number 77)

20. Which of the following is least likely to be a characteristic of a high-risk lifestyle?
   a. drinking alcohol
   b. taking drugs
   c. participating in sports
   d. involvement in crime
   (Answer = c, page number 77)

21. Lifestyle impacts the opportunity for crime because it controls a person's:
   a. proximity to criminals
   b. time of exposure to criminals
   c. attractiveness as a target
   d. all of the above
   (Answer = d, page number 77)

22. Deviant places are:
    a. poor
    b. densely populated
    c. highly transient neighborhoods
    d. all of the above
    (Answer = d, page number 79)

23. In Routine Activities Theory, police and homeowners would be an example of:
    a. suitable targets
    b. motivated offenders
    c. capable guardians
    d. all of the above
    (Answer = c, page number 80)

24. In Routine Activities Theory, a large number of unemployed teenagers would be and example of:
    a. suitable targets
    b. motivated offenders
    c. capable guardians
    d. all of the above
    (Answer = b, page number 80)

25. Which of the following is the best example of a suitable target?
    a. middle-aged men
    b. police officers
    c. expensive cars
    d. homeowners
    (Answer = c, page number 80)

26. According to Routine Activities Theory, a home that contained easily salable objects (for example, laptop computers, stereos, and television sets) would be classified as a:
    a. motivated offender
    b. suitable target
    c. victimologist
    d. chronic offender
    (Answer = b, page number 80)

27. Places where there is an elevated chance of being the victim of crime are known as:
    a. hot targets
    b. hot spots
    c. suitable targets
    d. chronic spots
    (Answer = b, page number 80)

28. A person's lifestyle has _____ impact on their risk of victimization.
   a. little
   b. somewhat of an
   c. a great deal of
   d. it is unclear what the impact level is
   (Answer = c, page number 80)

29. Cohen and Felson argue that crime rates _____ between 1960-1980 because the number of adult caretakers at home during the day decreased as a result of increased female participation in the workforce.
   a. decreased
   b. stayed the same
   c. did not change
   d. increased
   (Answer = d, page number 81)

30. Skyrocketing drug use in the _____ created an excess of motivated offenders, and the rates of some crimes, such as robbery, increased dramatically.
   a. 1960's
   b. 1980's
   c. 1990's
   d. 2000's
   (Answer = b, page number 83)

31. A local program to assist victims/witnesses with applying for compensation, transportation, crisis intervention, and other needs caused by the crime is known as:
   a. social services
   b. a Victim-Witness Assistance Program
   c. a Rape Crisis Center
   d. a Guardian Ad Litem Program
   (Answer = b, page number 84)

32. Which of the following is typically not covered by victim compensation programs?
   a. replacement costs for stolen property
   b. loss of wages
   c. counseling expenses
   d. medical expenses
   (Answer = a, page number 84)

33. What is the largest area of award from victim compensation programs?
   a. medical expenses
   b. support for lost wages
   c. funeral expenses
   d. mental health counseling
   (Answer = a, page number 84)

34. Which of the following is a primary aim of victim-offender reconciliation programs?
    a. restitution agreements
    b. reconciliation between the two parties
    c. recovery of stolen property
    d. a and b are both correct
    (Answer = d, page number 85)

35. The victim's ability to address the sentencing judge and tell of his or her experiences as a result of the victimization is known as a(n):
    a. compensation request
    b. reconciliation program
    c. restitution agreement
    d. impact statement
    (Answer = d, page number 85)

36. Which of the following is a private, nonprofit organization committed to the recognition and implementation of victim rights and services?
    a. VOCA
    b. NOVA
    c. NCVS
    d. VORP
    (Answer = b, page number 85)

37. Which of the following is not part of the Crime Victims' Bill of Rights?
    a. the right to be reasonably protected from the accused
    b. the right not to be excluded from any such public proceeding
    c. the right to full and timely restitution as provided in the law
    d. all of the above are included
    (Answer = d, page number 86)

38. Making one's home and business crime proof through locks, bars, alarms, and other devices is known as:
    a. target hardening
    b. suitable targets
    c. active hardening
    d. desistence
    (Answer = a, page number 87)

39. About _____ of households in the U.S. contain guns.
    a. one-fourth
    b. one-third
    c. one-half
    d. three-fourths
    (Answer = b, page number 88)

40. Studies have shown that when neighborhood patrols focus directly on crime problems, they are:
    a. very effective
    b. somewhat effective
    c. not very effective
    d. the findings are unclear
    (Answer = c, page number 88)

True/False

1. The National Crime Victimization Survey indicates that the annual number of victimizations in the U.S. is about 24 million.
    (Answer = true, page number 70)

2. If the cost of the justice system, legal costs, treatment costs, and so on, are added up, the cost per U.S. citizen is about $100 annually.
    (Answer = false, page number 70)

3. Research shows that both boys and girls are more likely to engage in violent behavior if they were the target of physical abuse, exposed to violent behavior among adults they know or live with, or exposed to weapons.
    (Answer = true, page number 73)

4. The NCVS reports higher rates of violent victimizations than of property victimizations for persons over age 12.
    (Answer = false, page number 73)

5. Between 1993 and 2003, the violent crime victimization rate decreased by 55 percent.
    (Answer = true, page number 73)

6. The NCVS shows that violent crimes are slightly more likely to take place in dark, closed places in the middle of the night.
    (Answer = false, page number 74)

7. The NCVS tells us that rural, white homes in the Northeast are the most likely to contain crime victims or be the target of theft offenses, such as burglary or larceny.
    (Answer = false, page number 74)

8. Individuals who have been crime victims maintain a significantly higher chance of future victimization than people who have remained nonvictims.
    (Answer = true, page number 76)

9. Victims reported that a single offender over age 20 committed most crimes.
    (Answer = true, page number 76)

10. Crime tends to be interracial.
　　(Answer = false, page number 76)

11. Victimization commonly occurs within families and involves parents, children, and extended family.
　　(Answer = true, page number 76)

12. According to the victim precipitation view, some people may actually initiate the confrontation that eventually leads to their injury or death.
　　(Answer = true, page number 77)

13. According to Deviant Place Theory, victims encourage crime and are victim prone because they live in safe, nice neighborhoods.
　　(Answer = false, page number 79)

14. Motivated people, such as teenage males, drug users, and unemployed adults, are the ones most likely to commit crime.
　　(Answer = true, page number 80)

15. Some criminologists support the idea that moral beliefs and socialization may influence the routine activities that produce crime.
　　(Answer = true, page number 81)

Essay Questions

1. Describe the problems which most crime victims suffer. What are some of the remedies that a victim can use to help his or her plight?
　　(page numbers 70-73)

2. Define the nature of victimization. Are there certain characteristics which predispose one to becoming a victim? Are victims and criminals similar in their characteristics?
　　(page numbers 73-77)

3. Compare and contrast the various theories of victimization. Give examples of sensational crimes for which each theory applies.
　　(page numbers 77-83)

4. Should society participate in the care of victims? What has been the government's response to caring for victims? In your opinion, is this sufficient?
　　(page numbers 83-88)

5. Describe victim service programs. Are they effective? If they are not effective, how can they be improved?
　　(page numbers 84-88)

Chapter Four

Choice Theories

Summary

Chapter Four examines the development of Rational Choice Theory. Particular attention is paid to the issue of whether crime is rational or irrational. Methods of eliminating crime are introduced and the chapter concludes with a discussion of public policy implications of Choice Theory.

Chapter Objectives

After reading this chapter the student should be able to:

- Be familiar with the concept of rational choice
- Know the work of Beccaria
- Be familiar with the concept of offense-specific crime
- Be familiar with the concept of offender-specific crime
- Be able to discuss why violent and drug crimes are rational
- Know the various techniques of situational crime prevention
- Be able to discuss the association between punishment and crime
- Be familiar with the concepts of certainty, severity, and speed of punishment
- Know what is meant by specific deterrence
- Be able to discuss the issues involving the use of incapacitation
- Understand the concept of just desert

Chapter Overview

Introduction
The Development of Rational Choice Theory
    The Classical Theory of Crime
    Choice Theory Emerges
The Concepts of Rational Choice
    Offense- and Offender-Specific Crimes
    Structuring Criminality
    Structuring Crime
Is Crime Rational?
    Is Theft Rational?
    Is Drug Use Rational?

The Criminological Enterprise: Hector Vega: A Life in the Drug Trade
Is Violence Rational?
Eliminating Crime
Situational Crime Prevention
Comparative Criminology: CCTV or Not CCTV? Comparing Situational Crime Prevention Efforts in Great Britain and the United States
General Deterrence
The Criminological Enterprise: Does Capital Punishment Deter Murder?
Specific Deterrence
Race, Culture, Gender, and Criminology: Deterring Domestic Violence
Incapacitation
Public Policy Implications of Choice Theory
Just Desert
Summary

Chapter Outline

I. Introduction
    A. The Development of Rational Choice Theory
        1. View that crime is a decision to violate any law and is made for a variety of reasons, including greed, revenge, need, anger, lust, jealousy, thrill-seeking, or vanity.
II. The Development of Rational Choice Theory
    A. Rational Choice Theory
        1. Rooted in the classical school developed by Cesare Beccaria.
            a. called for fair and certain punishment to deter crime.
            b. if crime and punishment are not proportional, people will commit more serious offenses.
        2. Marginal deterrence - if petty offenses were subject to the same punishment as serious crimes, offenders would choose the worst.
    B. The Classical Theory of Crime
        1. Beccaria got others to think that criminals chose to commit crime.
        2. Jeremy Bentham (1748-1833) popularized Beccaria's views
            a. utilitarianism - people choose actions based on whether they receive pleasure and avoid pain.
        3. Punishment - has four objectives:
            a. to prevent all criminal offenses.
            b. when it does not prevent, to convince offenders to commit lesser offenses.
            c. to ensure that a criminal uses no more force than is necessary.
            d. to prevent crime as cheaply as possible.
        4. By the end of the 19th century, the classical approach declined.
    C. Choice Theory Emerges
        1. Mid-1970's classical approach becomes popular again.
            a. rehabilitation of known criminals came under attack.

b. significant increase in reported crime rate.

c. prison disturbances.

    2. Thinking About Crime

      a. 1970's - thinking began to reflect that criminals are rational actors who plan their crimes, fear punishment, and deserve to be penalized for their misdeeds.

      b. James Q. Wilson wrote *Thinking About Crime* in which he states that unless we react forcefully to crime, those "sitting on the fence" will decide that crime pays.

    3. Impact on Crime Control - shift in U.S. public policy.

      a. tougher laws were passed including mandatory sentences.

      b. stiffer penalties enacted leading to huge prison populations.

III. The Concepts of Rational Choice - law-violating behavior occurs when an offender decides to risk breaking the law after considering both personal factors and situation factors.

  A. Offense- and Offender-Specific Crimes

    1. Offense-specific crime - offenders will react selectively to the characteristics of particular offenses.

    2. Offender-specific crime - criminals are not simply automatons who, for one reason or another, engage in random acts of antisocial behavior.

    3. Crime versus criminality:

      a. crime is an event.

      b. criminality is a personal trait.

  B. Structuring Criminality - a number of personal factors condition people to choose crime.

    1. Economic opportunity - crime occurs when one feels they will profit.

    2. Learning and experience - career criminal learn their limits; when to take a chance and when to be cautious.

    3. Knowledge of criminal techniques - to avoid detection.

  C. Structuring Crime - criminals choose where and when to commit crime.

    1. Choosing the type of crime - some criminals are specialists.

    2. Choosing the time and place of crime - criminals select times that are better and are selective in the location of the crime.

    3. Choosing the target of crime - select more vulnerable targets.

IV. Is Crime Rational? - crimes are the product of rational, objective thought.

  A. Is Theft Rational? - seems more like random acts of criminal opportunity than well-thought-out conspiracies.

    1. Boosters - professional shoplifters who use complex methods to avoid detection.

    2. Permeable neighborhoods - neighborhoods with greater than usual number of access streets; the choice of most burglars.

  B. Is Drug Use Rational? - at the onset, drug use is controlled by rational decision making; it is treated like a business.

  C. Is Violence Rational? - there are cases of rational, thought-out violence.

1. Rational robbers? - choose victims who are vulnerable, have low coercive poser, and do not pose any threat.
2. Rational killers? - many homicides are the result of careful planning.
3. Rational rapists? - serial rapists show rationality to avoid detection.
4. Attraction of crime - crime may produce sensations that are reinforcing
   a. edgework - the exhilarating, momentary integration of danger, risk, and skill that motivates people to try dangerous criminal and noncriminal behaviors.

V. Eliminating Crime - if crime is rational, then offenders should be able to be convinced to make different choices.
A. Situational Crime Prevention - criminal acts will be avoided if potential targets are carefully guarded, the means to commit crime are controlled, and potential offenders are carefully monitored.
   1. Defensible space - coined in the early 1970's by Oscar Newman; crime can be prevented or displaced through the use of residential architectural designs that reduce criminal opportunity.
   2. Targeting specific crimes - 4 categories:
      a. increase the effort needed to commit crime.
      b. increase the risks of committing crime.
      c. reduce the rewards for committing crime.
      d. induce guilt or shame for committing crime.
   3. Increase efforts - target hardening and reducing opportunities for crime.
   4. Reduce rewards - reduce the value of crime to the potential criminal.
   5. Increase risk - make criminals think committing crime is risky.
      a. crime discouragers - guardians who monitor targets, handlers who monitor potential offenders, and managers who monitor places.
   6. Increase guilt - set strict rules to embarrass offenders.
   7. Situational crime prevention: costs and benefits.
      a. diffusion - when efforts to prevent one crime unintentionally prevent another and crime control efforts in one locale reduce crime in other nontarget areas.
      b. discouragement - when crime control efforts targeting one locale help reduce crime in surrounding areas and groups.
      c. crime displacement - doing something in one area which may re-direct the crime to another area.
      d. extinction - crime reduction programs may produce a short-term positive effect, but benefits dissipate as criminals adjust to new conditions.
B. General Deterrence - crime rates are influence and controlled by the threat of punishment. If people fear punishment, they will not break the law.
   1. Certainty of punishment - or the "tipping point;" will only deter if likelihood of getting caught reaches a critical point.
      a. deterrence theory states the crime rate should decrease with the certainty of punishment. However, crime continues because criminals believe:

    i. there is only a small chance they will get arrested.

    ii. police officers are sometimes reluctant to make arrests even if they are aware of the crime.

    iii. even if apprehended there is a good chance of receiving a lenient punishment.

2. Does increasing police activity deter crime?
    a. Kansas City, MO experiment found patrol techniques had little effect on crime patterns.
    b. crackdowns - sudden changes in police activity designed to increase the communicated threat or actual certainty of punishment to lower crime.
        i. while crime rates lower initially, they increase again after the crackdown ends.

3. Severity of punishment and deterrence - increasing the punishment for specific crimes can reduce their occurrence.

4. Capital punishment
    a. immediate impact - studies show that the overall impact of executions might actually increase the incidence of homicide.
    b. comparative research - states with and without the death penalty show no difference in their murder rates.
    c. time-series studies - look at the long-term association between capital sentencing and murder. Studies show no relationship between the deterrence of capital sentencing and the murder rate.
    d. rethinking the deterrent effect of capital punishment - some found that increasing the number of executions has helped reduce the murder rate.

5. Informal sanctions
    a. may have a greater deterrent impact than formal legal punishment.
    b. occur when significant others, such as parents, peers, neighbors, and teachers, direct their disapproval, stigma, anger, and indignation toward an offender.

6. Shame and humiliation - can be a powerful deterrent to crime.
    a. personal shame over violating the law and fear of public humiliation.

7. Critique of general deterrence
    a. rationality - deterrence theory assumes a rational offender weighs the costs and decides on their course of action.
    b. need - many offenders are members of the underclass.
    c. greed - some are immune to deterrence because they feel the profits are worth the risk.
    d. severity and speed - Beccaria said punishments should be severe, certain, and swift; ours are not.

C. Specific Deterrence - criminal sanctions should be so powerful that known criminals will never repeat their criminal acts.
   1. Does specific deterrence deter crime? - chronic offenders continue to offend.
D. Incapacitation - some feel that sending more to prison would reduce crime.
   1. Can incapacitation reduce crime? - studies show the results would be minimal.
   2. The logic behind incarceration - may not work as a deterrent.
      a. little evidence that incapacitating criminals will deter them from future criminality.
      b. first time offenders are exposed to more experienced inmates.
      c. older offenders are usually sentenced and may be kept beyond the time they are a threat to society.
      d. very expensive to incarcerate everyone.
      e. incarceration may have the long-term effect of accelerating crime rates when they are released.
   3. Selective incapacitation - for chronic career criminals.
      a. problems with Three Strives and You're Out policies:
         i. will age out soon anyway.
         ii. violent sentences are already severe.
         iii. more prisoners lead to more costs.
         iv. racial disparity in sentencing.
         v. police in danger from two-time offenders who have nothing to lose.
         vi. highest -frequency offenders already are in prison.

VI. Public Policy Implications of Choice Theory
A. Just Desert - Andrew Von Hirsch in his book *Doing Justice*.
   1. Those who violate others' rights deserve to be punished.
   2. We should not deliberately add to human suffering; punishment makes those punished suffer.
   3. Punishment may prevent more misery than it inflicts.

VII. Summary

Key Terms

Boosters - Professional shoplifters who steal with the intention of reselling stolen merchandise.

Crackdowns - The concentration of police resources on a particular problem area, such as street-level drug dealing, to eradicate or displace criminal activity.

Crime Discouragers - Discouragers can be grouped into three categories: guardians, who monitor targets (such as store security guards); handlers, who monitor potential offenders (such as parole officers and parents); and managers, who monitor places (such as homeowners and doorway attendants).

Crime Displacement - An effect of crime prevention efforts in which efforts to control crime in one area shift illegal activities to another.

Criminality - A personal trait of the individual as distinct from a "crime," which is an event.

Defensible Space - The principle that crime prevention can be achieved through modifying the physical environment to reduce the opportunity individuals have to commit crime.

Deterrence Theory - The view that if the probability of arrest, conviction, and sanctioning increases, crime rates should decline.

Diffusion - An effect that occurs when an effort to control one type of crime has the unexpected benefit of reducing the incidence of another.

Discouragement - An effect that occurs when an effort to eliminate one type of crime also controls others, because it reduces the value of criminal activity by limiting access to desirable targets.

Edgework - The excitement or exhilaration of successfully executing illegal activities in dangerous situations.

Extinction - The phenomenon in which a crime prevention effort has an immediate impact that then dissipates as criminals adjust to new conditions.

General Deterrence - A crime control policy that depends on the fear of criminal penalties. General deterrence measures, such as long prison sentences for violent crimes, are aimed at convincing the potential law violator that the pains associated with crime outweigh its benefits.

Incapacitation Effect - The idea that keeping offenders in confinement will eliminate the risk of their committing further offenses.

Informal Sanctions - Disapproval, stigma, or anger directed toward an offender by significant others (parents, peers, neighbors, teachers), resulting in shame, embarrassment, and loss of respect.

Just Desert - The philosophy of justice that asserts that those who violate the rights of others deserve to be punished. The severity of punishment should be commensurate with the seriousness of the crime.

Marginal Deterrence - The concept that a penalty for a crime may prompt commission of a marginally more severe crime because that crime receives the same magnitude of punishment as the original one.

Offender-Specific Crime - The idea that offenders evaluate their skills, motives, needs, and fears before deciding to commit crime.

Offense-Specific Crime - The idea that offenders react selectively to the characteristics of particular crimes.

Permeable Neighborhood - Areas with a greater than usual number of access streets from traffic arteries into the neighborhood.

Rational Choice - The view that crime is a function of a decision-making process in which the potential offender weighs the potential costs and benefits of an illegal act.

Reasoning Criminal - According to the rational choice approach, law-violating behavior occurs when an offender decides to risk breaking the law after considering both personal factors (such as the need for money, revenge, thrills, and entertainment) and situational factors (how well a target is protected and the efficiency of the local police force).

Selective Incapacitation - The policy of creating enhanced prison sentences for the relatively small group of dangerous chronic offenders.

Situational Crime Prevention - A method of crime prevention that stresses tactics and strategies to eliminate or reduce particular crimes in narrow settings, such as reducing burglaries in a housing project by increasing lighting and installing security alarms.

Specific Deterrence - A crime control policy suggesting that punishment be severe enough to convince convicted offenders never to repeat their criminal activity.

Discussion Exercises

1. Discuss recent films such as *Natural Born Killers, Hannibal* and *Blow*. Were these criminals rational? Did they make a choice to be a criminal or were there other contributing elements to their criminality? Could any of these individuals have avoided criminal behaviors or was it beyond their control?

2. Provide students with information on the "hot spots" of crime on your campus. Then, break them into groups and ask the students to apply concepts from situational crime prevention and defensible space in an effort to reduce criminal incidents in these areas.

3. Although most Americans support the death penalty, there remains an ongoing debate as to its effectiveness as a deterrent against murder. Divide the class into two groups. Have one group develop a presentation in support of the deterrent effect of capital punishment and the other group against the deterrent effect. Students, then, can discuss which position is the stronger of the two.

InfoTrac Assignment

GETTING STARTED: Search term words for subject guide: Rational Choice Theory, Street Crimes, Drug Use, Situation Crime, Deterrence, Incapacitation, Just Desert.

CRITICAL THINKING PROJECT: Using the search term "Street Crimes," find articles that discuss this aspect of crime.

Here are three articles:

Lafree, Gary. "Social Institutions and the Crime 'Bust' of the 1990s." *Journal of Criminal Law and Criminology*.

Surratt, Hilary. "Street Kids, Street Drugs, Street Crime: An examination of drug use and serious delinquency in Miami." *Social Forces*.

Young, Thomas J. "Parricide Rates and Criminal Street Violence in the United States: Is there a correlation." *Adolescence*.

Test Bank

Fill in the Blank

1. The policy of giving individuals convicted of three violent offenses a mandatory life term without parole is known as **Three Strikes**.
    (page number 98)

2. **Rational Choice Theory** states that criminals make a rational choice to commit crime.
    (page number 98)

3. **Utilitarianism** is the philosophy which emphasizes that behavior occurs when the actor considers it useful, purposeful, and reasonable.
    (page number 98)

4. **Situational crime prevention** policies convince potential criminals to desist from criminal activities, delay their actions, or avoid a particular target.
    (page number 107)

5. The idea that crime can be prevented or displaced through the use of residential architectural designs that reduce criminal opportunity is known as **defensible space**.
    (page number 107)

6. Techniques and technology used to make it more difficult to commit crime is known as **target hardening**.
    (page number 108)

7. Examples of **crime discouragers** are guardians, handlers, and managers.
    (page number 109)

8. **Difussion** occurs when efforts to prevent one crime unintentionally prevents another.
    (page number 110)

9. Crime reduction programs which may produce a short-term positive effect, but the benefits dissipate as criminals adjust to new conditions is known as **extinction**.
    (page number 112)

10. **General deterrence** says that crime rates are influenced and controlled by the threat of punishment.
    (page number 112)

11. The **tipping point** is when the likelihood of getting caught reaches a certain level and the offender is deterred.
    (page number 112)

12. **Crackdowns** are sudden changes in police activity designed to increase the communicated threat or actual certainty of punishment.
    (page number 113)

13. **Informal sanctions** occur when significant others, such as parents, peer, neighbors, and teachers direct their disapproval, stigma, anger, and indignation toward the offender.
    (page number 115)

14. **Selective incapacitation** is the model that proposes that if a small number of people account for a relatively large percentage of the nation's crime, then an effort to incapacitate these few troublemakers might have a significant payoff.
    (page number 121)

15. **Just desert** is the philosophy of justice that asserts that those who violate the rights of others deserve to be punished.
    (page number 122)

Multiple Choice

1. The policy of giving individuals convicted of three violent offenses a mandatory life term without parole is known as:
    a. the death penalty
    b. probation
    c. parole
    d. Three Strikes
    (Answer = d, page number 98)

2. The belief that criminals choose to commit crimes is supported by:
    a. Choice Theory
    b. Deterrence Theory
    c. Classical Theory
    d. Crime Displacement Theory
    (Answer = a, page number 98)

3. Rational Choice Theory has its roots in the classical school of criminology developed by:
    a. Sigmund Freud
    b. Karl Marx
    c. Mark Martin
    d. Cesare Beccaria
    (Answer = d, page number 98)

4. If petty offenses were subject to the same punishment as more serious crimes, offenders would choose the worse crime. This is known as:
    a. marginal deterrence
    b. motivated criminals
    c. specific deterrence
    d. general deterrence
    (Answer = a, page number 98)

5. The philosophy which emphasized that behavior occurs when the actor considers it useful, purposeful, and reasonable is known as:
    a. Utilitarianism
    b. Rational Choice Theory
    c. Deterrence Theory
    d. Discouragement Theory
    (Answer = a, page number 98)

6. Who wrote *Thinking about Crime?*
    a. Charles Murray
    b. Louis Cox
    c. James Q. Wilson
    d. Mark Twain
    (Answer = c, page number 99)

7. According to Rational Choice Theory, the potential criminals in a population are known as:
    a. victims
    b. defendants
    c. suitable criminals
    d. reasoning criminals
    (Answer = d, page number 100)

8. The view that criminals make a rational choice to commit crime is supported by:
    a. Deterrence Theory
    b. Crime Displacement Theory
    c. Rational Choice Theory
    d. Classical Theory
    (Answer = c, page number 100)

9. Offenders reacting selectively to the characteristics of particular offenses is known as:
    a. offense specific
    b. offender specific
    c. rational choice
    d. altruistic fear
    (Answer = a, page number 100)

10. The notion that criminals are not simply automatons who, for one reason or another, engage in random acts of antisocial behavior is known as:
   a. altruistic fear
   b. rational choice
   c. offense specific
   d. offender specific
   (Answer = d, page number 100)

11. Personal factors which may influence people to commit crime are:
   a. economic opportunities
   b. learning and experience
   c. learning criminal techniques
   d. all of the above
   (Answer = d, page number 101)

12. The exhilarating, momentary integration of danger, risk, and skill that motivates people to try a variety of dangerous criminal and non-criminal behaviors is known as:
   a. discouragers
   b. edgework
   c. suitable targets
   d. defensible space
   (Answer = b, page number 107)

13. The principle that crime prevention can be achieved through modifying the physical environment to reduce the opportunity individuals have to commit crime is called:
   a. crime displacement
   b. edgework
   c. crime discouragers
   d. defensible space
   (Answer = d, page number 107)

14. Policies that convince potential criminals to desist from criminal activities, delay their actions, or avoid a particular target are known as:
   a. situational crime prevention
   b. crime displacement
   c. crime discouragers
   d. deterrence
   (Answer = a, page number 107)

15. Which of the following is not a crime prevention strategy used today?
   a. increase the effort needed to commit crime
   b. increase the risks for committing crime
   c. reduce the rewards for committing crime
   d. reduce guilt or shame for committing crime
   (Answer = d, page number 108)

16. Techniques and technology used to make it more difficult to commit a crime is known as:
    a. diffusion
    b. formal surveillance
    c. suitable target
    d. target hardening
    (Answer = d, page number 108)

17. Which of the following is the best example of target hardening?
    a. steering locks
    b. formal surveillance
    c. gender-neutral phone lines
    d. graffiti cleaning
    (Answer = a, page number 109)

18. Reducing anticipated rewards may include which of the following?
    a. target removal
    b. identifying property
    c. all of the above
    d. none of the above
    (Answer = c, page number 109)

19. Parole officers and parents are the best examples of:
    a. guardians
    b. handlers
    c. managers
    d. none of the above
    (Answer = b, page number 109)

20. People whose behavior directly influences crime prevention are known as:
    a. capable guardians
    b. legal guardians
    c. chronic offenders
    d. crime discouragers
    (Answer = d, page number 109)

21. When efforts to prevent one crime unintentionally prevents another and crime control efforts in one locale reduce crime in other nontarget areas, this is known as:
    a. Choice Theory
    b. diffusion of benefits
    c. crackdowns
    d. discouragement
    (Answer = b, page number 110)

22. This occurs when efforts to eliminate one type of crime convince would-be lawbreakers to forgo other criminal activity because crime no longer pays:
    a. persistence
    b. desistance
    c. discouragement
    d. passive precipitation
    (Answer = c, page number 111)

23. Preventing crime in one location, but having that crime then relocated to another location is known as:
    a. crime discouragers
    b. edgework
    c. crime displacement
    d. Deterrence Theory
    (Answer = c, page number 112)

24. Crime reduction programs which may produce a short-term positive effect, but the benefits dissipate as criminals adjust to new conditions is known as:
    a. crackdowns
    b. loss
    c. deterrence
    d. extinction
    (Answer = d, page number 112)

25. According to _____, crime rates are influenced and controlled by the threat of punishment.
    a. specific deterrence
    b. general deterrence
    c. diffusion of benefits
    d. crime displacement
    (Answer = b, page number 112)

26. According to _____, the severity of punishment is inversely proportional to the level of crime benefits.
    a. defensible space
    b. Deterrence Theory
    c. discouragement
    d. diffusion of benefits
    (Answer = b, page number 112)

27. Crime persists because most offenders believe that:
    a. there is only a small chance they will be arrested for committing a crime
    b. police officers are sometimes reluctant to arrest even when aware of crime
    c. even if apprehended there is a good chance of receiving a lenient punishment
    d. all of the above
    (Answer = d, page number 113)

28. The most famous police experiment concerning the impact of police activities on crime rates was conducted where?
   a. Kansas City, Missouri
   b. Kansas City, Kansas
   c. Fayetteville, North Carolina
   d. Las Cruces, New Mexico
   (Answer = a, page number 113)

29. Sudden changes in police activity designed to lower crime rates through an increase in the communicated threat or actual certainty of punishment are known as:
   a. crime discouragers
   b. edgework
   c. crackdowns
   d. crime displacement
   (Answer = c, page number 113)

30. Between 1993 - 1997 the probability of going to prison for murder increased:
   a. 6%
   b. 20%
   c. 65%
   d. 17%
   (Answer = d, page number 114)

31. Between 1993 - 1997 the murder rate dropped:
   a. 6%
   b. 20%
   c. 23%
   d. 65%
   (Answer = c, page number 114)

32. Between 1993 - 1997 robbery declined:
   a. 1%
   b. 2%
   c. 21%
   d. 4%
   (Answer = c, page number 114)

33. Between 1993 - 1997 the probability of going prison after a conviction increased:
   a. 2%
   b. 4%
   c. 10%
   d. 14%
   (Answer = d, page number 114)

34. _____ occur when significant others, such as parents, peer, neighbors, and teachers, direct their disapproval, stigma, anger, and indignation toward the offender.
    a. Informal sanctions
    b. Formal sanctions
    c. Delayed sanctions
    d. Reactive sanctions
    (Answer = a, page number 115)

35. Which of the following is the best example of inducing guilt or shame?
    a. rule setting
    b. strengthening moral condemnation
    c. all of the above
    d. none of the above
    (Answer = c, page number 115)

36. The type of study which has been conducted on the impact of capital punishment is called:
    a. immediate impact
    b. comparative research
    c. time series analysis
    d. all of the above
    (Answer = d, page number 116)

37. Research which compares the murder rates in jurisdictions that have abolished the death penalty with the rates of those that employ the death penalty is called:
    a. immediate impact
    b. comparative research
    c. time series analysis
    d. discouragement
    (Answer = b, page number 116)

38. The use of sanctions to keep criminals from reoffending is known as:
    a. specific deterrence
    b. special deterrence
    c. particular deterrence
    d. all of the above
    (Answer = d, page number 116)

39. The model that proposes that if a small number of people account for a relatively large percentage of the nation's crime, then an effort to incapacitate these few troublemakers might have a significant payoff is known as:.
    a. Deterrence Theory
    b. Classical Theory
    c. Rational Choice Theory
    d. Selective Incapacitation
    (Answer = d, page number 121)

40. The philosophy of justice that asserts that those who violate the rights of others deserve to be punished is known as:
    a. crime discouragers
    b. just desert
    c. crackdowns
    d. none of the above
    (Answer = b, page number 122)

True/False

1. The view that crime is a matter of rational choice is held by a number of criminologists who believe that the decision to violate any law is made for a variety of personal reasons including greed, revenge, need, anger, lust, jealousy, thrill-seeking, or vanity.
    (Answer = true, page number 98)

2. Rational Choice Theory has roots in the Chicago School of Sociology developed by the Italian social thinker Cesare Beccaria.
    (Answer = false, page number 98)

3. To deter people from committing more serious offenses, Beccaria believed punishment should be lenient.
    (Answer = false, page number 98)

4. Britain philosopher Jeremy Bentham helped popularize Beccaria's views in his writings on utilitarianism.
    (Answer = true, page number 98)

5. The purpose of law is to produce and support the total happiness of the community it serves.
    (Answer = true, page number 98)

6. Selling hours means learning how to hide drugs on their person, in the street, or home.
    (Answer = false, page number 102)

7. Stashing means that drug dealers are aware of those times of the day when it is best to sell their drugs.
    (Answer = false, page number 102)

8. Routine activities means that dealers camouflaged their activities within the bustle of their daily lives.
    (Answer = true, page number 102)

9. The peep game is scooping out the terrority to make sure the turf is free from anything out of place that may be a potential threat.
    (Answer = true, page number 102)

10. Most burglars commit crime in impermeable neighborhoods.
    (Answer = false, page number 104)

11. Edgework is the exhilarating, momentary integration of danger, risk, and skill that motivates people to try a variety of dangerous criminal and non-criminal behavior.
    (Answer = true, page number 107)

12. Informal sanctions are less effective at reducing crime then is fear of formal legal punishment.
    (Answer = false, page number 115)

13. Fear of the death penalty has been an effective tool in reducing homicide in recent years.
    (Answer = false, page numbers 116-117)

14. The Minneapolis domestic violence study showed that arresting offenders was an ineffective means of reducing recidivism.
    (Answer = false, page number 118)

15. Today, more than 2 million Americans are incarcerated.
    (Answer = true, page number 120)

Essay Questions

1. Describe the concepts of Rational Choice Theory. Trace the origin of this theory and its implications on our policies today.
    (page numbers 98-100)

2. Differentiate between offense-specific crimes and offender-specific crimes. Incorporate examples for each.
    (page numbers 100-101)

3. Is crime a rational choice? Give specific examples for your discussion.
    (page numbers 104-107)

4. Describe deterrence. What is the difference between general and specific deterrence. Do deterrence strategies work in eliminating crime?
    (page numbers 112-119)

5. What are the policy implications of choice theory? Define choice theory and how it emerged.
    (page numbers 122-123)

Chapter Five

Trait Theories

Summary

Chapter Five examines the Trait Theories of criminology. A discussion of the foundations and explanations of the various biological trait theories is key. This chapter also looks at the psychological trait theories and their implications. The chapter concludes with the public policy implications that these theories have had in our society.

Chapter Objectives

After reading this chapter the student should be able to:

- Be familiar with the concept of sociobiology
- Know what is meant by the term *equipotentiality*
- Be able to discuss the relationship between diet and crime
- Be familiar with the association between hormones and crime
- Be able to discuss why violent offenders may suffer from neurological problems
- Know the factors that make up the ADHD syndrome
- Be able to discuss the role genetics plays in violent behavior
- Be familiar with the concepts of evolutionary theory
- Be able to discuss the psychodynamics of criminality
- Understand the association between media and crime
- Discuss the role of personality and intelligence in antisocial behaviors

Chapter Overview

Introduction
Foundations of Trait Theory
    Impact of Sociobiology
    Modern Trait Theories
Biological Trait Theories
    Biochemical Conditions and Crime
Comparative Criminology: Diet and Crime: An International Perspective
    Neurophysiological Conditions and Crime
    Arousal Theory
    Genetics and Crime
    Evolutionary Theory
    Evaluation of the Biosocial Branch of Trait Theory

Psychological Trait Theories
      Psychodynamic Theory
      Behavioral Theories
The Criminological Enterprise: The Media and Violence
      Cognitive Theory
      Personality and Crime
The Criminological Enterprise: The Antisocial Personality
      Intelligence and Crime
Public Policy Implications of Trait Theory
Summary

Chapter Outline

I. **Introduction**
II. **Foundations of Trait Theory**
    A. The earliest supporters of biological theory.
        1. Cesare Lombroso and his "born criminal."
        2. Raffaele Garofalo and his notion that criminals are less sensitive to physical pain.
        3. Enrico Ferri and his view that criminals should not be held responsible for forces outside their control.
        4. The inheritance school traced the activities of several generations of families believed to have an especially large number of criminal members.
        5. William Sheldon, 50 years ago, of the somatotype school, held that criminals manifest distinct physiques that makes them susceptible to particular types of delinquent behavior.
           a. mesomorphs - have well-developed muscles and an athletic appearance; active, aggressive, and most likely to be criminal.
           b. endomorphs - heavy builds and are slow moving; less likely to commit violent crime, possibly engage in less strenuous crimes.
           c. ectomorphs - tall, thin, less social, and more intellectual than other types.
    B. Impact of Sociobiology
        1. Biological explanations of crime fell out of favor in the early 20th century.
        2. Biophobia - the belief that no serious consideration should be given to biological factors when attempting to understand human nature.
        3. In the early 1970's criminologist Edmund O. Wilson published *Sociobiology* and the biological basis for crime reemerged.

4. Sociobiologists view the gene as ultimate unit of life that controls all human destiny.
5. People are controlled by the need to have their genetics survive and dominate others.
6. Reciprocal altruism - people are motivated by believing that their actions will be reciprocated and that their gene survival will be enhanced.

C. Modern Trait Theories - each offender is unique, physically and mentally.
1. Trait theorists are not overly concerned with legal definitions of crime.
2. Trait theorists focus on basic human behavior and drives like aggression, violence, and the tendency to act on impulse.
3. Trait theorists argue that chronic offenders suffer some biological/psychological condition that renders them incapable of resisting social pressures and problems.

III. **Biosocial Trait Theories** - believe that physical, environmental, and social conditions work together to produce human behavior.
A. Core principles:
1. Genetic makeup contributes significantly to human behavior.
2. Not all humans are born with equal potential to learn and achieve (equipotentiality).
3. No two people are alike; the combination of genes and environment produce individual behavior patterns.

B. Learning Potential and its Effect on Individual Behavior Patterns
1. Social behavior is learned; each individual organism has a unique potential for learning.
2. Learning takes place when physical changes occur in the brain.
3. Instinct - some believe that learning is influenced by instinctual drives.
   a. instincts are inherited, natural, and unlearned dispositions that activate specific behavior patterns designed to reach certain goals.

C. Biochemical Conditions and Crime
1. Chemical and mineral influences - minimum levels of minerals and chemicals are needed for normal brain functioning and growth, especially in the early years of life.
2. Diet and crime - malnourished or those lacking in certain vitamins may be predisposed to learning and behavior disorders.
3. Sugar and crime - diets high in sugar and carbohydrates have been linked to violence and aggression, although some studies have found no link.
4. Glucose metabolism/hypoglycemia
   a. Research indicates that persistent abnormality in the way the brain metabolizes glucose (sugar) can be linked to antisocial behaviors, such as substance abuse.
   b. hypoglycemia - when glucose in the blood falls below levels necessary for normal and efficient brain functioning; linked to outbursts of antisocial behavior and violence.

5. Hormonal influences - James Q. Wilson feels that hormones may be the key to understanding human behavior.
    a. androgens - male sex hormones which may produce aggressive behavior.
    b. testosterone - the most abundant androgen.
6. How hormones may influence behavior - hormones cause areas of the brain to become less sensitive to environmental stimuli.
    a. neocortex - part of the brain that controls sympathetic feelings toward others.
7. Premenstrual Syndrome - PMS - the onset of the menstrual cycle triggers excessive amounts of the female sex hormones, which affects antisocial, aggressive behavior.
8. Allergies - unusual or excessive reactions of the body to foreign substances.
    a. cerebral allergies - cause an excessive reaction of the brain.
    b. neuroallergies - affect the nervous system.
9. Environmental contaminants - dangerous amounts of copper, cadmium, mercury and inorganic gases, such as chlorine and nitrogen dioxide, are found in the ecosystem and can influence behavior.
10. Lead levels - studies have shown that lead ingestion can cause aggressive behavior.

D. Neurophysiological Conditions and Crime - neurophysiology is the study of brain activity.
    1. Neurological impairments and crime - numerous ways to test neurological functioning.
        a. electroencephalograph (EEG) - the most important measure of neurophysiological functioning.
    2. Minimal Brain Dysfunction (MBD) - related to an abnormality in cerebral structure.
        a. linked to serious antisocial acts, dyslexia, visual perception problems, hyperactivity, poor attention span, temper tantrums, and aggressiveness.
    3. Attention Deficit/Hyperactivity Disorder (ADHD) - a child shows a developmentally inappropriate lack of attention, impulsivity, and hyperactivity.
        a. 3 % of U.S. children, most often boys, suffer from ADHD.
        b. it is the most common reason children are referred to mental health clinics.
        c. conduct disorder - many ADHD children continually engage in aggressive and antisocial behavior in early childhood and disorders are sustained over the life course.
    4. Tumors, lesions, injury, and disease
        a. tumors and lesions of the brain - linked to wide variety of psychological problems, including personality changes, hallucinations, and psychotic episodes.

b. head injuries - linked to personality reversals marked by outbursts of antisocial and violent behavior.

c. central nervous system diseases - cerebral arteriosclerosis, epilepsy, senile dementia, Korsakoff's syndrome, and Huntington's chorea linked to affective disturbances.

5. Brain chemistry - neurotransmitters are chemical compounds that influence or activate brain functions.

    a. abnormal levels of chemicals lead to aggression.

    b. low supply of enzymes linked to violence and property crime.

    c. violent prone people often treated with Haldol, Stelazine, Prolizin, and Risperdal - they help control levels of neurotransmitters and are often referred to as chemical restraints or chemical straightjackets.

E. Arousal Theory - obtaining thrills is a crime motivator.

1. Jack Katz - immediate gratifications from criminality that he calls the "seductions of crime."

2. Some people's brains function differently in response to environmental stimuli; all seek to maintain a preferred level of arousal.

    a. too much stimulation leaves us anxious and stressed out.

    b. too little stimulation leaves us bored and weary.

3. Sensation seekers seek out stimulating activities, which may include aggressive and violent behavior.

F. Genetics and Crime - data suggest that human traits associated with criminality have a genetic basis.

1. Parental deviance - idea that if criminal tendencies are inherited, then criminal parents will produce criminal children.

2. Sibling similarities - if criminal behavior is inherited, it stands to reason that the behavior of siblings would be similar.

3. Twin behavior - studies found that similarities between twins due to genes, not the environment; twins reared apart are so similar, the environment, if anything makes them different.

4. Evaluating genetic research

    a. contagion effect - the genetic predisposition and early experiences which make some people, including twins, susceptible to deviant behavior which is transmitted by the presence of antisocial siblings in the household.

5. Adoption studies - if adopted children behave more like their biological parents, then their adopted parents it would show a biological basis for crime and vice versa an environmental basis for crime.

G. Evolutionary Theory - some believe that human traits that produce violence and aggression are produced through the long process of human evolution.

1. Violence and evolution - some believe that violent offenses are often driven by evolutionary and reproductive factors.

2. Gender and evolution - aggressive males tend to mate with more partners thus producing more aggressive individuals.

3. Theories of evolutionary criminology

a. Rushton's Theory of Race and Evolution - as people migrated north from Africa, they learned to adapt to the harsher climates and their brain mass increased; this explains crime rate differences between the races.

b. R/K Selection Theory - "R" end males reproduce rapidly and invest little in their offspring while "K" end females have fewer offspring and give them more care and devotion.

c. Cheater Theory - a subpopulation of men evolved with genes that incline them toward extremely low parental involvement; they have to use stealth to gain sexual access since they are not chosen willingly as mates.

H. Evaluation of the Biosocial Branch of Trait Theory
   1. Critics find some theories racist and dysfunctional.
   2. Supporters suggest behavior is a product of interacting biological and environmental events.
   3. Most significant criticism is the lack of adequate empirical testing.

IV. **Psychological Trait Theories -** focuses on the psychological aspects of crime including the association between intelligence, personality, learning, and criminal behavior.

A. Charles Goring (1870-1919) uncovered a relationship between crime and defective intelligence which involves such traits as feeblemindedness, epilepsy, insanity, and defective social instinct.

B. Psychological views of antisocial behavior:
   1. Psychoanalytic or psychodynamic perspective - focus is on early childhood experience and its effect on personality.
   2. Behaviorism - stresses social learning and behavior modeling.
   3. Cognitive theory - analyzes human perception and how it affects behavior.

C. Psychodynamic Perspective (or psychoanalytic psychology) - originated by Viennese psychiatrist Sigmund Freud (1856-1939).
   1. Elements of psychodynamic theory - human personality contains a three part structure:
      a. id - primitive part of people's mental makeup present at birth.
         i. represents unconscious biological drives for sex, food, and other life-sustaining necessities.
         ii. follows the pleasure principle; it requires instant gratification without concern for the rights of others.
      b. ego - develops early in life, when a child learns that their wishes cannot be instantly gratified.
         i. part of the personality that compensates for the demands of the id.
         ii. guided by the reality principle; it takes into account what is practical and conventional by societal standards.

       c. superego - develops as a result of incorporating within the personality the moral standards and values of parents, community, and significant others.
          i. the moral aspect of people's personality; passes judgment on behavior.
          ii. divided into 2 parts: conscience (deals with right and wrong) and ego ideal (forced to control the id and directs people into morally acceptable and responsible behaviors).

D. Psychosexual Stages of Human Development
    1. Eros - most basic human drive present at birth; the instinct to preserve and create life; expressed sexually by seeking pleasure for the body.
    2. Stages of development:
       a. oral stage - first year of life, a child attains pleasure by sucking and biting.
       b. anal stage - second and third years of life, the focus of sexual attention is on bodily wastes.
       c. phallic stage - third year when children focus their attention on their genitals.
          i. Oedipus complex - males begin to have sexual feelings for their mother.
          ii. Electra complex - girls begin to have sexual feelings for their father.
       d. latency - age six when children repress their feelings of sexuality until the genital stage begins at puberty.
    3. If conflicts are encountered during any of the psychosexual stages, a person can become fixated at that point and trouble could arise later.
    4. The Psychodynamics of Antisocial Behavior
       a. Alfred Adler (1870-1937), founder of individual psychology, coined term the inferiority complex - people who have feelings of inferiority and compensate for them with a drive for superiority.
       b. Erik Erikson (1902-1984) described the identity crisis - a period of serious personal questioning people undertake in an effort to determine their own values and sense of direction.
       c. August Aichorn - latent delinquency found in youth whose personality seeks immediate gratification, consider satisfying their personal needs more important than relating to others, and satisfy instinctive urges.
       d. psychodyamics of criminal behavior
          i. depicts an aggressive, frustrated person dominated by events that occurred early in childhood.
          ii. bipolar disorder - moods alternate between periods of wild elation and deep depression.

    iii. crime is a manifestation of feelings of oppression and an inability to develop proper psychological defenses and rationales to control feelings.
  5. Mood disorders and crime
    a. disruptive behavior disorder (DBD) - 2 elements:
      i. oppositional defiant disorder (ODD) - children are uncooperative, defiant, and hostile towards authority figures.
      ii. conduct disorder (CD) - children have difficulty following rules and behaving in socially acceptable ways.
  6. Crime and mental illness
    a. most serious forms of personality disturbance referred to as psychosis.
      i. including depression, bipolar disorder, and schizophrenia.
    b. schizophrenics - exhibit illogical and incoherent thought processes and a lack of insight into their behavior.
    c. paranoid schizophrenics - suffer complex behavior delusions involving wrongdoing or persecution; they think everyone is out to get them.
  7. Is the link valid?
    a. the mentally ill may be more likely to withdraw or harm themselves than act aggressively.
    b. the mental illness/crime link may be spurious.
    c. the mentally ill may lack resources for treatment.
E. Behavioral Theories - human actions are developed through learning experiences.
  1. Social Learning Theory - branch of behavior theory most relevant to criminology.
    a. social learning and violence - violence as learned through a process of behavior modeling; three principal sources:
      i. family interaction.
      ii. environmental experiences.
      iii. mass media.
    b. four factors may contribute to violent and/or aggressive behavior:
      i. an event that heightens arousal.
      ii. aggressive skills.
      iii. expected outcomes.
      iv. consistency of behavior with values.
F. Cognitive Theory
  1. Psychologists focus on mental processes and how people perceive and mentally represent the world around them and solve problems.

2. Subdivisions:
   a. moral development branch - concerned with the way people morally represent and reason around the world.
   b. humanistic psychology - stresses self-awareness and getting in touch with feelings.
   c. information processing branch - focuses on the way people process, store, encode, retrieve, and manipulate information to make decisions and solve problems.
3. Moral and intellectual development theory
   a. founder Jean Piaget (1896-1980) hypothesized that people's reasoning processes develop in an orderly fashion, beginning at birth and continuing until they are 12 years old.
   b. Lawrence Kohlberg applied the concept of moral development to issues in criminology.
      i. found people travel through stages of moral development with criminals at the lowest levels of moral reasoning.
4. Information processing
   a. when people make decisions, they engage in a sequence of cognitive thought processes:
      i. they encode information.
      ii. they search for a proper response.
      iii. they act on their decision.
   b. people who use information properly, who are better conditioned to make reasoned judgments, and can make quick and reasoned decisions are better able to avoid antisocial behavior choices.
5. Shaping perceptions
   a. skewed cognitive processes may be the result of "scripts" learned in childhood.
   b. treatments focus on recognizing scripts, controlling impulses, and problem-solving skills.
G. Personality and Crime - reasonably stable patterns of behavior, including thoughts and emotions, that distinguish one person from another.
   1. Hans Eysenck identified 2 antisocial personality traits:
      a. extraversion-introversion.
      b. stability-instability.
   2. Antisocial personality/psychopathy/sociopathy- terms used interchangeably.
      a. sociopaths are a product of a destructive home environment.
      b. psychopaths are a product of a defect or aberration within themselves.
   3. Research on personality
      a. Minnesota Multiphasic Personality Inventory (MMPI) - measures different personality traits.

    b. California Personality Inventory (CPI) - distinguish deviant from nondeviant groups.

    c. Multidimensional Personality Questionnaire (MPQ) - assesses personality traits as control, aggression, alienation, and well-being.

  H. Intelligence and crime - testing to determine if correlation between IQ and crime.

    1. Nature theory - intelligence is largely determined genetically and low IQ or intelligence is linked to criminal behavior.

    2. Nurture theory - intelligence viewed as partly biological, but primarily sociological.

    3. Rediscovering IQ and criminality - Hirschi and Hindelang published in 1977 a paper linking the two.

    4. Cross-national studies

      a. Weschsler Adult Intelligence Scale - standard IQ test; has found lower IQ levels among delinquents.

    5. IQ and crime reconsidered

      a. recent studies have questioned the strength of the IQ-crime link.

      b. Herrnstein and Murray, in *The Bell Curve*, argue that those with lower IQs are more likely to commit crime, get caught, and be sent to prison.

V. Public Policy Implications of Trait Theory - biological and psychological views of criminality have influenced crime control and prevention policy.

  A. Primary Prevention Programs - seek to treat personal problems before they manifest themselves as crimes.

  B. Secondary Prevention Programs - provide treatment after they have violated the law.

    1. Biologically oriented therapy - programs altered diet, changed lighting, compensated for learning disabilities, treated allergies, and more.

VI. Summary

Key Terms

Anal Stage - In Freud's schema, the second and third years of life, when the focus of sexual attention is on the elimination of bodily wastes.

Androgens - Male sex hormones.

Arousal Theory - A view of crime suggesting that people who have a high arousal level seek powerful stimuli in their environment to maintain an optimal level of arousal. These stimuli are often associated with violence and aggression. Sociopaths may need greater than average stimulation to bring them up to comfortable levels of living; this need explains their criminal tendencies.

Attention Deficit Hyperactivity Disorder (ADHD) - A psychological disorder in which a child shows developmentally inappropriate impulsivity, hyperactivity, and lack of attention.

Behavior Modeling - Process of learning behavior (notably aggression) by observing others. Aggressive models may be parents, criminals in the neighborhood, or characters on television or in video games and movies.

Behaviorism - The branch of psychology concerned with the study of observable behavior rather than unconscious motives. It focuses on the relationship between particular stimuli and people's responses to them.

Biophobia - Sociologists who held the view that no serious consideration should be given to biological factors when attempting to understand human nature.

Bipolar Disorder - An emotional disturbance in which moods alternate between periods of wild elation and deep depression.

California Personality Inventory (CPI) - A frequently administered personality test used to distinguish deviants from nondeviant groups.

Cerebral Allergies - A physical condition that causes brain malfunction due to exposure to some environmental or biochemical irritant.

Chemical Restraints - Antipsychotic drugs such as Haldol, Stelazine, Prolixin, and Risperdal, which help control levels of neurotransmitters (such as serotonin/dopamine), that are used to treat violence-prone people; also called chemical straightjackets.

Chemical Straightjackets - Another term for chemical restraints; antipsychotic drugs used to treat violence-prone people.

Cognitive Theory - The study of the perception of reality and of the mental processes required to understand the world in which we live.

Conduct Disorder (CD) - A psychological condition marked by repeated and severe episodes of antisocial behaviors.

Conscience - One of two parts of the superego; it distinguishes between what is right and wrong.

Contagion Effect - Genetic predispositions and early experiences made some people, including twins, susceptible to deviant behavior, which is transmitted by the presence of antisocial siblings in the household.

Defective Intelligence - Traits such as feeblemindedness, epilepsy, insanity, and defective social instinct, which Goring believed had a significant relationship to criminal behavior.

Disorders - Any type of psychological problem (formerly labeled neuroses or psychoses), such as anxiety disorders, mood disorders, and conduct disorders.

Ego - The part of the personality, developed in early childhood, that helps control the id and keep people's actions within the boundaries of social convention.

Ego Ideal - Part of the superego; directs the individual into morally acceptable and responsible behaviors, which may not be pleasurable.

Electra Complex - A stage of development when girls begin to have sexual feelings for their fathers.

Electroencephalograph (EEG) - A device that can record the electronic impulses given off by the brain, commonly called brain waves.

Equipotentiality - View that all individuals are equal at birth and are thereafter influenced by their environment.

Eros - The instinct to preserve and create life; eros is expressed sexually.

Fixated - An adult that exhibits behavior traits characteristic of those encountered during infantile sexual development.

Humanistic Psychology - A branch of psychology that stresses self-awareness and "getting in touch with feelings."

Hypoglycemia - A condition that occurs when glucose (sugar) levels in the blood fall below the necessary level for normal and efficient brain functioning.

Id - The primitive part of people's mental makeup, present at birth, that represents unconscious biological drives for food, sex, and other life-sustaining necessities. The id seeks instant gratification without concern for the rights of others.

Identity Crisis - A psychological state, identified by Erikson, in which youth face inner turmoil and uncertainty about life roles.

Inferiority Complex - People who have feelings of inferiority and compensate for them with a drive for superiority.

Information Processing - A branch of cognitive psychology that focuses on the way people process, store, encode, retrieve, and manipulate information to make decisions and solve problems.

Inheritance School - Advocates of this view trace the activities of several generations of families believed to have an especially large number of criminal members.

Latency - A developmental stage that begins at age 6. During this period, feelings of sexuality are repressed until the genital stage begins at puberty; this marks the beginning of adult sexuality.

Latent Delinquency - A psychological predisposition to commit antisocial acts because of an id-dominated personality that renders an individual incapable of controlling impulsive, pleasure-seeking drives.

Minnesota Multiphasic Personality Inventory (MMPI) - A widely used psychological test that has subscales designed to measure many different personality traits, including psychopathic deviation (Pd scale), schizophrenia (Sc scale), and hypomania (Ma scale).

Moral Development - The way people morally represent and reason about the world.

Multidimensional Personality Questionnaire (MPQ) - A test that allows researchers to assess such personality traits as control, aggression, alienation, and well-being. Evaluations using this scale indicate that adolescent offenders who are crime prone maintain negative emotionality, a tendency to experience aversive affective states such as anger, anxiety, and irritability.

Nature Theory - The view that intelligence is largely determined genetically and that low intelligence is linked to criminal behavior.

Neocortex - A part of the human brain; the left side of the neocortex controls sympathetic feelings toward others.

Neuroallergies - Allergies that affect the nervous system and cause the allergic person to produce enzymes that attack wholesome foods as if they were dangerous to the body. They may also cause swelling of the brain and produce sensitivity in the central nervous system - conditions that are linked to mental, emotional, and behavioral problems.

Neurophysiology - The study of brain activity.

Nurture Theory - The view that intelligence is not inherited but is largely a product of environment. Low IQ scores do not cause crime but may result from the same environmental factors.

Oedipus Complex - A stage of development when males begin to have sexual feelings for their mothers.

Oral Stage - In Freud's schema, the first year of life, when a child attains pleasure by sucking and biting.

Paranoid Schizophrenics - Individuals who suffer complex behavior delusions involving wrongdoing or persecution - they think everyone is out to get them.

Personality - The reasonably stable patterns of behavior, including thoughts and emotions, that distinguish one person from another.

Phallic Stage - In Freud's schema, the third year, when children focus their attention on their genitals.

Pleasure Principle - According to Freud, a theory in which id-dominated people are driven to increase their personal pleasure without regard to consequences.

Premenstrual Syndrome (PMS) - The stereotype that several days prior to and during menstruation females are beset by irritability and poor judgment as a result of hormonal changes.

Primary Prevention Programs - Treatment programs that seek to correct or remedy personal problems before they manifest themselves as crime.

Psychoanalytic (Psychodynamic) Perspective - Branch of psychology holding that the human personality is controlled by unconscious mental processes developed early in childhood.

Psychosis - A mental state in which the perception of reality is distorted. People experiencing psychosis hallucinate, have paranoid or delusional beliefs, change personalities, exhibit disorganized thinking, and engage in unusual or bizarre behavior.

Reality Principle - According to Freud, the ability to learn about the consequences of one's actions through experience.

Reciprocal Altruism - According to sociobiology, acts that are outwardly designed to help others but that have at their core benefits to the self.

Schizophrenia - A type of psychosis often marked by bizarre behavior, hallucinations, loss of thought control, and inappropriate emotional responses. Schizophrenic types include catatonic, which characteristically involves impairment of motor activity; paranoid, which is characterized by delusions of persecution; and hebephrenic, which is characterized by immature behavior and giddiness.

Secondary Prevention Programs - Treatment programs aimed at helping offenders after they have been identified.

Social Learning - The view that human behavior is modeled through observation of human social interactions, either directly from observing those who are close and from intimate contact, or indirectly through the media. Interactions that are rewarded are copied, while those that are punished are avoided.

Somatotype - A system developed for categorizing people on the basis of their body build.

Superego - Incorporation within the personality of the moral standards and values of parents, community, and significant others.

Testosterone - The principal male steroid hormone. Testosterone levels decline during the life cycle and may explain why violence rates diminish over time.

Thanatos - According to Freud, the instinctual drive toward aggression and violence.

Trait Theory - The view that criminality is a product of abnormal biological and/or psychological traits.

Wechsler Adult Intelligence Scale - One of the standard IQ tests.

Wernicke-Korsakoff Disease - A deadly neurological disorder.

Discussion Exercises

1. Can personality traits predispose an individual to commit crimes? Divide the class into groups. One group is to describe a successful individual. Another group is to describe a not so successful individual. A third group is to describe a criminal. Are there distinct traits for the successful individual, the not so successful individual, and the criminal individual?

2. Many states provide pictures on the Internet of those criminals who are registered as a sex offender. Select four such pictures making sure that three of them fit Lombroso's "born criminal" and Sheldon's "mesomorph" typologies. The fourth picture should look like your traditional college-aged student. Then, have the students decide who is and is not a sex offender among the group. Discussions can center on the usefulness of physical characteristics in identifying criminals and the stereotypes that are predominate within our society concerning offender types.

3. As stated in this chapter, a variety of mental disorders have been linked to criminal activities. Have students discuss whether those criminals who have been deemed mentally ill should be incarcerated for their offenses or be housed in a mental health facility. Is it appropriate to incarcerate someone with a mental illness? Are they "getting away" with the crime if they are housed in a mental health facility instead of a prison?

InfoTrac Assignment

GETTING STARTED: Search term words for subject guide: Sociobiology, Genetics, Psychodynamic Perspective, Behavioral Theories, Cognitive Theory, Mental Illness, Personality, Intelligence.

CRITICAL THINKING PROJECT: Using the search term "Mental Illness," find articles that discuss how the criminal justice system deals with offenders who are mentally ill.

Here are three articles:

Morse, Stephen J. "Preventive Confinement of Dangerous Offenders." *Journal of Law, Medicine & Ethics*.

Szegedy-Maszak, Marianne. "Psychosis and Punishment." *U.S. News & World Report.*

Williams, Erin. "Patient Rights: Mentally disordered offenders may refuse medication." *Journal of Law, Medicine & Ethics.*

Test Bank

Fill in the Blank

1. The view developed by William Sheldon that criminals manifest distinct physiques that make them susceptible to particular types of delinquent behavior is known as a **somatotype**.
    (page number 134)

2. **Equipotentiality** is the view that all individuals are equal at birth and are thereafter influenced by their environment.
    (page number 135)

3. The view of crime causation that some individuals are unable to control their urges and passions is known as **Trait Theories**.
    (page number 135)

4. **Hypoglycemia** is a condition that occurs when glucose (sugar) in the blood falls below levels necessary for normal and efficient brain functioning.
    (page number 140)

5. The principal male hormone is **testosterone**.
    (page number 140)

6. The study of brain activity is **neurophysiology**.
    (page number 142)

7. Children are often said to have a **conduct disorder** when they continually engage in aggressive and anti-social behavior in early childhood.
    (page number 143)

8. **Eros** is the most basic human drive present at birth; the instinct to preserve and create life.
    (page number 151)

9. During the second and third years of life, the focus of sexual attention is on the elimination of bodily wastes. This is known as the **anal stage.**
    (page number 152)

10. During the phallic stage, a male begins to have sexual feelings for his mother, known as the **Oedipus Complex**.
    (page number 152)

11. According to Freud, at age six children develop feelings of sexuality which are repressed until the genital stage begins at puberty. This is known as the **latency stage**.
    (page number 152)

12. **Schizophrenia** is a type of psychosis often marked by bizarre behavior, hallucinations, loss of thought control, and inappropriate emotional responses.
   (page number 153)

13. Individuals who suffer complex behavior delusions involving wrongdoing or persecution are known as **paranoid schizophrenics**.
   (page number 153)

14. **Cognitive Theory** focuses on the mental processes and how people perceive and mentally represent the world around them to solve problems.
   (page number 155)

15. Personality conditions linked to aggression, impulsivity, and neuroticism are called **psychopathy**.
   (page number 162)

Multiple Choice

1. The view of crime causation that some individuals are unable to control their urges and passions is known as:
   a. Arousal Theory
   b. Electra Complex
   c. Nature Theory
   d. Trait Theory
   (Answer = d, page number 134)

2. The view developed by William Sheldon that criminals manifest distinct physiques that make them susceptible to particular types of delinquent behavior is known as:
   a. psychopathy
   b. somatotype
   c. Nurture Theory
   d. Nature Theory
   (Answer = b, page number 134)

3. The study of the activities of several generations of families believed to have an especially large number of criminal members is the:
   a. Nature Theory
   b. Nurture Theory
   c. Inheritance school
   d. Classical school
   (Answer = c, page number 134)

4. Individuals that have well-developed muscles and an athletic appearance are:
     a. mesomorphs
     b. endomorphs
     c. ectomorphs
     d. somatotypes
     (Answer = a, page number 134)

5. Individuals that have heavy builds and are slow-moving are:
     a. mesomorphs
     b. ectomorphs
     c. somatotypes
     d. endomorphs
     (Answer = d, page number 134)

6. Individuals that are tall, thin, less social, and more intellectual are:
     a. mesomorphs
     b. somatotypes
     c. ectomorphs
     d. endomorphs
     (Answer = c, page number 134)

7. The belief that no serious consideration should be given to biological factors when attempting to understand human nature is known as:
     a. Choice Theory
     b. biophobia
     c. Nature Theory
     d. Nurture Theory
     (Answer = b, page number 135)

8. The belief that when we come to the aid of others that our actions will be reciprocated and our gene survival capability will be enhanced is known as:
     a. biochemical
     b. Arousal Theory
     c. reciprocal altruism
     d. all of the above
     (Answer = c, page number 135)

9. The belief that all humans are born with equal potential to learn and achieve is known as:
     a. eros
     b. equipotentiality
     c. Electra Complex
     d. androgens
     (Answer = b, page number 135)

10. The Biosocial theorists believe human behavior is produced by:
    a. physical conditions
    b. environmental conditions
    c. social conditions
    d. all of the above
    (Answer = d, page number 136)

11. A condition that occurs when glucose in the blood falls below levels necessary for normal and efficient brain functioning is known as:
    a. conduct disorder
    b. hypoglycemia
    c. phallic stage
    d. testosterone
    (Answer = b, page number 140)

12. Abnormal levels of these male sex hormones have been linked to aggressive behavior.
    a. androgens
    b. eros
    c. somatotypes
    d. hypoglycemia
    (Answer = a, page number 140)

13. The principal male hormone is:
    a. hypoglycemia
    b. somatotype
    c. neurophysiology
    d. testosterone
    (Answer = d, page number 140)

14. The part of the brain that controls sympathetic feelings towards others is called the:
    a. hormone
    b. androgen
    c. testosterone
    d. neocortex
    (Answer = d, page number 140)

15. The condition which at the onset of the menstrual cycle triggers excessive amounts of hormones affecting antisocial, aggressive behavior is known as:
    a. premenstrual syndrome
    b. Oedipus Complex
    c. neurophysiology
    d. latency
    (Answer = a, page number 141)

16. The study of brain activity is known as:
    a. Nature Theory
    b. neurophysiology
    c. Nuture Theory
    d. somatotype
    (Answer = b, page number 142)

17. The most important measure of neurophysiological functions is an:
    a. identity crisis
    b. inferiority complex
    c. eros
    d. electroencephalograph
    (Answer = d, page number 142)

18. A disorder in which a child shows a developmentally inappropriate lack of attention and impulsivity is known as:
    a. attention deficit hyperactivity disorder
    b. Oedipus Complex
    c. hypoglycemia
    d. psychopathy
    (Answer = a, page number 143)

19. Many children continually engage in aggressive and anti-social behavior in early childhood. This is called:
    a. the Arousal Theory
    b. an attention deficit hyperactivity disorder
    c. a conduct disorder
    d. neurophysiology
    (Answer = c, page number 143)

20. The notion that some individuals may engage in crime due to the attraction of "getting away with it" is known as:
    a. biophobia
    b. the Arousal Theory
    c. the Nature Theory
    d. the Nurture Theory
    (Answer = b, page number 144)

21. The mental processes and how people perceive and mentally represent the world around them to solve problems is known as:
    a. a conduct disorder
    b. cognitive processing
    c. biophobia
    d. the Arousal Theory
    (Answer = b, page number 151)

22. The most basic human drive present at birth is:
   a. eros
   b. biophobia
   c. the Electra Complex
   d. testosterone
   (Answer = a, page number 151)

23. During the second and third years of life, the focus of sexual attention is on the elimination of bodily wastes. This is known as:
   a. the oral stage
   b. premenstrual syndrome
   c. eros
   d. the anal stage
   (Answer = d, page number 152)

24. According to Freud, during the first year of life a child attains pleasure by sucking and biting. This is known as:
   a. the anal stage
   b. the Electra Complex
   c. latency
   d. the oral stage
   (Answer = d, page number 152)

25. If conflict is encountered during any of the psychosexual stages of development, an adult will exhibit behavior traits characteristic of those encountered during infantile sexual development. This is known as:
   a. the anal stage
   b. the oral stage
   c. the Electra Complex
   d. fixation
   (Answer = d, page number 152)

26. When males begin to have sexual feelings for their mother this is called the:
   a. Electra Complex
   b. oral stage
   c. anal stage
   d. Oedipus Complex
   (Answer = d, page number 152)

27. According to Freud, at age six children develop feelings of sexuality which are repressed until the genital stage begins at puberty. This is known as:
   a. the phallic stage
   b. the oral stage
   c. latency
   d. the anal stage
   (Answer = c, page number 152)

28. According to Freud, during the third year when children focus their attention on their genitals, this is known as:
    a. latency
    b. the oral stage
    c. the anal stage
    d. the phallic stage
    (Answer = d, page number 152)

29. When individuals experience serious personal questions, they are having an:
    a. eros
    b. inferiority complex
    c. Oedipus Complex
    d. identity crisis
    (Answer = d, page number 152)

30. The concept used to describe people who have feelings of inferiority and compensate for them with a drive for superiority is:
    a. identity crisis
    b. phallic stage
    c. psychopathy
    d. inferiority complex
    (Answer = d, page number 152)

31. A type of psychosis often marked by bizarre behavior, hallucinations, loss of thought control, and inappropriate emotional responses is known as:
    a. psychopathy
    b. testosterone
    c. hypoglycemia
    d. schizophrenia
    (Answer = d, page number 153)

32. Individuals who suffer complex behavior delusions involving wrongdoing or persecution are said to be:
    a. psychopathic
    b. neurophysiological
    c. paranoid schizophrenic
    d. hypoglycemic
    (Answer = c, page number 153)

33. The theory which argues that intelligence is largely determined genetically is the:
    a. Nurture Theory
    b. Inheritance school
    c. Classical school
    d. Nature Theory
    (Answer = d, page number 161)

34. One of the most widely used psychological tests that is designed to measure many different personality traits, including psychopathic deviation, schizophrenia, and hypomania is known as the:
    a. Minnesota Mutiphasic Personality Inventory
    b. Multidimensional Personality Questionnaire
    c. California Personality Inventory
    d. Wechsler Adult Intelligence Scale
    (Answer = a, page number 161)

35. A frequently administered personality test which has been used to distinguish deviants from nondeviant groups is the:
    a. Minnesota Multiphasic Personality Inventory
    b. Multidimensional Personality Questionnaire
    c. California Personality Inventory
    d. Weschler Adult Intelligence Scale
    (Answer = c, page number 161)

36. The questionnaire which allows researchers to assess such personality traits as control, aggression, alienation, and well-being is known as the:
    a. Minnesota Multiphasic Personality Inventory
    b. California Personality Inventory
    c. Wechsler Adult Intelligence Scale
    d. Multidimensional Personality Questionnaire
    (Answer = d, page number 161)

37. The assumption that intelligence must be viewed as partly biological, but primarily sociological is part of the:
    a. Nature Theory
    b. Inheritance school
    c. Nuture Theory
    d. Classical school
    (Answer = c, page number 161)

38. Personality conditions tied to aggression, impulsivity, and neuroticism are known as:
    a. psychopathy
    b. equipotentiality
    c. biophobia
    d. neurotic
    (Answer = a, page number 162)

39. A common IQ test is the:
    a. California Personality Inventory
    b. Wechsler Adult Intelligence Scale
    c. Minnesota Multiphasic Personality Inventory
    d. Multidimensional Personality Questionnaire
    (Answer = b, page number 164)

40. Programs which alter diet, change lighting, compensate for learning disabilities, and treat allergies are known as:
    a. biophobia
    b. equipotentiality
    c. biologically oriented therapy
    d. neurophysiology
    (Answer = c, page number 165)

True/False

1. Cesare Lombroso's work on the classification of the "born criminal" was a direct offshoot of applying the scientific method to the study of crime.
    (Answer = false, page number 134)

2. Memsomorphs have heavy builds and are slow-moving.
    (Answer = false, page number 134)

3. Biophobia is the belief that no serious consideration should be given to biological factors when attempting to understand human nature.
    (Answer = true, page number 135)

4. Trait theories can be divided into two major sub-divisions: one that stresses psychological functioning and the other that stresses biological make-up.
    (Answer = true, page number 136)

5. The biosocial view states that behavior is a product of interacting social and environmental events.
    (Answer = false, page number 136)

6. Biosocial criminologists maintain that minimum level of minerals and chemicals are needed for normal brain functioning and growth, especially in the early years of life.
    (Answer = true, page number 137)

7. Neuroallergies cause an excessive reaction of the brain.
    (Answer = false, page number 141)

8. The study of brain activity is nitrophysiology.
    (Answer = false, page number 142)

9. Traditionally, the most important measure of neurophysiological functioning is the electroencephalograph.
    (Answer = true, page number 142)

10. Minimal brain dysfunction is related to an abnormality in the cerebral structure.
    (Answer = true, page number 142)

11. Strong egos are associated with immaturity, poor social skills, and excessive dependence on others.
(Answer = false, page number 151)

12. Individuals who have feelings of inferiority and compensate for them with a drive for superiority have an inferiority complex.
(Answer = true, page number 152)

13. Latent delinquency is found in youngsters whose personality requires them to seek immediate gratification, consider satisfying their personal needs more important than relating to others, and satisfy instinctive urges without considering right and wrong.
(Answer = true, page number 152)

14. Behavior Theory maintains that human actions are developed through learning experiences.
(Answer = true, page number 154)

15. Social learning is the branch of Behavior Theory most relevant to criminology.
(Answer = true, page number 154)

Essay Questions

1. Describe sociobiology and its impact on criminal justice, social policy, and society.
(page numbers 134-136)

2. Compare and contrast biochemical/neurophysiological conditions and their relationship to crime in our society.
(page numbers 137-144)

3. What have researchers found in regards to the effect of mental illness and crime? Which area of the Psychological Trait Theories seems more likely to be the cause of crime?
(page numbers 150-165)

4. What is the psychodynamic perspective of the Psychological Trait Theories? Who wrote this theory and what is its implication for us?
(page numbers 151-152)

5. Describe Cognitive Theory. Compare Cognitive Theory to the Behavioral Theories. Is there a relationship?
(page numbers 154-159)

Chapter Six

Social Structure Theories

Summary

Chapter Six explains in detail the Social Structure Theories. The chapter begins with an analysis of the socioeconomic structure and crime and then examines the various components of each of the theories. Particular emphasis is devoted to the Social Disorganization Theories, Strain Theories, and the Cultural Deviance Theories. The chapter concludes with an evaluation of the Social Structure Theories and their implication on public policy.

Chapter Objectives

After reading this chapter the student should be able to:

- Be familiar with the concept of social structure
- Have knowledge of the socioeconomic structure of American society
- Be able to discuss the concept of social disorganization
- Be familiar with the works of Shaw and McKay
- Know the various elements of ecological theory
- Be able to discuss the association between collective efficacy and crime
- Know what is meant by the term *anomie*
- Be familiar with the concept of strain
- Understand the concept of cultural deviance

Chapter Overview

Introduction
Socioeconomic Structure and Crime
      Child Poverty
      The Underclass
      Minority Group Poverty
Race, Culture, Gender, and Criminology: Bridging the Racial Divide
Social Structure Theories
Social Disorganization Theories
      The Work of Shaw and McKay
      The Social Ecology School
The Criminological Enterprise: Random Family
Strain Theories
      The Definition of Anomie

Theory of Anomie
Institutional Anomie Theory
Relative Deprivation Theory
General Strain Theory
Sources of Strain
Coping with Strain
Evaluating GST
Cultural Deviance Theories
Conduct Norms
Focal Concerns
Race, Culture, Gender, and Criminology: The Code of the Streets
Theory of Delinquent Subcultures
Theory of Differential Opportunity
Evaluating Social Structure Theories
Public Policy Implications of Social Structure Theory
Summary

Chapter Outline

I. Introduction
  A. According to this view, it is social forces and not individual traits that cause crime.
  B. The Chicago School
    1. The work of Robert Ezra Park (1864-1944), Ernest W. Burgess (1886-1966), and Louis Wirth (1897-1952) at the University of Chicago.
    2. Work on the social ecology of the city led to the conclusion that social forces operating in urban areas create criminal interactions.

II. Socioeconomic Structure and Crime
  A. People in U.S. live in a stratified society.
    1. Social strata - created by unequal distribution of wealth, power, and prestige.
    2. Social classes - segments of population that have similar portions of things and share attitudes, values, norms, and lifestyles.
    3. Problems of the lower-class include inadequate housing and healthcare, disrupted family lives, underemployment, despair, depression, less likely to have achievement motivation, less likely to put off immediate gratification, and less willing to stay in school.
  B. Child Poverty
    1. Poverty during early childhood may have a more severe impact than if experienced later in life.
    2. Children have the highest rate of poverty
      a. many studies have found an association between family poverty and children's health, achievement, and behavior impairments.
      b. 25% of children under six live in poverty.

        c. 6% of white children are extremely poor versus 50% of black children.

  C. The Underclass

      1. In 1966, Oscar Lewis argued the crushing lifestyle of slum areas produces a culture of poverty, which is passed through generations.

          a. culture of poverty - apathy, cynicism, helplessness, and mistrust of social institutions.

          b. identified at-risk children and adults.

      2. In 1970, Gunnar Myrdal described a worldwide underclass of members cut off from society and lacking the education and skills to be in demand.

  D. Minority Group Poverty

      1. More than 20% of African Americans and Latino Americans live in poverty compared to less than 10% of whites.

      2. In some jurisdictions, up to half of all minority males are under criminal justice control.

      3. Interracial crime rate differentials can be explained by differences in standard of living; end economic disparity and differences in the crime rate would decrease.

      4. In 1987, William Julius Wilson labeled the lowest levels of the underclass the "truly disadvantaged."

III. Social Structure Theories - view that the disadvantaged economic class position is a primary cause of crime.

  A. Branches of Social Structure Theory

      1. Social Disorganization Theory - focuses on the urban environmental conditions that affect crime

          a. disorganized areas are ones in which institutions of social control have broken down.

          b. indicators of disorganization include high unemployment, school dropout rates, deteriorated housing, low income levels, and large numbers of single-parent households.

      2. Strain Theory - crime is a function of the conflict between goals people have and their means to legally obtain them.

          a. while social and economic goals are common, the ability to obtain these goals is class dependent.

          b. lower class are unable to achieve goals so they experience strain - anger, frustration, and resentment.

      3. Cultural Deviance Theory - combines strain and social disorganization.

          a. subcultures - unique lower-class cultures that develop in disorganized neighborhoods; values and beliefs in conflict with conventional values.

          b. cultural transmission - process where subcultural values are handed down from one generation to the next.

IV. Social Disorganization Theories - links crime rates to neighborhood ecological characteristics; highest rates in neighborhoods that are highly transient, mixed-use, and/or changing.

A. The Work of Shaw and McKay - Chicago sociologists in the 1920's who linked life in transitional slum areas to the inclination to commit crime.
   1. Transitional neighborhoods - poverty ridden, suffered high rates of population turnover, and were incapable of inducing people to stay and defend the neighborhood against criminals.
   2. Concentric zones - Zones I and II (central city and a transitional area) exhibited higher rates of crime, even with ethnic changes.
   3. The Legacy of Shaw and McKay
      a. crime is a constant fixture in areas of poverty regardless of the racial or ethnic identity of its residents.
      b. both adult and juvenile criminality is a normal response to adverse social conditions in urban slum areas.
      c. critics challenge the assumed stability of neighborhoods and their definition of social disorganization.
B. The Social Ecology School - emphasizes the association of community deterioration and economic decline to criminality but places less emphasis on value conflict.
   1. Community deterioration - deserted houses, houses needing repair, and abandoned buildings are magnets for crime.
   2. Poverty concentration - in the same area.
      a. concentration effect - when working- and middle-class families flee inner-city poverty areas it results in the most disadvantaged population being consolidated in urban ghettos.
         i. conflicts Shaw and McKay's assumption that crime rates increase in transitional neighborhoods.
   3. Chronic unemployment - aggregate crime rates and aggregate unemployment rates seem weakly related.
   4. Community fear - those living in disorganized neighborhoods suffer social and civil incivilities: rowdy youth, trash and litter, graffiti, drunks, etc.
      a. race and fear - fear is highest in areas undergoing rapid and unexpected racial and age-composition changes.
      b. gangs and fear - gangs openly engage in activities in deteriorated neighborhoods.
      c. mistrust and fear - people in high crime neighborhoods become suspicious and mistrusting.
         i. siege mentality - residents become suspicious of authority; the outside world is considered the enemy out to destroy the neighborhood.
   5. Community change - as areas decline, residents flee to more stable locales.
   6. The cycles of community change - infra-structure may change with urban life cycles.
      a. gentrification - urban renewal.

7. Change and decline - neighborhoods at highest risk for crime have single-parent families, rental units, and lost jobs.
8. Collective efficacy - cohesive communities with high levels of social control develop mutual trust and shared responsibilities.
    a. informal social control - direct criticism, ridicule, ostracism, desertion, or physical punishment.
    b. institutional social control - businesses, stores, schools, churches, and social service and volunteer organizations.
    c. public social control - policing.
9. Social support/altruism - neighborhoods providing strong social supports help young people cope with life's stressors.
    a. social altruism - indications of generosity such as the ratio of contributions given to a charity by area income levels has been linked to crime rates.
    b. crime rates are lower in altruistic areas.

V. Strain Theories
A. The Definition of Anomie - traced to Emile Durkheim; an anomic society is one where rules, or norms, have broken down or become inoperative due to rapid social change.
    1. Anomie is more likely to occur in societies moving from mechanical to organic solidarity.
        a. mechanical solidarity - preindustrial society; traditions, shared values, and unquestioned beliefs.
        b. organic solidarity - connected by interdependent needs and division of labor.
B. Theory of Anomie - applied by Robert Merton; found two culture elements interact to produce anomic conditions: culturally defined goals and socially approved means of obtaining them.
    1. Social adaptations - each has own concept of the goals of society and how to attain them.
        a. conformity - individuals embrace conventional social goals and have the means to attain them.
        b. innovation - individual accepts social goals, but rejects or is incapable of attaining them through legitimate means.
        c. ritualism - those that receive pleasure from practicing traditional ceremonies regardless of whether they have a goal.
        d. retreatism - reject both the goals and means of society.
        e. rebellion - substituting an alternative set of goals and means for conventional ones.
    2. Evaluation of Anomie Theory - number of questions unanswered by Merton.
        a. no explanation as to why people choose certain crimes.
        b. anomie assumes all share same goals, which everyone does not.
    3. Anomie reconsidered - many Americans may feel anomic due to economic displacement in a shifting economy.

C. Institutional Anomie Theory - anomie theory view antisocial behavior as a function of cultural and institutional influences in American society.
    1. Impact of anomie - social institutions have been rendered powerless.
        a. non-economic functions and roles have been devalued.
        b. when conflict emerges, non-economic roles become subordinate to economic roles.
        c. economics penetrates into non-economic realms.
        d. according to Messner and Rosenfield, high crime rates are due to the relationship between culture and institutions.
    2. Supporting research
        a. Chamlin and Cochran found areas of high church membership, lower divorce rates, and high voter turnout enjoy a lower crime rate.
D. Relative Deprivation Theory
    1. Lower-class people may feel deprived as they compare their life to the affluent.
    2. Frustration increases as does the likelihood that the poor will choose illegitimate life enhancing activities.
    3. Affluent may feel deprived if they fail to achieve lofty and unlimited goals.
E. General Strain Theory (GST) - Sociologist Robert Agnew explains individuals who feel stress and strain are more likely to commit crime.
    1. Multiple sources of stress - criminality is the result of:
        a. negative affective states - anger, frustration and adverse emotions.
        b. strain caused by failure to achieve positively valued goals.
        c. strain caused by disjunction of expectations and achievements.
        d. strain from the removal of positively valued stimuli.
        e. strain from the presentation of negative stimuli.
F. Sources of Strain
    1. Social sources:
        a. may feel strain due to groups one associates with.
    2. Community sources of strain:
        a. they influence the goals people pursue and the ability to achieve.
        b. they influence feelings of relative deprivation and exposure to adverse stimuli.
        c. they influence the likelihood of angry, strain-filled individuals will interact with one another.
G. Coping with Strain
    1. Not all that experience strain will commit crime.
        a. crime may provide relief and satisfaction for one living in stressful life.
    2. Strain and criminal careers
        a. certain people are more sensitive to strain and thus more crime prone.

H. Evaluating GST
    1. Adds to literature describing how social and life history influence offending patterns; empirical support for GST.
    2. Gender issues
        a. evidence indicates that females under strain commit less crime than like men.
        b. criminal behavior is more prevalent with men than women.

VI. Cultural Deviance Theories - combines social disorganization and strain to explain how people living in deteriorated neighborhoods react to social isolation and economic deprivation.
  A. Conduct Norms - rules governing daily living conditions within subcultures.
    1. Culture conflict - occurs when rules expressed in the criminal law clash with the demands of group conduct norms.
  B. Focal Concerns - unique value system that dominates lower-class culture.
    1. Miller's Lower Class Focal Concerns
        a. trouble, toughness, smartness, excitement, fate, and autonomy.
  C. Theory of Delinquent Subcultures - Albert Cohen.
    1. Status frustration - lower-class youth experience culture conflict because social conditions make them incapable of achieving success legitimately.
    2. The development of the delinquent subculture is a consequence of socialization practices found in the ghetto or slum environment.
    3. Middle-class measuring rods - standards set by authority figures.
    4. The formation of deviant subcultures - lower-class boys suffer rejection by middle-class decision makers leading boys to join one of these subcultures:
        a. corner boy - not a chronic offender, but a truant engaging in petty or status offenses.
        b. college boy - embraces the cultural and social values of the middle class and actively strives to be successful by those standards.
        c. delinquent boy - adopts norms and principles in direct opposition to middle-class values.
            i. reaction formation - frustrated by their inability to succeed, individuals develop overly intense responses that seem disproportionate to the stimuli that trigger them.
  D. Theory of Differential Opportunity - Richard Cloward and Lloyd Ohlin wrote *Delinquency and Opportunity*; combining strain and social disorganization principles into a portrayal of a gang-sustaining criminal subculture.
    1. Differential opportunities - people in all strata of society share the same success goals; however, those in the lower class have limited means of achieving them.
    2. Because of differential opportunity, kids are likely to join a gang:

a. criminal gangs - in slum areas where close connections between adolescent and adult offenders create an environment for successful criminal enterprise.

b. conflict gangs - develop in communities unable to provide either legitimate or illegitimate opportunities. Crime in this area is individualistic, unorganized, petty, poorly paid, and unprotected.

c. retreatist gangs - double failures, unable to gain success through legitimate means and unwilling to do so through illegal ones.

3. Analysis of Differential Opportunity - important because it integrates cultural deviance and social disorganization variables and it recognizes different modes of criminal adaptation.

E. Evaluating Social Structure Theories - influenced criminological theory and crime prevention strategies.

1. Is the structural approach valid? - questionable.

VII. Public Policy Implications of Social Structure Theory

A. Social structure theory has a significant influence on social policy.

1. Provide welfare and AFDC.
2. Chicago Area Project - crime prevention effort.
3. Kennedy and Johnson's Administrations - War on Poverty.
4. Operation Weed and Seed - weed out criminals then bring human services into the area.

VIII. Summary

Key Terms

American Dream - The goal of accumulating material goods and wealth through individual competition; the process of being socialized to pursue material success and to believe it is achievable.

At Risk - Children and adults who lack the education and skills needed to be effectively in demand in modern society.

Collective Efficacy - Social control exerted by cohesive communities, based on mutual trust, including intervention in the supervision of children and maintenance of public order.

College Boy - A disadvantaged youth who embraces the cultural and social values of the middle class and actively strives to be successful by those standards. This type of youth is embarking on an almost hopeless path, because he is ill-equipped academically, socially, and linguistically to achieve the rewards of middle-class life.

Concentration Effect - As working- and middle-class families flee inner-city poverty areas, the most disadvantaged population is consolidated in urban ghettos.

Conduct Norms - Behaviors expected of social group members. If group norms conflict with those of the general culture, members of the group may find themselves described as outcasts or criminals.

Corner Boy - According to Cohen, a role in the lower-class culture in which young men remain in their birth neighborhood, acquire families and menial jobs, and adjust to the demands of their environment.

Cultural Deviance Theory - Branch of social structure theory that sees strain and social disorganization together resulting in a unique lower-class culture that conflicts with conventional social norms.

Cultural Transmission - The concept that conduct norms are passed down from one generation to the next so that they become stable within the boundaries of a culture. Cultural transmission guarantees that group lifestyle and behavior are stable and predictable.

Culture Conflict - According to Sellin, a condition brought about when the rules and norms of an individual's subcultural affiliation conflict with the role demands of conventional society.

Culture of Poverty - The view that people in the lower class of society form a separate culture with its own values and norms that are in conflict with conventional society; the culture is self-maintaining and ongoing.

Delinquent Boy - A youth who adopts a set of norms and principles in direct opposition to middle-class values, engaging in short-run hedonism, living for today and letting "tomorrow take care of itself."

Differential Opportunity - The view that lower-class youths, whose legitimate opportunities are limited, join gangs and pursue criminal careers as alternative means to achieve universal success goals.

Focal Concerns - According to Miller, the value orientations of lower-class cultures; features include the needs for excitement, trouble, smartness, fate, and personal autonomy.

General Strain Theory (GST) - According to Agnew, the view that multiple sources of strain interact with an individual's emotional traits and responses to produce criminality.

Gentrification - A residential renewal stage in which obsolete housing is replaced and upgraded; areas undergoing such change seem to experience an increase in their crime rates.

Incivilities - Rude and uncivil behavior; behavior that indicates little caring for the feelings of others.

Institutional Anomie Theory - The view that anomie pervades U.S. culture because the drive for material wealth dominates and undermines social and community values.

Mechanical Solidarity - A characteristic of a pre-industrial society, which is held together by traditions, shared values, and unquestioned beliefs.

Middle-Class Measuring Rods - According to Cohen, the standards by which teachers and other representatives of state authority evaluate lower-class youths. Because they cannot live up to middle-class standards, lower-class youths are bound for failure, which gives rise to frustration and anger at conventional society.

Negative Affective States - According to Agnew, the anger, depression, disappointment, fear, and other adverse emotions that derive from strain.

Organic Solidarity - Postindustrial social systems, which are highly developed and dependent upon the division of labor; people are connected by their interdependent needs for one another's services and production.

Reaction Formation - According to Cohen, rejecting goals and standards that seem impossible to achieve. Because a boy cannot hope to get into college, for example, he considers higher education a waste of time.

Relative Deprivation - The condition that exists when people of wealth and poverty live in close proximity to one another. Some criminologists attribute crime rate differentials to relative deprivation.

Siege Mentality - Residents who become so suspicious of authority that they consider the outside world to be the enemy out to destroy the neighborhood.

Social Altruism - Voluntary mutual support systems, such as neighborhood associations and self-help groups, that reinforce moral and social obligations.

Social Disorganization Theory - Branch of social structure theory that focuses on the breakdown of institutions such as the family, school, and employment in inner-city neighborhoods.

Social Structure Theory - The view that disadvantaged economic class position is a primary cause of crime.

Status Frustration - A form of culture conflict experienced by lower-class youths because social conditions prevent them from achieving success as defined by the larger society.

Strain - The emotional turmoil and conflict caused when people believe they cannot achieve their desires and goals through legitimate means. Members of the lower class might feel strain because they are denied access to adequate educational opportunities and social support.

Strain Theorists - Criminologists who view crime as a direct result of lower-class frustration and anger.

Strain Theory - Branch of social structure theory that sees crime as a function of the conflict between people's goals and the means available to attain them.

Stratified Society - Grouping according to social strata or levels. American society is considered stratified on the basis of economic class and wealth.

Subculture - A group that is loosely part of the dominant culture but maintains a unique set of values, beliefs, and traditions.

Theory of Anomie - A modified version of the concept of anomie developed by Merton to fit social, economic, and cultural conditions found in modern U.S. society. He found that two elements of culture interact to produce potentially anomic conditions: culturally defined goals and socially approved means for obtaining them.

Transitional Neighborhood - An area undergoing a shift in population and structure, usually from middle-class residential to lower-class mixed use.

Truly Disadvantaged - Wilson's term for the lowest level of the underclass; urban, inner-city, socially isolated people who occupy the bottom rung of the social ladder and are the victims of discrimination.

Underclass - The lowest social stratum in any country, whose members lack the education and skills needed to function successfully in modern society.

Discussion Exercises

1. Examine the Los Angeles Riot of April 29, 1992. What components of Strain Theory are evident in this devastating event? Would other theories such as Differential Opportunity be relevant to this riot?

2. Strain Theory proposes that lower-class citizens turn to crime, in part, as a result of frustrations they face when attempting to achieve socially approved goals. Have students investigate the various agencies and programs in your community that are oriented towards providing assistance to this group of citizens. Students should pay close attention to barriers that may interfere with the agency's ability to provide services to all in need (for example, limited resources, limited space, regulations concerning substance use, and financial need requirements).

3. Cohen provides an explanation for the development of deviant subcultures among young, lower-class males who are unable to "measure up" to the middle-class measuring rods. Ask students to reflect upon the various subcultures they saw within their high school. How might these vary according to how urban or rural the community was, the economic status of the students, the gender ratio within the school, and whether the school was public or private.

InfoTrac Assignment

GETTING STARTED: Search term words for subject guide: Social Structure Theory, Social Disorganization Theory, Social Ecology School, Anomie Theory, Relative Deprivation Theory, Strain Theory, Social Norms.

CRITICAL THINKING PROJECT: Using the search term "Anomie Theory," find articles that discuss this important Social Structure Theory. Examine this theory and compare it to other theories of crime.

Here are three articles:

Arts, Wil, Piet Hermkens, and Peter Van Wijck. "Anomie, Distributive Injustice and Dissatisfaction with Material Well-Being in Eastern Europe: A comparative study." *International Journal of Comparative Sociology*.

Einstadter, Werner. "The Legacy of Anomie Theory: Advances in criminological theory, vol. 6." *Social Forces*.

Messner, Steven F. and Richard Rosenfeld. "Political Restraint of the Market and Levels of Criminal Homicide: A cross-national application of institutional-anomie theory." *Social Forces*.

Test Bank

Fill in the Blank

1. **Social classes** are segments of the population whose members have a relatively similar portion of desirable things and who share attitudes, values, norms, and an identifiable lifestyle.
   (page number 178)

2. **Social strata** are created by the unequal distribution of wealth, power, and prestige.
   (page number 178)

3. Gunnar Myrdal described a worldwide **underclass** that was cut off from society, its members lacking the education and skills needed to be effectively in demand in modern society.
   (page number 180)

4. Apathy, cynicism, helplessness, and mistrust of social institutions, such as schools, government agencies, and the police mark the **culture of poverty**.
   (page number 180)

5. Children and adults who are more likely to be a part of the culture of poverty are considered **at-risk**.
   (page number 180)

6. The third variation of Structural Theory, **Cultural Deviance Theory** combines elements of both strain and social disorganization.
   (page number 183)

7. The view that the outside world is considered the enemy out to destroy the neighborhood is supported by a **siege mentality.**
   (page number 190)

8. According to Durkheim, an **anomic** society is one in which rules of behavior have broken down or become inoperative during periods of rapid social change or social crisis, such as war or famine.
   (page number 194)

9. **Relative deprivation** is the condition that exists when people of wealth and poverty live in close proximity to one another.
   (page numbers 196-197)

10. According to Robert Agnew, **General Strain Theory** states that individuals who feel stress and strain are more likely to commit crimes.
    (page number 197)

11. The anger, frustration, and adverse emotions that emerge in the wake of negative and destructive social relationships are known as **negative affective states**.
(page number 197)

12. **Conduct norms** are the rules governing day-to-day living conditions with a culture, group, or political structure.
(page number 202)

13. **Focal concerns** are the unique value system that dominates life among the lower class.
(page number 202)

14. **Culture conflict** occurs when the rules expressed in the criminal law clash with the demands of group conduct norms.
(page number 202)

15. Standards set by authority figures such as teachers, employers or supervisors are called **middle-class measuring rods**.
(page number 203)

Multiple Choice

1. People in the United States live in what type of society?
   a. unified
   b. verified
   c. unstratified
   d. stratified
   (Answer = d, page number 178)

2. The unequal distribution of wealth, power, and prestige create:
   a. social harmony
   b. social peace
   c. social joy
   d. social strata
   (Answer = d, page number 178)

3. Segments of the population whose members have a relatively similar portion of desirable things and who share attitudes, values, norms, and an identifiable lifestyle are known as:
   a. social strata
   b. social harmony
   c. social joy
   d. social classes
   (Answer = d, page number 178)

4. What percentage of children under the age of 6 now live in poverty?
   a. 5%
   b. 25%
   c. 50%
   d. 75%
   (Answer = b, page number 180)

5. What percentage of white children now live in poverty?
   a. 25%
   b. 50%
   c. 6%
   d. 75%
   (Answer = c, page number 180)

6. What percentage of black children now live in poverty?
   a. 50%
   b. 25%
   c. 6%
   d. 75%
   (Answer = a, page number 180)

7. Children and adults who are more likely to be a part of the culture of poverty are considered to be:
   a. focal concerns
   b. at-risk
   c. middle-class measuring rods
   d. negative affective states
   (Answer = b, page number 180)

8. The view of apathy, cynicism, helplessness, and mistrust of social institutions, such as schools, government agencies, and the police, is termed:
   a. culture conflict
   b. culture of poverty
   c. focal concerns
   d. negative affective states
   (Answer = b, page number 180)

9. Members of the underclass who are socially isolated, live in urban inner cities, and occupy the bottom rung of the social ladder are known as:
   a. business people
   b. the truly disadvantaged
   c. the truly advantaged
   d. the successful
   (Answer = b, page number 182)

10. Social Disorganization Theory focuses on which of the following conditions in the environment?
  a. unequal distribution of wealth
  b. deteriorated neighborhoods
  c. frustration levels
  d. all of the above
  (Answer = b, page number 182)

11. A branch within the social structure perspective is:
  a. Social Disorganization
  b. Strain Theory
  c. Cultural Deviance Theory
  d. all of the above
  (Answer = d, page number 182

12. The theory which holds that crime is a function of the conflict between the goals people have and the means they can use to legally obtain them is:
  a. Cultural Conflict
  b. Cultural Deviance Theory
  c. Social Disorganization
  d. Strain Theory
  (Answer = d, page numbers 182-183)

13. The third variation of Structural Theory which combines elements of both strain and social disorganization is known as:
  a. Anomie Theory
  b. Cultural Deviance Theory
  c. Culture of Poverty Theory
  d. Social Structure Theory
  (Answer = b, page number 183)

14. Strain Theory focuses on which of the following conflicts between goals and means?
  a. inadequate social control
  b. deteriorated neighborhoods
  c. frustration levels
  d. all of the above
  (Answer = c, page number 183)

15. Cultural Deviance Theory focuses on which of the following factors?
  a. development of subcultures as a result of disorganization and stress
  b. subcultural values in opposition to conventional values
  c. all of the above
  d. none of the above
  (Answer = c, page number 183)

16. Social Disorganization Theory was popularized by:
    a. Martin and Gordon
    b. Winfree and Mays
    c. Sutherland and Durkeim
    d. McKay and Shaw
    (Answer = d, page number 184)

17. Poverty-ridden neighborhoods which suffer high rates of population turnover and are incapable of inducing residents to remain are known as:
    a. suburbs
    b. gated communities
    c. transitional neighborhoods
    d. college campuses
    (Answer = c, page number 185)

18. The view that the outside world is considered the enemy out to destroy the neighborhood is known as:
    a. anomie
    b. culture conflict
    c. middle-class measuring rods
    d. a siege mentality
    (Answer = d, page number 190)

19. A renewal stage in which obsolete housing is replace and upgraded is known as:
    a. gentrification
    b. turnover
    c. transitional neighborhoods
    d. none of the above
    (Answer = a, page number 190)

20. Informal control mechanisms include which of the following:
    a. direct criticism
    b. ridicule
    c. ostracism
    d. all of the above
    (Answer = d, page number 191)

21. Institutional social control includes which of the following?
    a. schools
    b. gangs
    c. MTV
    d. nightclubs
    (Answer = a, page number 191)

22. Public social control includes which of the following?
    a. schools
    b. churches
    c. police
    d. gangs
    (Answer = c, page number 191)

23. According to Durkheim, _____ occurs in a society in which rules of behavior have broken down or become inoperative during periods of rapid social change or social crisis, such as war or famine.
    a. anomie
    b. at-risk
    c. pathology
    d. all of the above
    (Answer = a, page number 194)

24. _____ is a characteristic of pre-industrial society, held together by traditions, shared values and unquestioned beliefs.
    a. Organic solidarity
    b. Solidarity
    c. Mechanic solidarity
    d. none of the above
    (Answer = c, page number 194)

25. When individuals embrace conventional social goals and have the means at their disposal to attain them, this is known as:
    a. innovation
    b. ritualism
    c. conformity
    d. rebellion
    (Answer = c, page number 194)

26. When an individual accepts the goals of society, but rejects or is incapable of attaining them through legitimate means, it is called:
    a. conformity
    b. ritualism
    c. innovation
    d. rebellion
    (Answer = c, page number 194)

27. Which of the following are means to attaining goals according to Merton?
    a. conformity
    b. innovation
    c. ritualism
    d. all of the above
    (Answer = d, page numbers 194-195)

28. Those who reject both the goals and the means of society are called:
    a. conformists
    b. ritualists
    c. rebels
    d. retreatists
    (Answer = d, page number 195)

29. Those who gain pleasure from practicing traditional ceremonies regardless of whether they have a real purpose or a goal are known as:
    a. conformists
    b. ritualists
    c. retreatists
    d. rebels
    (Answer = b, page number 195)

30. Substituting an alternative set of goals and means for conventional ones is common with:
    a. ritualists
    b. rebels
    c. retreatists
    d. realists
    (Answer = b, page number 195)

31. The condition that exists when people of wealth and poverty live in close proximity to one another is known as:
    a. general strain
    b. anomie
    c. siege mentality
    d. relative deprivation
    (Answer = d, page number 196-197)

32. The view, according to Robert Agnew, that individuals who feel stress and strain are more likely to commit crimes is called:
    a. the Electra Complex
    b. negative affective states
    c. relative deprivation
    d. the General Strain Theory
    (Answer = d, page number 197)

33. The anger, frustration, and adverse emotions that emerge in the wake of negative and destructive social relationships is known as:
    a. negative affective states
    b. positive affective states
    c. anomie
    d. siege mentality
    (Answer = a, page number 197)

34. Who developed General Strain Theory?
    a. Sellin
    b. Durkheim
    c. Agnew
    d. Merton
    (Answer = c, page number 197)

35. Which of the following is not an element of General Strain Theory?
    a. achievement of positively valued goals
    b. disjunction of expectations and achievements
    c. removal of positively valued stimuli
    d. presentation of negative stimuli
    (Answer = a, page number 198)

36. The rules which govern day-to-day living conditions with a culture, group, or political structure are known as:
    a. policies
    b. social policies
    c. middle-class measuring rods
    d. conduct norms
    (Answer = d, page number 202)

37. This occurs when the rules expressed in the criminal law clash with the demands of group conduct norms.
    a. culture conflict
    b. culture of poverty
    c. cultural deviance
    d. relative deprivation
    (Answer = a, page number 202)

38. The unique value system that dominates life among the lower classes is known as:
    a. focal concerns
    b. middle-class measuring rods
    c. the culture of poverty
    d. culture conflict
    (Answer = a, page number 202)

39. Standards set by authority figures such as teachers, employers, or supervisors are:
    a. anomies
    b. middle-class measuring rods
    c. conduct norms
    d. focal concerns
    (Answer = b, page number 203)

40. Which of the following gangs develop in stable lower-class areas that allow for successful criminal enterprise?
   a. criminal gangs
   b. conflict gangs
   c. retreatist gangs
   d. none of the above
   (Answer = a, page number 206)

True/False

1. People in the United States live in a stratified society.
   (Answer = true, page number 178)

2. Social strata are segments of the population whose members have a relatively similar portion of desirable things and who share attitudes, values, norms, and an identifiable lifestyle.
   (Answer = false, page number 178)

3. Lower-class areas are scenes of inadequate housing and health care, disrupted family lives, underemployment, and despair.
   (Answer = true, page number 178)

4. In the year 2003, the poverty rate rose to 22.3 percent, the highest since 1979.
   (Answer = false, page number 179)

5. Children who grow up in low-income homes are less likely to achieve in school and are less likely to complete their schooling than children with more affluent parents.
   (Answer = true, page number 179)

6. Strain Theory holds that the conditions within the urban environment affect crime rates.
   (Answer = false, page numbers 182-183)

7. Cultural Deviance Theory links crime rates to neighborhood ecological characteristics.
   (Answer = false, page number 183)

8. Subcultural values are handed down from one generation to the next in a process called cultural transmission.
   (Answer = true, page number 183)

9. Graffiti would be an example of a physical incivility.
   (Answer = true, page number 189)

10. Cohesive communities with high levels of social control develop collective efficacy.
    (Answer = true, page number 190)

11. Sources of institutional social control include businesses, stores, schools, churches, and social service and volunteer organizations.
(Answer = true, page number 191)

12. Mechanical solidarity is a characteristic of postindultrial society.
(Answer = false, page number 194)

13. Feelings of relative deprivation can be found only among the lower-class.
(Answer = false, page number 197)

14. According to Sellin, culture conflict occurs when the rules expressed in criminal law clash with the demands of group conduct norms.
(Answer = true, page number 202)

15. According to Cohen, the "delinquent boy" adopts a set of norms in direct opposition to middle-class values.
(Answer = true, page number 205)

Essay Questions

1. Describe the socioeconomic structure and its relationship to crime. If one is a member of the lower class, does it predispose them to a life of crime?
(page numbers 178-181)

2. Define the Social Structure Theories. What are the various branches of Social Structure Theory? What is their impact on criminal justice, social policy and society?
(page numbers 181-184)

3. What is the Social Ecology School? Describe the work of Shaw and McKay. What influence has their study had on social policy?
(page numbers 184-193)

4. Compare and contrast Relative Deprivation Theory and General Strain Theory. What are the differences? What are the similarities? Are these theories important to social policy making?
(page numbers 196-201)

5. Compare and contrast the Theory of Delinquent Subcultures with the Theory of Differential Opportunity. How do they compliment each other?
(page numbers 203-206)

Chapter Seven

Social Process Theories

Summary

Chapter Seven examines the Social Process Theories: Learning, Control, and Reaction. The chapter begins with a discussion of socialization and crime and then shifts to describing the various social process theories. Chapter Seven concludes with an evaluation of Social Process Theory and the impact of these theories on public policy.

Chapter Objectives

After reading this chapter the student should be able to:

- Be familiar with the concept of socialization
- Discuss the effect of schools, family, and friends on crime
- Be able to discuss the differences of learning, control, and reaction
- Be familiar with the concept of differential association
- Be able to discuss what is meant by a definition toward criminality
- Understand the concept of neutralization
- Be able to discuss the relationship between self-concept and crime
- Know the elements of the social bond
- Describe the labeling process and how it leads to criminal careers
- Be familiar with the concepts of primary and secondary deviance

Chapter Overview

Introduction
Socialization and Crime
      Family Relations
      Child Abuse and Crime
      Educational Experience
Policy and Practice in Criminology: Keeping Kids in Schools: The Communities In Schools Program
      Peer Relations
      Institutional Involvement and Belief
      The Effects of Socialization on Crime
Social Learning Theory
      Differential Association Theory
      Differential Reinforcement Theory
      Neutralization Theory

Are Learning Theories Valid?

Social Control Theory

Self-Concept and Crime

Hirschi's Social Bond Theory

Social Reaction Theory

Crime and Labeling Theory

Differential Enforcement

Becoming Labeled

Consequences of Labeling

Primary and Secondary Deviance

Research on Social Reaction Theory

Is Labeling Theory Valid?

Evaluating Social Process Theories

Public Policy Implications of Social Process Theory

Policy and Practice in Criminology: Head Start

Summary

Chapter Outline

I. Introduction
II. Socialization and Crime

A. Social Process Theories

1. Criminality is a function of individual socialization.
2. People are influenced by interactions with various organizations, institutions, and processes of society such as education, employment, and family life and peer relations.
3. All people have the potential to become delinquents or criminals.

B. Family Relations

1. Youth from home with conflict and tension more likely to become criminal.
2. Lack of love can lead to criminality.
3. Children with strong, positive role models are less likely to become criminal.
4. Parental efficacy - supportive parents who effectively control their children are more likely to raise children who refrain from delinquency.

C. Child Abuse and Crime - link between child abuse, neglect, sexual abuse, and crime.

D. Educational Experience

1. Children who do poorly in school, lack educational motivation, and feel alienated are more likely to engage in criminality.
2. Schools label problem youth, which contributes to criminality.
    a. the "track system" perpetuates stigmatization.
3. More than 10% of Americans aged 16-24 have left school early; national graduation rate of 68%.

    a. Communities in Schools network is designed to reduce the number of dropouts.
4. Many crimes occur on school grounds.
    a. 2003 estimates of 1.5 million violent incidents in public elementary and secondary schools each year.
E. Peer Relations
    1. Peer groups influence decision making and behavior choices.
    2. Cliques - small groups of friends who share activities and confidences.
    3. Crowds - loosely organized groups of children who share interests and activities.
    4. Adolescents feel pressure to conform to group values.
    5. Peer rejection/peer acceptance
        a. peer rejection may increase and sustain antisocial behaviors.
        b. associating with prosocial friends and coworkers can lure adolescents away from delinquent peer networks.
    6. Peers and criminality
        a. delinquent friends my cause law-abiding youth to get into trouble.
        b. deviant peers sustain and amplify delinquent careers.
        c. antisocial friends help youths maintain delinquent careers and obstruct the aging-out process.
        d. troubled kids choose delinquent peers out of necessity.
F. Institutional Involvement and Belief
    1. Studies show that participation in institutions such as religion eschew crime and anti-social behavior.
G. The Effects of Socialization on Crime
    1. Anyone with a positive self-image; learned moral values; support of their parents, peers, teachers, and neighbors can resist inducement to crime.
    2. Social process approach - an individual's socialization determines the likelihood of criminality.
        a. social learning theory - crime is a learned behavior.
        b. social control theory - everyone has the potential to become a criminal, but most are controlled by the bond to society.
        c. social reaction theory - people become criminal when significant members of society label them as such and they accept those labels as a personal identity.
III. **Social Learning Theory** - crime is a product of learning the norms, values, and behaviors associated with criminal activity.
    A. Differential Association Theory - Edwin H. Sutherland published in 1939 *Principles of Criminality*.
        1. Principles of Differential Association:
            a. criminal behavior is learned.
            b. criminal behavior is learned as a by-product of interacting with others.

      c. learning criminal behavior occurs within intimate personal groups.

      d. learning criminal behavior involves learning the techniques of committing the crime, which are sometimes very complicated and sometimes very simple.

      e. the specific direction of motives and drives is learned from perceptions of various aspects of the legal code as being favorable or unfavorable.

      f. differential associations may vary in frequency, duration, priority, and intensity.

  2. Testing Differential Association Theory - research has been fairly sparse, however, some testing has some that there is a correlation between:

      a. having deviant friends.

      b. holding deviant attitudes.

      c. committing deviant acts.

  3. Analysis of Differential Association Theory

      a. cultural deviance critique - differential association is invalid because it suggests that criminals are people properly socialized into a deviant subculture.

      b. fails to explain why one exposed to delinquency succumbs and another does not.

      c. possible that the internalization of deviant attitudes follows, rather than precedes, criminality.

B. Differential Reinforcement Theory - Akers and Burgess (1966); employs both differential association concepts with learning theory.

  1. Also known as direct conditioning - occurs when behavior is reinforced either by being rewarded or punished while interacting with others.

  2. When behavior is punished, this is known as negative reinforcement.

  3. Testing Differential Reinforcement - testing showed that learning deviant behavior is not static.

C. Neutralization Theory - Matza and Sykes

  1. View the process of becoming a criminal as a learning experience, in which potential delinquents and criminals master techniques that enable them to counterbalance or neutralize conventional values and drift back and forth between illegitimate and conventional behavior.

  2. Subterranean values - morally tinged influences, which have become entrenched in the culture but are publicly condemned.

  3. Drift - the movement from one extreme of behavior to another.

  4. Model based on:

      a. criminals sometimes voice a sense of guilt over their illegal acts.

      b. offenders frequently respect and admire honest, law-abiding persons.

        c. criminals draw a line between those whom they can victimize and those whom they cannot.

        d. criminals are not immune to the demands of conformity.

    5. Techniques of neutralization:

        a. denial of responsibility.

        b. denial of injury.

        c. denial of victim.

        d. condemnation of the condemners.

        e. appeal to higher loyalties.

    6. Testing Neutralization Theory - attempts have been made to test, but the results have been inconclusive.

  D. Are Learning Theories Valid?

    1. Little evident to substantiate that people learn the techniques that enable them to become criminals before they actually commit criminal acts.

IV. Social Control Theory

  A. Maintain that people have the potential to violate the law and that modern society presents many opportunities for illegal activity.

    1. Some have self-control, which keeps them from hurting others violating social norms.

    2. Others develop a commitment to conformity - adhered to because of a real, present, and logical reason to obey the rules of society.

    3. Their attachment and commitment to conventional institutions, individuals, and processes control people's behavior.

  B. Self-Concept and Crime

    1. Containment Theory - proposed by Walter Reckless; argued that a strong self-image insulates a youth from the pressures and pulls of criminogenic influences in the environment.

    2. Self-Enhancement Theory - proposed by Howard Kaplan

        a. youth with poor self-concepts are most likely to engage in delinquent behavior; successful participation in criminality actually helps raise their self-esteem.

  C. Hirschi's Social Bond Theory - Travis Hirschi (1969) *Causes of Delinquency*

    1. Links the onset of criminality to the weakening of the ties that bind people to society.

    2. Elements of the social bond:

        a. attachment - a person's sensitivity to and interest in others.

        b. commitment - the time, energy, and effort expended in conventional lines of action such as getting an education and saving money for the future.

        c. involvement - when individuals are involved in school, recreation and family, they are insulated from the lure of criminal behavior.

        d. belief - those who live in the same social setting often share common moral beliefs.

3. Testing Social Bond Theory - Hirschi tested youth in self-report survey.
  a. found youth strongly attached to parents are less likely to commit criminal acts.
  b. commitment to conventional values were indicative of conventional behavior.
  c. youth involved in conventional behavior were less likely to commit crime.
  d. youth involved in nonconventional behavior were more delinquency-prone.
  e. youth who had poor relationships with people tended toward delinquency.
  f. those who shunned unconventional acts were attached to their peers.
  g. delinquents and nondelinquents shared similar beliefs about society.
4. Supporting research - corroborated by numerous research studies showing that delinquent youth often feel detached from society.
5. Opposing views - question some or all of the elements of the theory. Some have questioned the relationship of the following to the theory:
  a. friendship.
  b. not all elements of the bond are equal.
  c. deviant peers and parents.
  d. restricted in scope.
  e. changing bonds.
  f. crime and social bonds.

V. Social Reaction Theory - commonly called Labeling Theory.
  A. Explains how criminal careers form based on destructive social interactions and encounters.
  B. Roots found in symbolic interaction theory - people communicate via symbols (gestures, signs, words, or images that stand for or represent something else).
  C. Crime and Labeling Theory
    1. Crime and deviance are defined by the social audience's reaction to people and their behavior and the subsequent effects of that reaction; they are not defined by the moral content of the illegal act itself.
    2. Moral entrepreneurs - people who create rules.
  D. Differential Enforcement - the law is differentially applied, benefiting those who hold economic and social power and penalizing the powerless.
  E. Becoming Labeled - the less personal power and fewer resources a person has, the greater the chance he or she will become labeled.
  F. Consequences of Labeling

1. Creation of stigma - labeled deviant becomes a social outcast who may be prevented from enjoying higher education, well-paying jobs, and other social benefits.
2. Such alienation leads to a low self-image.
3. Differential social control
    a. the process of labeling may produce a re-evaluation of the self, which reflects actual or perceived appraisals made by others.
    b. reflective role-taking - informal and institutional social control processes.
4. Joining deviant cliques - when children are labeled as deviant, they may join similarly outcast delinquent peers.
5. Retrospective reading - process of the past of the labeled person being reviewed and reevaluated to fit his or her current status.
6. Dramatization of evil - the person becomes the thing he or she is labeled.

G. Primary and Secondary Deviance - Edwin Lemert
1. Primary deviance - involves norm violations or crimes that have very little influence on the actor and can be quickly forgotten.
2. Secondary deviance - occurs when a deviant event comes to the attention of significant others or social control agents who apply a negative label.
    a. deviance amplification effect - offenders feel isolated from the mainstream of society and become firmly locked within their deviant role.

H. Research on Social Reaction Theory
1. Who gets labeled?
    a. the poor and powerless are victimized by the law and justice system; labels are not equally distributed across class and racial lines.
    b. contextual discrimination - refers to judges' practices in some jurisdictions to impose harsher sentences on African-Americans only in some instances such as when they victimize whites and not other African-Americans.
2. The effects of labeling - empirical evidence that negative labels actually have a dramatic influence on the self-image of offenders.
3. Labeling and criminal careers - evidence that labeling plays an important role in persistent offending.

I. Is Labeling Theory Valid? - some found little to support the theory.
1. Labeling Reexamined - others found supporting evidence of the theory.
    a. Labeling Theory identifies the role played by social control agents in the process of crime causation.
    b. Labeling Theory recognizes that criminality is not a disease or pathological behavior.

c. Labeling Theory distinguishes between criminal acts and criminal careers and shows that these concepts are interrelated and treated differently.

VI. Evaluating Social Process Theories
A. The three branches are compatible because they suggest that criminal behavior is part of the socialization process.

VII. Public Policy Implications of Social Process Theory
A. Major influence on social policy-making since 1950's.
B. Resulting programs include:
    1. Head Start programs.
    2. Diversion programs - designed to remove both juvenile and adult offenders from the normal channels of the criminal justice process by placing them in programs designed for rehabilitation.
    3. Restitution - an offender is asked to either pay back the victim of the crime for any loss incurred, or do some useful work in the community in lieu of receiving court-ordered sentence.

VIII. Summary

Key Terms

Commitment to Conformity - A strong personal investment in conventional institutions, individuals, and processes that prevents people from engaging in behavior that might jeopardize their reputation and achievements.

Containment Theory - The idea that a strong self-image insulates a youth from the pressures and pulls of crimogenic influences in the environment.

Contextual Discrimination - A practice in which African Americans receive harsher punishments in some instances (as when they victimize whites) but not in others (as when they victimize other blacks).

Differential Association Theory - According to Sutherland, the principle that criminal acts are related to a person's exposure to an excess amount of antisocial attitudes and values.

Differential Reinforcement - Behavior is reinforced by being either rewarded or punished while interacting with others; also called direct conditioning.

Differential Reinforcement Theory - An attempt to explain crime as a type of learned behavior. First proposed by Akers in collaboration with Burgess in 1966, it is a version of the social learning view that employs differential association concepts as well as elements of psychological learning theory.

Differential Social Control - A process of labeling that may produce a reevaluation of the self, which reflects actual or perceived appraisals made by others.

Direct Conditioning - Behavior is reinforced by being either rewarded or punished while interacting with others; also called differential reinforcement.

Diversion Programs - Programs of rehabilitation that remove offenders from the normal channels of the criminal justice system, thus avoiding the stigma of a criminal label.

Dramatization of Evil - As the negative feedback of law enforcement agencies, parents, friends, teachers, and other figures amplifies the force of the original label, stigmatized offenders may begin to reevaluate their own identities. The person becomes the thing he is described as being.

Drift - According to Matza, the view that youths move in and out of delinquency and that their lifestyles can embrace both conventional and deviant values.

Labeling Theory - Theory that views society as creating deviance through a system of social control agencies that designate certain individuals as deviants. The stigmatized individual is made to feel unwanted in the normal social order. Eventually, the individual begins to believe that the label is accurate, assumes it as a personal identity, and enters into a deviant or criminal career.

Negative Reinforcement - Using either negative stimuli (punishment) or loss of reward (negative punishment) to curtail unwanted behaviors.

Neutralization Theory - Neutralization theory holds that offenders adhere to conventional values while "drifting" into periods of illegal behavior. In order to drift, people must first overcome (neutralize) legal and moral values.

Normative Groups - Groups, such as the high school in-crowd, that conform to the social rules of society.

Primary Deviance - According to Lemert, deviant acts that do not help redefine the self-image and public image of the offender.

Reflective Role Taking - According to Matsueda and Heimer, the phenomenon that occurs when youths who view themselves as delinquents give an inner voice to their perceptions of how significant others feel about them.

Retrospective Reading - The reassessment of a person's past to fit a current generalized label.

Secondary Deviance - According to Lemert, accepting deviant labels as a personal identity. Acts become secondary when they form a basis for self-concept, as when a drug experimenter becomes and addict.

Self-Control - A strong moral sense that renders a person incapable of hurting others or violating social norms.

Social Bond - Ties a person has to the institutions and processes of society. According to Hirschi, elements of the social bond include commitment, attachment, involvement, and belief.

Social Control Theory - The view that people commit crime when the forces that bind them to society are weakened or broken.

Social Process Theory - The view that criminality is a function of people's interactions with various organizations, institutions, and processes in society.

Social Reaction Theory - The view that people become criminals when significant members of society label them as such and they accept those labels as a personal identity. Also known as labeling theory.

Stigma - An enduring label that taints a person's identity and changes him or her in the eyes of others.

Subterranean Values - Morally tinged influences that have become entrenched in the culture but are publicly condemned. They exist side by side with conventional values and while condemned in public may be admired or practiced in private.

Symbolic Interaction Theory - The sociological view that people communicate through symbols. People interpret symbolic communication and incorporate it within their personality. A person's view of reality, then, depends on his or her interpretation of symbolic gestures.

Discussion Exercises

1. Examine the career and life of Robert Downey, Jr. Downey, a renowned actor, has a serious addiction to drugs. Has Downey been labeled as an addict or a criminal? Has labeling theory been a factor in the treatment of Downey? What elements of social process theory apply to the Downey situation?

2. Hirschi proposes that the stronger the social bond to society, the less likely one is to offend. Ask students to investigate what agencies and programs are available in their community to strengthen each of the four elements of the social bond. The following provides examples: attachment - Big Brothers/Big Sisters, commitment - banks that advertise special savings accounts for children, involvement - midnight basketball, and belief - youth leaders who are members of community boards.

3. The following is a quick exercise to demonstrate the power of a label. Ask students to close their eyes and visualize a police officer (you may have to ask them to humor you here). Then, one-by-one, tell them the police officer is a female, Hispanic, 47 years of age, and a lesbian. The point is not how common this combination of characteristics exists, but rather how drastically their perception changes once a new "label" is revealed.

InfoTrac Assignment

GETTING STARTED: Search term words for subject guide: Differential Association Theory, Neutralization Theory, Social Control Theory, Labeling Theory.

CRITICAL THINKING PROJECT: Using the search term "Social Control Theory," find articles that discuss this important Social Process Theory. Examine this theory and compare it to other theories of crime.

Here are three articles:

Alston, Reginald J., Debra Harley, and Karen Lenhoff. "Hirschi's Social Control Theory: A sociological perspective on drug abuse among persons with disabilities." *The Journal of Rehabilitation.*

Brezina, Timothy. "Adolescent Maltreatment and Delinquency: The question of intervening processes." *Journal of Research in Crime and Delinquency.*

Junger, Marianne and Ineke Haen Marshall. "The Interethnic Generalizability of Social Control Theory: An empirical test." *Journal of Research in Crime and Delinquency*.

Test Bank

Fill in the Blank

1. **Social Process Theories** hold that criminality is a function of individual socialization.
    (page number 218)

2. When behavior is punished, this is referred to as **negative reinforcement**.
    (page number 229)

3. According to Akers, **differential reinforcement** is the principle that both deviant and conventional behavior is learned.
    (page number 229)

4. **Neutralization Theory** offers the principle that becoming a criminal is a learning process in which potential delinquents and criminals master techniques that enable them to counterbalance or neutralize conventional value and drift back and forth between illegitimate and conventional behavior.
    (page number 230)

5. **Subterranean values** are the morally tinged influences which have become entrenched in the culture but are publicly condemned.
    (page number 230)

6. According to Neutralization Theory, **techniques of neutralization** are used by delinquent youth to neutralize moral constraints so they may drift into criminal acts.
    (page number 230)

7. Some individuals have **self-control**, manifested through a strong moral sense, which renders them incapable of hurting others and violating social norms.
    (page number 232)

8. **Attachment** refers to a person's sensitivity to and interest in others.
    (page number 234)

9. People who create the rules are called **moral entrepreneurs**.
    (page number 238)

10. Garfinkle called transactions that produce irreversible, permanent labels **degradation ceremonies**.
    (page number 239)

11. **Reflective role-taking** is when one believes that others view them as antisocial or troublemakers, and they take on attitudes and roles that reflect this assumption.
    (page number 239)

12. A youth's self-evaluation based on his or her perceptions of how others evaluate him or her is called a **reflected appraisal**.
    (page number 239)

13. **Primary deviance** involves norm violations or crimes that have very little influence on the actor and can be quickly forgotten.
    (page number 240)

14. **Secondary deviance** occurs when a deviant event comes to the attention of significant others or social control agents who apply a negative label.
    (page number 240)

15. **Contextual discrimination** refers to judges' practices in some jurisdictions of imposing harsher sentences on African Americans in specific instances.
    (page number 241)

Multiple Choice

1. Today, more than _____ million Americans live in poverty.
    a. 1
    b. 2
    c. 10
    d. 30
    (Answer = d, page number 218)

2. The process of human development and enculturation is known as:
    a. stigma
    b. socialization
    c. drift
    d. primary deviance
    (Answer = b, page number 218)

3. Children in homes where a parent suffers from mental impairment are at risk for:
    a. success
    b. delinquency
    c. scholarships
    d. successful careers
    (Answer = b, page number 220)

4. A 2003 national survey on school crime estimates how many violent incidents occurring in public elementary and secondary schools each year?
    a. 1.5 million
    b. 2 million
    c. 150,000
    d. 2.5 million
    (Answer = a, page number 221)

5. One national survey found that about ____ percent of public schools report one or more serious violent incidents to the police each year.
    a. 10
    b. 5
    c. 15
    d. 40
    (Answer = c, page number 221)

. One national survey found that about ____ percent of public schools report one or more thefts to the police each year.
    a. 12
    b. 20
    c. 28
    d. 52
    (Answer = c, page number 221)

7. Small groups of friends who share activities and confidences are called:
    a. cliques
    b. crowds
    c. gangs
    d. friends
    (Answer = a, page number 221)

8. Loosely organized groups of children who share interests and activities are known as:
    a. cliques
    b. gangs
    c. friends
    d. crowds
    (Answer = d, page numbers 221-222)

9. _____ states that people learn the techniques and attitudes of crime from close and intimate relationships with criminal peers.
    a. Social Reaction Theory
    b. Social Learning Theory
    c. Social Control Theory
    d. Labeling Theory
    (Answer = b, page numbers 225-226)

10. _____ states that criminal behavior is learned through human interaction.
    a. Control Theory
    b. Labeling Theory
    c. Social Control Theory
    d. Social Learning Theory
    (Answer = d, page numbers 225-226)

11. According to Sutherland, the principle that criminal acts are related to a person's exposure to an excess amount of antisocial attitudes and values is part of the:
    a. Labeling Theory
    b. Differential Reinforcement Theory
    c. Social Learning Theory
    d. Differential Association Theory
    (Answer = d, page number 226)

12. When friends or parents demonstrate their disapproval of crime:
    a. associations occur
    b. disassociations occur
    c. definitions favorable toward criminality occur
    d. definitions unfavorable toward criminality occur
    (Answer = d, page numbers 226-227)

13. Differential associations may vary in:
    a. frequency
    b. duration
    c. priority
    d. all of the above
    (Answer = d, page number 227)

14. The age of children when they first encounter definitions of criminality impacts the _____ of an association.
    a. frequency
    b. duration
    c. priority
    d. intensity
    (Answer = c, page number 227)

15. The importance and prestige attributed to individuals or groups from whom the definitions are learned is the _____ element of an association.
    a. priority
    b. duration
    c. intensity
    d. frequency
    (Answer = c, page number 227)

16. When behavior is punished, this is referred to as:
    a. direct conditioning
    b. reconditioning
    c. labeling
    d. negative reinforcement
    (Answer = d, page number 229)

17. The view, according to Ackers, that both deviant and conventional behavior is learned is called:
     a. Differential Association Theory
     b. Labeling Theory
     c. Social Reaction Theory
     d. Differential Reinforcement Theory
     (Answer = d, page number 229)

18. The morally tinged influences, which have become entrenched in the culture but are publicly condemned, are known as:
     a. techniques of neutralization
     b. symbolic interaction
     c. subterranean behaviors
     d. labeling
     (Answer = c, page number 230)

19. The movement from one extreme of behavior to another, resulting in behavior that is sometimes unconventional, free, or deviant and at other times constrained and sober is called:
     a. stigma
     b. conduct disorder
     c. drift
     d. relative deprivation
     (Answer = c, page number 230)

20. The principle that becoming a criminal is a learning process in which potential delinquents and criminals master techniques that enable them to counterbalance conventional value and drift back and forth between illegitimate and conventional behavior is known as:
     a. a conduct disorder
     b. Labeling Theory
     c. reflected appraisal
     d. techniques of neutralization
     (Answer = d, page number 230)

21. The ability of delinquent youth to neutralize moral constraints so they may drift into criminal acts is known as:
     a. symbolic interaction
     b. techniques of neutralization
     c. subterranean behaviors
     d. Labeling Theory
     (Answer = b, page number 230)

22. When young offenders claim their unlawful acts were simply not their fault, it is known as:
    a. denial of responsibility
    b. denial of injury
    c. denial of victim
    d. condemnation of the condemners
    (Answer = a, page number 230)

23. By denying the wrongfulness of an act, criminals are able to neutralize illegal behavior. This is known as:
    a. denial of responsibility
    b. denial of victim
    c. condemnation of the condemners
    d. denial of injury
    (Answer = d, page number 230)

24. Criminals sometimes neutralize wrongdoing by maintaining that the victim of crime "had it coming." This is known as:
    a. denial of responsibility
    b. denial of injury
    c. denial of victim
    d. condemnation of the condemners
    (Answer = c, page number 230)

25. When an offender views the world as a corrupt place with a dog-eat-dog code, it is called:
    a. denial of responsibility
    b. denial of injury
    c. condemnation of the condemners
    d. denial of victim
    (Answer = c, page number 230)

26. Novice criminals often argue that they are caught in the dilemma of being loyal to their own peer group while at the same time attempting to abide by the rules of the larger society. This is known as:
    a. denial of responsibility
    b. appeal to higher loyalties
    c. denial of injury
    d. denial of victim
    (Answer = b, page number 231)

27. A strong moral sense which renders individuals incapable of hurting others and violating social norms is known as:
      a. self-control
      b. out of control
      c. drift
      d. reflected appraisal
      (Answer = a, page number 232)

28. The theory which maintains that everyone has the potential to become a criminal, but that their bond to society controls most people, is known as:
      a. Social Learning Theory
      b. Differential Association theory
      c. Differential Reinforcement Theory
      d. Social Control Theory
      (Answer = d, page number 232)

29. Human behavior is controlled through close associations with institutions and individuals. This is part of the:
      a. Control Theory
      b. Social Learning Theory
      c. Labeling Theory
      d. Social Control Theory
      (Answer = a, page number 232)

30. People's behavior, including criminal activity, is controlled by their attachment and commitment to conventional institutions, individuals, and processes. This is known as:
      a. commitment to conformity
      b. negative affective states
      c. positive affective states
      d. primary deviance
      (Answer = a, page number 234)

31. Communication via symbols is known as:
      a. symbolic interaction
      b. Labeling Theory
      c. subterranean behaviors
      d. techniques of neutralization
      (Answer = a, page numbers 236-237)

32. Some people are labeled "criminal" by police and court authorities; labeled people are known as troublemakers and are shunned by conventional society. This is part of:
      a. Social Learning Theory
      b. Control Theory
      c. Labeling Theory
      d. Social Control Theory
      (Answer = c, page number 238)

33. People become criminals when significant members of society label them as such and they accept those labels as a personal identity. This is part of the:
   a. Social Strata Theory
   b. Social Learning Theory
   c. Social Control Theory
   d. Social Reaction Theory
   (Answer = d, page number 238)

34. People who create rules are called:
   a. poor definers
   b. moral entrepreneurs
   c. deviants
   d. academics
   (Answer = b, page number 238)

35. An enduring label that taints a person's identity and changes him or her in the eyes of others is known as:
   a. socialization
   b. drift
   c. a clique
   d. a stigma
   (Answer = d, page number 239)

36. Social Reaction theorists are most concerned with:
   a. the creation of stigma
   b. the effect of stigma on self image
   c. all of the above
   d. none of the above
   (Answer = c, page number 239)

37. A youth's self-evaluation based on his or her perceptions of how others evaluate him or her is known as:
   a. reflected appraisal
   b. primary deviance
   c. secondary deviance
   d. stigma
   (Answer = a, page number 239)

38. When one believes that others view them as antisocial or a troublemaker, he or she then takes on attitudes and roles that reflect this assumption. This is known as:
   a. reflected appraisal
   b. reflective role-taking
   c. stigma
   d. primary deviance
   (Answer = b, page number 239)

39. The view that involves norm violations or crimes that have very little influence on the actor and can be quickly forgotten is known as:
    a. anomie
    b. primary deviance
    c. secondary deviance
    d. social control
    (Answer = b, page number 240)

40. This occurs when a deviant event comes to the attention of significant others or social control agents who then apply a negative label.
    a. secondary deviance
    b. primary deviance
    c. anomie
    d. social control
    (Answer = a, page number 240)

True/False

1. Children growing up in homes where a parent suffers from a mental impairment are also at risk for delinquency.
    (Answer = true, page number 220)

2. There is no link between child abuse, neglect, sexual abuse, and crime.
    (Answer = false, page number 220)

3. Schools have no contribution to criminality when they label problem youths and set them apart from conventional society.
    (Answer = false, page number 220)

4. Research indicates that many school dropouts, especially those who have been expelled, face a significant chance of entering a criminal career.
    (Answer = true, page number 220)

5. A popular government supported program designed to reduce the number of students who drop out of school is the Communities in Schools network.
    (Answer = true, page number 221)

6. Cliques refer to the movement from one extreme of behavior to another.
    (Answer = false, page number 221)

7. Social Learning Theories assume people are born "bad" and learn to be "good."
    (Answer = false, page number 225)

8. One of the most prominent social learning theories is Karl Marx's Differential Association Theory.
    (Answer = false, page number 226)

9. When behavior is punished, this is referred to as negative reinforcement.
    (Answer = true, page number 229)

10. Subterranean values are the morally tinged influences which have become entrenched in the culture but are publicly condemned.
    (Answer = true, page number 230)

11. Offenders frequently respect and admire honest, law-abiding persons.
    (Answer = true, page number 230)

12. When young offenders sometimes claim their unlawful acts were simply not their fault, it is known as denial of responsibility.
    (Answer = true, page number 230)

13. When an offender views the world as a corrupt place with a dog-eat-dog code, it is known as denial of injury.
    (Answer = false, page number 230)

14. Some individuals have self-control, manifested through a strong moral sense, which renders them incapable of hurting others and violating social norms.
    (Answer = true, page number 232)

15. Hirschi argues that the social bond a person maintains with society is divided into four main elements: attachment, commitment, involvement, and belief.
    (Answer = true, page number 234)

Essay Questions

1. Describe the relationship between socialization and crime. What are the prominent elements of socialization that contribute or not to a criminal career?
    (page numbers 218-225)

2. Compare and contrast the Social Learning Theories. Are the Learning Theories valid? Why or why not?
    (page numbers 225-232)

3. Define Differential Association. Describe the basic principles of differential association. Does Differential Association have any impact on current social policy?
    (page numbers 226-229)

4. Describe Social Control Theory. What is the relationship between crime and self-concept? Define the elements of the social bond and their relationship to deviance.
    (page numbers 232-236)

5. What is Labeling Theory? What are the consequences of labeling an individual? Differentiate between primary and secondary deviance.   (page numbers 236-242)

Chapter Eight

Social Conflict Theories
Critical Criminology and Restorative Justice

Summary

Chapter Eight begins with a discussion of Marxist thought. The development of conflict-based theory is presented, as is Social Conflict Theory and Critical Criminology. More contemporary forms of Critical Theory are examined. Chapter Eight concludes with the implications of Social Conflict Theory, more specifically Restorative Justice, on public policy.

Chapter Objectives

After reading this chapter the student should be able to:

- Be familiar with the concept of social conflict and how it shapes behavior
- Be able to discuss elements of conflict in the justice system
- Be familiar with the idea of critical criminology
- Be able to discuss the difference between structural and instrumental Marxism
- Know the various techniques of critical research
- Be able to discuss the term *left realism*
- Understand the concept of patriarchy
- Know what is meant by feminist criminology
- Be able to discuss peacemaking
- Understand the concept of restorative justice

Chapter Overview

Introduction
Marxist Thought
      Productive Forces and Productive Relations
      Surplus Value
      Marx on Crime
Developing a Conflict-Based Theory of Crime
      The Contribution of Willem Bonger
      The Contribution of Ralf Dahrendorf
      The Contribution of George Vold
Social Conflict Theory
      Social Conflict Research

Critical Criminology
> Fundamentals of Critical Criminology
> Instrumental versus Structural Theory
> Research on Critical Criminology
> Critique of Critical Criminology

Contemporary Forms of Critical Theory
> Left Realism
> Critical Feminist Theory

Race, Culture, Gender, and Criminology: Capitalism and Patriarchy
> Power-Control Theory
> Postmodern Theory
> Peacemaking Theory

Public Policy Implications of Social Conflict Theory: Restorative Justice
> Reintegrative Shaming
> The Concept of Restorative Justice
> The Process of Restoration

Comparative Criminology: Practicing Restorative Justice Abroad
> The Challenge of Restorative Justice

Summary

Chapter Outline

I. Introduction
A. Social conflict theorists view crime as a function of social conflict and economic rivalry.
B. Marxist criminologists or radical criminologists, but using the generic term critical criminologists and the field of study as critical criminology.
C. Conflict theorists goals:
  1. To explain crime within economic and social contexts.
  2. To express the connection between the nature of social class, crime and social control.
D. Conflict theorists concerned with:
  1. The role government plays in creating a crimogenic environment.
  2. The relationship between personal or group power and the shaping of criminal law.
  3. The prevalence of bias in the justice system operations.
  4. The relationship between a capitalist free-enterprise economy and crime rates.

II. Marxist Thought
A. Karl Marx - lived in time of unrestrained capitalist expansion.
B. Friedrich Engels (1820-1895) - friend and economic patron.
C. Marx and Engels joined the Communist League by 1847.
D. Productive Forces and Productive Relations
  1. 1848 - Marx published his famous communist manifesto.

a. focused on the economic conditions perpetuated by the capitalist system.

b. development had turned workers into a dehumanized mass that merely existed at the mercy of the capitalist employers.

c. identified the economic structures in society that control all human relations.

2. Production has two components:

a. productive forces - technology, energy sources and material resources.

b. productive relations - the relationships that exist among the people producing goods and services.

3. Most important relations in industrial culture between:

a. capitalist bourgeoisie - the owners of production.

b. proletariat - people who do the actual work.

c. lumpen proletariat - the bottom of society - the fringe members who produce nothing and live off the work of others.

4. Class - does not refer to an attribute or characteristic of a person or group; rather, it denotes position in relation to others.

a. not necessary to have wealth or prestige to be part of capitalist class; it is more important to have the power to exploit.

5. Societies and their structures are not stable, thus can change through slow evolution or sudden violence.

E. Surplus Value

1. Marx held that laboring class produces goods that exceed wages in value - the theory of surplus value.

a. excess value goes to capitalists as profit.

2. Capitalists find ways to produce cheaply:

a. pay workers lowest possible wages.

b. replace workers with labor-saving machinery.

3. Dialectic method of Hegel - for every idea or thesis there is an opposing argument or antithesis; a synthesis is the merger of the two.

F. Marx on Crime

1. The product of law enforcement policies akin to a labeling process theory.

2. A connection between criminality and the inequities found in the capitalist system.

III. Developing a Conflict-Based Theory of Crime

A. Marx influenced the development of social conflict thinking.

B. Conflict theory first applied to Bonger, Dahrendorf, and Vold.

C. The Contribution of Willem Bonger

1. Born 1876 in Holland and committed suicide in 1940 rather than submit to Nazi rule.

2. Believed crime is of social origin and crime lies within the boundaries of normal human behavior.

3. No act is naturally immoral or criminal.

4. Society is divided into have and have not groups.
   a. every society that is divided into the ruling class and an inferior class, the penal law serves the will of the ruling class.
5. The legal system discriminates against the poor by defending the actions of the wealthy and it is the proletariat who are deprived.
6. Upper-class individuals will commit crime if:
   a. they have a good opportunity to make a financial gain.
   b. their lack of moral sense enables them to violate social rules.
7. When wealth is distributed unequally, those who are poor will be crime-prone.
8. Concluded that crime will disappear if society progresses from competitive capitalism to monopoly capitalism - relatively few enterprises control the means of production.
D. The Contribution of Ralf Dahrendorf
   1. Argues that modern society is organized into imperatively coordinated associations.
      a. those who posses authority and those who lack authority.
   2. Domination of one society does not mean dominating another; society is a plurality of competing interest groups.
   3. Wrote *Class and Class Conflict in Industrial Society*.
      a. attempted to show how society changed since Marx's works.
      b. argued that Marx did not foresee the changes occurring in the labor classes.
      c. workers divided into unskilled, skilled, and semiskilled.
   4. Proposed a unified conflict theory of human behavior:
      a. social change is everywhere, all of the time.
      b. social conflict is everywhere, all of the time.
      c. every element in society contributes to its disintegration and change.
      d. others base every society on the coercion of some of its members.
E. The Contribution of George Vold
   1. Argued that crime can be explained by social conflict.
   2. Laws created by politically-oriented groups who seek the government's assistance to help them defend their rights and protect their interests.
   3. Criminal acts are a consequence of direct contact between forces struggling to control society.
IV. Social Conflict Theory - became prominent during the 1960's.
   A. Criminologists began to view the justice system as a mechanism to control the lower class and maintain the status quo.
   B. William Chambliss and Robert Seidman wrote *Law, Order and Power* - documented how the justice system protects the rich and powerful.
      1. Described how the control of the political and economic system affects how criminal justice is administered.

        2. Showed how the definitions of crime favor those who control the justice system.

        3. Analyzed the role of conflict in contemporary society.

  C. According to Richard Quinney and his social reality of crime, laws represent the interests of those who hold power in society.

        1. Power - the ability of persons and groups to determine and control the behavior of others and to shape public opinion to meet their personal needs.

        2. Unequal distribution of power causes conflict.

  D. Social Conflict Research

        1. Comparing crime rates of members of powerless groups with those of member of the elite classes.

            a. economic marginalization turns people to violent crime for survival.

            b. examining the criminal justice systems operations.

                i. studies that show that the criminal justice system is quick to take action when the victim of crime is wealthy, white and male, but it is disinterested when the victim is poor, black, and female.

V. Critical Criminology

  A. 1968 - British sociologists formed the National Deviancy Conference.

  B. 1973 - critical theory published in *The New Criminology* by Ian Taylor, Paul Walton, and Jock Young.

  C. Scholars in America started following a critical approach to criminology.

        1. Primarily at University of California at Berkeley.

  D. 1980's - the Left Realism School was started by scholars of the Middlesex Polytechnic and the University of Edinburgh in Great Britain.

  E. Since the 1980's - critical criminologists have been concerned with the conservative trend in American politics and the creation of an American empire.

        1. Have turned their attention to the threat of competitive capitalism to the working class.

  F. Fundamentals of Critical Criminology

        1. Critical criminologists - view crime as a function of the capitalist mode of production and not the social conflict that might occur in any society.

        2. Critical criminology - capitalism produces haves and have-nots, each engaging in a particular branch of criminality.

        3. In a capitalist society, those with economic and political power control the definition of crime and the manner in which the criminal justice system enforces the law.

        4. Globalization - refers to the process of creating transnational markets, politics, and legal systems; creating a global economy.

  G. Instrumental versus Structural Theory

1. Instrumental critical theory - views the criminal justice system as a method of controlling the poor, have-not members of society; the state is the tool of the capitalists.
   a. the poor may or may not commit more crimes, but they are arrested and punished more often because of a natural frustration.
   b. demystify law and justice - to unmask its true purpose.
2. The structural view - the relationship between law and capitalism is unidirectional, not always working for the rich and against the poor.
   a. law is used to maintain the long-term interests of the capitalist system.
   b. law is used to control members of any class who pose a threat to its existence.
   c. law is designed to keep the capitalist system working efficiently.

H. Research on Critical Criminology
1. They believe mainstream research is designed to unmask the weak and powerless members of society so they can be better dealt with by the legal system.
2. Critical research tends to be historical and analytical, not quantitative and empirical.
   a. macrolevel issues - how the accumulation of wealth affects crime rates.
   b. microlevel issues - the effect of criminal interactions on the lives of individuals living in a capitalist society.
3. Crime, the individual, and the state
   a. crime and its control are a function of capitalism.
   b. the justice system is biased against the working class and favors upper-class interests.
4. Historical analysis
   a. to show changes in criminal law correspond to the development of capitalist economy and investigate the development of modern police agencies.
   b. research between nineteenth century convict work and capitalism.

I. Critique of Critical Criminology
1. Great deal of criticism.
2. Some charge that critical criminologists unfairly neglect the efforts of the capitalist system to regulate itself.
3. Refuse to address the problems that exist in socialist countries.

VI. Contemporary Forms of Critical Theory
A. Left Realism - connected to British scholars John Lea and Jock Young
1. Relative deprivation equals discontent; discontent plus lack of political solution equals crime.
2. Crime protection

a. preemptive deterrence - an approach of community efforts trying to eliminate or reduce crime before it becomes necessary to employ police.

b. marginalized youth - youth that feel they are not a part of society and have nothing to lose by committing crime.

B. Critical Feminist Theory - a number of feminist writers have attempted to explain the cause of crime, gender differences in the crime rate, and the exploitation of female victims.

1. Critical feminist - view gender inequality as stemming from the unequal power of men and women in a capitalist society.

a. patriarchy, or male supremacy, continues to be supported by capitalists.

2. Patriarchy and crime - link criminal behavior patterns to the gender conflict created by the economic and social struggles common in post-industrial societies.

a. double marginality - capitalists control the labor of workers, while men control women both economically and biologically.

b. females in a capitalist society commit fewer crimes than males; they are isolated in families and have fewer opportunities than men.

c. doing gender - dominating women to prove their manliness.

d. female victimization should decline as women's place in society is elevated.

3. Exploitation and criminality - exploitation triggers the onset of female delinquent and deviant behavior.

4. How the justice system penalizes women:

a. juvenile system views the majority of female delinquents as sexually precocious girls who have to be brought under control.

b. females more likely to be arrested for sexual misconduct than their male counterpart.

c. girls more likely to undergo physical exam then boys.

d. girls more likely to be sent to a detention facility before trial.

e. longer detention for girls than boys.

C. Power-Control Theory - John Hagan and associates.

1. Crime and delinquency are a function of:

a. class position (power).

b. family functions (control).

2. Parents reproduce the power relationships they hold in the workplace.

3. Paternalistic families - fathers assume the traditional role of breadwinners, while mothers tend to have menial jobs or remain at home to supervise domestic matters.

a. role exit behaviors - unhappy girls are likely to run away or commit suicide.

4. Egalitarian families - the husband and wife share similar positions of power at home and in the workplace.
   a. daughters gain a freedom that reflects reduced parental control.

5. Evaluating power-control - received a great deal of attention.
   a. not all research is supportive.

VII. Postmodern Theory

A. Post-modernists, or deconstructionists, have embraced semiotics or deconstructionist analysis as a method of understanding all human relations including human behavior.
   1. Semiotics - using language as signs or symbols beyond their literal meaning.
B. Post-modernists believe that language is value-laden and can promote inequities that are present in the rest of the social structure.
C. Peacemaking Theory
   1. The purpose of criminology is to promote a peaceful and just society.
   2. Peacemakers view the efforts of the state to punish and control as crime encouraging rather than crime discouraging.
   3. Advocate rather than prison, policies such as mediation and conflict resolution.

VIII. Public Policy Implications of Social Conflict Theory: Restorative Justice

A. Conflict causes crime.
B. Restorative Justice - peacemaking movement which has adopted non-violent methods and applied them
C. Reintegrative shaming
   1. John Braithwaite's book *Crime, Shame, and Reintegration*.
   2. Shame - power tool of informal social control.
      a. stigmatization - an ongoing process of degradation in which the offender is branded as an evil person and cast out of society.
      b. reintegrative shaming - disapproval is extended to the offenders' evil deeds, while at the same time they are cast as respected people who can be reaccepted by society.
D. The Concept of Restorative Justice
   1. Zehr - we address victims' harm and needs, hold offenders accountable, and involve victims, offenders, and communities; at the core is respect.
E. The Process of Restoration
   1. Redefine crime in terms of a conflict among the offender, the victim, and the affected constituencies (families, schools, etc.).
   2. The resolution must take place within the context in which the conflict originally occurred.
   3. Developing restoration
      a. the offender is asked to recognize the injury caused and to accept responsibility.
      b. a commitment to material restitution and symbolic reparation.

        c. community support for both victim and offender.
    4. Restoration programs
        a. sentencing circles - crime victims and their families are brought together with offenders and their families in an effort to formulate a sanction that addresses the needs of each party.
        b. programs within communities, schools, police, and courts.
    5. Balanced and Restorative Justice (BARJ) - restorative justice should be centered on the principle of balance.
        a. offender accountability.
        b. competency development.
        c. community protection.
  F. The Challenge of Restorative Justice
    1. The difficult task of balancing the needs of offenders with those of their victims.
    2. May risk ignoring the offender's need and increasing the likelihood of re-offending.
    3. Programs, which focus on the offender, may turn off victims.

IX. Summary

Key Terms

Antithesis - An opposing argument.

Capitalist Bourgeoisie - The owners of the means of production.

Communist Manifesto - In this document, Marx focused his attention on the economic conditions perpetuated by the capitalist system. He stated that its development had turned workers into a dehumanized mass who lived an existence that was at the mercy of their capitalist employers.

Critical Criminologists - Researchers who view crime as a function of the capitalist mode of production and not the social conflict that might occur in any society regardless of its economic system.

Critical Criminology - The view that capitalism produces haves and have-nots, each engaging in a particular branch of criminality. The mode of production shapes social life. Because economic competitiveness is the essence of capitalism, conflict increases and eventually destabilizes social interactions and the individuals within them.

Critical Feminist - Scholars, both male and female, who focus on the effects of gender inequality and the unequal power of men and women in a capitalist society.

Deconstructionist - An approach that focuses on the use of language by those in power to define crime based on their own values and biases; also called postmodernist.

Demystify - To unmask the true purpose of law, justice, or other social institutions.

Dialectic Method - For every idea, or thesis, there exists an opposing argument, or antithesis. Because neither position can ever be truly accepted, the result is a merger of the two ideas, a synthesis. Marx adapted this analytic method for his study of class struggle.

Egalitarian Families - Families in which spouses share similar positions of power at home and in the workplace.

Globalization - The process of creating transnational markets, politics, and legal systems in an effort to form and sustain a global economy.

Imperatively Coordinated Associations - These associations are composed of two groups: those who possess authority and use it for social domination and those who lack authority and are dominated.

Instrumental Critical Theory - The view that criminal law and the criminal justice system are capitalist instruments for controlling the lower class.

Left Realism - An approach that views crime as a function of relative deprivation under capitalism and that favors pragmatic, community-based crime prevention and control.

Lumpen Proletariat - The fringe members at the bottom of society who produce nothing and live, parasitically, off the work of others.

Marginalization - Displacement of workers, pushing them outside the economic and social mainstream.

Marxist Criminologists - Criminologists who view crime as a product of the capitalist system.

Paternalistic Families - Traditional family model in which fathers assume the role of breadwinners, while mothers tend to have menial jobs or remain at home to supervise domestic matters.

Patriarchy - A society in which men dominate public, social, economic, and political affairs.

Peacemaking - An approach that considers punitive crime control strategies to be counterproductive and favors the use of humanistic conflict resolution to prevent and control crime.

Postmodernist - Approach that focuses on the use of language by those in power to define crime based on their own values and biases; also called deconstructionist.

Power - The ability of people and groups to control the behavior of others, to shape public opinion, and to define deviance.

Power-Control Theory - The view that gender differences in crime are a function of economic power (class position, one- versus two-earner families) and parental control (paternalistic versus egalitarian families).

Preemptive Deterrence - Efforts to prevent crime through community organization and youth involvement.

Productive Forces - Technology, energy sources, and material resources.

Productive Relations - The relationships that exist among the people producing goods and services.

Radical Criminologists - Criminologists who view crime as a product of the capitalist system.

Reintegrative Shaming - A method of correction that encourages offenders to confront their misdeeds, experience shame because of the harm they caused, and then be reincluded in society.

Restorative Justice - Using humanistic, nonpunitive strategies to right wrongs and restore social harmony.

Role Exit Behaviors - In order to escape from a stifling life in male-dominated families, girls may try to break away by running away and/or even attempting suicide.

Semiotics - The use of language elements as signs or symbols beyond their literal meaning.

Sentencing Circle - A peacemaking technique in which offenders, victims, and other community members are brought together in an effort to formulate a sanction that addresses the needs of all.

Social Conflict Theory - The view that crime is a function of class conflict and power relations. Laws are created and enforced by those in power to protect their own interests.

Social Reality of Crime - The view that the main purpose of criminology is to promote a peaceful, just society.

Structural Critical Theory - The view that criminal law and the criminal justice system are means of defending and preserving the capitalist system.

Surplus Value - The Marxist view that the laboring classes produce wealth that far exceeds their wages and goes to the capitalist class as profits.

Synthesis - A merger of two opposing ideas.

Thesis - In the philosophy of Hegel, an original idea or thought.

Discussion Exercises

1. Divide the class into three groups. Have each group review one of the Conflict theorists: Bonger, Dahrendorf, or Vold. Compare and contrast the theorists, the culture in which they lived, the economic times, and the relevance of their theory in today's pop culture.

2. Taking a recent case of a female offender that was featured in the local newspaper, ask students to explain her offense as a radical feminist would. That is, examine the extent to which the offender may have been disadvantaged by a patriarchal society in her various educational, economic, and social endeavors. Was her crime a reflection of her less valued position in society? Is there any mention of her being a crime victim in the past?

3. The peacemaking movement advocates for more "humanist solutions to crime." Break students into groups and have them brainstorm as to what these humanist solutions might look like. Remember that Pepinsky and Quinney advocate for mediation and conflict resolution policies.

InfoTrac Assignment

GETTING STARTED: Search term words for subject guide: Marx, Ralf Dahrendorf, Critical Criminology, Left Realism, Critical Feminist Theory, Power-Control Theory, Restorative Justice.

CRITICAL THINKING PROJECT: Using the search term "Restorative Justice," examine the public policy implications of Social Conflict Theory.

Here are three articles:

Burford, Gale and Paul Adams. "Restorative Justice, Responsive Regulation and Social Work." *Journal of Sociology & Social Welfare.*

Grauwiler, Peggy and Linda G. Mills. "Moving Beyond the Criminal Justice Paradigm: A radical restorative justice approach to intimate abuse." *Journal of Sociology & Social Welfare.*

Viano, Emilio C. "Restorative Justice for Victims Offenders: A return to American traditions." *Corrections Today.*

Fill in the Blank

1. In 1848, Marx issued his famous **Communist Manifesto**.
    (page number 257)

2. **Productive forces** include such things as technology, energy sources, and material resources.
    (page number 257)

3. The relationships, which exist among the people producing the goods and services, are known as **productive relations**.
    (page number 257)

4. The owners of the means of production are the **capitalist bourgeoisie**.
    (page number 257)

5. The **proletariat** are the people who do the actual labor.
    (page number 257)

6. Hegel argued that for every idea, or thesis, there exists an opposing argument, or **antithesis**.
    (page number 259)

7. **Ralf Dahrendorf** argued that modern society is organized into imperatively coordinated associations: those who possess authority and those who lack authority.
    (page number 260)

8. According to Richard Quinney, **The Social Reality of Crime** is that criminal definitions (law) represent the interests of those who hold power in society.
    (page number 261)

9. **Marginalization** thrusts people outside of the economic mainstream.
    (page number 262)

10. **Globalization** is the process of creating transnational markets, politics, and legal systems.
    (page number 264)

11. **Left Realism School** began in the 1980's by scholars affiliated with the Middlesex Polytechnic and the University of Edinburgh in Great Britain.
    (page number 268)

12. **Critical Feminist Theory** is the area of criminology where a number of feminist writers have attempted to explain the cause of crime, gender differences in the crime rate, and the exploitation of female victims.
(page number 268)

13. The purpose of **Peacemaking Criminology** is to promote a peaceful and just society.
(page number 272)

14. **Reintegrative shaming** is when disapproval is extended to offenders' evil deeds, while at the same time they are cast respected people who can be reaccepted by society.
(page number 274)

15. The most common form of shaming typically involves **stigmatization**.
(page number 274)

Multiple Choice

1. Conflict theorists are concerned with which of the following?
   a. the role government plays in creating a crimiogenic environment
   b. the relationship between personal or group power and the shaping of criminal law
   c. the prevalence of bias in the justice system operations
   d. all of the above
   (Answer = d, page number 257)

2. The view that the inter-group conflicts and rivalry that exists in every society causes crime is known as:
   a. Social Conflict Theory
   b. Radical Feminist Theory
   c. Surplus Value Theory
   d. Peacemaking Criminology
   (Answer = a, page number 257)

3. In 1848 Karl Marx issued his famous:
   a. Communist Manifesto
   b. Declaration of Independence
   c. Constitution
   d. Declaration of War
   (Answer = a, page number 257)

4. Productive forces include such things as:
   a. technology
   b. energy sources
   c. material resources
   d. all of the above
   (Answer = d, page number 257)

5. The relationships which exist among the people producing goods and services are known as:
   a. productive forces
   b. productive relations
   c. capitalist bourgeoisie
   d. the proletariat
   (Answer = b, page number 257)

6. The owners of the means of production are called:
   a. productive forces
   b. productive relations
   c. capitalist bourgeoisie
   d. the proletariat
   (Answer = c, page number 257)

7. The people who do the actual work are called:
   a. productive forces
   b. productive relations
   c. capitalist bourgeoisie
   d. the proletariat
   (Answer = d, page number 257)

8. In Marxist theory, what term refers to position in relation to others?
   a. stigma
   b. productive force
   c. class
   d. label
   (Answer = c, page number 257)

9. The view held by Marx that the laboring class produces goods that exceed wages in value is known as:
   a. left realism
   b. surplus value
   c. stigma
   d. drift
   (Answer = b, page number 258)

10. Hegel argued that for every idea, or thesis, there exists an opposing argument or:
    a. antithesis
    b. subthesis
    c. hypothesis
    d. dialectic method
    (Answer = a, page number 259)

11. Which theorist believed that crime is of social and not biological origin and that, with a few exceptions, crime lies within the boundaries of normal human behavior?
    a. Karl Marx
    b. George Vold
    c. Ralf Dahrendorf
    d. Willem Bonger
    (Answer = d, page number 260)

12. Which theorist argued that modern society is organized into imperatively coordinated associations: those who possess authority and those who lack authority?
    a. Willem Bonger
    b. Ralf Dahrendorf
    c. George Vold
    d. Karl Marx
    (Answer = b, page number 260)

13. Dahrendorf proposed a unified conflict theory of human behavior, which says which of the following?
    a. every society is at every point subject to processes of change.
    b. every society displays at every point dissent and conflict.
    c. every element in a society renders a contribution to its disintegration and change.
    d. all of the above
    (Answer = d, page number 261)

14. Which theorist argued that crime could also be explained by social conflict?
    a. Willem Bonger
    b. George Vold
    c. Ralf Dahrendorf
    d. Karl Marx
    (Answer = b, page number 261)

15. The theory according to Richard Quinney that criminal definitions represent the interests of those who hold power in society is known as:
    a. Marxist Feminism
    b. Radical Feminism
    c. Social Reality of Crime
    d. Integrative-Constitutive Theory
    (Answer = c, page number 261)

16. Quinney wrote that criminal definitions are based on which of the following factors?
    a. changing social conditions
    b. emerging interests
    c. all of the above
    d. none of the above
    (Answer = c, page number 261)

17. The ability of persons and groups to determine and control the behavior of others and to shape public opinion to meet their personal interests is known as:
    a. class
    b. status
    c. power
    d. stigma
    (Answer = c, page number 262)

18. This occurs when people are thrust outside of the economic mainstream.
    a. techniques of neutralization
    b. symbolic interaction
    c. marginalization
    d. subterranean behaviors
    (Answer = c, page number 262)

19. A group of Marxists who view the criminal law and criminal justice system solely as an instrument for controlling the poor, have-not members of society is known as:
    a. Instrumentalists
    b. Peacemakers
    c. Left Realists
    d. surplus values
    (Answer = a, page number 265)

20. According to the Instrumental Critical Theory, the agency of control for the state is:
    a. the police
    b. the courts
    c. the correctional system
    d. all of the above
    (Answer = d, page number 265)

21. To unmask the true purpose of law and justice is to:
    a. socialize
    b. educate
    c. label
    d. demystify
    (Answer = d, page number 265)

22. Which theory states the relationship between law and capitalism is unidirectional?
    a. Critical Feminist Theory
    b. Marxist Criminology
    c. Left Realism
    d. Structural Critical Theory
    (Answer = d, page number 265)

23. Critical research tends to be:
    a. historical
    b. quantitative
    c. empirical
    d. all of the above
    (Answer = a, page number 266)

24. Critical criminologists devote considerable attention to the study of relationships between which of the following?
    a. crimes
    b. victims
    c. the state
    d. all of the above
    (Answer = d, page number 266)

25. The branch of Conflict Theory which holds that crime is a "real" social problem experienced by the lower classes and radical scholars must address those lower-class concerns about crime is known as:
    a. Marginalization
    b. Social Learning Theory
    c. Social Control Theory
    d. Left Realism
    (Answer = d, page number 268)

26. This school of thought was begun in the 1980's by scholars affiliated with the Middlesex Polytechnic and the University of Edinburgh in Great Britain.
    a. Left Realism School
    b. School of Hard Knocks
    c. Social Reality School
    d. Peacemaker School
    (Answer = a, page number 268)

27. The area of criminology where a number of feminist writers have attempted to explain the cause of crime, gender differences in the crime rate, and the exploitation of female victims is called:
    a. Differential Association
    b. Labeling Theory
    c. Social Reaction Theory
    d. Critical Feminist Theory
    (Answer = d, page number 268)

28. Those theorists who view gender inequality as a function of female exploitation by fathers and husbands are known as:
   a. Left Realists
   b. Critical Feminists
   c. Peacemakers
   d. Instrumentalists
   (Answer = b, page number 268)

29. Male supremacy is also known as:
   a. paternalism
   b. patriarchy
   c. left realism
   d. marginalization
   (Answer = b, page number 269)

30. According to critical feminists, females in a capitalist society commit fewer crimes than males due to their:
   a. double marginality
   b. stigmatization
   c. reintegration
   d. surplus value
   (Answer = a, page number 269)

31. Hagan's view is that crime and delinquency rates are a function of:
   a. class position
   b. family functions
   c. all of the above
   d. none of the above
   (Answer = c, page number 270)

32. Which of the following is the best example of a role exit behavior?
   a. running away from home
   b. hanging out with deviant peers
   c. living in an egalitarian family
   d. all of the above
   (Answer = a, page number 270)

33. In what type of families do husbands and wives share similar positions of power at home and the workplace?
   a. conflict
   b. patriarchal
   c. paternalistic
   d. egalitarian
   (Answer = d, page numbers 270-271)

34. When capitalists agreed to pay men enough money to support wives and children, this was known as the:
   a. double wage
   b. family wage
   c. patriarchal wage
   d. none of the above
   (Answer = b, page number 271)

35. For members of this movement, the main purpose of criminology is to promote a peaceful and just society.
   a. Peacemaking Criminology
   b. Marxist Feminists
   c. Left Realism School
   d. Integrative-Constitutive Theory
   (Answer = a, page number 272)

36. Which theory is most likely to draw its inspiration from Quakerism and Zen?
   a. Peacemaking
   b. Left Realism
   c. Power-Control
   d. Critical Feminist
   (Answer = a, page number 272)

37. What is the best example of symbolic reparation?
   a. performing a service
   b. the presentation of a gift
   c. monetary payment
   d. an apology
   (Answer = d, page number 275)

38. Used in schools, _____ programs strive to improve the person's relationships with key figures in the community who may have been harmed by the student's actions.
   a. shaming
   b. sentencing circle
   c. relational rehabilitation
   d. reintegrative shaming
   (Answer = c, page number 276)

39. According to the Balanced and Restorative Justice Approach, the justice system should give weight to:
   a. offender accountability
   b. competence development
   c. community protection
   d. all of the above
   (Answer = d, page numbers 276-277)

40. Which of the following is not a concern victims have expressed concerning restorative justice programs?
   a. too much focus may be placed on the victim
   b. it may be another way that offender's rights are protected more than those of victims
   c. they may be victimized all over again by the process
   d. many victims do want an apology, if it is heartfelt
   (Answer = a, page number 277)

True/False

1. Marx concludes that the character of every civilization is determined by its mode of production.
   (Answer = true, page number 257)

2. According to Marxist theory, class does not refer to an attribute of a person, rather it is a position in relation to others.
   (Answer = true, page number 257)

3. Willem Bonger believed that crime is of a biological origin not a social origin.
   (Answer = false, page number 260)

4. Upper-class individuals will commit crime if they sense a poor opportunity to make a financial gain and their abundance of moral sense enables them to violate social rules.
   (Answer = false, page number 260)

5. Conflict theory came into criminological prominence during the 1960's.
   (Answer = true, page number 261)

6. Globalization is the process of creating transnational markets, politics, and legal systems.
   (Answer = true, page number 264)

7. Instrumentalists view the criminal law and criminal justice system solely as an instrument for controlling the elite members of society.
   (Answer = false, page number 265)

8. According to the instrumental view, capitalist justice serves the powerful and rich and enables them to impose their morality and standards of behavior on the entire society.
   (Answer = true, page number 265)

9. Left realists argue that crime victims in the lower-class need and deserve the most protections.
   (Answer = false, page number 268)

10. Critical feminists focus on the social forces that shape women's lives and experiences to explain female criminality.
(Answer = true, page number 268)

11. Patriarchy first emerged in pre-capitalist agricultural societies in which a male head presided over his family, controlling work and the marriages of its members.
(Answer = true, page number 268)

12. Girls are more likely to be sent to a detention facility before trial, and the length of their detention averaged three times that of the boys.
(Answer = true, page number 270)

13. Post-modernists rely on semiotics to conduct their research efforts.
(Answer = true, page number 272)

14. Restorative justice advocates support the methods of punishment that include probation and imprisonment.
(Answer = false, page number 274)

15. The most common form of shaming typically involves reintegrative shaming.
(Answer = false, page number 274)

Essay Questions

1. Describe Karl Marx's theory on crime. What influence has Marx had on current social policy?
(page numbers 256-259)

2. Compare and contrast the theory contributions of Willem Bonger, Ralf Dahrendorf, and George Vold.
(page numbers 259-261)

3. Define Social Conflict Theory. What research has been conducted to validate conflict theory? Provide the current analysis of conflict theory.
(page numbers 261-263)

4. What is Critical Criminology? Which criminologists influenced this theory?
(page numbers 263-267)

5. What is Left Realism theory? What are the roots of left realism and how did it evolve? What are the current social implications of left realism theory?
(page number 268)

Chapter Nine

Developmental Theories
Life Course and Latent Trait

Summary

Chapter Nine examines the Developmental Theories, which can be divided into either Life Course Theories or Latent Trait Theories. The Life Course view examines such topics as the Glueck's research, the Social Development Model, and Sampson and Laub's Age-Graded Theory. The Latent Trait view includes the General Theory of Crime, Differential Coercion Theory, and Control Balance Theory. The chapter concludes with a discussion of public policy implications of the Developmental Theories.

Chapter Objectives

After reading this chapter the student should be able to:

- Be familiar with the concept of developmental theory
- Know the factors that influence the life course
- Recognize that there are different pathways to crime
- Be able to discuss the social development model
- Describe what is meant by interactional theory
- Be familiar with the "turning points in crime"
- Be able to discuss the influence of social capital on crime
- Know what is meant by a latent trait
- Be able to discuss Gottfredson and Hirschi's General Theory of Crime
- Be familiar with the concepts of impulsivity and self-control

Chapter Overview

Introduction
The Life Course View
> The Glueck Research
> Life Course Concepts
> Problem Behavior Syndrome
> Pathways to Crime
> Age of Onset/Continuity of Crime
The Criminological Enterprise: Desisting from Crime
Theories of the Criminal Life Course
> The Social Development Model
> Farrington's ICAP Theory

Interactional Theory
General Theory of Crime and Delinquency (GTCD)
Sampson and Laub: Age-Graded Theory
The Criminological Enterprise: Shared Beginnings, Divergent Lives
Latent Trait View
Crime and Human Nature
Latent Trait Theories
General Theory of Crime
Differential Coercion Theory
Control Balance Theory
Evaluating Developmental Theories
Public Policy Implications of Developmental Theory
Policy and Practice in Criminology: The Fast Track Project
Summary

Chapter Outline

I. Introduction - Developmental theories fall into two groups: life course and latent trait theories.
    A. Life Course Theories - view criminality as a dynamic process, influenced by a multitude of individual characteristics, traits, and social experiences.
    B. Latent Trait Theories - hold that human development is controlled by a "master trait" present at birth or soon after.
II. The Life Course View
    A. Even as toddlers, people begin relationships and behaviors that determine their adult life course.
        1. People must learn to conform to social rules and function effectively in society.
        2. Transitions are expected to occur in order: finish school, marriage, etc.
    B. Disruptions in life's major transitions can be destructive and may cause criminality.
        1. Positive life experience may help some criminals desist from crime for a while; a negative life experience may cause them to resume their activities.
    C. As people mature, the factors that influence their behavior change.
    D. Multidimensional theories - criminality has multiple roots, including maladaptive personality traits, educational failure, and family relations.
    E. The Glueck Research - Sheldon and Eleanor Glueck at Harvard University in the 1930's popularized research on the life cycle of delinquent careers.
        1. Conducted longitudinal research studies to determine the factors that predicted persistent offending.
        2. Found children who are antisocial early in life are most likely to continue their offending careers into adulthood.
        3. Identified a number of personal and social factors related to persistent offending - the most important family relations.

4. Measured biological and psychological traits such as body type, intelligence, and personality.
5. Found children with low intelligence, with a background of mental disease, and had a powerful physique were the most likely to become persistent offenders.
6. Research was ignored for 30 years until 1990s when rediscovered by Sampson and Laub.

F. Life Course Concepts - the factors that produce crime and delinquency at one point in the life cycle may not be relevant at another; as people mature, the social, physical, and environmental influences on their behavior are transformed.

G. Problem Behavior Syndrome - a group of antisocial behaviors that cluster together and typically involve:
1. Family dysfunction.
2. Sexual and physical abuse.
3. Substance abuse.
4. Smoking.
5. Precocious sexuality.
6. Early pregnancy.
7. Educational underachievement.
8. Suicide attempts.
9. Sensation seeking.
10. Unemployment.

H. Pathways to Crime - Rolf Loeber and associates identified paths to crime:
1. Authority conflict pathway - begins at an early age with stubborn behavior which leads to defiance and then to authority avoidance.
2. Covert pathway - begins with minor, underhanded behavior (lying, shoplifting) that leads to property damage then to more serious criminality.
3. Overt pathway - escalates to aggressive acts beginning with aggression leading to physical fighting and then to violence.

I. Age of Onset/Continuity of Crime - early onset of deviance strongly predicts later and more serious criminality.
1. Continuity and desistance - children repeatedly in trouble will continue to be antisocial throughout their life course.
2. Gender similarities and differences:
   a. similarities - both who have early experiences with antisocial behavior are the ones most likely to continue involvement throughout the life course.
   b. differences:
      i. males - early onset to problems at work and substance abuse.
      ii. females - early onset to relationship problems, depression, suicide, and poor health.
3. Adolescent-limiteds and life course persisters

          a. adolescent-limited offenders - begin to mimic the antisocial
             behavior of more troubled teens, only to reduce the
             frequency of their offending as they mature to around age
             18.
          b. life course persisters - those who begin offending at an early
             age and continue to offend well into adulthood.
      4. Supporting research
          a. support for Moffitt's views that early-onset delinquents are both
             more prevalent and more generalized in their delinquent
             activity.
          b. life course persisters have more mental health problems than
             adolescent-limited offenders.
          c. early onset delinquents more influenced by individual-level
             traits and negative personality, are more violent, and
             experiment with substance abuse and sexuality earlier; late-
             onset delinquents more influenced by peers and conflict
             with parents.
III. **Theories of the Criminal Life Course**
   A. The Social Development Model (SDM)
      1. A number of community-level risk factors make some people more
         susceptible to developing antisocial behaviors.
      2. As children mature, elements of socialization control their
         developmental process.
          a. perceived opportunities for involvement in activities and
             interactions with others.
          b. the degree of involvement and interaction with parents.
          c. the children's ability to participate in these interactions.
          d. the reinforcement they perceive for their participation.
      3. To control the risk of antisocial behavior, a child must maintain
         prosocial bonds.
      4. Children's antisocial behavior also depends on the quality of their
         attachments to parents and other influential relations.
      5. SDM holds that commitment and attachment to conventional
         institutions, activities, and beliefs insulate youth from crime
         influences.
   B. Farrington's ICAP Theory - longitudinal study since 1982 that uses self-report
      data, interviews, and psychological testing of London boys born in 1953.
      1. Found traits present in persistent offenders can be observed as early as
         age 8.
      2. Future criminals receive poor parental supervision.
      3. Deviant behavior tends to be versatile rather than specialized.
      4. By age 30, former delinquents are likely to be separated or divorced
         and an absent parent.
      5. Nonoffenders and desisters:
          a. nonoffenders - those who exhibit factors that put them at risk
             of offending, but remain a nonoffender.

b. desisters - those who begin a criminal career and then later desist.

6. What caused offenders to desist?
    a. holding a good job.
    b. physical relocation.
    c. marriage.

7. The ICAP Theory
    a. antisocial potential (AP) - key element of ICAP; refers to the potential to commit antisocial acts.
    b. long-term AP:
        i. increases when people desire material goods, want to increase their status, and seek excitement and sexual satisfaction yet lack legitimate means for their attainment.
        ii. depends on attachment and socialization.
        iii. changing life events can lower AP.
    c. short term AP - a person may be influenced by situational inducements to crime; reflects criminal opportunities and the availability of victims.
    d. AP and crime - the commission of offenses depends on the interaction between the individual and the social environment.
    e. long-term offending patterns are caused when people with high AP also experience increases in their long-term motivation, increases in physical capabilities and skills, and changes in socialization influences.
    f. short-term offending patterns are caused by increasing short-term motivation and increasing opportunities for offending because of changes in routine activities.

C. Interactional Theory - Terrence Thornberry, an age-graded view of crime.
    1. Seriously delinquent youths form belief systems that are consistent with their deviant lifestyle.
    2. Delinquents form a criminal peer group of individuals with the same interests as their own.
    3. Testing Interactional Theory
        a. current testing and ample evidence supportive of its premise: crime and social relations are interactional.
        b. research indicates association with delinquents does increase delinquent involvement.
        c. delinquency related to weakened attachments to family and education.
        d. suggests criminality is part of a dynamic social process and not just an outcome.

D. General Theory of Crime and Delinquency (GTCD) - Agnew finds crime is an interactional phenomenon.

1. Life domains or 5 key elements of human development:
   a. self.
   b. family.
   c. school.
   d. peers.
   e. work.
2. As success within these life domains change, so does one's criminality.

E. Sampson and Laub: Age-Graded Theory
   1. Robert Sampson and John Laub (1993) *Crime in the Making*.
   2. The stability of delinquent behavior can be affected by events that occur later in life.
   3. Turning points - life events that enable an adult offender to desist from crime (marriage, career).
   4. Social capital - positive relations with individuals and institutions that are life sustaining.
      a. building social capital and strong social bonds reduces the likelihood of long-term deviance.
   5. Testing Age-Graded Theory
      a. empirical research shows people change over the life course and factors which predict delinquency in adolescence may have less of an impact on adult crime.
      b. evidence supports once begun, criminal careers can be reversed if life conditions improve.
      c. research supports accumulating social capital reduces crime rates.
   6. The marriage factor - people who maintain a successful marriage and become parents are the most likely to mature out of crime.
   7. Future research directions - questions continue.

IV. **Latent Trait Theories** - explain the flow of crime over the life cycle.
   A. Latent traits - either present at birth or established early in life and remain stable over time. Suspected latent traits include:
      1. Defective intelligence.
      2. Impulsive personality.
      3. Genetic abnormalities.
      4. The physical-chemical functioning of the brain.
      5. Environmental influences on brain function - drugs, chemicals, injuries.
   B. Crime and Human Nature
      1. James Q. Wilson and Richard Herrnstein (1985) wrote *Crime and Human Nature*.
      2. Personal traits, genetics, intelligence, and body build outweigh social variables as predictors of criminal activity.
   C. General Theory of Crime - Michael Gottfredson and Travis Hirschi wrote *A General Theory of Crime* - they modified Hirschi's Social Control Theory with biosocial, psychological, routine activities, and rational choice theories.
      1. The act and the offender

   a. the criminal offender and the criminal act are separate concepts.

2. What makes people crime-prone?
   a. the tendency to commit crime to a person's level of self-control.
   b. people with limited self-control tend to be impulsive.
   c. those with low self-control enjoy risky, exciting, or thrilling behaviors with immediate gratification - more likely to enjoy criminal acts.
   d. root of poor self-control to inadequate child-rearing practices.
   e. low self-control develops early in life and remains stable into adulthood.

3. Self-control and crime
   a. principles of self-control theory explain all varieties of criminal behavior.

4. Supporting evidence for GTC
   a. research identified indicators of impulsiveness and self-control to determine if the correlated with criminal activity.
   b. a number of studies have indicated successfully this correlation.

5. Analyzing the General Theory of Crime - several questions remain unanswered:
   a. tautological - may involve circular reasoning.
   b. different classes of criminals - this would contradict the GTC vision that a single factor causes crime and that there is a single class of offender.
   c. ecological/individual differences - GTC fails to address individual and ecological patterns in the crime rate.
   d. racial and gender differences - little evidence that males are more impulsive than girls; Gottfredson and Hirschi explain racial differences as a failure of African-Americans in child-rearing.
   e. moral beliefs - GTC ignores the moral concept of right and wrong.
   f. peer influence - findings that kids who lack self-control have trouble maintaining friendships with law-abiding peers contradicts the GTC which suggests the influence of friends should be stable.
   g. people change - GTC assumes that criminal propensity does not change; opportunities change.
   h. modest relationship - self-control is a modest fact and there are other forces which predict the onset of criminal behavior.
   i. cross-cultural differences - evidence shows the criminals in other countries do not lack self-control and GTC may be culturally limited.
   j. misreads human nature - makes flawed assumptions about people; assumes that people are selfish, self-serving and hedonistic and must be controlled.

        k. personality disorder - saying one lacks self-control implies a personality defect making them impulsive or rash.

D. Differential Coercion Theory

    1. Mark Colvin wrote *Crime and Coercion* - suggested that self-control is produced by experiences a person has with destructive forces called coercion.

    2. Two types of coercion:

        a. inter-personal coercion - direct, involving the use or threat of force and intimidation from parents, peers, and significant others.

        b. impersonal coercion - involves pressures beyond individual control, such as economic and social pressure caused by unemployment, poverty, or competition among businesses or other groups.

    3. A person's ability to maintain self-control is a function of the amount, type and consistency of coercion they experience as they go through life.

    4. Coercion and criminal careers - Colvin found that chronic offenders grew up with parents using erratic control and in an inconsistent fashion.

        a. coercive ideation - a mind-set in which the world is conceived as full of coercive forces that can only be overcome through the application of equal or greater coercive responses.

    5. Social support and differential coercion - Colvin, Cullen, and Ven proposed a modified version of the coercion view called Differential Social Support and Coercion Theory (DSSCT).

        a. social support comes in 2 forms:

            i. expressive, which includes the sharing of emotions and the affirmation of self-worth and dignity.

            ii. instrumental, which includes material and financial assistance and the giving of advice, guidance, and connections for positive social advancement in legitimate society.

        b. to reduce crime rates, societies must enhance the legitimate sources of social support and reduce the forces of coercion.

E. Control-Balance Theory - Charles Tittle

    1. Control has 2 elements:

        a. the amount of control one can exercise over others.

        b. the amount of control one is subject to by others.

    2. Conformity results when these 2 elements are in balance; control imbalances produce deviant and criminal behaviors.

    3. Control deficit - occurs when one's desires or impulses are limited by others ability to regulate or punish their behavior.

4. Control surplus - occurs when the amount of control one exercises over others is in excess of the ability others have to control or modify the person's behavior.
5. People sensing a deficit of control turn to 3 types of behavior to restore balance:
    a. predation - direct forms of physical violence such as robbery, sexual assault or other forms of physical violence.
    b. defiance - designed to challenge and control mechanisms but stop short of physical harm: vandalism, curfew violations, and unconventional sex.
    c. submission - passive obedience to the demands of others such as submitting to physical or sexual abuse without response.
6. Those with an excess of control may engage in:
    a. exploitation - using others to commit crime, such as contract killers or drug runners.
    b. plunder - using power without regard for others, such as committing a hate crime or polluting the environment.
    c. decadence - involves spur of the moment, irrational acts such as child molesting.

V. Evaluating Developmental Theories
A. A criminal career has a beginning and an ending.
B. Factors affecting criminal careers could include:
    1. Structural factors - income and status.
    2. Socialization factors - family and peer relations.
    3. Biological factors - size and strength.
    4. Psychological factors - intelligence and personality.
    5. Opportunity factors - free time, inadequate police protection, and a supply of easily stolen merchandise.
C. Latent trait theories assume that it is not people but criminal opportunities that change.

VI. Public Policy Implications of Developmental Theory
A. Initiatives typically feature multi-systemic treatment efforts designed to provide at-risk kids with personal, social, educational, and family services.
B. Many of the most successful programs are aimed at strengthening children's social-emotional competence and positive coping skills and suppressing the development of antisocial, aggressive behavior.

VII. Summary

Key Terms

Adolescent-Limited Offenders - Offenders who follow the most common criminal trajectory, in which antisocial behavior peaks in adolescence and then diminishes.
Authority Conflict Pathway - The path to a criminal career that begins with early stubborn behavior and defiance of parents.

Coercive Ideation - The world is conceived as full of coercive forces that can only be overcome through the application of equal or even greater coercive responses.

Control Balance Theory - According to Tittle, a developmental theory that attributes deviant and criminal behaviors to imbalances between the amount of control that the individual has over others and that others have over him or her.

Covert Pathway - A path to a criminal career that begins with minor underhanded behavior and progresses to fire starting and theft.

Decadence - Spur of the moment, irrational acts such as child molesting.

Defiance - Challenging control mechanisms but stopping short of physical harm: for example, vandalism, curfew violations, and unconventional sex.

Desist - To spontaneously stop committing crime.

Developmental Theories - A branch of criminology that examines change in a criminal career over the life course. Developmental factors include biological, social, and psychological change. Among the topics of developmental criminology are desistance, resistance, escalation, and specialization.

Differential Social Support and Coercion Theory (DSSCT) - According to Colvin, a theory that holds that perceptions of coercion become ingrained and guide reactions to adverse situations that arise in both family and nonfamily settings.

General Theory of Crime (GTC) - According to Gottfredson and Hirschi, a developmental theory that modifies social control theory by integrating concepts from biosocial, psychological, routine activities, and rational choice theories.

Human Nature Theory - A belief that personal traits, such as genetic makeup, intelligence, and body build, may outweigh the importance of social variables as predictors of criminal activity.

Impersonal Coercion - Pressures beyond individual control, such as economic and social pressure caused by unemployment, poverty, or business competition.

Integrated Theories - Models of crime causation that weave social and individual variables into a complex explanatory chain.

Interactional Theory - The idea that interaction with institutions and events during the life course determines criminal behavior patterns; crimogenic influences evolve over time.

Interpersonal Coercion - The use of force, threat of force, or intimidation by parents, peers, or significant others.

Latent Trait - A stable feature, characteristic, property, or condition, present at birth or soon after, that makes some people crime prone over the life course.

Latent Trait Theories - Theoretical views that criminal behavior is controlled by a master trait, present at birth or soon after, that remains stable and unchanging throughout a person's lifetime.

Life Course Persister - One of the small group of offenders whose criminal career continues well into adulthood.

Life Course Theories - Theoretical views studying changes in criminal offending patterns over a person's entire life. Are there conditions or events that occur later in life that influence the way people behave, or is behavior predetermined by social or personal conditions at birth?

Life Domains - According to Agnew, the five key elements that influence human behavior involving self, education, work, peers, and family relations.

Overt Pathway - Pathway to a criminal career that begins with minor aggression, leads to physical fighting, and eventually escalates to violent crime.

Plunder - Using power without regard for others, such as committing a hate crime or polluting the environment.

Predation - Direct forms of physical violence, such as robbery, sexual assault, or other forms of physical violence.

Problem Behavior Syndrome (PBS) - A cluster of antisocial behaviors that may include family dysfunction, substance abuse, smoking, precocious sexuality and early pregnancy, educational underachievement, suicide attempts, sensation seeking, and unemployment, as well as crime.

Prosocial Bonds - Socialized attachment to conventional institutions, activities, and beliefs.

Self-Control Theory - According to Gottfredson and Hirschi, the view that the cause of delinquent behavior is an impulsive personality. Kids who are impulsive may find that their bond to society is weak.

Social Capital - Positive relations with individuals and institutions that are life sustaining.

Social Development Model (SDM) - A developmental theory that attributes criminal behavior patterns to childhood socialization and pro- or antisocial attachments over the life course.

Submission - Passive obedience to the demands of others, such as submitting to physical or sexual abuse without response.

Turning Points - According to Laub and Sampson, the life events that alter the development of a criminal career.

Discussion Exercises

1. Conduct an anonymous survey of student's deviant behavior as adolescents. Have the class analyze results and discuss delinquent behavior in terms of the developmental theories.

2. The chapter notes how a successful marriage is a key variable in a person's ability to "mature out of crime." Ask your married students to discuss how their life has changed since their wedding day and compare that with the lifestyles of your single students. Of specific interest will be topics of responsibility, commitment, time, duty, etc.

3. Find an article in the local newspaper featuring a crime committed by a very young offender. Explain the case to the students and have them develop a timeline for this person's life according to life course theories. That is, what might we expect from someone who has started a criminal career so early in life? What would be necessary for this person to age out of offending in the future?

GETTING STARTED: Search term words for subject guide: Developmental Theories, Latent Trait Theories, Glueck Research, Social Development Model, Sampson and Laub.

CRITICAL THINKING PROJECT: Using the search term "Developmental Theory," find articles that discuss childhood violence and school failure.

Here are three articles:

Allen, Joseph P., Gabe Kuperminc, Susan Philliber, and Kathy Herre. "Programmatic Prevention of Adolescent Problem Behaviors: The role of autonomy, relatedness, and volunteer service in the teen outreach program." *American Journal of Community Psychology.*

Bolger, Kerry E. and Charlotte J. Patterson. "Developmental Pathways from Child Maltreatment to Peer Rejection." *Child Development.*

Schickedanz, Judith A. "Helping Children Develop Self-Control." *Childhood Education.*

Test Bank

Fill in the Blank

1. **Latent trait** is a stable feature, characteristic, property, or condition present at birth or soon after that makes some people crime-prone over the life course.
    (page numbers 288-289)

2. **Life-course persister** is the small group of offenders who begin their career at an early age and then continue to offend well into adulthood.
    (page number 296)

3. **Interactional Theory** is a view that seriously delinquent youths form belief systems that are consistent with their deviant lifestyles.
    (page number 301)

4. A view that both biological and psychological traits influence the crime-noncrime choice is the **Human Nature Theory**.
    (page number 307)

5. As part of the **General Theory of Crime** Gottfredson and Hirschi consider the criminal offender and the criminal act as separate concepts.
    (page number 309)

6. When a theory involves circular reasoning, it is **tautological**.
    (page number 312)

7. **Interpersonal coercion** is direct, involving the use or threat of force and intimidation from parents, peers, and significant others.
    (page number 314)

8. **Impersonal coercion** involves pressures beyond individual control, such as economic and social pressure caused by unemployment, poverty, or competition among businesses or other groups.
    (page number 314)

9. **Coercive ideation** is where the world is conceived as full of coercive forces that can only be overcome through the application of equal or even greater coercive responses.
    (page number 314)

10. **Control deficit** occurs when a person's desires or impulses are limited by other people's ability to regulate or punish their behavior.
    (page number 315)

11. **Control surplus** occurs when the amount of control one can exercise over others is in excess of the ability others have to control or modify the person's behavior.
    (page number 315)

12. **Predation** involves direct forms of physical violence such as robbery, sexual assault, or other forms of physical violence.
    (page number 315)

13. **Defiance** is designed to challenge control mechanisms but stop short of physical harm.
    (page number 315)

14. **Submission** involves passive obedience to the demands of others such as submitting to physical or sexual abuse without response.
    (page number 315)

15. **Decadence** involves spur of the moment, irrational acts such as child molesting.
    (page number 316)

Multiple Choice

1. What is another term for aging out of crime?
    a. desist
    b. submission
    c. defiance
    d. predation
    (Answer = a, page number 288)

2. The branch of criminology that examines change in a criminal career over the life course is known as the:
    a. Social Development Model
    b. Developmental Criminology
    c. General Theory of Crime
    d. Social Control Theory
    (Answer = b, page number 288)

3. The view that even as toddlers, people begin relationships and behaviors that will determine their adult life course is known as the:
    a. Social Development Model
    b. Life Course Theory
    c. Interactional Theory
    d. Human Nature Theory
    (Answer = b, page number 288)

4. A stable feature, characteristic, property, or condition present at birth or soon after that makes some people crime-prone over the life course is known as a(n):
   a. life-course persister
   b. overt pathway
   c. social capital
   d. latent trait
   (Answer = d, page numbers 288-289)

5. According to the Gluecks, the most important factor that impacts offending is:
   a. school performance
   b. family relations
   c. psychological stability
   d. peer relations
   (Answer = b, page number 290)

6. Some theorists believe that criminality may be a part of a group of antisocial behaviors that cluster together and typically involve family dysfunction, sexual and physical abuse, substance abuse, smoking, precocious sexuality and early pregnancy, educational underachievement, suicide attempts, sensation seeking, and unemployment. This is known as:
   a. problem behavior syndrome
   b. General Theory of Crime
   c. Social development Model
   d. Human Nature Theory
   (Answer = a, page number 291)

7. Life course theorists conclude which of the following factors influence criminality?
   a. social
   b. personal
   c. economic
   d. all of the above
   (Answer = d, page number 291)

8. When one has problem behaviors in the social realm, they may exhibit which of the following?
   a. family dysfunction
   b. unemployment
   c. educational underachievement
   d. all of the above
   (Answer = d, page number 291)

9. When one has problem behaviors in the personal realm, they may exhibit which of the following?
   a. family dysfunction
   b. unemployment
   c. substance abuse
   d. all of the above
   (Answer = c, page number 291)

10. When one has problem behaviors in the environmental realm, they may exhibit which of the following?
    a. family dysfunction
    b. substance abuse
    c. racism
    d. all of the above
    (Answer = c, page number 291)

11. Which of the following are pathways to crime?
    a. authority conflict pathway
    b. covert pathway
    c. overt pathway
    d. all of the above
    (Answer = d, page number 292)

12. The pathway to crime that begins at an early age, usually with stubborn behavior, is known as:
    a. the authority conflict pathway
    b. the covert pathway
    c. the overt pathway
    d. social capital
    (Answer = a, page number 292)

13. The pathway to crime that begins with minor, underhanded behavior that leads to property damage is known as:
    a. social capital
    b. the authority conflict pathway
    c. the overt pathway
    d. the covert pathway
    (Answer = d, page number 292)

14. A pathway of crime where aggressive acts begin with aggression, lead to physical fighting, and then to violence is known as:
    a. social capital
    b. the authority conflict pathway
    c. the overt pathway
    d. the covert pathway
    (Answer = c, page number 293)

15. Which of the following is more typical of early-onset boys than early-onset girls?
     a. suicide
     b. depression
     c. substance abuse
     d. relationship problems
     (Answer = c, page number 295)

16. Most offenders' antisocial behavior peaks during adolescence and then diminishes. This is known as:
     a. adolescent-limited
     b. life-course persister
     c. an overt pathway
     d. social capital
     (Answer = a, page number 296)

17. A small group of offenders who begin their career at an early age and then continue to offend well into adulthood are known as:
     a. adolescent-limiteds
     b. life-course persisters
     c. social capitals
     d. none of the above
     (Answer = b, page number 296)

18. "Early starters" are those youth who begin offending before age:
     a. 10
     b. 14
     c. 16
     d. 18
     (Answer = b, page number 296)

19. Which group of delinquents begin to mimic the antisocial behavior of more troubled teens, only to reduce the frequency of their offending as they mature to around age 18?
     a. life-course persisters
     b. subjects
     c. authorities
     d. adolescent limiteds
     (Answer = d, page number 296)

20. According to which theory do a number of community-level risk factors make some people susceptible to developing antisocial behaviors?
     a. General Theory of Crime
     b. Differential Association Theory
     c. Social Development Model
     d. Labeling Theory
     (Answer = c, page number 296)

21. Children are socialized and develop bonds to their families through which of the following interactions and processes?
  a. perceived opportunities for involvement in activities and interactions with others
  b. the degree of involvement and interaction with parents
  c. the children's ability to participate in these interactions
  d. all of the above
  (Answer = d, page number 297)

22. Which theorist is associated with Interactional Theory?
  a. Terence Thornberry
  b. Karl Marx
  c. Travis Hirschi
  d. Edwin Sutherland
  (Answer = a, page number 301)

23. Which theory holds that seriously delinquent youth form belief systems that are consistent with their deviant lifestyle?
  a. Differential Association Theory
  b. Labeling Theory
  c. Social Conflict Theory
  d. Interactional Theory
  (Answer = d, page number 301)

24. Life events which enable adult offenders to desist from crime are known as:
  a. anniversaries
  b. birthdays
  c. special occasions
  d. turning points
  (Answer = d, page number 303)

25. Positive relations with individuals and institutions that are life sustaining are known as:
  a. adolescent-limiteds
  b. the social development model
  c. social capital
  d. turning points
  (Answer = c, page number 305)

26. Age-graded theory states that people who _____ are most likely to mature out of crime.
  a. get married
  b. become a parent
  c. all of the above
  d. none of the above
  (Answer = c, page number 306)

27. The view that both biological and psychological traits influence the crime-noncrime behavior is known as:
    a. Human Nature Theory
    b. Peacemaking Criminology
    c. Marxist Feminists
    d. Left Realism School
    (Answer = a, page number 307)

28. The theory where Gottfredson and Hirschi consider the criminal offender and the criminal act as separate concepts is called:
    a. Differential Association Theory
    b. Labeling Theory
    c. Social Reaction Theory
    d. General Theory of Crime
    (Answer = d, page number 309)

29. According to the General Theory of Crime, an impulsive personality would consist of which of the following:
    a. unstable social relations
    b. insensitivity
    c. risk-taking
    d. all of the above
    (Answer = d, page numbers 309-310)

30. When a theory involves circular reasoning it is called:
    a. ecological
    b. tautological
    c. biological
    d. psychological
    (Answer = b, page number 312)

31. Which of the following are types of coercion?
    a. interpersonal
    b. impersonal
    c. all of the above
    d. none of the above
    (Answer = c, page number 314)

32. Coercion that is direct, involving the use or threat of force and intimidation from parents, peers, and significant others is known as:
    a. interpersonal
    b. impersonal
    c. latent
    d. personal
    (Answer = a, page number 314)

33. Coercion that involves pressures beyond individual control, such as economic and social pressure caused by unemployment, poverty, or competition among businesses or other groups is known as:
    a. personal
    b. latent
    c. interpersonal
    d. impersonal
    (Answer = d, page number 314)

34. This occurs when a person's desires or impulses are limited by other people's ability to regulate or punish their behavior.
    a. control deficit
    b. control surplus
    c. exploitation
    d. defiance
    (Answer = a, page number 315)

35. When the amount of control one can exercise over others is in excess of the ability others have to control or modify the person's behavior, this is known as:
    a. defiance
    b. exploitation
    c. control deficit
    d. control surplus
    (Answer = d, page number 315)

36. Direct forms of physical violence, such as robbery and sexual assault, are known as:
    a. submission
    b. predation
    c. defiance
    d. all of the above
    (Answer = b, page number 315)

37. _____ is designed to challenge control mechanisms but stops short of physical harm (for example, vandalism, curfew violations, and unconventional sex).
    a. Predation
    b. Submission
    c. Defiance
    d. All of the above
    (Answer = c, page number 315)

38. Passive obedience to the demands of others, such as submitting to physical or sexual abuse without response, is called:
    a. predation
    b. defiance
    c. exploitation
    d. submission
    (Answer = d, page number 315)

39. Those who have an excess of control and involve others to commit crime are known as having the power of:
    a. predation
    b. defiance
    c. submission
    d. exploitation
    (Answer = d, page number 316)

40. Spur of the moment, irrational acts are known as:
    a. exploitation
    b. predation
    c. defiance
    d. decadence
    (Answer = d, page number 316)

True/False

1. Life course theories are inherently integrated theories.
    (Answer = true, page number 288)

2. Life course theories recognize that as people mature, the factors that influence their behavior never change.
    (Answer = false, page number 288)

3. Disruptions in life's major transitions can be constructive and ultimately can promote success.
    (Answer = false, page number 289)

4. The Gluecks identified a number of personal and social factors related to persistent offending, the most important of which was family relations.
    (Answer = true, page number 290)

5. The Gluecks research was highly praised for nearly 30 years as the study of crime and delinquency shifted almost exclusively to social factors.
    (Answer = false, page number 290)

6. As they reach their mid-teens, adolescent-limited delinquents begin to mimic the antisocial behavior of more troubled teens, only to reduce the frequency of their offending as they mature to around age 18.
(Answer = true, page number 296)

7. Early-onset delinquents also appear to be more violent than their older peers, who are likely to be involved in nonviolent crimes such as theft.
(Answer = true, page number 296)

8. As children mature within their environment, elements of socialization control their developmental process.
(Answer = true, page number 296)

9. To control the risk of antisocial behavior, a child must maintain prosocial bonds.
(Answer = true, page number 297)

10. Gottfredson and Hirschi suggest that low self-control is a function of an impulsive personality.
(Answer = true, page number 310)

11. Interpersonal coercion involves pressures beyond individual control, such as economic and social pressure caused by unemployment, poverty, or competition among businesses or other groups.
(Answer = false, page number 314)

12. Impersonal coercion is direct, involving the use or threat of force and intimidation from parents, peers, and significant others.
(Answer = false, page number 314)

13. Control Balance Theory expands upon the concept of personal control as a predisposing element for criminality.
(Answer = true, page number 315)

14. Control deficit occurs when a person's desires or impulses are limited by other people's ability to regulate or punish their behavior.
(Answer = true, page number 315)

15. Policy-based initiatives based on premises of Developmental Theory typically feature multi-systemic treatment efforts.
(Answer = true, page number 318)

Essay Questions

1. Compare and contrast the Developmental Theories: Life Course and Latent Trait. What are the commonalities and distinctions?
(page numbers 288-319)

2. Describe Latent Trait Theories. Where did they get their origin? What is the foundation for Latent Trait Theories? Are they valid theories?
    (page numbers 307-316)

3. Define the General Theory of Crime. Which theorist is this theory attributed to and what is the foundation?
    (page numbers 308-314)

4. What are the areas of General Theory of Crime, which remain unanswered? Do these unanswered areas truly matter in our study of crime causation?
    (page numbers 311-314)

5. Define Differential Coercion Theory. What is its origin and which theorist is credited with this theory? Distinguish between the various types of coercion.
    (page numbers 314-315)

Chapter Ten

Violent Crime

Summary

Chapter Ten discusses the various types of violent crime in our society. The chapter begins with an examination of the roots of violence and various factors that predispose individuals to violence. The common-law crimes of forcible rape, murder, assault and battery, and robbery are explained. Other emerging forms of violence including hate crimes, workplace violence, and stalking also are presented. The chapter concludes with a discussion on terrorism and the various forms and causes.

Chapter Objectives

After reading this chapter the student should be able to:

- Be familiar with the various causes of violent crime
- Know the concept of the brutalization process
- Be able to discuss the history of rape and know the different types of rape
- Be able to discuss the legal issues in rape prosecution
- Recognize that there are different types of murder
- Be able to discuss the differences among serial killing, mass murder, and spree killing
- Be familiar with the nature of assault in the home
- Understand the careers of armed robbers
- Be able to discuss newly emerging forms of violence such as stalking, hate crimes, and workplace violence
- Understand the different types of terrorism and what is being done to combat terrorist activities

Chapter Overview

Introduction
Comparative Criminology: World Report on Violence
The Causes of Violence
      Personal Traits and Makeup
      Evolutionary Factors/Human Instinct
      Substance Abuse
      Socialization and Upbringing
      Exposure to Violence
      Cultural Values/Subculture of Violence

The Criminological Enterprise: Violent Land

Forcible Rape
> History of Rape
> Rape and the Military
> Incidence of Rape
> Types of Rape and Rapists
> The Causes of Rape
> Rape and the Law

Murder and Homicide
> Degrees of Murder
> The Nature and Extent of Murder
> Murderous Relations
> Serial Murder

The Criminological Enterprise: Mass Murder and Serial Killing

Assault and Battery
> Nature and Extent of Assault
> Assault in the Home

Robbery
> Acquaintance Robbery
> Rational Robbery

The Criminological Enterprise: Armed Robbers in Action

Emerging Forms of Interpersonal Violence
> Hate Crimes
> Workplace Violence
> Stalking

Terrorism
> What is Terrorism?
> A Brief History of Terrorism
> Contemporary Forms of Terrorism

Comparative Criminology: Transnational Terrorism in the New Millennium
> What Motivates Terrorists?
> Responses to Terrorism

Summary

Chapter Outline

I. Introduction
> A. Expressive Violence - acts that vent rage, anger, or frustration.
> B. Instrumental Violence - acts designed to improve the financial or social position of the criminal.

II. The Causes of Violence
> A. Personal Traits and Makeup - Psychologist Dorothy Otnow Lewis and her associates found murderous youths suffer:
>> 1. Major neurological impairment - abnormal EEGs, multiple psychomotor impairment, and severe seizures.

2. Low intelligence.
3. Psychotic close relatives.
4. Psychotic symptoms - paranoia, illogical thinking, hallucinations.
B. Evolutionary Factors/Human Instinct
   1. Freud believed that human aggression and violence are produced by instinctual drives.
      a. eros - life instinct; drives people to self-fulfillment and enjoyment.
      b. thanatos - death instinct; produces self-destruction.
         i. externally - violence or sadism.
         ii. internally - suicide, alcoholism, or other self-destructive habits.
   2. Evolutionary theories suggest that violent behavior is mostly committed by males.
C. Substance Abuse - influences violence by the following:
   1. Psychopharmacological relationship - high does of PCP and amphetamines may produce violent, aggressive behavior. Alcohol abuse associated with all forms of violence.
   2. Economic compulsive behavior - drug users resort to violence to support their habit.
   3. Systemic link - violence escalates when gangs try to dominate a territory.
D. Socialization and Upbringing - the following are linked to persistent violent offending:
   1. Absent or deviant parents.
   2. Inconsistent discipline.
   3. Lack of supervision.
   4. Physical punishment without support, warmth, and care.
   5. Abused children
      a. research indicates that abused children engage in delinquent behaviors more than unabused children.
   6. The brutalization process
      a. Lonnie Athens, criminologist, links violence to child abuse and classifies aggressive people into the following:
         i. nonviolent.
         ii. violent - those who attack others physically with the intention of harming them.
         iii. incipiently violent - those who are willing and ready to attack but limit themselves to violent ultimatums and/or intimidating physical gestures.
      b. Athens, found 4 distinct types of violent acts:
         i. physically defensive - perpetrator sees his violent act as one of self-defense.
         ii. frustrative - offender acts out of anger due to frustration when they cannot get their way.

             iii. malefic - victim is considered to be extremely evil or malicious.

             iv. frustrative-malefic - a combined type.

       c. antisocial careers are created in a series of stages that begin with brutal episodes:

             i. brutalization process - young victim begins the process of developing a belligerent, angry demeanor. Brutalization can result from subjugation, personal horrification, and violent coaching by peers.

             ii. brutalized youth may become belligerent and angry. They respond with violent performances of angry, hostile behavior.

             iii. virulency stage - emerging criminals develop a violent identity that makes them feared; they enjoy intimidating others.

       d. violentization process - one must complete the full cycle - belligerence, violence performances, and virulencey to become socialized into violence.

   E. Exposure to Violence - those constantly exposed to violence are more likely to adopt violent methods.

      1. Crusted over - condition children living in violence adopt; they do not let others inside, nor do they express their feelings. They exploit others and allow themselves to be exploited.

   F. Cultural Values/Subculture of Violence

      1. Subculture of violence - areas where violence seems to cluster together. Violence influences lifestyles, socialization, and interpersonal relationships. Usually found in areas with concentrated poverty and social disorganization.

      2. Peer group influences

         a. gangs - members likely to own guns, drug traffic, and turf protection.

      3. Regional values - South has higher rates of violence and homicide; although the southern subculture of violence is still debated.

      4. National values - Some nations have higher rates of violence: United States, Sri Lanka, Angola, Uganda, and the Philippines.

III. Forcible Rape - the carnal knowledge of a female forcibly and against her will.

   A. History of Rape - under Babylonian Law rape was punishable by death.

   B. Rape and the Military - throughout history, rape has been associated with armies and warfare.

   C. Incidence of Rape

      1. UCR data - 93,000 rapes or attempted rapes reported to police in 2003.

      2. NCVS data - 200,000 rapes and attempted rapes took place in 2003.

   D. Types of Rape and Rapists

      1. Anger rape - sexuality becomes a way of expressing and discharging pent-up anger and rage.

2. Power rape - does not want to harm the victim, but wants to possess her sexually.
3. Sadistic rape - involves sexuality and aggression. Victim may be tormented, bound, or tortured.
4. Gangs versus individual rape:
    a. 25% of rapes involve multiple offenders.
    b. gang rapes usually more severe. Victim are more likely to call police and to consider suicide.
5. Serial rape - rapists who commit more than one rape in their lifetime.
6. Acquaintance rape - involves someone known to the victim, including family members and friends.
    a. date rape - sexual attack during a courting relationship.
    b. statutory rape - the victim is underage.
    c. martial rape - forcible sex between people who are legally married.
7. Date rape - frequent on college campuses.
    a. 15-20% of all college women are victims of rape or attempted rape.
8. Marital rape:
    a. marital exception - traditionally a married husband could not be charged with raping his wife.
    b. today, almost every state recognizes it as a crime.
9. Statutory rape - sexual relations between an underage minor female and an adult male.

E. The Causes of Rape
    1. Evolutionary, biological factors - rape may be instinctual, developed over the ages as a means of perpetuating the species.
    2. Male socialization - a function of modern male socialization.
        a. virility mystique - belief that males must separate their sexual feelings from needs for love, respect, and affection.
    3. Hypermasculinity - men who have a callous sexual attitude and believe that violence is manly.
    4. Psychological abnormality - view that rapists suffer from a personality disorder or mental illness.
    5. Social learning - perspective that men learn to commit rapes as they learn other behavior.
    6. Sexual motivation - older criminals may rape for power and control, while younger offenders may rape for sexual gratification.

F. Rape and the Law - created the most conflict in the legal system.
    1. Proving rape - extremely challenging for prosecutors.
    2. Consent - must prove that the attack was forced and the victim did not give voluntary consent to the attacker.
    3. Reform - efforts include:
        a. changing the language of statutes.
        b. dropping the condition of victim resistance.

    c. changing the requirement of use of force to include threat of force or injury.

    d. shield laws - protect women from being questioned about sexual history unless it directly bears on the case.

  4. The limits of reform - prosecutors may still be influenced in their decision by the circumstances of the crime.

IV. Murder and Homicide - the unlawful killing of a human being with "malice aforethought;" the most serious crime and can be punished by death.

 A. Degrees of Murder

   1. First-degree murder - person kills after premeditation and deliberation.

    a. premeditation - killing considered beforehand and it was motivated by more than a desire to engage in violence.

    b. deliberation - killing planned after careful thought rather than impulse.

   2. Second-degree murder - killer must have malice aforethought but not premeditation or deliberation.

   3. Manslaughter - homicide without malice.

    a. voluntary manslaughter - killing committed in heat of passion or during a sudden quarrel that provoked violence.

    b. involuntary manslaughter - killing that occurs when one is negligent and without regard for the harm they may cause others.

   4. "Born and Alive" - whether a murder victim can be a fetus that has not been delivered; feticide.

 B. The Nature and Extent of Murder

   1. In the U.S. in 2003, about 16,500 murders for a murder rate of 5.76 per 100,000; this is an increase since 1999.

   2. Murder tends to be an urban crime.

   3. Victims and offenders tend to be males.

   4. About 1/3 of murder victims are under 25; about 1/2 of murder offenders are under 25.

   5. Half of murder victims are African-American and half are Caucasian.

    a. murder tends to be intra-racial.

   6. Infanticide - murders which involve very young children.

   7. Eldercide - murders which involve senior citizens.

 C. Murderous Relations - murders occur more frequently among people with relationships rather than strangers.

   1. Spousal relations.

   2. Personal relations.

   3. Stranger relations.

   4. Student relations.

 D. Serial Murder

   1. Serial killers operate over a long period of time, while the mass murderer kills many victims in a single, violent outburst.

   2. Serial murderers and their motivations

    a. long histories of violence.

      b. maintain superficial relationships with others.

      c. have trouble relating to the opposite sex.

      d. feel guilty about their interest in sex.

      e. sociopaths, who from early childhood demonstrate bizarre behavior and this behavior extends to the pleasure they reap from killing, their ability to ignore or enjoy their victims' suffering, and their propensity for basking in the media limelight when apprehended for their crimes.

   3. Female serial killers:

      a. estimated 10-15% of serial killers are women.

      b. more likely to poison or smother their victims.

      c. more likely to lure victims to their death.

   4. Controlling serial killers

      a. FBI developed a profiling system to identity potential suspects.

      b. Justice Department's Violent Criminal Apprehension Program - computerized information service, gathers information and matches offense characteristics on violent crimes around the country.

V. Assault and Battery

   A. Battery - offensive touching, such as slapping, hitting, or punching a victim.

   B. Assault - requires no actual touching, but involves either attempted battery or intentionally frightening the victim by word or deed.

   C. Aggravated Assault - an unlawful attack by one person upon another for the purpose of inflicting severe or aggravated bodily injury.

   D. Nature and Extent of Assault

      1. Road rage - motorists who assault each other.

      2. FBI recorded 857,000 assaults in year 2003; assaults on the decline.

      3. Offenders are more often young, male, and white.

   E. Assault in the Home - intrafamily violence is an enduring problem in U.S.

      1. Child abuse

         a. actual physical beatings administered to a child by hands, feet, weapons, belts, sticks, burning, and so on.

         b. neglect - not providing a child with the care and shelter to which he or she is entitled.

         c. causes of child abuse:

            i. family violence perpetuated from one generation to the next.

            ii. abusive parent behavior can often be traced to negative childhood experiences.

            iii. blended families have been linked to abuse.

            iv. parents may become abusive if isolated from friends, neighbors or relatives.

      2. Sexual abuse - exploitation of children through rape, incest, and molestation by parents or other adults.

      3. Parental abuse - parents who are targets of abuse from own children.

      4. Spousal abuse - has occurred throughout recorded history.

5. The nature and extent of spousal abuse
    a. 60-70% of evening calls to police involve domestic disputes.
    b. 1 in 5 high school girls suffered sexual or physical abuse from a boyfriend.
    c. batterers tend to fall into 2 categories:
        i. Pit Bulls - emotions are quick to erupt, are driven by deep insecurity and dependence on the wives and partners they abuse; tend to become stalkers, unable to let go of relationships once they have ended.
        ii. Cobras - coolly and methodically inflict pain and humiliation on their mates. See violence as an unavoidable part of life.

VI. Robbery - the taking or attempting to take anything of value for the care, custody or control of a person or persons by force or threat of force or violence and/or by putting the victim in fear.
    A. In 2003, FBI recorded 413,000 robberies, a rate of 142 per 100,000 population.
    B. The typical armed robber is unlikely to be a professional; therefore seem diverted by modest defensive measures.
    C. Acquaintance Robbery - robbing people one knows is attractive
        1. Victims may be reluctant to report.
        2. The robber settles a dispute by stealing the victim's property.
        3. The robber has inside information about the property.
        4. These are convenient targets.
    D. Rational Robbery - not merely a random act.
        1. Robbery peaks during the winter months.
        2. Robbers choose vulnerable victims.

VII. Emerging Forms of Interpersonal Violence
    A. Hate Crimes - violent acts directed toward a particular person or members of a group because the targets share a discernible racial, ethnic, religious or gender characteristic; bias crimes.
        1. The roots of hate - McDevit and Levin identify 3 types of hate crimes:
            a. thrill-seeking hate crimes.
            b. reactive hate crimes.
            c. mission hate crimes.
        2. Recent research uncovered retaliatory hate crimes - offenses committed in response to a hate crime, whether real or perceived.
        3. Nature and extent of hate crime
            a. during 2002, FBI reported 8,832 hate crime offenses.
            b. about half were motivated by race, 18% by religion, 15% by ethnicity or national origin, and .5% by disability.
            c. 60% of hate crimes were violent and 40% property.
        4. Controlling hate crimes - some argue that punishment should be more severe than the same crime without the bias.

202

B. Workplace Violence - third leading cause of occupational injury or death; typical offender is middle-aged white male who faces termination in a worsening economy.
1. Creating workplace violence - causal factors:
   a. management style that is cold and insensitive to workers.
   b. refused romantic relationships.
   c. loss of position with company.
   d. poor service.
2. The extent of workplace violence:
   a. 1.7 million U.S. residents become victims of violent workplace crime.
   b. violent occupations include police officer, correctional officer, taxicab driver, private security worker, and bartender.
3. Can workplace violence be controlled?
   a. use of restorative justice tactics is helpful.
   b. aggressive job retraining.
   c. continued medical coverage after layoffs.
C. Stalking - a course of conduct directed at a specific person that involves repeated physical or visual proximity, nonconsensual communication, or verbal, written, or implied threats sufficient to cause fear in a reasonable person.
1. Affects 1.4 million victims annually.
2. Most victims know their stalker.
3. Women are most likely to be stalked by an intimate partner.

VIII. Terrorism
A. What is Terrorism?
1. Involves the illegal use of force against innocent people to achieve a political objective.
2. U.S. State Department says terrorism means premeditated, politically motivated violence perpetrated against noncombatant targets by sub-national groups or clandestine agents usually intended to influence an audience.
3. International terrorism - terrorism involving citizens or the territory of more than one country.
4. Terrorist Group - any group practicing, or that has significant subgroups that practice, international terrorism.
B. Terrorist and Guerilla
1. Terrorists:
   a. urban focus.
   b. operate in small bands or cadres - 3 to 5 members.
   c. target the property or person of their enemy.
2. Guerillas:
   a. located in rural areas.
   b. attack the military, police, and government officials.
   c. organizations grow large.

C. A Brief History of Terrorism - throughout history.
  1. Assassination of Julius Caesar - March 15, 44 BCE.
  2. Middle Ages.
  3. French Revolution.
  4. World War II.
D. Contemporary Forms of Terrorism
  1. Revolutionary terrorists - use violence to frighten those in power and to replace the existing government with a regime that holds acceptable political or religious views.
  2. Political terrorists - directed at those who oppose the terrorists' political ideology.
  3. Nationalist terrorism - promotes the interests of a minority ethnic or religious group that feels it has been persecuted under majority rule and wants independence.
  4. Cause-based terrorism - against individuals and/or governments to whom they object.
  5. Environmental terrorism - acts to prevent the use of land or animals for human consumption.
  6. State-sponsored terrorism - occurs when a repressive governmental regime forces its citizens into obedience, oppresses minorities, and stifles political dissent.
  7. Criminal terrorism - sometimes terrorist groups become involved in common law crimes such as drug dealing and kidnapping to fund their activities.
E. What Motivates Terrorists?
  1. Emotionally disturbed individuals who act out their psychosis within the confines of violent groups.
  2. Hold extreme ideological beliefs that prompt their behavior.
  3. May be motivated by feelings of alienation and failure to comprehend post-technological society.
F. Responses to Terrorism
  1. Difficulty of gaining information about highly secretive groups and sealing our borders.
  2. Post 9/11 efforts
      a. 1994 Violent Crime Control Act authorized the death penalty for international terrorists who kill U.S. citizens abroad.
      b. legal efforts - USA Patriot Act (USAPA).
          i. aim was to give new powers to domestic law enforcement and international intelligence agencies in order to fight terrorism, to expand the definition of terrorism, and to alter sanctions for violent terrorism.
      c. law enforcement responses - Foreign Terrorist Tracking Task Force.
          i. aids in closing the borders to any illegal alien who is associated with a terrorist organization.

d. Department of Homeland Security - mission is to unify the organizations involved in national security.

e. The 9/11 Commission Report - one goal was to create a plan so no further attacks will take place.

IX.   Summary

<u>**Key Terms**</u>

Acquaintance Rape - Forcible sex in which offender and victim are acquainted with each other.

Acquaintance Robbery - Robbers who focus their thefts on people they know.

Aggravated Rape - Rape involving multiple offenders, weapons, and victim injuries.

Bias Crimes - Violent acts directed toward a particular person or members of a group merely because the targets share a discernable racial, ethnic, religious, or gender characteristic; also called hate crimes.

Child Abuse - Any physical, emotional, or sexual trauma to a child for which no reasonable explanation, such as an accident, can be found. Child abuse can also be a function of neglecting to give proper care and attention to a young child.

Consent - In prosecuting rape cases, it is essential to prove that the attack was forced and that the victim did not give voluntary consent to her attacker. In a sense, the burden of proof is on the victim to show that her character is beyond question and that she in no way encouraged, enticed, or misled the accused rapist. Proving victim dissent is not a requirement in any other violent crime.

Crusted Over - Children who have been victims or witnesses to violence and do not let people inside, nor do they express their feelings. They exploit others and in turn are exploited by those older and stronger; as a result, they develop a sense of hopelessness.

Death Squads - Government troops used to destroy political opposition parties.

Deliberation - Planning a homicide after careful thought, however brief, rather than acting on sudden impulse.

Eldercide - The murder of a senior citizen.

Expressive Violence - Violence that is designed not for profit or gain but to vent rage, anger, or frustration.

Felony Murder - A homicide in the context of another felony, such as robbery or rape; legally defined as first-degree murder.

Feticide - Endangering or killing an unborn fetus.

Gang Rape - Forcible sex involving multiple attackers.

Guerrilla - The term means "little war" and developed out of the Spanish rebellion against French troops after Napoleon's 1808 invasion of the Iberian Peninsula. Today the term is used interchangeably with the term terrorist.

Hate Crimes - Acts of violence or intimidation designed to terrorize or frighten people considered undesirable because of their race, religion, ethnic origin, or sexual orientation.

Hypermasculine - Men who typically have a callous sexual attitude and believe that violence is manly. They perceive danger as exciting and are overly sensitive to insult and ridicule. They are also impulsive, more apt to brag about sexual conquests, and more likely to lose control, especially when using alcohol.

Infanticide - The murder of a very young child.

Instrumental Violence - Violence used in an attempt to improve the financial or social position of the criminal.

International Terrorism - Terrorism involving citizens or the territory of more than one country.

Involuntary Manslaughter - A homicide that occurs as a result of acts that are negligent and without regard for the harm they may cause others, such as driving under the influence of alcohol or drugs.

Manslaughter - A homicide without malice.

Martial Exemption - The practice in some states of prohibiting the prosecution of husbands for the rape of their wives.

Martial Rape - Forcible sex between people who are legally married to each other.

Mass Murder - The killing of a large number of people in a single incident by an offender who typically does not seek concealment or escape.

Mission Hate Crimes - Violent crimes committed by disturbed individuals who see it as their duty to rid the world of evil.

Murder - The unlawful killing of a human being (homicide) with malicious intent.

Narcissistic Personality Disorder - A condition marked by a persistent pattern of self-importance, need for admiration, lack of empathy, and preoccupation with fantasies of unlimited success, power, brilliance, beauty, or ideal love.

Neglect - Not providing a child with the care and shelter to which he or she is entitled.

Negligent Manslaughter - A homicide that occurs as a result of acts that are negligent and without regard for the harm they may cause others, such as driving under the influence of alcohol or drugs; also called involuntary manslaughter.

Nonnegligent Manslaughter - A homicide committed in the heat of passion or during a sudden quarrel; although intent may be present, malice is not; also called voluntary manslaughter.

Premeditation - Consideration of a homicide before it occurs.

Reactive (Defensive) Hate Crimes - Perpetrators believe they are taking a defensive stand against outsiders who they believe threaten their community or way of life.

Retaliatory Hate Crimes - A hate crime motivated by revenge for another hate crime, either real or imaginary, which may spark further retaliation.

Road Rage - A term used to describe motorists who assault each other.

Second-Degree Murder - A homicide with malice but not premeditation or deliberation, as when a desire to inflict serious bodily harm and a wanton disregard for life result in the victim's death.

Serial Murder - The killing of a large number of people over time by an offender who seeks to escape detection.

Serial Rape - Multiple rapes committed by one person over time.

Sexual Abuse - Exploitation of a child through rape, incest, or molestation by a parent or other adult.

Shield Laws - Laws designed to protect rape victims by prohibiting the defense attorney from inquiring about their previous sexual relationships.

Statutory Rape - Sexual relations between an underage minor female and an adult male; though not coerced, an underage partner is considered incapable of giving informed consent.

Subculture of Violence - Norms and customs that, in contrast to society's dominant value system, legitimize and expect the use of violence to resolve social conflicts.

Sufferance - The aggrieved party does nothing to rectify a conflict situation; over time, the unresolved conflict may be compounded by other events that cause an eventual eruption.

Terrorism - The illegal use of force against innocent people to achieve a political objective.

Terrorist Group - Any group practicing, or that has significant subgroups that practice, international terrorism.

Thrill-Seeking Hate Crimes - Acts by hate-mongers who join forces to have fun by bashing minorities or destroying property; inflicting pain on others gives them a sadistic thrill.

USA Patriot Act (USAPA) - Legislation giving U.S. law enforcement agencies a freer hand to investigate and apprehend suspected terrorists.

Virility Mystique - The belief that males must separate their sexual feelings from needs for love, respect, and affection.

Workplace Violence - Irate employees or former employees attack coworkers or sabotaging machinery and production lines; now considered the third leading cause of occupational injury or death.

Discussion Exercises

1. Assign groups to various terrorism events that have occurred in the last 10 years in the United States and abroad. Key events may include the September 11, 2001 attack on the United States, the Oklahoma City Bombing, events in the Middle East, and the Unabomber. How have these events changed the United States?

2. Workplace violence costs American businesses billions of dollars each year. While the chapter identifies such occupations as police officer, correctional officer, and taxicab driver as most dangerous, have students discuss violence they may have witnessed in the jobs they have held.

3. The web site http://www.tolerance.org provides a map of hate groups for the nation and by state. Print off the map for your state and bring it to class for discussion. Are students even aware of the number and range of recognized hate groups in their state? How active are these groups?

GETTING STARTED: Search term words for subject guide: Violence, Forcible Rape, Murder, Homicide, Assault, Battery, Robbery, Hate Crimes, Terrorism.

CRITICAL THINKING PROJECT: Using the search term "Workplace Violence," find relevant articles.

Here are three articles:

Johnson, Pamela R. and Julie Indvik. "Rudeness at Work: Impulse over restraint." *Public Personnel Management*.

Kondrasuk, Jack N., Herff L. Moore, and Hua Wang. "Negligent Hiring: The emerging contributor to workplace violence in the public sector." *Public Personnel Management*.

Lipscomb, Jane, Barbara Silverstein, Thomas J. Slavin, Eileen Cody, and Lynn Jenkins. "Perspectives on Legal Strategies to Prevent Workplace Violence." *Journal of Law, Medicine & Ethics*.

Fill in the Blank

1. **Expressive violence** is violence that is designed not for profit or gain but to vent rage, anger, or frustration.
     (page number 332)

2. **Eros** is the most basic human drive present at birth; the instinct to preserve and create life.
     (page number 333)

3. According to Freud, **thanatos** is the instinctual drive toward aggression and violence.
     (page number 333)

4. **Systemic link** reflects the violent behavior that results from the conflict inherent in the drug trade.
     (page number 334)

5. **Subculture of violence** occurs where a potent theme of violence influences lifestyles, the socialization process, and interpersonal relationships.
     (page number 337)

6. Rape involving people in some form of courting relationship is known as **date rape**.
     (page number 342)

7. **Statutory rape** occurs when there are sexual relations between an underage minor female and an adult male.
     (page number 343)

8. **Shield laws** are laws that protect women from being questioned about their sexual history unless it directly bears upon the case.
     (page number 345)

9. **Felony murder** is killing a human being with malice aforethought.
     (page number 346)

10. **Serial murder** involves the killing of a large number of people over time by an offender who seeks to escape detection.
     (page number 350)

11. Serial killers who strive for either sexual sadism or dominance are known as **thrill killers**.
     (page number 350)

12. **Sexual abuse** is the exploitation of children through rape, incest, and molestation by parents or other adults.
  (page number 354)

13. **Hate crimes or bias crimes** are violent acts directed toward a particular person or members of a group merely because the targets share a discernible racial, ethnic, religious, or gender characteristic.
  (page number 359)

14. An act that must carry with it the intent to disrupt and change the government and must not be merely a common-law crime committed for greed or egotism is known as **terrorism**.
  (page number 364)

15. **Guerillas** are individuals located in rural areas that attack the military, the police, and government officials.
  (page number 364)

Multiple Choice

1. Violence that is designed not for profit or gain but to vent rage, anger, or frustration is known as:
  a. terrorism
  b. expressive violence
  c. stalking
  d. gang banging
  (Answer = b, page number 332)

2. Violence designed to improve the financial or social position of the criminal is known as:
  a. subculture of violence
  b. expressive violence
  c. hate crimes
  d. instrumental violence
  (Answer = d, page number 332)

3. According to Freud, the instinctual drive toward aggression and violence is known as:
  a. terrorism
  b. thanatos
  c. thrill killing
  d. hate crimes
  (Answer = b, page number 333)

4. The most basic human drive present at birth; the instinct to preserve and create life is known as:
    a. ego
    b. id
    c. superego
    d. eros
    (Answer = d, page number 333)

5. Violent behavior that results from the conflict inherent in the drug trade is known as:
    a. the subculture of violence
    b. shield laws
    c. sexual abuse
    d. systemic link
    (Answer = d, page number 334)

6. According to Athens, the first stage in a violent career during which parents victimize children, causing them to develop a belligerent, angry demeanor is known as:
    a. the honeymoon stage
    b. verbal abuse
    c. child abuse
    d. the brutalization process
    (Answer = d, page number 336)

7. Which of the following is a classification category based on aggressive tendencies that is used by Athens?
    a. nonviolent
    b. brutalization
    c. frustrative-malefic
    d. malefic
    (Answer = a, page number 336)

8. Which of the following are types of violent acts?
    a. physically defensive
    b. frustrative
    c. malefic
    d. all of the above
    (Answer = d, page number 336)

9. A potent theme of violence that influences lifestyles, the socialization process, and interpersonal relationships is known as:
    a. thanatos
    b. subculture of violence
    c. terrorism
    d. serial killers
    (Answer = b, page number 337)

10. The carnal knowledge of a female forcibly and against her will is known as:
       a. robbery
       b. murder
       c. felony murder
       d. rape
       (Answer = d, page number 338)

11. According to the most recent UCR data, about _____ rapes or attempted rapes were reported to U.S. police in 2003.
       a. 9,300,000
       b. 930,000
       c. 93,000
       d. 930
       (Answer = c, page number 340)

12. When an attacker does not want to harm his victim as much as he wants to possess her sexually, it is known as:
       a. anger rape
       b. gang rape
       c. serial rape
       d. power rape
       (Answer = d, page number 341)

13. Which rapist is bound up in ritual: tormenting their victim, binding her, or torturing her?
       a. sadistic rapist
       b. anger rapist
       c. gang rapist
       d. power rapist
       (Answer = a, page number 341)

14. Men who engage in multiple rapes are known as:
       a. gang rapists
       b. power rapists
       c. anger rapists
       d. serial rapists
       (Answer = d, page number 342)

15. Rape by someone known to the victim, possibility including family members and friends, is known as:
       a. acquaintance rape
       b. date rape
       c. stranger rape
       d. gang rape
       (Answer = a, page number 342)

16. Rape involving people in some form of courting relationship is called:
    a. stranger rape
    b. gang rape
    c. serial killer rape
    d. date rape
    (Answer = d, page number 342)

17. The rape of a woman by her husband is known as:
    a. gang rape
    b. serial rape
    c. marital rape
    d. sexual abuse
    (Answer = c, page number 342)

18. The practice in some states of prohibiting the prosecution of husbands for the rape of their wives is known as:
    a. shield laws
    b. marital rape
    c. the marital exemption
    d. sexual abuse
    (Answer = c, page number 343)

19. Sexual relations between an underage minor female and an adult male are known as:
    a. consent
    b. marital rape
    c. statutory rape
    d. gang rape
    (Answer = c, page number 343)

20. The belief that males must separate their sexual feelings from needs for love, respect, and affection is called:
    a. hypermasculinity
    b. the martial exemption
    c. the virility mystique
    d. the subculture of violence
    (Answer = c, page number 344)

21. Men who typically have a callous sexual attitude and believe that violence is manly are known as:
    a. hypermasculine
    b. feminist
    c. virility mystique
    d. all of the above
    (Answer = a, page number 344)

22. Which of the following are explanations of sexually assaultive behavior?
   a. hypermasculinity
   b. the virulency mystique
   c. all of the above
   d. none of the above
   (Answer = c, page number 344)

23. In a rape case, the absence of _____ is essential to the proof that a rape did occur.
   a. assault
   b. penetration
   c. consent
   d. all of the above
   (Answer = c, page number 345)

24. Laws that protect women from being questioned about their sexual history unless it directly bears on the case are called:
   a. statutory laws
   b. marital laws
   c. sexual laws
   d. shield laws
   (Answer = d, page number 345)

25. Killing a human being with malice aforethought is known as:
   a. assault
   b. battery
   c. felony murder
   d. misdemeanor murder
   (Answer = c, page number 346)

26. The killing of a large number of people over time by an offender who seeks to escape detection is known as:
   a. mass murder
   b. hate crimes
   c. serial murder
   d. martial rape
   (Answer = c, page number 350)

27. The killing of a large number of people in a single incident by an offender who typically does not seek concealment or escape is which of the following?
   a. rape
   b. serial murder
   c. gang banging
   d. mass murder
   (Answer = d, page number 350)

28. The most common form of serial murder where the killer strives for either sexual sadism or dominance is known as:
   a. thrill killing
   b. random killing
   c. accidental killing
   d. felony murder
   (Answer = a, page number 350)

29. The crime which requires offensive touching, such as hitting a victim, is known as:
   a. battery
   b. assault
   c. rape
   d. murder
   (Answer = a, page number 352)

30. This crime requires no actual touching, but involves either attempted battery or intentionally frightening the victim by word or deed.
   a. battery
   b. rape
   c. murder
   d. assault
   (Answer = d, page number 352)

31. Any physical, emotional, or sexual trauma to a child for which no reasonable explanation, such as an accident, can be found is known as:
   a. child abuse
   b. elder abuse
   c. hate crimes
   d. cruelty to animals
   (Answer = a, page number 353)

32. The exploitation of children through rape, incest, and molestation by parents or other adults is known as:
   a. terrorism
   b. thrill killing
   c. robbery
   d. sexual abuse
   (Answer = d, page number 354)

33. The taking or attempting to take anything of value from the care, custody, or control of a person or persons by force or threat of force or violence is known as:
   a. robbery
   b. rape
   c. murder
   d. felony murder
   (Answer = a, page numbers 355-356)

34. Which of the following is not a factor that predicts spousal abuse?
   a. a stepchild in the home
   b. the man has served in the military
   c. the presence of alcohol
   d. all of the above are predictors
   (Answer = d, page number 356)

35. Violent acts directed toward a particular person or members of a group merely because the targets share a discernible racial, ethnic, religious, or gender characteristic are known as:
   a. forms of instrumental violence
   b. felony murders
   c. subcultures of violence
   d. hate crimes
   (Answer = d, page number 359)

36. Another name for hate crime is:
   a. terrorism
   b. bias crime
   c. serial killing
   d. gang rape
   (Answer = b, page number 359)

37. When irate employees or former employees attack coworkers or sabotage machinery and production lines it is known as:
   a. terrorism
   b. workplace violence
   c. stalking
   d. instrumental violence
   (Answer = b, page number 362)

38. A course of conduct directed at a specific person that involves repeated physical or visual proximity, nonconsensual communication, or verbal, written, or implied threats is known as:
   a. hypermasculinity
   b. hate crimes
   c. terrorism
   d. stalking
   (Answer = d, page number 363)

39. An act that must carry with it the intent to disrupt and change the government and must not be merely a common-law crime committed for greed or egotism is known as:
>   a. statutory rape
>   b. felony murder
>   c. assault
>   d. terrorism
>   (Answer = d, page number 364)

40. Individuals located in rural areas who attack the military, police, and government officials are known as:
>   a. guerillas
>   b. Cobras
>   c. Pit-bulls
>   d. Snakes
>   (Answer = a, page number 364)

True/False

1. Evolutionary theories in criminology suggest that violent behavior is predominantly committed by males because over the course of human existence, sexually aggressive males have been the ones most likely to produce children.
>   (Answer = true, page number 333)

2. Substance abuse has no link to violence in our society.
>   (Answer = false, page number 333)

3. People who are constantly exposed to violence at home, at school, or in the environment will never adopt violent methods themselves.
>   (Answer = false, page number 336)

4. The virility mystique states that men typically have a callous sexual attitude and believe that violence is manly.
>   (Answer = false, page number 344)

5. Hypermasculine men typically believe that males must separate their sexual feelings from needs for love, respect, and affection.
>   (Answer = false, page number 344)

6. A number of states and the federal government have replaced rape laws with the more sexually neutral crimes of sexual assault.
>   (Answer = true, page number 345)

7. Most states and the federal government have developed shield laws which protect women from being questioned about their sexual history unless it directly bears on the case.
>   (Answer = true, page number 345)

8. Murder is defined as the lawful killing of a human being with malice aforethought.
     (Answer = false, page number 346)

9. Murders in which senior citizens are the victims are referred to as eldercide.
     (Answer = true, page number 348)

10. The younger the child the greater the risk for infanticide.
     (Answer = true, page number 348)

11. Most murders occur among strangers.
     (Answer = false, page number 348)

12. Thrill killers strive for either sexual sadism or dominance.
     (Answer = true, page number 350)

13. An estimated 10 to 15 percent of serial killers are women.
     (Answer = true, page number 352)

14. The term "road rage" has been coined to refer to motorists who assault each other.
     (Answer = true, page number 353)

15. Membership in radical political and social movements contributes to violence.
     (Answer = true, page number 360)

Essay Questions

1. Compare and contrast assault and battery. Where do these crimes occur most frequently and what are the some of the precipitators?
     (page numbers 352-356)

2. What are hate crimes? Give three examples of recent hate crimes. How should we punish hate crime offenders? What can be done to prevent hate crimes?
     (page numbers 358-362)

3. Define workplace violence. Which occupations are most likely to encounter workplace violence? What are some methods that may be used to cut-down or eliminate violence in the workplace?
     (page numbers 362-363)

4. Define terrorism. What are the various forms of terrorism? What is the United States plan against terrorism? Is this sufficient?
     (page numbers 363-372)

5. Describe the events of 9/11 in the United States. What type of terrorist acts were committed? Who was responsible and what was the purpose of the attack? What type of terrorist were involved in the 9/11 attack against the United States?   (page numbers 369-372)

Chapter Eleven

Property Crime

Summary

Chapter Eleven describes the various property crimes in our society. The chapter begins with a brief history of theft and an explanation of modern thieves. The various types of larceny/theft are defined with special emphasis on the crime of burglary. Chapter Eleven concludes with a description of arson and the various types of arsonists.

Chapter Objectives

After reading this chapter the student should be able to:

- Be familiar with the history of theft offenses
- Recognize the differences between professional and amateur thieves
- Know the similarities and differences between the various types of larceny
- Understand the different forms of shoplifting
- Be able to discuss the concept of fraud
- Know what is meant by a confidence game
- Understand what it means to burgle a home
- Know what it takes to be a good burglar
- Understand the concept of arson

Chapter Overview

Introduction
A Brief History of Theft
Modern Thieves
    Occasional Criminals
    Professional Criminals
    Sutherland's Professional Criminal
The Criminological Enterprise: Transforming Theft: Train Robbers and Safecrackers
    The Professional Fence
    The Nonprofessional Fence
Larceny/Theft
    Larceny Today
    Shoplifting
    Bad Checks
    Credit Card Theft
The Criminological Enterprise: Credit Card Theft

Auto Theft
False Pretenses or Fraud
Confidence Games
Embezzlement
Burglary
    The Nature and Extent of Burglary
    Residential Burglary
Race, Culture, Gender, and Criminology: Are There Gender Differences in Burglary?
    Commercial Burglary
    Careers in Burglary
Arson
The Criminological Enterprise: What Motivates Juvenile Fire Setters?
Summary

Chapter Outline

I. Introduction

II. A Brief History of Theft

    A. Economic crimes - acts in violation of the criminal law designed to bring financial reward to the offender.

    B. Theft has been recorded throughout history.

        1. 11th Century Crusades - inspired peasants and noblemen to prey upon passing pilgrims.

        2. 13th Century - peasants poached the king's game and robbed strangers.

        3. 14th Century - livestock thieves.

        4. 15th and 16th Century - Hundred Years War - foreign mercenaries looted and pillaged the countryside.

        5. 18th Century - 3 groups of property criminals were active:

            a. skilled thieves - worked in larger cities. Pickpockets, forgers and counterfeiters. Gathered in flash houses-public meeting places. Gang headquarters.

            b. smugglers - transported goods without bothering to pay tax or duty.

            c. poachers - lived in the country and lived on game that belonged to the landlord.

III. Modern Thieves

    A. Occasional Criminals - do not see self as criminal.

        1. Commit most of the annual property and theft-related crimes and do not see themselves as criminals.

        2. Situational inducement - short-term influences on a person's behavior that increase risk-taking.

    B. Professional Criminals - skilled, theft-oriented, career criminal.

    C. Sutherland's Professional Criminal - thieves who use no force or physical violence in their crimes and live solely by their wits and skill.

D. The Professional Fence - earns a living by buying and reselling stolen merchandise.
   1. Upfront cash - all deals are cash transactions.
   2. Knowledge of dealing-learning the ropes - knowledge of the trade.
   3. Connections with suppliers of stolen goods - able to engage in long-term relationships with suppliers of high-value stolen goods.
   4. Connections with buyers - must have continuous access to buyers of stolen merchandise.
   5. Complicity with law enforcers - must work out a relationship with law enforcement officials to stay in business.
E. The Nonprofessional Fence - significant portion of all fencing is done by amateur or occasional criminals.
   1. Associational fences - amateur bartering stolen goods for services.
   2. Neighborhood hustlers - buy and sell stolen property as one way to make a living.
   3. Amateur receivers - strangers approached publicly by one offering a deal on commodities.

IV. **Larceny/Theft** - early common-law crime created by English judges; act where one took for his or her own uses the property of another.
   A. Larceny Today
      1. Petit (petty) larceny:
         a. small amounts of money or property.
         b. punished as a misdemeanor.
      2. Grand larceny:
         a. involves merchandise of greater value.
         b. considered a felony.
         c. punished in state prison.
      3. Probably the most common criminal offense; 7 million acts of larceny in 2003.
   B. Shoplifting - common form of theft involving taking of goods from retail stores.
      1. Profile of a shoplifter
         a. boosters or heels - professional shoplifters who steal intending to resell stolen merchandise to pawnshops or fences.
         b. snitches - majority of shoplifters - amateur pilfers - systematic shoplifters who steal for their own use.
      2. Controlling shoplifting
         a. less than 10% of shoplifting incidents are detected by store employees.
         b. customers are unwilling to report crimes.
      3. Prevention Strategies:
         a. target removal strategies - using display dummy goods while locking up the "real" merchandise.
         b. target hardening strategies - locking goods into place or having them monitored by electronic systems.

      c. electronic article surveillance systems - tags with small electronic sensors that trip sound and light alarms if not removed.

      d. source tagging - process of manufacturers embedding the tag in packaging or in the product itself.

      e. situational measures - place the most valuable goods in the least vulnerable places, use warning signs and closed-circuit cameras.

      f. create specialized programs like community service, restitution, writing essays, apology letters, and counseling.

C. Bad Checks - knowingly and intentionally drawing money on a nonexistent or underfunded bank account.

    1. Naïve check forgers - amateurs who do not believe their actions will hurt anyone; usually have a financial crisis that demands an immediate resolution.

      a. closure - naïve check writers who have a financial crisis such as pressing bills or lost money at the track.

    2. Systemic forgers - make a substantial living by passing bad checks.

D. Credit Card Theft - major problem in the U.S.

E. Auto Theft - common larceny offense.

    1. In 2003, about 1.2 million auto thefts for a loss of $8 billion.

    2. Categories of auto theft

      a. joyriding - do not steal for profit, but to experience the benefits associated with owning an automobile. Often teenagers.

      b. short-term transportation - similar to joyriding. Theft of a car to go from one place to another.

      c. long-term transportation - intend to keep cars for personal use.

      d. profit - for monetary gain. Some are professionals who resell expensive cars; others are amateurs who may strip the vehicle of parts.

      e. commission of another crime - some steal cars to use in other crimes.

    3. Which cars are taken most? according to National Insurance Crime Bureau top 3:

      a. Toyota Camry.

      b. Honda Accord.

      c. Honda Civic.

    4. Carjacking - type of auto theft where gunmen approach car and force the owner to give up the keys.

    5. Combating auto theft:

      a. increase the risk of apprehension.

      b. information hot-lines.

      c. Lojack System - hidden tracking device installed in cars.

      d. publicity campaigns.

F. False Pretense or Fraud - misrepresenting a fact that a victim willingly gives up property to the offender, who keeps it.

1. False pretense - differs from traditional larceny because victim willingly gives possession to offender and it does not involve "trespass in the taking."
2. Fraud - may also occur when people conspire to cheat a third party or institution.
G. Confidence Games - run by swindlers who aspire to separate the victim from his or her money.
1. Mark - that target of a con man or woman.
2. Pigeon drop - most common con game.
H. Embezzlement - when one who is trusted with property fraudulently keeps it for their own use or the use of others.

V. **Burglary** - forcible entry into a home or place of work for theft.
A. The Nature and Extent of Burglary - UCR reports 2.1 million burglaries in 2003; NVCS reported 3.3 million residential burglaries in 2003.
1. Residential burglary.
2. Commercial burglary.
B. Careers in Burglary
1. Good burglar - professional burglars distinguished themselves:
    a. technical competence.
    b. maintenance of personal integrity.
    c. specialization in burglary.
    d. financial success.
    e. ability to avoid prison sentences.
2. The Burglary "Career Ladder:"
    a. young novices - learn the trade from older more experienced burglars.
    b. novices - continue to get tutoring as long as they develop their own markets (fences) for stolen goods.
    c. journeyman stage - forays in search of lucrative targets and careful planning.
3. Repeat burglary - research indicates that many burglars will return to the "scene of the crime" in order to repeat their offenses.

VI. **Arson** - willful and malicious burning of a home, public building, vehicle, or commercial building.
A. FBI reports 71,000 known arsons in 2003.
B. Motives for Arson
1. Adult arsonists - severe emotional turmoil or angry.
2. Juvenile arsonists - associated with conduct problems, disobedience, aggressiveness, anger, hostility and resentment over parental rejection.
3. Professional arsonist - engage in arson for profit. People looking to collect insurance money, but afraid to set the fire, may hire a professional arsonist.
4. Arson fraud - a business owner burning his or her own property, or hiring someone to do it, to escape financial problems.

VII. **Summary**

Key Terms

Arson For Profit - People looking to collect insurance money, but who are afraid to set the fire themselves, hire professional arsonists. These professionals have acquired the skills to set fires yet make the cause seem accidental.

Arson Fraud - A business owner burns his or her property, or hires someone to do it, to escape financial problems.

Boosters - Professional shoplifters who steal with the intention of reselling stolen merchandise.

Carjacking - Theft of a car by force or threat of force.

Closure - A term used by Lemert to describe people from a middle-class background who have little identification with a criminal subculture but cash bad checks because of a financial crisis that demands an immediate resolution.

Confidence Games - A swindle, usually involving a get-rich-quick scheme, often with illegal overtones, so that the victim will be afraid or embarrassed to call the police.

Constructive Possession - In the crime of larceny, willingly giving up temporary physical possession of property but retaining legal ownership.

Economic Crime - An act in violation of the criminal law that is designed to bring financial gain to the offender.

Embezzlement - A type of larceny that involves taking the possessions of another (fraudulent conversion) that have been placed in the thief's lawful possession for safekeeping, such as a bank teller misappropriating deposits or a stockbroker making off with a customer's account.

False Pretenses - Illegally obtaining money, goods, or merchandise from another by fraud or misrepresentation.

Fence - A buyer and seller of stolen merchandise.

Flash Houses - Public meeting places in England, often taverns, that served as headquarters for gangs.

Fraud - Taking the possessions of another through deception or cheating, such as selling a person a desk that is represented as an antique but is known to be a copy.

Good Burglar - Professional burglars use this title to characterize colleagues who have distinguished themselves as burglars. Characteristics of the good burglar include technical competence, maintenance of personal integrity, specialization in burglary, financial success, and the ability to avoid prison sentences.

Grand Larceny - Theft of money or property of substantial value, punished as a felony.

Heels - Professional shoplifters who steal with the intention of reselling stolen merchandise to pawnshops or fences, usually at half the original price.

Mark - The target of a con man or woman.

Naive Check Forgers - Amateurs who cash bad checks because of some financial crisis but have little identification with a criminal subculture.

Occasional Criminals - Offenders who do not define themselves by a criminal role or view themselves as committed career criminals.

Petit (Petty) Larceny - Theft of a small amount of money or property, punished as a misdemeanor.

Pigeon Drop - A con game in which a package or wallet containing money is "found" by a con man or woman. A passing victim is stopped and asked for advice about what to do, and soon another "stranger," who is part of the con, approaches and enters the discussion. The three decide to split the money; but first, one of the swindlers goes off to consult a lawyer. The lawyer claims the money can be split up, but each party must prove he or she has the means to reimburse the original owner, should one show up. The victim then is asked to give some good-faith money for the lawyer to hold. When the victim goes to the lawyer's office to pick up a share of the loot, he or she finds the address bogus and the money gone. In the new millennium, the pigeon drop has been appropriated by corrupt telemarketers, who contact typically elderly people over the phone to bilk them out of their savings.

Poachers - Early English thieves who typically lived in the country and supplemented their diet and income with game that belonged to a landlord.

Professional Criminals - Offenders who make a significant portion of their income from crime.

Professional Fence - An individual who earns his or her living solely by buying and reselling stolen merchandise.

Shoplifting - The taking of goods from retail stores.

Situational Inducement - Short-term influence on a person's behavior, such as financial problems or peer pressure, that increases risk taking.

Smugglers - Thieves who move freely in sparsely populated areas and transport goods, such as spirits, gems, gold, and spices, without bothering to pay tax or duty.

Snitches - Amateur shoplifters who do not self-identify as thieves but who systematically steal merchandise for personal use.

Street Crime - Common theft-related offenses such as larcenies and burglaries, embezzlement, and theft by false pretenses.

Systematic Forgers - Professionals who make a living by passing bad checks.

Target Hardening Strategies - Making one's home or business crime proof through the use of locks, bars, alarms, and other devices.

Target Removal Strategies - Displaying dummy or disabled goods as a means of preventing shoplifting.

Discussion Exercises

1. Have the class research current statistics for petty property crimes and white-collar property crimes. Discuss the results. What are the similarities? What are the differences?

2. Credit card abuse has become a billion dollar industry in the United States. Ask the students how many credit and debit cards they have in their name. Discuss their use in both secure and nonsecure sites on the Internet, over the telephone, and in various stores. How easy would it be for someone to gain access to their account?

3. Although the victim of a confidence game may loose large amounts of money, to what extent can we hold them partially responsible? Are they truly innocent victims of the con man or woman, or are they partly to blame because they participated in the get-rich-quick scheme? If we do hold the victim partly responsible, does this reduce the amount of culpability we place on the offender?

InfoTrac Assignment

GETTING STARTED: Search term words for subject guide: Theft, Thieves, Professional Criminals, Larceny, Auto Theft, False Pretenses, Fraud, Embezzlement, Burglary, Arson.

CRITICAL THINKING PROJECT: Using the search term "Arson," find relevant articles.

Here are three articles:

Becker, Kimberly D., Jeffrey Stuewig, Veronica M. Herrera, and Laura A. McCloskey. "A Study of Firesetting and Animal Cruelty in Children: Family influences and adolescent outcomes." *Journal of American Academy of Child and Adolescent Psychiatry.*

Cahn, Susan. "Spirited Youth or Fiends Incarnate: The Samarcand arson case and female adolescence in the American South." *Journal of Women's History.*

Carter, Carolyn S. "Church Burning in African American Communities: Implications for empowerment practice." *Social Work.*

Test Bank

Fill in the Blank

1. Common theft-related offenses are referred to as **street crimes**.
   (page number 384)

2. A **fence** is a buyer and seller of stolen merchandise.
   (page number 384)

3. **Flash houses** are public meeting places that served as headquarters for gangs in the 18th century.
   (page number 385)

4. **Professional criminals** are criminals who make a significant portion of their income from crime.
   (page number 385)

5. **Occasional criminals** are amateur criminals whose decision to steal is spontaneous and whose acts are unskilled, unplanned, and haphazard.
   (page number 385)

6. **Situational inducement** is the concept that describes occasional property crimes occurring when there is an opportunity to commit crime.
   (page number 385)

7. **Snitches** are usually respectable persons who do not conceive of themselves as thieves, but are systematic shoplifters who steal merchandise for their own use.
   (page number 391)

8. **Heels** are professional shoplifters who steal with the intention of reselling stolen merchandise to pawnshops or fences.
   (page number 391)

9. **Naïve check forgers** are the majority of check forgers who do not believe their actions will hurt anyone.
   (page number 392)

10. **Joyriding** is a type of car theft usually motivated by a teenager's desire to acquire the power, prestige, sexual potency, and recognition associated with an automobile.
    (page number 394)

11. **False pretense** involves misrepresenting a fact in a way that causes a victim to willingly give his or her property to the wrongdoer, who then keeps it.
    (page number 396)

12. **Fraud** is another name for false pretense.
    (page number 396)

13. A common method of swindling money out of an innocent victim is known as the **pigeon drop**.
    (page number 397)

14. The **good burglar** is a burglar who has technical competence, maintains personal integrity, specializes in burglary, and has financial success and the ability to avoid prison sentences.
    (page number 401)

15. **Arson fraud** involves a business owner burning his or her property, or hiring someone to do it, to escape financial problems.
    (page number 403)

Multiple Choice

1. Common theft-related offenses which usually include larceny, embezzlement, and theft by false pretense are known as:
    a. snitches
    b. street crimes
    c. terrorism
    d. burglary
    (Answer = b, page number 384)

2. A buyer and seller of stolen merchandise is known as a:
    a. snitch
    b. professional criminal
    c. occasional criminal
    d. fence
    (Answer = d, page number 384)

3. Criminal acts designed to bring financial reward to an offender are known as:
    a. street crimes
    b. situational inducements
    c. economic crimes
    d. snitches
    (Answer = c, page number 384)

4. Public meeting places, often taverns, that served as headquarters for gangs in the 18th century were known as:
   a. flash houses
   b. pigeon drops
   c. boosters
   d. heels
   (Answer = a, page number 385)

5. By the 18th century, which of the following property criminals were active?
   a. skilled thieves
   b. smugglers
   c. poachers
   d. all of the above
   (Answer = d, page number 385)

6. Thieves who typically worked in the larger cities and were often pickpockets, forgers, and counterfeiters were known as:
   a. smugglers
   b. poachers
   c. burglars
   d. skilled thieves
   (Answer = d, page number 385)

7. Thieves who moved freely in sparsely populated areas and transported goods, such as spirits, gems, gold, and spices, without bothering to pay tax or duty were known as:
   a. skilled thieves
   b. poachers
   c. smugglers
   d. burglars
   (Answer = c, page number 385)

8. Thieves who typically lived in the county and supplemented their diet and income with game that belonged to a landlord were known as:
   a. poachers
   b. skilled thieves
   c. smugglers
   d. burglars
   (Answer = a, page number 385)

9. Criminals who make a significant portion of their income from crime are known as:
   a. occasional criminals
   b. professional criminals
   c. naïve check forgers
   d. snitches
   (Answer = b, page number 385)

10. Amateur criminals whose decision to steal is spontaneous and whose acts are unskilled, unplanned, and haphazard are known as:
     a. professional criminals
     b. systematic forgers
     c. snitches
     d. occasional criminals
     (Answer = d, page number 385)

11. Occasional property crimes, which occur when there is an opportunity to commit crime, are known as:
     a. situational inducements
     b. systematic forgers
     c. false pretenses
     d. burglaries
     (Answer = a, page number 385)

12. Who wrote the classic book, *The Professional Thief*?
     a. Sigmund Freud
     b. Karl Marx
     c. Charles Darwin
     d. Edwin Sutherland
     (Answer = d, page number 387)

13. According to the Typology of Professional Thieves, which of the following do professional thieves engage in?
     a. pickpocketing
     b. shoplifting
     c. stealing jewels
     d. all of the above
     (Answer = d, page number 387)

14. A successful fence must meet which of the following conditions?
     a. upfront cash
     b. knowledge of dealing
     c. connections with buyers
     d. all of the above
     (Answer = d, page number 389)

15. Amateur fences who barter stolen goods for services are known as:
     a. neighborhood hustlers
     b. professional fences
     c. associational fences
     d. amateur receivers
     (Answer = c, page number 389)

16. Those who buy and sell property as one of the many ways they make a living are known as:
    a. associational fences
    b. amateur receivers
    c. professional fences
    d. neighborhood hustlers
    (Answer = d, page number 389)

17. Complete strangers approached in a public place by one offering a great deal on valuable commodities would be called:
    a. amateur receivers
    b. associational fences
    c. professional fences
    d. neighborhood hustlers
    (Answer = a, page number 389)

18. A form of larceny is which of the following?
    a. petit larceny
    b. grand larceny
    c. all of the above
    d. none of the above
    (Answer = c, page number 390)

19. The FBI reports about how many larcenies each year?
    a. 1 million
    b. 10 million
    c. 7 million
    d. 1 billion
    (Answer = c, page number 390)

20. In England about what percent of the population has been convicted of shoplifting by the age of 40?
    a. 100
    b. 50
    c. 5
    d. 1
    (Answer = c, page number 391)

21. Another name for boosters is:
    a. arsons
    b. heels
    c. snitches
    d. fences
    (Answer = b, page number 391)

22. Usually respectable persons who do not conceive of themselves as thieves, but are systematic shoplifters who steal merchandise for their own use are called:
    a. systematic forgers
    b. professional criminals
    c. burglars
    d. snitches
    (Answer = d, page number 391)

23. Professional shoplifters who steal with the intention of reselling stolen merchandise to pawnshops or fences are known as:
    a. naïve check forgers
    b. good burglars
    c. heels
    d. snitches
    (Answer = c, page number 391)

24. Using dummy or disabled goods on display while having the "real" merchandise kept under lock and key is known as:
    a. target removal strategies
    b. target hardening strategies
    c. electronic surveillance systems
    d. source tagging
    (Answer = a, page number 392)

25. Which of the following are prevention strategies to reduce or eliminate shoplifting?
    a. electronic article surveillance systems
    b. source tagging
    c. target removal strategies
    d. all of the above
    (Answer = d, page number 392)

26. Locking goods into place or having them monitored by electronic systems is known as:
    a. target removal strategies
    b. electronic surveillance systems
    c. source tagging
    d. target hardening strategies
    (Answer = d, page number 392)

27. Cashing forged checks for a financial crisis is known as:
    a. boosters
    b. heels
    c. closure
    d. constructive possession
    (Answer = c, page number 392)

28. The majority of check forgers who do not believe their actions will hurt anyone and usually cash bad checks because of a financial crisis are known as:
    a. professional criminals
    b. systematic forgers
    c. good burglars
    d. naïve check forgers
    (Answer = d, page number 392)

29. Professionals who make a substantial living by passing bad checks are:
    a. snitches
    b. occasional criminals
    c. systematic forgers
    d. naïve check forgers
    (Answer = c, page number 392)

30. Car theft usually motivated by a teenager's desire to acquire the power, prestige, sexual potency, and recognition associated with an automobile is known as:
    a. carjacking
    b. joyriding
    c. closure
    d. situational inducement
    (Answer = b, page number 394)

31. A type of auto theft involving gunmen approaching a car and forcing the owner to give up the keys is known as:
    a. carjacking
    b. situation inducement
    c. joyriding
    d. false pretenses
    (Answer = a, page number 396)

32. Another name for fraud is:
    a. fence
    b. flash house
    c. fake
    d. false pretense
    (Answer = d, page number 396)

33. Misrepresenting a fact in a way that causes a victim to willingly give his or her property to the wrongdoer, who then keeps it, is known as:
    a. street crimes
    b. false pretense
    c. naïve check forgers
    d. joyriding
    (Answer = b, page number 396)

34. The target of a con man or woman is known as the:
    a. smuggler
    b. poacher
    c. pigeon
    d. mark
    (Answer = d, page number 397)

35. Cons run by swindlers who aspire to separate a victim from his or her hard-earned money are known as:
    a. constructive possessions
    b. confidence games
    c. carjackings
    d. closures
    (Answer = b, page number 397)

36. A common method of swindling money out of an innocent victim is known as a:
    a. situation inducement
    b. systematic forger
    c. false pretense
    d. pigeon drop
    (Answer = d, page number 397)

37. Unlawful entry of a structure to commit theft or a felony is known as:
    a. arson
    b. murder
    c. homicide
    d. burglary
    (Answer = d, page number 398)

38. A burglar who has technical competence, maintains personal integrity, specializes in burglary, has financial success, and has the ability to avoid prison sentences is known as:
    a. a good burglar
    b. an occasional criminal
    c. a snitch
    d. a shoplifter
    (Answer = a, page number 401)

39. The willful and malicious burning of a home, public or commercial building, or vehicle for criminal purposes such as profit, revenge, fraud, or crime concealment is known as:
    a. arson
    b. burglary
    c. robbery
    d. murder
    (Answer = a, page number 403)

40. When a business owner burns his or her property, or hires someone to do it, to escape financial problems is known as:
    a. arson fraud
    b. closure
    c. burglary
    d. carjacking
    (Answer = a, page number 403)

True/False

1. Economic crimes can be defined as acts in violation of the criminal code designed to bring financial reward to an offender.
    (Answer = true, page number 384)

2. National surveys indicate that between 55 and 75 percent of the U.S. population are victims of theft offenses each year.
    (Answer = false, page number 384)

3. Theft is a phenomenon unique to modern times; the theft of personal property has not been known throughout recorded history.
    (Answer = false, page number 385)

4. By the eighteenth century, three separate groups of property criminals were active: skilled thieves, smugglers, and poachers.
    (Answer = true, page number 385)

5. Occasional property crime occurs when there is an opportunity or situational inducement to commit crime.
    (Answer = true, page number 385)

6. Larceny is usually separated by state statute into big larceny and small larceny.
    (Answer = false, page number 390)

7. Shoplifting is a common form of theft involving the taking of goods from retail stores.
    (Answer = true, page number 391)

8. One major problem with combating shoplifting is that many customers who observe pilferage gladly report it to security agents.
    (Answer = false, page number 391)

9. Retail security measures add to the already high cost of crime, all of which is passed on to the consumer.
    (Answer = true, page number 392)

10. Motor vehicle theft is another common larceny offense.
    (Answer = true, page number 393)

11. Thieves who steal cars for long-term transportation intend to keep the cars for their personal use.
(Answer = true, page number 394)

12. A large portion of auto thieves steal cars to use in other crimes, such as robberies and thefts.
(Answer = false, page number 395)

13. About 50,000 carjackings occur each year.
(Answer = true, page number 396)

14. Both the victims and offenders in carjackings tend to be young black men.
(Answer = true, page number 396)

15. Burglary was one of the earliest common-law crimes created by English judges to define acts in which one person took for his or her own use the property of another.
(Answer = false, page number 398)

Essay Questions

1. Provide a brief history of theft. Define theft. What is the common-law definition of theft?
(page numbers 384-385)

2. Who would be considered modern thieves? Compare and contrast occasional criminals with professional criminals.
(page numbers 385-390)

3. What is larceny/theft? Describe the varieties of larceny?
(page numbers 390-393)

4. Define auto theft? What are the various categories of auto theft? What types of individuals are most likely to commit which types of auto theft?
(page numbers 393-396)

5. What is the nature and extent of burglary? How does one make a career out of this crime?
(page numbers 398-402)

Chapter Twelve

Enterprise Crime
White-Collar, Cyber, and Organized Crime

Summary

Chapter Twelve provides a discussion of white-collar, cyber, and organized crime. The history of white-collar crime and its current components are included. Various causes and methods of control of white-collar crime are emphasized. Internet crime and other forms of computer crime are presented. Efforts at controlling cyber crime are discussed. The chapter concludes with a discussion of organized crime. The various characteristics and activities of organized crime are included, as are methods of control.

Chapter Objectives

After reading this chapter the student should be able to:

- Understand the concept of enterprise crime
- Be familiar with the various types of white-collar crime
- Be familiar with the various types of corporate crime
- Recognize the extent and various causes of white-collar crime
- Be able to discuss the different approaches to combating white-collar crime
- Recognize new types of cyber crime
- Describe the methods being used to control Internet and computer crime
- List the different types of illegal behavior engaged in by organized crime figures
- Describe the evolution of organized crime
- Explain how the government is fighting organized crime

Chapter Overview

Introduction
Enterprise Crime
    Crimes of Business Enterprise
White-Collar Crime
    Redefining White-Collar Crime
Components of White-Collar Crime
    Stings and Swindles
    Chiseling
    Individual Exploitation of Institutional Position

Chapter Outline

I. Introduction

II. Enterprise Crime - crimes of the marketplace.
- A. Crimes of Business Enterprise
  1. Cyber crime, organized crime, and white-collar crime often overlap.
     a. all three forms can involve violence.

III. White-Collar Crime - 1930's, Edwin Sutherland described the criminal activities of the rich and powerful. White-collar crime - crime committed by a respectable, high social status person in the course of his occupation.
- A. Redefining White-Collar Crime
  1. Much broader than Sutherland's original definition and include middle-income Americans and corporate titans who use their marketplace for criminal activity.
  2. Crimes included are tax evasion, credit card fraud, bankruptcy fraud, pilfering, soliciting bribes or kickbacks, embezzlement, land swindles, securities theft, medical fraud, antitrust violations, price-fixing, and false advertising.
  3. Difficult to state the cost of white-collar crime, but estimates are in the hundreds of billions of dollars.
  4. White-collar crimes often damage property and kill people.

IV. Components of White-Collar Crime
- A. Stings and Swindles - stealing through deception by individuals who use their institutional or business position to bilk people out of their money.
  1. Religious swindles - an example a swindle.
- B. Chiseling - regularly cheating an organization, its consumers, or both.
  1. Professional chiseling - professionals who use their positions to cheat their clients.
  2. Securities fraud - brokers using their position to cheat individual clients.
     a. churning - by repeated, excessive, and unnecessary buying and selling of stock
     b. front running - brokers place personal orders ahead of a large customer's order to profit from the market effects of the trade.
     c. bucketing - skimming customer-trading profits by falsifying trade information.
     d. insider trading - using one's position of trust to profit from inside business information.
- C. Individual Exploitation of Institutional Position - occurs when victim has a right to service and offender threatens to withhold service unless a payment or bribe is forthcoming.
  1. Exploitation in government and private industry.
- D. Influence Peddling and Bribery
  1. Taking of kickbacks - from contractors in return for awarding them contracts they could not have won on merit.

2. Exploitation - forcing victims to pay for services to which they have a clear right.
3. Influence peddling in government
    a. HUD - 1980's - officials tried to defraud the government of $4 billion to $8 billion.
    b. Knapp Commission - found corrupt police officers in New York City.
4. Influence peddling in business
    a. Gulf Oil paid $4 million to South Korean ruling party and Burroughs Corporation paid $1.5 million to foreign officials.
    b. Foreign Corrupt Practices Act (FCPA) - 1977 - a criminal offense to bribe foreign officials or to make questionable overseas payments.
E. Embezzlement and Employee Fraud - individuals' use their positions to embezzle company funds or appropriate company property for themselves.
    1. Blue-collar fraud
        a. pilferage - systematic theft of company property by employees.
        b. employee theft may amount to almost $35 billion per year.
    2. Management fraud
        a. converting company assets for personal benefit.
        b. fraudulently receiving increases in compensation (such as raises and bonuses).
        c. fraudulently increasing personal holdings of company stock.
        d. retaining one's present position within the company by manipulating accounts.
        e. concealing unacceptable performance from stockholders.
F. Client Fraud - theft by an economic client from an organization that advances credit to its clients or reimburses them for services rendered.
    1. Health care fraud - in obtaining patients and administering treatment.
    2. Bank fraud - to knowingly execute or attempt to execute a scheme to fraudulently obtain money or property from a financial institution.
    3. Tax evasion - the victim is the government.
        a. passive neglect - not paying taxes, not reporting income, or not paying taxes when due.
        b. affirmative tax evasion - keeping double books, making false entries, destroying books or records, concealing assets, or covering up sources of income.
G. Corporate Crime - (or organizational crime) socially injurious acts committed by people who control companies to further their business interests.
    1. For a corporation to be held criminally liable, the employee must be acting within the scope of job and must have authority to engage in act.
        a. actual authority - when a corporation knowingly gives authority to an employee.

  b. apparent authority - if a third party reasonably believes the agent has authority to perform act.

 2. Illegal restraint of trade and price-fixing - regulated by the Sherman Antitrust Act.

  a. restraint of trade - involves a contract or conspiracy designed to stifle competition, create a monopoly, artificially maintain prices, or otherwise interfere with free market competition.

  b. division of markets - firms divide a region into territories and each firm agrees not to compete in the others' territories.

  c. tying arrangement - corporation requires customers of one of its services to use other services it offers.

  d. group boycotts - company boycotts retail stores that do not comply with its rules or desires.

  e. price-fixing - conspiracy to set and control the price of a necessary commodity; is considered an absolute violation of the act.

 3. Deceptive pricing - when contractors provide the government or other corporations with incomplete or misleading information on how much it actually cost to fulfill the contracts they were bidding on or use mischarges once the contracts are signed.

 4. False claims and advertising - illegal to knowingly and purposely advertise a product as possessing qualities that the manufacturer realizes that it does not have.

 5. Worker safety/environmental crimes - maintaining unsafe working conditions and intentional or negligent environmental pollution.

  a. Environmental Protection Agency (EPA) - major enforcement arm against environmental crimes.

V. Causes of White-Collar Crime

 A. Some individuals rationalize their behavior.

 B. Some see no harm; since they see that it does not hurt anyone.

 C. Some do not see their actions as crimes.

 D. Some feel justified; everyone else does it, too.

 E. Greedy or Needy?

  1. Corporate culture view - some business enterprises cause crime by placing excessive demands on employees while at the same time maintaining a business climate tolerant of employee deviance.

  2. Self-control view - Hirschi and Gottfredson maintain the motives that produce white-collar crimes are the same as those that produce any other criminal behaviors: the desire for relatively quick, relatively certain benefit, with minimal effort.

VI. White-Collar Law Enforcement Systems - detection is primarily in the hands of administrative departments and agencies like the FBI.

 A. Controlling White-Collar Crime - rarely prosecuted and when convicted, receives relatively light sentences.

  1. Compliance strategies - aim for law conformity without the necessity of detecting, processing, or penalizing individual violators.

    a. set up administrative agencies to oversee business activity.

    b. force corporate boards to police themselves.

   2. Deterrence strategies - involve detecting criminal violations, determining who is responsible, and penalizing the offenders to deter future violations.

  B. Is the Tide Turning? - Growing evidence that white-collar crime deterrence strategies have become normative.

VII. Cyber Crime

  A. Use emerging forms of technology typically for the theft of information, resources, or funds.

VIII. Internet Crime

  A. Survey by Computer Security Institute found 78% of the employers contacted had detected employee abuse of Internet access.

  B. Distributing Sexual Material

   1. Internet is an ideal venue for selling and distributing obscene material.

    a. Landslide Productions case.

  C. Denial of Service Attack

   1. Threats to flood an Internet site with bogus messages so services will be tied up unless pay extortion.

  D. Illegal Copyright Infringement

   1. Warez - illegally obtaining software and then cracking its copyright protections before posting it on the Internet for other members to use.

   2. Computer Fraud and Abuse Act (CFAA) - criminalizes accessing computer systems without authorization to obtain information.

   3. Digital Millennium Copyright Act (DMCA) - a crime to circumvent antipiracy measures and outlaws the manufacture, sale, or distribution of code-cracking devices.

  E. Internet Securities Fraud

   1. Market manipulation - individual tries to control the price of stock by interfering with the natural forces of supply and demand.

    a. pump and dump - erroneous and deceptive information is posted online to get unsuspecting investors to become interested in a stock, while those spreading the information sell previously purchased stock at an inflated price.

    b. cyber-smear - reverse pump and dump; negative information is spread online about a stock driving down its price and allowing people to buy it at an artificially low price before rebuttals by the company's officers re-inflate the price.

   2. Fraudulent offerings of securities - cyber criminals create websites to fraudulently sell securities.

   3. Illegal touting - individuals make securities recommendations and fail to disclose they are being paid to disseminate their favorable opinions.

F. Identity Theft - person uses the Internet to steal someone's identity and/or impersonate them in order to open a new credit card account or conduct some other financial transaction.
   1. Phishing - a process to gather identity information.
   2. Identity Theft Penalty Enhancement Act of 2004 - increases existing penalties for identity theft.
G. Internet Fraud
   1. Ponzi/Pyramid Schemes - investors are promised abnormally high profits on their investments; no investment is actually made. Early investors are paid returns with the investment money from the later investors.
   2. Nondelivery of goods or services - not delivering promised purchases or services, which were purchased through the Internet.

IX. Computer Crime
A. Computer-Related Thefts - new trend in employee theft and embezzlement.
B. Computer crime falls into one of five categories:
   1. Theft of services - computer used for unauthorized purposes or an unauthorized user penetrates the computer system.
   2. Use of data in a computer system for personal gain.
   3. Unauthorized use of computers employed for various types of financial processing to obtain assets.
   4. Theft of property by computer for personal use or conversion to profit.
   5. Making the computer itself the subject of a crime - planting a virus.
   6. Computer theft styles and methods:
      a. the Trojan horse - one computer is used to reprogram another for illicit purposes.
      b. the salami slice - employee sets up dummy account in the company's computerized records. A small amount is subtracted from customers' accounts and added to the account of the thief.
      c. super-zagging - tinkering with the company computer program to issue checks to ones personal account.
      d. the logic bomb - program looking for an error in company computer. When error occurs, the thief exploits the situation and steals money, secrets, commits sabotage or the like.
      e. impersonation - unauthorized person uses the identity of an authorized person to access the computer system.
      f. data leakage - person illegally obtains data from a computer system by leaking it out in small amounts.
   7. Computer virus - a program that disrupts or destroys existing programs and networks, causing them to perform the task for which the virus was designed.
   8. Computer worms - similar to viruses but use computer networks or the Internet to self-replicate and "send themselves" to other users.
C. The Extent of Computer Crime

1. The Computer Crime and Security Survey found that overall computer-related financial losses total more than $140 million; denial of services and theft of intellectual property were the two most significant causes of loss.
2. The Business Software Alliance (BSA) found that 36% of the software installed on computers worldwide was pirated; a loss of nearly $29 billion.

X. **Controlling Cyber Crime**
   A. New laws, enforcement processes, and organizations have been set up to control cyber crime.
      1. Counterfeit Access Device and Computer Fraud and Abuse Law of 1984 - treat computer related crime as a distinct federal offense.

XI. **Organized Crime** - the ongoing criminal enterprise groups whose ultimate purpose is personal economic gain through illegitimate means.
   A. Characteristics of Organized Crime
      1. A conspiratorial activity, involving the coordination of numerous persons in the planning and execution of illegal acts or in the pursuit of a legitimate objective by unlawful means.
      2. Has economic gain as its primary goal.
      3. Not limited to providing illicit services.
      4. Employs predatory tactics, such as intimidation, violence and corruption.
      5. Groups are very quick and effective in controlling their members, associates, and victims.
      6. Not synonymous with the Mafia. The Mafia is a common stereotype of organized crime.
      7. Does not include terrorists dedicated to political change.
   B. Activities of Organized Crime
      1. Activities include the following: providing illicit materials, using force to enter into and maximize profits in legitimate businesses, narcotic distribution, loansharking, prostitution, gambling, theft rings, pornography, and other illegal enterprises.
   C. The Concept of Organized Crime
      1. Alien Conspiracy Theory - organized crime is a direct offshoot of a criminal society - the Mafia - that first originated in Italy and Sicily and now controls racketeering in major U.S. cities.
         a. the Mafia is centrally coordinated by a national committee that settles disputes, dictates policy, and assigns territory.
   D. Alien Conspiracy Theory
      1. La Cosa Nostra - national syndicate of 25 or so Italian-dominated crime families.
      2. Sees organized crime as being run by an ordered group of ethnocentric criminal syndicates, maintaining unified leadership and shared values.
   E. Contemporary Organized Crime Groups

1. View organized crime as a loose confederation of ethnic and regional crime groups, bound together by a commonality of economic and political objectives.
            2. Eastern European crime groups - growth since the fall of the Soviet Union.
    F. The Evolution of Organized Crime - it is simplistic to view organized crime in the U.S. as a national syndicate that controls all illegitimate rackets in an orderly fashion.
    G. Controlling Organized Crime
            1. Interstate and Foreign Travel or Transportation in Aid of Racketeering Enterprises Act (Travel Act) - aimed directly at organized crime.
            2. Organized Crime Control Act - 1970 - called Racketeer Influenced and Corrupt Organization Act (RICO).
                    a. created new categories of offenses in racketeering activity.
                    b. enterprise theory of investigation (ETI) - used by the FBI; focus is on criminal enterprise and investigation attacks on the structure of the criminal enterprise rather than on criminal acts viewed as isolated incidents.
    H. The Future of Organized Crime
            1. Indications that organized crime is on the decline.
            2. Some large gangs are becoming similar to traditional organized crime.
            3. Due to the demand for certain illegal goods and services, organized crime will never be totally eliminated.

XII. Summary

Key Terms

Actual Authority - The authority a corporation knowingly gives to an employee.
Alien Conspiracy Theory - The view that organized crime was imported to the United States by Europeans and that crime cartels have a policy of restricting their membership to people of their own ethnic background.
Apparent Authority - Authority that a third party, like a customer, reasonably believes the agent has to perform the act in question.
Bucketing - A form of stockbroker chiseling in which brokers skim customer trading profits by falsifying trade information.
Chiseling - Crimes that involve using illegal means to cheat an organization, its consumers, or both, on a regular basis.
Churning - A white-collar crime in which a stockbroker makes repeated trades to fraudulently increase commissions.
Computer Virus - A program that disrupts or destroys existing programs and networks, causing them to perform the task for which the virus was designed.
Computer Worm - A program that attacks computer networks (or the Internet) by self-replicating and "sending" itself to other users, generally via e-mail without the aid of the operator.

Corporate Crime - White-collar crime involving a legal violation by a corporate entity, such as price fixing, restraint of trade, or hazardous waste dumping.

Cyber Crime - The use of modern technology for criminal purpose.

Division of Markets - Firms divide a region into territories, and each firm agrees not to compete in the others' territories.

Enterprise Crime - The use of illegal tactics to gain profit in the marketplace. Enterprise crimes can involve both the violation of law in the course of an otherwise legitimate occupation or the sale and distribution of illegal commodities.

Enterprise Theory of Investigation (ETI) - A standard investigation tool of the FBI that focuses on criminal enterprise and investigation attacks on the structure of the criminal enterprise rather than on criminal acts viewed as isolated incidents.

Front Running - A form of stockbroker chiseling in which brokers place personal orders ahead of a large order from a customer to profit from the market effects of the trade.

Group Boycott - A company's refusal to do business with retail stores that do not comply with its rules or desires.

Influence Peddling - Using an institutional position to grant favors and sell information to which their co-conspirators are not entitled.

Insider Trading - Illegal buying of stock in a company based on information provided by someone who has a fiduciary interest in the company, such as an employee or an attorney or accountant retained by the firm. Federal laws and the rules of the Securities and Exchange Commission require that all profits from such trading be returned and provide for both fines and a prison sentence.

La Cosa Nostra - A national syndicate of twenty-five or so Italian-dominated crime families who control crime in distinct geographic areas.

Mafia - A criminal society that originated in Sicily, Italy, and is believed to control racketeering in the United States.

Organizational Crime - Crime that involves large corporations and their efforts to control the marketplace and earn huge profits through unlawful bidding, unfair advertising, monopolistic practices, or other illegal means.

Organized Crime - Illegal activities of people and organizations whose acknowledged purpose is profit through illegitimate business enterprise.

Phishing - Sometimes called "carding" or "brand spoofing," phishing is a scam where the perpetrator sends out e-mails appearing to come from legitimate web enterprises such as eBay, Amazon, PayPal, and America Online in an effort to get the recipient to reveal personal and financial information.

Pilferage - Theft by employees through stealth or deception.

Price Fixing - A conspiracy to set and control the price of a necessary commodity.

Racketeer Influenced and Corrupt Organization (RICO) Act - Federal legislation that enables prosecutors to bring additional criminal or civil charges against people whose multiple criminal acts constitute a conspiracy. RICO features monetary penalties that allow the government to confiscate all profits derived from criminal activities. Originally intended to be used against organized criminals, RICO has also been used against white-collar criminals.

Sherman Antitrust Act - Law that subjects to criminal or civil sanctions any person "who shall make any contract or engage in any combination or conspiracy" in restraint of interstate commerce.

Sting or Swindle - A white-collar crime in which people use their institutional or business position to trick others out of their money.

Tying Arrangement - A corporation requires customers of one of its services to use other services it offers.

Viatical Investments - The selling of a death benefit policy, at less than face value, by a terminally ill person to a third party.

Warez - A term computer hackers and software pirates use to describe a game or application that is made available for use on the Internet in violation of its copyright protection.

White-Collar Crime - Illegal acts that capitalize on a person's status in the marketplace. White-collar crimes can involve theft, embezzlement, fraud, market manipulation, restraint of trade, and false advertising.

Discussion Exercises

1. Have the class review various groups of organized crime. Discuss the different characteristics of the groups, their areas of operation, and their specific crime specializations.

2. This chapter spends quite a bit of time on white-collar crimes. These are crimes that are committed because of access within a business structure. While few students will have held white-collar positions, they will have had experience in blue- and pink-collar jobs. Discuss the various forms of crime they or other coworkers were able to commit because of the jobs they held.

3. The vast majority of persons with a computer connected to the Internet and e-mail have had experience with some form of a computer virus. Discuss those activities that place our personal computers at highest risk. What can we do to better protect our computer system? Allow the students to discuss how their computer got "infected."

InfoTrac Assignment

GETTING STARTED: Search term words for subject guide: White-Collar Crime, Swindles, Embezzlement, Fraud, Cyber Crime, Organized Crime.

CRITICAL THINKING PROJECT: Using the search term "Computer Crimes," find relevant articles.

Here are three articles:

Goldsborough, Reid. "Fighting Back Against Cyberstalking." *Black Issues in Higher Education*.

Lunsford, Dale L., Walter A. Robbins, and Pascal A. Bizarro. "Protecting Information Privacy when Retiring Old Computers." *The CPA Journal*.

O'Rourke, Morgan. "Cyber-Extortion Evolves." *Risk Management*.

Test Bank

Fill in the Blank

1. **Insider trading** is information that is used to buy and sell securities, giving the trader an unfair advantage over the general public.
     (page number 415)

2. **Churning** is a white-collar crime in which a stockbroker makes repeated trades to fraudulently increase his or her commissions.
     (page number 415)

3. **Bucketing** is when a broker skims customer trading profits by falsifying trade information.
     (page number 415)

4. **Front running** is when brokers place personal orders ahead of a large customer's order to profit from the market effects of the trade.
     (page number 415)

5. **Viatical investments** are interests in the death benefits of terminally ill patients.
     (page number 415)

6. **Exploitation** involves forcing victims to pay for services to which they have a clear right.
     (page number 416)

7. When government employees take **kickbacks**, they are taking money from contractors in return for awarding them contracts.
     (page number 416)

8. **Check kiting** is a scheme whereby a client with accounts in two or more banks takes advantage of the time required for checks to clear in order to obtain unauthorized use of bank funds.
     (page number 419)

9. **Corporate or organizational crime** is a component of white-collar crime which involves situations in which powerful institutions or their representatives willfully violate the laws that restrain these institutions from doing social harm or require them to do social good.
     (page number 422)

10. **Compliance** is a white-collar enforcement strategy that encourages law-abiding behavior through both the threat of economic sanctions and the promise of rewards for conformity.
     (page number 427)

11. **The Trojan horse** is a computer crime whereby one computer is used to reprogram another for illicit purposes.
(page number 432)

12. A computer program that disrupts or destroys existing programs and networks is known as a **virus**.
(page number 432)

13. **Computer worms** use computer networks or the Internet to self-replicate and "send themselves" to other users.
(page number 433)

14. The **Alien Conspiracy Theory** supports the notion that organized crime is the direct offshoot of a criminal society known as the Mafia.
(page number 436)

15. A national syndicate of 25 or so Italian-dominated crime families call themselves **La Cosa Nostra**.
(page number 436)

Multiple Choice

1. When one is willing to take risks for profit in the marketplace, this is known as:
   a. entrepreneurship
   b. enterprise
   c. compliance
   d. a tying arrangement
   (Answer = a, page number 412)

2. According to Sutherland, a crime committed by a person of respectability and high status in the course of his occupation, this is known as:
   a. white-collar crime
   b. a division of labor
   c. organized crime
   d. enterprise
   (Answer = a, page number 413)

3. Regularly cheating an organization, its consumers, or both is known as:
   a. churning
   b. compliance
   c. corporate crime
   d. chiseling
   (Answer = d, page number 414)

4. A white-collar crime in which a stockbroker makes repeated trades to fraudulently increase his or her commissions is known as:
   a. compliance
   b. churning
   c. forfeiture
   d. pilferage
   (Answer = b, page number 415)

5. Skimming customer trading profits by falsifying trade information is known as:
   a. front running
   b. churning
   c. chiseling
   d. bucketing
   (Answer = d, page number 415)

6. Information used to buy and sell securities, giving the trader an unfair advantage over the general public is called:
   a. group boycott
   b. a division of markets
   c. enterprise
   d. insider trading
   (Answer = d, page number 415)

7. Broker fraud, in which brokers place personal orders ahead of a large customer's order to profit from the market effects of the trade, is known as:
   a. front running
   b. bucketing
   c. churning
   d. all of the above
   (Answer = a, page number 415)

8. When government employees take money from contractors in return for awarding them contracts, it is known as:
   a. exploitation
   b. the taking of kickbacks
   c. front running
   d. churning
   (Answer = b, page number 416)

9. Forcing victims to pay for services to which they have a clear right is known as:
   a. churning
   b. front running
   c. exploitation
   d. the taking of kickbacks
   (Answer = c, page number 416)

10. Which Act makes it a criminal offense to bribe foreign officials or to make other questionable overseas payments?
      a. Sherman Antitrust Act
      b. 1977 White-Collar Crime Act
      c. RICO Act
      d. Foreign Corrupt Practices Act
      (Answer = d, page number 417)

11. Theft by employees through stealth or deception is known as:
      a. price-fixing
      b. pilferage
      c. insider trading
      d. forfeiture
      (Answer = b, page number 418)

12. How much is lost each year due to employee theft?
      a. $350,000
      b. $3.5 million
      c. $3.5 billion
      d. $35 billion
      (Answer = d, page number 418)

13. Which of the following are types of management fraud?
      a. converting company assets for personal benefit
      b. fraudulently receiving increases in compensation
      c. all of the above
      d. none of the above
      (Answer = c, page number 418)

14. Bank fraud can encompass which of the following?
      a. check kiting
      b. check forging
      c. sale of stolen checks
      d. all of the above
      (Answer = d, page number 419)

15. A scheme whereby a client with accounts in two or more banks takes advantage of the time required for checks to clear in order to obtain unauthorized use of bank funds is known as:
      a. check forging
      b. sale of stolen checks
      c. auto title fraud
      d. check kiting
      (Answer = d, page number 419)

16. Simply not paying taxes, not reporting income, or not paying taxes when due is known as:
    a. affirmative tax evasion
    b. check forging
    c. check kiting
    d. passive neglect
    (Answer = d, page number 420)

17. Keeping double books, making false entries, destroying books or records, concealing assets, or covering up sources of income is known as:
    a. passive neglect
    b. check kiting
    c. check forging
    d. affirmative tax evasion
    (Answer = d, page numbers 420-421)

18. A component of white-collar crime, which involves situations in which powerful institutions or their representatives willfully violate the laws that restrain these institutions from doing social harm or require them to do social good, is known as:
    a. corporate crime
    b. insider trading
    c. enterprise
    d. a tying arrangement
    (Answer = a, page number 422)

19. Crime that involves large corporations and their efforts to control the marketplace and earn huge profits through unlawful bidding, unfair advertising, monopolistic practices, or other illegal means is known as:
    a. organizational crime
    b. a tying arrangement
    c. insider trading
    d. enterprise
    (Answer = a, page number 422)

20. An act associated with corporate crime is:
    a. price-fixing
    b. illegal restraint of trade
    c. all of the above
    d. none of the above
    (Answer = c, page number 422)

21. A contract or conspiracy designed to stifle competition, create a monopoly, artificially maintain prices, or otherwise interfere with free market competition is known as:
    a. a division of markets
    b. a tying arrangement
    c. group boycotts
    d. restraint of trade
    (Answer = d, page number 422)

22. The legal basis which restrains trade violations and subjects criminal or civil sanctions on any person who shall make any contract or engage in any combination or conspiracy in restraint of interstate commerce is known as:
    a. RICO
    b. a division of markets
    c. arbitrage
    d. the Sherman Antitrust Act
    (Answer = d, page numbers 422-423)

23. When firms divide a region into territories and each firm agrees not to compete in the others' territories, this is known as:
    a. compliance
    b. churning
    c. forfeiture
    d. a division of markets
    (Answer = d, page number 423)

24. When an organization or company boycotts retail stores that do not comply with its rules or desires it is known as:
    a. forfeiture
    b. group boycott
    c. enterprise
    d. entrepreneurship
    (Answer = b, page number 423)

25. When a corporation requires customers of one of its services to use other services it offers it is known as:
    a. price-fixing
    b. a tying arrangement
    c. enterprise
    d. compliance
    (Answer = b, page number 423)

26. A conspiracy to set and control the price of a necessary commodity is known as:
    a. arbitrage
    b. churning
    c. compliance
    d. price-fixing
    (Answer = d, page number 423)

27. A white-collar enforcement strategy that encourages law-abiding behavior through the threat of economic sanctions and the promise of rewards for conformity is known as:
    a. churning
    b. enterprise
    c. compliance
    d. pilferage
    (Answer = c, page number 427)

28. According to a survey by the Computer Security Institute, what percentage of employers reported they had detected employee abuse of Internet access?
    a. about 25%
    b. about 50%
    c. about 75%
    d. 100%
    (Answer = c, page number 429)

29. When an individual tries to control the price of stock by interfering with the natural forces of supply and demand, it is called:
    a. market manipulation
    b. fraudulent offerings of securities
    c. illegal touting
    d. enterprises
    (Answer = a, page number 430)

30. Which of the following is a type of market manipulation?
    a. pump and dump
    b. cyber-smear
    c. all of the above
    d. none of the above
    (Answer = c, page number 430)

31. When erroneous and deceptive information is posted online to get unsuspecting investors to become interested in a stock, while those spreading the information sell previously purchased stock at an inflated price, this is called:
    a. cyber-smear
    b. fraudulent offerings of securities
    c. pump and dump
    d. illegal touting
    (Answer = c, page number 430)

32. A reverse pump and dump is when negative information is spread online about a stock driving down its price and allowing people to buy it at an artificially low price before rebuttals by the company's officers re-inflate the price. This is known as:
   a. illegal touting
   b. pump and dump
   c. cyber-smear
   d. fraudulent offerings of securities
   (Answer = c, page number 430)

33. When individuals make securities recommendations and fail to disclose that they are being paid to disseminate their favorable opinions, this is known as:
   a. fraudulent offerings of securities
   b. cyber-smear
   c. pump and dump
   d. illegal touting
   (Answer = d, page number 430)

34. When a person uses the Internet to steal someone's identity and/or impersonate them in order to open a new credit card account or conduct some other financial transaction, it is known as:
   a. identity theft
   b. cyber-smear
   c. pump and dump
   d. illegal touting
   (Answer = a, page number 430)

35. Schemes where investors are promised abnormally high profits, no investments are made, and only early investors are paid returns with investment money from later investors are known as:
   a. ponzi schemes
   b. pyramid schemes
   c. all of the above
   d. none of the above
   (Answer = c, page number 431)

36. The fraud attributable to the misrepresentation of a product advertised for sale through an Internet auction site or the non-delivery of merchandise or goods purchased through an Internet auction site is known as:
   a. non-delivery of goods/services
   b. pyramid schemes
   c. credit card theft
   d. online auction/retail
   (Answer = a, page number 432)

37. An organized crime group that profits from the sale of illegal goods and services, such as narcotics, pornography, and prostitution is participating in:
     a. entrepreneurship
     b. enterprise crime
     c. compliance
     d. a tying arrangement
     (Answer = b, page number 433)

38. A conspiratorial activity, involving the coordination of numerous persons in the planning and execution of illegal acts or in the pursuit of a legitimate objective by unlawful means is known as:
     a. enterprise
     b. a division of markets
     c. organized crime
     d. corporate crime
     (Answer = c, page number 434)

39. The view organized crime is made up of a national syndicate of 25 or so Italian - dominated crime families that call themselves La Cosa Nostra is known as:
     a. the alien conspiracy theory
     b. a division of markets
     c. the Sherman Antitrust Act
     d. a tying arrangement
     (Answer = a, page number 436)

40. In 1970, Congress passed the Organized Crime Act also known as:
     a. a division of markets
     b. arbitrage
     c. the Sherman Antitrust Act
     d. RICO
     (Answer = d, page number 437)

True/False

1. Exploitation involves taking money from contractors in return for awarding them contracts they could have won on merit.
     (Answer = false, page number 416)

2. The taking of kickbacks involves forcing victims to pay for services to which they have a clear right.
     (Answer = false, page number 416)

3. Blue-collar employees may be involved in systematic theft of company property, commonly called pilferage.
     (Answer = true, page number 418)

4. Bank fraud can encompass such diverse schemes as check kiting, check forgery, false statements on loan applications, sale of stolen checks, bank credit card fraud, unauthorized use of ATMs, auto title fraud, and illegal transactions with offshore banks.
(Answer = true, page number 419)

5. Affirmative tax evasion occurs when an individual fails to pay taxes or does not report all income.
(Answer = false, page numbers 420-421)

6. Group boycotts occur when an organization or company refuses to do business in a retail store that does not comply with its rules or desires.
(Answer = true, page number 423)

7. A division of markets involves a contract or conspiracy designed to stifle competition, create a monopoly, artificially maintain prices, or otherwise interfere with free market competition.
(Answer = false, page number 423)

8. A tying arrangement is where an organization or company boycotts retail stores that do not comply with its rules or desires.
(Answer = false, page number 423)

9. Price-fixing is a conspiracy to set and control the price of a necessary commodity.
(Answer = true, page number 423)

10. Deceptive pricing occurs when contractors provide the government or other corporations with incomplete or misleading information on how much it will actually cost to fulfill the contracts they are bidding on or use mischarges once they are signed.
(Answer = true, page number 423)

11. Phishing is the process of gathering identity information.
(Answer = true, page number 430)

12. Ponzi/Pyramid Schemes are the unauthorized use of a credit/debt card or credit/debt card number to fraudulently obtain money or property.
(Answer = false, page number 431)

13. When a computer is used to reprogram another for illicit purposes, it is known as the Trojan horse.
(Answer = true, page number 432)

14. Super-zapping is the process of enabling a computer system to issue checks to one's private account.
(Answer = true, page number 432)

15. The Mafia are a good example of current organized crime groups.
       (Answer = false, page number 434)

Essay Questions

1. Define white-collar crime. Compare and contrast Sutherland's original definition of white-collar crime with today's more updated definition.
       (page number 413)

2. Describe the various components of white-collar crime. What are the various types of crimes that individuals commit under the heading of white-collar crime?
       (page numbers 413-424)

3. What is the cause of white-collar crime? Do individuals commit white-collar crime for need or for greed and why?
       (page numbers 424-425)

4. Discuss the relatively new forms of cyber crime. How do control efforts differ from other forms of crime?
       (page numbers 429-433)

5. What are the characteristics of organized crime? How has it evolved over the years? What attempts have been made to control organized crime?
       (page numbers 433-440)

Chapter Thirteen

Public Order Crime

Summary

Chapter Thirteen discusses the various public order crimes. The chapter opens with a section on law and morality. A definition of homosexuality is provided with various attitudes towards the behavior and the current laws in our society. Deviant sexual activities are discussed with a section on prostitution. Pornography is included and the impact that it is having on our society. Finally, Chapter Thirteen discusses the use of drugs in our culture. Different drugs are examined with explanations of the various federal drug laws.

Chapter Objectives

After reading this chapter the student should be able to:

- Be familiar with the association between law and morality
- Be able to discuss the legal problems faced by gay people
- Know what is meant by paraphilias
- Be able to discuss the various types of prostitution
- Describe the relationship between obscenity and pornography
- Know the various techniques being used to control pornography
- Discuss the history and extent of drug abuse
- Be able to discuss the cause of substance abuse
- Describe the different types of drug users
- Identify the various drug control strategies

Chapter Overview

Introduction
Law and Morality
      Debating Morality
      Social Harm
      Moral Crusaders
Homosexuality
      Attitudes toward Homosexuality
      Homosexuality and the Law
      Is the Tide Turning?
Paraphilias
Prostitution

Chapter Outline

I. Introduction
II. Law and Morality
    A. Debating Morality
        1. So-called victimless crimes are prohibited because one of the functions of criminal law is to express a shared sense of public morality.
    B. Social Harm
        1. Immoral acts can be distinguished from crimes on the basis of the social harm they cause.
        2. Acts believed to be extremely harmful to the public are outlawed; those which only harm the actor are tolerated.
    C. Moral Crusaders
        1. Vigilantes - held a strict standard of morality that, when they caught their prey, swift justice resulted.

2. Moral crusaders/entrepreneurs - rule creators operating with an absolute certainty that their way is right and that any means are justified to get their way.
  a. take on issues such as prayer in school, the right to legal abortions, and the distribution of sexually explicit books and magazines.
  b. risk engaging in immoral conduct trying to protect society from those considered immoral.

III. **Homosexuality** - erotic interest in members of one's own sex.
  A. Homosexuality - an adult motivated by a definite preferential erotic attraction to members of the same sex and who usually (but not necessarily) engage in overt sexual relations with them.
    1. Today there are more than 600,000 gay partnerships.
  B. Attitudes toward Homosexuality
    1. Throughout history, homosexuals have been the subjects of discrimination, sanction, and violence.
    2. Sodomy - deviant sexual intercourse.
    3. Bible forbids homosexuality.
    4. Gay bashing remains a common occurrence around the world.
    5. Homophobia - extremely negative overreaction to homosexuals.
  C. Homosexuality and the Law
    1. No longer a crime in the U.S.
    2. Military - don't ask, don't tell policy.
  D. Is the Tide Turning?
    1. Increased social tolerance.
    2. Many support gays in the military, as well as equal housing, employment, inheritance rights, and social security benefits for same sex couples.
    3. *Lawrence v. Texas* (2003) - made it impermissible for states to criminalize oral and anal sex; prohibited sodomy, deviant sexuality, and buggery laws.

IV. **Paraphilias**
  A. Bizarre or abnormal sexual practices involving recurrent urges focused on:
    1. Nonhuman objects.
    2. Humiliation or the experience of receiving or giving pain.
    3. Children or others that cannot give consent.
    4. Outlawed sexual behavior includes:
      a. transvestite fetishism - wearing clothes normally worn by the opposite sex.
      b. asphyxiophilia - using a noose, ligature, plastic bag, mask, volatile chemicals, or chest compression, attempting partial asphyxia and oxygen deprivation to the brain to enhance sexual gratification.
      c. frotteurism - rubbing against or touching a nonconsenting person in a crowd, elevator, or other public place.

      d. voyeurism - obtaining sexual pleasure from spying on a stranger while they disrobe or engage in sexual behavior with another.

      e. exhibitionism - deriving sexual pleasures from exposing the genitals to surprise or shock a stranger.

      f. sadomasochism - deriving pleasure from receiving pain or inflicting pain on another.

      g. pedophilia - attaining sexual pleasure through sexual activity with prepubescent children.

V. Prostitution - the granting of nonmarital sexual access, established by mutual agreement of the prostitutes, their clients, and their employers for remuneration.

  A. Incidence of Prostitution

     1. UCR indicates that about 80,000 prostitution arrests are made annually.

  B. International Sex Trade

     1. Sex tourism - men from wealthy countries frequent needy nations in order to procure young girls forced or sold into prostitution.

     2. Estimated 50,000 women and children are imported into the U.S. yearly.

  C. Types of Prostitutes

     1. Streetwalkers - prostitutes working the streets in plain sight; also known as hustlers or hookers.

     2. Bar girls - called B-girls spend time in bars, drinking and waiting to be picked up by customers.

     3. Brothel prostitutes - bordellos, cathouses, sporting houses, and houses of ill repute; large establishments usually run by a madam that house several prostitutes.

     4. Call girls - aristocrats of prostitution; some net over $100,000 annually.

     5. Escort services/call houses

       a. escort services are usually fronts for prostitution rings.

       b. call houses - madams receive calls and arrange for prostitution service.

     6. Circuit travelers - groups of 2 or 3 traveling to lumber, labor, and agricultural camps.

     7. Skeezers - women who barter drugs for sex.

     8. Massage parlors/photo studios - oral sex and manual stimulation are common.

     9. Cyber prostitute - set up personal websites or put listings on web boards; then select client through e-mail messages and chats on-line.

  D. Becoming a Prostitute

     1. Prostitutes often come from troubled homes.

     2. Most prostitutes grew up with absent fathers.

     3. Conflict with school authorities, poor grades.

     4. Drug abuse.

     5. Psychological disturbance.

        6. Child sexual abuse and prostitution:
            a. initiated into sex by family members at age 10 to 12.
            b. many flee an abusive home.
            c. vulnerable on the street.
    E. Controlling Prostitution
        1. The federal Mann Act (1925) prohibited bringing women into the country or transporting them across state lines for the purpose of prostitution. Often called the "white slave act."
        2. Prostitution, today, is a misdemeanor punishable by a fine or a short jail sentence.
            a. illegal in all states but Nevada.
    F. Legalize Prostitution?
        1. Sexual equality view - considers the prostitute a victim of male dominance.
        2. Free choice view - prostitution, if freely chosen, expresses women's equality and is not a symptom of subjugation.
        3. Both positions argue that prostitution should be decriminalized.

VI. Pornography
    A. Obscenity - deeply offensive to morality or decency; designed to incite lust or depravity.
        1. Who is to judge what is obscene?
    B. Child pornography - estimated that each year over a million children are believed to be used in pornography or prostitution.
    C. Does pornography cause violence?
        1. Some studies indicate that viewing sexually explicit material actually has little effect on sexual violence.
        2. Violent pornography
            a. men exposed to violent pornography are more likely to act aggressively and hold aggressive attitudes toward women.
    D. Pornography and the law
        1. All states and the federal government prohibit the sale and production of pornographic material.
        2. Punishing obscenity creates moral and legal dilemmas.
            a. art or pornography.
            b. the 1st Amendment and a variety of cases protect people's right of free expression.
    E. Controlling Pornography - little evidence that it can be controlled or eliminated by legal means alone.
        1. Technological change - adult CD-ROMs, Internet sex services, obscene films via satellite.

VII. Substance Abuse
    A. 1.5 million drug-related arrests occur today.
    B. When Did Drug Use Begin? - has been around for thousands of years.
    C. Alcohol and Its Prohibition

1. Temperance movement - at the turn of the century was fueled by the belief that the purity of the U.S. agrarian culture was being destroyed by the growth of the city and the heavy drinkers therein.
2. 18th Amendment - 1919 - prohibited the sale of alcoholic beverages.
3. 21st Amendment - 1933 - repealed prohibition.

D. The Extent of Substance Abuse
   1. Monitoring the Future (MTF)
      a. annual self-report survey of drug abuse of high school students conducted by the Institute of Social Research (ISR) at the University of Michigan.
      b. nearly 50,000 high school students - 8th, 10th, and 12th grades.
      c. drug use declined from 1980 until 1990, increased until 1996, and currently has either stabilized or declined.
      d. marijuana is currently on the decrease.
      e. ecstasy use has been decreasing.
      f. alcohol use has stabilized.
   2. National Survey on Drug Use and Health (NSDUH)
      a. conducted by the Department of Health and Human Services.
      b. collects information from all U.S. residents of households, noninstitutional group quarters, and civilians living on military bases.
      c. about 8% of the population are current illicit drug users.
   3. National Center on Addiction and Substance Abuse (CASA) Survey
      a. show that alcohol abuse begins at an early age and remains a serious problem over the life course.
      b. 31.5% of high school students admit to binge drinking at least once a month.
   4. Are the Surveys Accurate?
      a. respondents may overreport, underreport, forget, or be unaware.
      b. significant population missing - those who are homeless, in prison, in drug rehab clinics, in AIDS clinics, and those who refuse to participate.
      c. surveys administered yearly so problems should be consistent.

E. AIDS and Drug Use
   1. Intravenous drug use closely linked to the threat of AIDS.
   2. About 1/4th of adult AIDS cases have occurred among IV drug users.

F. What Causes Substance Abuse?
   1. Subcultural view - lower-class problem.
      a. racial prejudice.
      b. devalued identities.
      c. low self-esteem.
      d. poor socioeconomic status.
      e. high level of mistrust, negativism, and deviance found in poor areas.
   2. Psychodynamic view - suggest that drugs help youth control or express unconscious needs and impulses.

a. drinking alcohol may reflect on oral fixation.

b. weak ego.

c. low frustration tolerance.

d. anxiety.

e. fantasies of omnipotence.

3. Genetic factors

a. people whose parents are substance abusers may have a greater chance of developing a problem than children of nonusers.

4. Social learning

a. drug abuse may result from observing parental drug use.

5. Problem Behavior Syndrome (PBS) - for some substance abuse is one of many social problems.

6. Rational choice - some use drugs and alcohol to enjoy the effects.

G. Is There a Drug Gateway?

1. Most people fall into drug abuse slowly, beginning with alcohol and following with marijuana (the gateway drugs) and then more serious drugs.

H. Types of Drug Users

1. Adolescents who distribute small amounts of drugs - stash dealers.

2. Adolescents who frequently sell drugs.

3. Teenage drug dealers who commit other delinquent acts.

4. Adolescents who cycle in and out of the justice system.

5. Drug-involved youth who continue to commit crimes as adults.

6. Outwardly respectable adults who are top-level dealers.

7. Smugglers - import drugs into the United States.

a. generally men, middle-aged with strong organizational skills, established connections, capital to invest and a willingness to take large business risks.

8. Adult predatory drug users who are frequently arrested.

a. getting arrested, doing time, using multiple drugs, and committing predatory crimes are a way of life.

b. become street junkies.

9. Adult predatory drug users who are rarely arrested.

a. commit hundreds of crime each year and are rarely arrested.

b. sometimes referred to as stabilized junkies.

10. Less predatory drug-involved adult offenders.

a. petty criminals who avoid violent crime.

11. Women who are drug-involved offenders

a. often involved in prostitution and low-level drug dealing.

I. Drugs and Crime - research shows association between drug use and crime.

1. User surveys - show that people who take drugs have extensive involvement in crime.

2. Surveys of known criminals - testing known criminals to determine the extent of their substance abuse.

a. 80% of prison inmates are lifelong substance abusers.

3. The drug-crime connection

> a. police may apprehend muddle-headed substance abusers than clear-thinking abstainers.
>
> b. most criminals are substance abusers.
>
> c. drug use weakens the social bond that leads to antisocial behavior.

J. Drugs and the Law

1. Pure Food and Drug Act - 1906 - required manufacturers to list the amounts of habit-forming drugs in products on the labels, but did not restrict their use.

2. Harrison Narcotics Act - 1914 - restricted importation, manufacture, sale, and dispensing of narcotics.

   a. 1922 - revised to allow importation of opium and coca leaves for qualified medical practitioners.

3. Marijuana Tax Act - 1937 - required registration and tax payment by all that imported, sold, or manufactured marijuana.

4. Boggs Act of 1951 - provided mandatory sentences for violating federal drug laws.

5. Durham-Humphrey Act of 1951 - made it illegal to dispense barbiturates and amphetamines without a prescription.

6. Narcotic Control Act of 1956 - increased penalties for drug offenders.

7. Drug Abuse Control Act - 1965 - set up stringent guidelines for the legal use and sale of mood-modifying drugs.

8. Comprehensive Drug Abuse Prevention and Control Act - 1970 - set up unified categories of illegal drugs and associated penalties with their sale, manufacture, or possession.

9. 1984 Controlled Substances Act - set new, stringent penalties for drug dealers.

10. The Anti-Drug Abuse Act of 1986 - set new standards for minimum and maximum sentences for drug offenders.

11. Anti-Drug Abuse Act of 1988 - created national drug policy under a "drug czar," set treatment an prevention priorities and imposed the death penalty for drug-related killings.

K. Drug Control Strategies

1. Source control - deter drug sale and importation through the apprehension of dealers and enforcing laws with heavy penalties.

2. Interdiction strategies - using Border Patrol and military personnel to intercept drug suppliers as they enter the country.

3. Law enforcement strategies - local, state and federal law enforcement agencies fighting actively against drugs.

4. Punishment strategies - courts can severely punish known drug dealers and traffickers.

5. Community strategies - citizens and local community groups fighting against drugs.

   a. law enforcement type efforts - block watches, cooperative police-community efforts, and citizen patrols.

   b. civil justice system - to harass offenders.

   c. community-based treatment efforts - citizen volunteers
      participate in self-help support programs like NA or
      Cocaine Anonymous.
   d. activities to enhance the quality of life improve interpersonal
      relationships and upgrade the neighborhood's physical
      environment.
  6. Drug-testing programs - employees, government workers, and criminal
    offenders; is believed to deter substance abuse.
  7. Treatment Strategies.
   a. treatment programs.
   b. detoxification units.
   c. therapeutic programs.
  8. Employment programs - research indicates that abusers who obtain and
    keep employment will end or reduce the incidence of their
    substance abuse.
 L. Drug Legalization - or decriminalization of restricted drugs.
  1. The government would control price and distribution.
  2. The consequences of legalization:
   a. short-term effect would reduce the association of drug use and
     crime.
   b. might increase the nation's rate of drug usage.
   c. drug users might increase their daily intake.
  3. The lesson of alcohol - the problems of alcoholism should serve as a
    warning of what can happen when controlled substances are made
    readily available.

VIII. Summary

Key Terms

Brothel - A house of prostitution, typically run by a madam who sets prices and handles
  "business" arrangements.

Call Girls - Prostitutes who made dates via the phone and then service customers in hotel
  rooms or apartments. Call girls typically have a steady clientele who are repeat
  customers.

Gateway Model - An explanation of drug abuse that posits that users begin with a more
  benign drug (alcohol or marijuana) and progress to ever-more potent drugs.

Gay Bashing - Violent hate crimes directed toward people because of their sexual
  orientation.

Homophobia - Extremely negative overreaction to homosexuals.

Homosexuality - Erotic interest in members of one's own sex.

Madam - A woman who employs prostitutes, supervises their behavior, and receives a
  fee for her services.

Moral Crusaders - People who strive to stamp out behavior they find objectionable.
  Typically, moral crusades are directed at public order crimes, such as drug abuse
  or pornography.

Obscenity - According to current legal theory, sexually explicit material that lacks a serious purpose and appeals solely to the prurient interest of the viewer. While nudity per se is not usually considered obscene, open sexual behavior, masturbation, and exhibition of the genitals is banned in most communities.

Paraphilias - Bizarre or abnormal sexual practices that may involve recurrent sexual urges focused on objects, humiliation, or children.

Pornography - Sexually explicit books, magazines, films, or tapes intended to provide sexual titillation and excitement for paying customers.

Prostitution - The granting of nonmarital sexual access for remuneration.

Public Order Crimes - Acts that are considered illegal because they threaten the general well-being of society and challenge its accepted moral principles. Prostitution, drug use, and the sale of pornography are considered public order crimes.

Skeezers - Prostitutes who trade sex for drugs, usually crack.

Social Harm - A view that behaviors harmful to other people and society in general must be controlled. These acts are usually outlawed, but some acts that cause enormous amounts of social harm are perfectly legal, such as the consumption of tobacco and alcohol.

Sodomy - Illegal sexual intercourse. Sodomy has no single definition, and acts included within its scope are usually defined by state statute.

Temperance Movement - An effort to prohibit the sale of liquor in the United States that resulted in the passage of the Eighteenth Amendment to the Constitution in 1919, which prohibited the sale of alcoholic beverages.

Victimless Crimes - Crimes that violate the moral order but in which there is no actual victim or target. In these crimes, which include drug abuse and sex offenses, it is society as a whole and not an individual who is considered the victim.

Vigilantes - Individuals who go on moral crusades without any authorization from legal authorities. The assumption is that it is okay to take matters into your own hands if the cause is right and the target is immoral.

Discussion Exercises

1. Look at the statutes concerning various drugs. Have the class debate the issue of legalizing any or all types of drugs. Are the penalties currently in place appropriate? Why or why not?

2. Although this chapter reports an increased tolerance towards gays (for example, in the military and in housing rights), the November 2004 elections saw citizens in a number of states supporting amendments defining the family as a heterosexual union only. How can we resolve these contradictory views on homosexuals and what ramifications does it have for the criminal justice system?

3. Divide the class into two sections. Have one argue in favor of decriminalizing prostitution and the other argue against decriminalization. Obviously, key points in favor of decriminalization will include the ability to monitor the health status of the prostitutes, to generate tax dollars for the community, and to provide a safer working environment

for the prostitutes. Key points against decriminalization will include the possibility of youth being exposed to information on sexuality at a younger age, a disconnection between sex and love, and a general acceptance of sexual promiscuity in society.

InfoTrac Assignment

GETTING STARTED: Search term words for subject guide: Morality, Homosexuality, Paraphilias, Prostitution, Pornography, Substance Abuse, Alcohol, Drugs.

CRITICAL THINKING PROJECT: Using the search term "Prostitution," find relevant articles.

Here are three articles:

Nelson, William F. "Prostitution: A community solution alternative." *Corrections Today*.

Re, Richard. "A Persisting Evil: The global problem of slavery." *Harvard International Review*.

Sloss, Christine M. and Gary W. Harper. "When Street Sex Workers are Mothers." *Archives of Sexual Behavior*.

Test Bank

Fill in the Blank

1. Acts that are considered illegal because they threaten the general well-being of society and challenge its accepted moral principles are known as **public order crimes**.
   (page number 448)

2. **Victimless crimes** are crimes that violate the moral order but in which there is no actual victim or target.
   (page number 448)

3. Interest groups that attempt to control social life and the legal order to promote their own personal set of moral values are referred to as **moral crusaders**.
   (page number 450)

4. Deviant sexual intercourse is called **sodomy**.
   (page number 451)

5. **Homophobia** is an extremely negative overreaction to homosexuals.
   (page number 451)

6. **Paraphilias** are bizarre or abnormal sexual practices involving recurrent sexual urges.
   (page number 453)

7. **Transvestite fetishism** is wearing clothes normally worn by the opposite sex.
   (page number 453)
8. **Frotteurism** involves rubbing against or touching a nonconsenting person in a crowd, elevator, or other public area.
   (page number 453)

9. Obtaining sexual pleasure from spying on a stranger while he or she disrobes or engages in sexual behavior with another is known as **voyeurism**.
   (page number 453)

10. **Exhibitionism** is deriving sexual pleasure from exposing the genitals to surprise or shock a stranger.
    (page number 453)

11. **Prostitution** is the granting of nonmarital sexual access, established by mutual agreement, for renumeration.
    (page number 454)

12. Women who barter sex for drugs are called **skeezers**.
    (page number 455)

13. **Pornography** is material that is used to provide sexual titillation and excitement for paying customers.
   (page number 459)

14. **Obscenity** is sexually explicit material that lacks a serious purpose and appeals solely to the interest of the viewer.
   (page number 459)

15. The **temperance movement** was an effort to prohibit the sale of liquor in the United States that resulted in the passage of the 18th Amendment to the Constitution in 1919.
   (page number 463)

Multiple Choice

1. Acts that are considered illegal because they threaten the general well-being of society and challenge its accepted moral principles are known as:
   a. obscenities
   b. larcenies
   c. burglaries
   d. public order crimes
   (Answer = d, page number 448)

2. Which of the following are public-order crimes?
   a. prostitution
   b. drug use
   c. all of the above
   d. none of the above
   (Answer = c, page number 448)

3. Crimes that violate the moral order but in which there is no actual victim or target are known as:
   a. victimless crimes
   b. moral crusades
   c. larcenies
   d. burglaries
   (Answer = a, page number 448)

4. Interest groups that attempt to control social life and the legal order in order to promote their own personal set of moral values are known as:
   a. addicts
   b. call girls
   c. skeezers
   d. moral entrepreneurs
   (Answer = d, page number 450)

5. Efforts by interest-group members to stamp out behavior they find objectionable is known as:
    a. gay bashing
    b. moral crusades
    c. obscenities
    d. the temperance movement
    (Answer = b, page number 450)

6. Erotic interest in members of one's own sex is known as:
    a. prostitution
    b. pornography
    c. obscenity
    d. homosexuality
    (Answer = d, page number 451)

7. Violent acts directed at people because of their sexual orientation are known as:
    a. gay bashing
    b. corporate crimes
    c. insider trading
    d. tying arrangements
    (Answer = a, page number 451)

8. Extremely negative overreaction to homosexuals is referred to as:
    a. homosexuality
    b. racism
    c. sexism
    d. homophobia
    (Answer = d, page number 451)

9. Bizarre or abnormal sexual practices involving recurrent sexual urges are known as:
    a. homosexuals
    b. paraphilias
    c. call girls
    d. prostitution
    (Answer = b, page number 453)

10. Sex that involves unwilling or underage victims is known as:
    a. voyeurism
    b. sadomasochism
    c. pedophila
    d. paraphilia
    (Answer = d, page number 453)

11. Wearing clothing normally worn by the opposite sex is known as:
    a. asphyxiophilia
    b. transvestite fetishism
    c. frotteurism
    d. voyeurism
    (Answer = b, page number 453)

12. Using something to induce oxygen deprivation to the brain to enhance sexual gratification is known as:
    a. transvestite fetishism
    b. frotteurism
    c. asphyxiophilia
    d. voyeurism
    (Answer = c, page number 453)

13. Obtaining sexual pleasure from spying on a stranger while he or she disrobes or engages in sexual behavior with another is known as:
    a. transvestite fetishism
    b. frotteurism
    c. asphyxiophilia
    d. voyeurism
    (Answer = d, page number 453)

14. Deriving sexual pleasure from exposing the genitals to surprise or shock a stranger is known as:
    a. transvestite fetishism
    b. asphyxiophilia
    c. voyeurism
    d. exhibitionism
    (Answer = d, page number 453)

15. Deriving pleasure from receiving pain or inflicting pain on another is known as:
    a. transvestite fetishism
    b. voyeurism
    c. sadomasochism
    d. pedophila
    (Answer = c, page number 453)

16. Attaining sexual pleasure through sexual activity with prepubescent children is known as:
    a. transvestite fetishism
    b. voyeurism
    c. sadomasochism
    d. pedophila
    (Answer = d, page number 453)

17. Streetwalkers are also referred to as:
    a. hustlers
    b. hookers
    c. all of the above
    d. none of the above
    (Answer = c, page number 454)

18. Prostitutes who work the streets in plain sight of police, citizens, and customers are referred to as:
    a. streetwalkers
    b. hustlers
    c. hookers
    d. all of the above
    (Answer = d, page number 454)

19. Girls who spend their time in bars, drinking and waiting to be picked up by customers are referred to as:
    a. streetwalkers
    b. hustlers
    c. bar girls
    d. hookers
    (Answer = c, page number 455)

20. Large establishments usually run by a madam that houses several prostitutes is known as a:
    a. brothel
    b. bordello
    c. cathouse
    d. all of the above
    (Answer = d, page number 455)

21. A relatively new form of prostitution that combines brothels with call girl rings is known as:
    a. skeezers
    b. bar girls
    c. escort services
    d. call houses
    (Answer = d, page number 455)

22. A woman who employs prostitutes, supervises their behavior, and receives a fee for her services is known as a:
    a. prostitute
    b. madam
    c. call girl
    d. skeezer
    (Answer = b, page number 455)

23. Prostitutes who service upper-class customers and earn large sums of money are known as:
     a. streetwalkers
     b. call girls
     c. skeezers
     d. drug addicts
     (Answer = b, page number 455)

24. The aristocrats of prostitution are called:
     a. madams
     b. skeezers
     c. call girls
     d. bar girls
     (Answer = c, page number 455)

25. Prostitutes who move around in groups of two or three to lumber, labor, and agricultural camps are called:
     a. bar girls
     b. call girls
     c. circuit travelers
     d. skeezers
     (Answer = c, page number 455)

26. Women who barter drugs for sex are known as:
     a. bar girls
     b. circuit travelers
     c. skeezers
     d. call girls
     (Answer = c, page number 455)

27. The base of some prostitutes where they offer massages and some prostitution services for sale is known as:
     a. street corners
     b. brothels
     c. massage parlors
     d. none of the above
     (Answer = c, page number 456)

28. The 1925 federal Act which prohibited bringing women into the country or transporting them across state lines for the purposes of prostitution is known as the:
     a. Mann Act
     b. temperance movement
     c. moral crusades
     d. Sherman Antitrust Act
     (Answer = a, page number 458)

29. Material that is used to provide sexual titillation for paying customers is known as:
   a. homosexuality
   b. sodomy
   c. paraphilia
   d. pornography
   (Answer = d, page number 459)

30. According to current legal theory, sexually explicit material that lacks a serious purpose and appeals solely to the interest of the viewer is known as:
   a. obscenity
   b. homosexuality
   c. the Mann Act
   d. the Sherman Antitrust Act
   (Answer = a, page number 459)

31. Research indicates that each year, approximately how many children are used in pornography or prostitution?
   a. 25,000
   b. 50,000
   c. 500,000
   d. 1 million
   (Answer = d, page number 460)

32. Which Amendment protects free speech and prohibits police agencies from limiting the public's right of free expression?
   a. 1st
   b. 4th
   c. 5th
   d. 6th
   (Answer = a, page number 460)

33. How many drug-related arrests occur each year?
   a. 500,000
   b. 1.5 million
   c. 5 million
   d. 15 million
   (Answer = b, page number 463)

34. An effort to prohibit the sale of liquor in the United States that resulted in the passage of the 18th Amendment to the Constitution in 1919 is known as the:
   a. war on drugs
   b. rehabilitation movement
   c. Vietnam era
   d. temperance movement
   (Answer = d, page number 463)

35. Which Amendment prohibited the sale of alcoholic beverages?
    a. 1st
    b. 5th
    c. 14th
    d. 18th
    (Answer = d, page number 465)

36. Which Amendment repealed prohibition?
    a. 1st
    b. 5th
    c. 18th
    d. 21st
    (Answer = d, page number 465)

37. Which of the following is considered a gateway drug?
    a. alcohol
    b. marijuana
    c. all of the above
    d. none of the above
    (Answer = c, page number 469)

38. According to Tunnell, dealers who sold drugs to maintain a consistent access to drugs for their own consumption are known as:
    a. stash dealers
    b. front dealers
    c. drug-involved dealers
    d. none of the above
    (Answer = a, page number 469)

39. What percentage of violent crimes and fatal motor vehicle accidents involve alcohol?
    a. 10%
    b. 20%
    c. 30%
    d. 40%
    (Answer = d, page number 472)

40. Surveys indicate that _____ of prison inmates are lifelong substance abusers.
    a. 20%
    b. 40%
    c. 60%
    d. 80%
    (Answer = d, page number 472)

True/False

1. The military does not ban openly gay people from serving.
    (Answer = false, page number 452)

2. A significant majority of Americans now support equality in employment, housing, inheritance rights, and Social Security benefits for same-sex couples.
    (Answer = true, page number 452)

3. Asphyxiophilia is the wearing of clothes normally worn by the opposite sex.
    (Answer = false, page number 453)

4. Frotteurism is the rubbing against or touching of a nonconsenting person in a crowd, elevator, or other public place.
    (Answer = true, page number 453)

5. Voyeurism is obtaining sexual pleasure from spying on a stranger while he or she disrobes or engages in sexual behavior with another.
    (Answer = true, page number 453)

6. Prostitutes who work the streets in plain sight of police are called call girls.
    (Answer = false, page number 454)

7. Girls who spend their time in bars, drinking and waiting to be picked up by customers are called streetwalkers.
    (Answer = false, page number 455)

8. Brothels are large establishments, usually run by madams, that house several prostitutes.
    (Answer = true, page number 455)

9. Prostitutes known as circuit travelers move around in groups of two or three to lumber, labor, and agricultural camps.
    (Answer = true, page number 455)

10. Women who barter drugs for sex are called teasers.
    (Answer = false, page number 455)

11. According to the NSDUH, approximately 20 percent of Americans aged 12 or older are current illicit drug users.
    (Answer = false, page number 466)

12. Nearly one-third of high school students admit to binge drinking at least once a month.
    (Answer = true, page number 466)

13. Girls with boyfriends 2 or more years older are more likely to drink than girls whose boyfriends are less than 2 years older or who do not have a boyfriend.
   (Answer = true, page number 466)

14. About one-fourth of all adult AIDS cases have occurred among IV drug users.
   (Answer = true, page number 468)

15. Cocaine has been labeled a gateway drug.
   (Answer = false, page number 469)

Essay Questions

1. What is the correct definition of homosexuality? What is the origin and history of homosexuality? Describe the various attitudes towards homosexuality in our society.
   (page numbers 451-452)

2. Who are paraphilias? What are the various crimes that fall under the category of paraphilia? How should policy makers handle these types of crimes?
   (page numbers 452-453)

3. Define prostitution. What is the origin and history of prostitution? Debate the various aspects of legalizing prostitution.
   (page numbers 453-459)

4. What is pornography? What are the dangers of pornography? Does pornography cause violence in our society?
   (page numbers 459-462)

5. What is the extent of substance abuse in the U.S.? How has the legal system responded to drug users?
   (page numbers 462-478)

Chapter Fourteen

The Criminal Justice System

Summary

Chapter Fourteen examines the criminal justice system. The chapter begins with the origins of the criminal justice system and its development into the system that is operating today. The various components are described and the process of going through the system is outlined in detail. An analysis of criminal justice and the rule of law are explained in detail. The various models of justice are explained and Chapter Fourteen concludes with the concepts of justice today.

Chapter Objectives

After reading this chapter the student should be able to:

- Be familiar with the history of the criminal justice system
- Be familiar with the various stages in the process of justice
- Understand how criminal justice is shaped by the rule of law
- Know the elements of the crime control model
- Know what is meant by the justice model
- Discuss the elements of due process
- Be able to argue the merits of the rehabilitation model
- Understand the concept of nonintervention
- Know the elements of the restorative justice model

Chapter Overview

Introduction
Origins of the American Criminal Justice System
What Is the Criminal Justice System?
Policy and Practice in Criminology: The Juvenile Justice System in the New Millennium
The Process of Justice
      Going through the Justice Process
Criminal Justice and the Rule of Law
Concepts of Justice
      Crime Control Model
      Justice Model
      Due Process Model
      Rehabilitation Model
      Nonintervention Model

Restorative Justice Model
Concepts of Justice Today
Summary

Chapter Outline

I. Introduction
II. Origins of the American Criminal Justice System
    A. Early Origins of American Justice
        1. Common criminal justice agencies have existed for about 150 years.
        2. 1931 - President Hoover appointed National Commission of Law Observance and Enforcement, known today as Wickersham Commission.
            a. analyzed the American justice system.
            b. helped usher in era of treatment of rehabilitation.
    B. The Modern Era of Justice
        1. American Bar Association explored some of the hidden or low-visibility processes of justice operations.
            a. showed how informal decision-making and use of discretion are essential to the justice process.
            b. 1967 - President's Commission on Law Enforcement and Administration of Justice - published report titled The Challenge of Crime in a Free Society.
                i. resulted in Congress passing the Safe Streets and Crime Control Act of 1968 - provided federal funds for state and local crime control.
                ii. funded the Law Enforcement Assistance Administration - provided money to local and state agencies.
III. What is the Criminal Justice System? - agencies of government charged with enforcing law, adjudicating crime, and correcting criminal conduct; an instrument of social control.
    A. Contemporary Criminal Justice System
        1. Costs federal, state, and local governments about $150 billion per year for civil and criminal justice.
        2. Employs over 2 million people in over 55,000 agencies.
        3. It costs $70,000 to build a prison cell.
        4. It costs about $22,000 per year to house an adult inmate, $30,000 per year to house a juvenile inmate.
        5. More than 13.5 million people are arrested each year.
        6. Almost 7 million people are now under the control of the correctional system, with 2 million men and women in the nation's jails and prisons.
        7. Although there is less crime, people are more likely to be convicted and if sent to jail or prison to serve more of their sentence.

IV. The Process of Justice - series of decision points through which offenders flow; assembly-line justice.

A. Initial Contact - police may observe a crime or conduct an investigation where the offender comes into conduct with the justice system through the police.

B. Investigation - after a crime, police gather sufficient facts or evidence to identify the perpetrator, justify an arrest, and bring the offender to trial.

C. Arrest - police take a person into custody for allegedly committing a crime.
    1. Arrests are legal when:
        a. officer believes there is sufficient evidence (probable cause) that a crime has been committed and the suspect committed the crime.
        b. officer deprives the individual of freedom.
        c. suspect believes to be in custody of police and cannot voluntarily leave.

D. Custody - after arrest, suspect remains in police custody.
    1. Taken to police station.
    2. Booking - fingerprinted, photographed, and personal information recorded.
    3. Identification by witnesses in a lineup.
    4. Interrogation by police.

E. Complaint/Charging - with sufficient evidence, police turn case to prosecutor. Decision made to file complaint for court to have authority over case. Prosecutor determines the charges.

F. Preliminary Hearing/Grand Jury - constitution mandates that before standing trial for a serious crime, the state must prove probable cause that the accused committed the criminal act.
    1. Grand jury - group of citizens brought together to consider the case in a closed hearing where the prosecutor presents evidence. With sufficient evidence, grand jury issues a "true bill of indictment" - the accused must stand trial.
    2. Preliminary hearing - or probable cause hearing - prosecutor files a charging document called an information - hearing is then held to determine if there is sufficient evidence to actually try the case.

G. Arraignment - the accused is brought for the first time where they are informed of the charges against them, informed of their constitutional rights, have their bail considered, and have their trial date set.

H. Bail or Detention - a money bond, the amount of which is set by judicial authority; intended to ensure the defendant appears at trial while allowing freedom until that time.

I. Plea Bargaining - after arraignment, prosecution may offer the defense a possible guilty arrangement. The defendant agrees to plead guilty for reduced charges, a lenient sentence, or another consideration.

J. Trial/Adjudication - with no plea-bargain, defendant goes to trial. A full-scale inquiry into the facts of the case before a judge, a jury, or both. Defendant will be found either:

1. Guilty.
2. Not guilty.
3. Hung jury - when the jury fails to reach a decision; the case is then unresolved and open for possible retrial.
K. Disposition - guilty defendants are sentenced by the presiding judge. Dispositions may include a fine, community service, probation, incarceration, or death.
L. Postconviction Remedies - after disposition, defendants may appeal if they feel they were treated unfairly. If the court agrees, the defendant may be granted a new trial or possible release.
M. Correctional Treatment - offenders who are found guilty and are formally sentenced come under the jurisdiction of correction authorities.
N. Release - at the end of the correctional sentence, offenders are released into society.
O. Postrelease/Aftercare - some offenders are released to community correctional centers - to bridge the gap between a secure treatment facility an absolute freedom.
P. Going through the Justice Process
    1. Every stage of the process decisions are made whether to send the case further down the line.
    2. Decisions transform identities of individuals from an accused, to a defendant, to a convicted criminal, to an inmate, to an ex-con.
    3. Decision-making and discretion mark each stage of the system.
    4. Criminal justice system acts like a funnel in which the majority of cases are screened out before trial.
    5. Celebrity cases:
        a. receive a great deal of attention.
        b. courtroom work group - judges, prosecutors, and public defenders work together to keep the system flowing.
        c. "bargain justice" occurs in more than 90% of cases.

V. Criminal Justice and the Rule of Law
A. Hands-Off Doctrine - U.S. courts exercised little control over the operations of criminal justice agencies.
B. 1960's - under Chief Justice Earl Warren, U.S. Supreme Court became more active in the affairs of the justice system.
C. Law of Criminal Procedure - sets out and guarantees citizens certain rights and privileges when accused of a crime.
D. Procedural laws - control the actions of the agencies of justice and define the rights of criminal defendants.
    1. Most important source is the U.S. Constitution, specifically the first 10 amendments called the Bill of Rights.
    2. 14th Amendment - 1868 - made the first 10 amendments binding on the state governments.
E. Exclusionary Rule - illegally seized evidence cannot be used during a trial.
F. If Supreme Court has ruled on a procedural issue, lower court must follow; if not, lower courts are free to interpret the Constitution.

VI. Concepts of Justice

A. Crime Control Model - crime rates trend upwards when criminals do not sufficiently fear apprehension and punishment.
 1. If justice became efficient, then the criminal law would be toughened, and crime rates would decline.
 2. Expensive.
 3. Purpose of justice:
    a. protect the public.
    b. deter criminal behavior.
    c. incapacitate known criminals.
 4. Emphasizes protecting society and compensating victims.
 5. Crime control policies:
    a. became dominant in 1960's and 1970's.
    b. some states have recently enacted stiffer penalties for crimes.
    c. research indicates that strict crime control measures can have a deterrent effect.

B. Justice Model
 1. Most concerned about the presence of unequal treatment in the justice system.
 2. Concerned with racism and discrimination - which causes sentencing disparity and unequal treatment before the law.
 3. Calls for the adoption of sentencing policies, which require all offenders who commit the same type of crime, receive the same sentence (determinate sentencing).

C. Due Process Model
 1. Civil rights of the accused should be protected at all times.
 2. Requires practices such as strict scrutiny of police search and interrogation practices.
 3. Competent defense counsel, jury trials and other procedural safeguards be offered to every criminal defendant.
 4. Has not fared well with recent Supreme Court decisions expanding police ability to search and seize evidence.

D. Rehabilitation Model
 1. Believes that given proper care and treatment, criminals can be changed into productive, law-abiding citizens.
 2. Believes people commit crimes because they are victims of social injustice, poverty, and racism.
 3. Favors programs to help disadvantaged people who commit crime.
 4. Rehabilitation within the System:
    a. efforts should be made to treat criminals, rather than punish them.
    b. also known as Medical Model - view of dispensing "treatment" to needy "patients."
    c. effective treatment can make a significant difference in reducing offender recidivism.

E. Nonintervention Model
    1. When possible, justice agencies should limit their involvement with criminal defendants.
    2. Noninterventionists are fearful of the harmful effects of stigma and negative labels.
    3. Want to decriminalize (reduce penalties) and/or legalize non-serious victimless crimes such as small amounts of marijuana, public drunkenness, and vagrancy.
    4. Want non-violent offenders removed from the correctional system - deinstitutionalization.
    5. Want first offenders of minor crimes to be placed in informal, community-based treatment programs - pretrial diversion.
F. Restorative Justice Model
    1. Belief that the purpose of the criminal justice system is to promote a peaceful, just society.
    2. Advocate peacemaking, not punishment.
    3. Violent punishing acts of the state are similar to the violent acts of individuals.
    4. Mutual aid rather than coercive punishment is key.

VII. Concepts of Justice Today
A. Today, crime control and justice models have the support of the public and legislatures.

VIII. Summary

Key Terms

Appeal - Taking a criminal case to a higher court on the grounds that the defendant was found guilty because of legal error or violation of constitutional rights; a successful appeal may result in a new trial.

Arraignment - The step in the criminal justice process at which the accused are read the charges against them, asked how they plead, and advised of their rights. Possible pleas are guilty, not guilty, *nolo contendere*, and not guilty by reason of insanity.

Arrest - The taking of a person into the custody of the law, the legal purpose of which is to restrain the accused until he or she can be held accountable for the offense at court proceedings. The legal requirement for an arrest is probable cause. Arrests for investigation, suspicion, or harassment are improper and of doubtful legality. The police have the responsibility to use only the reasonable physical force necessary to make an arrest. The summons has been used as a substitute for arrest.

Bail - The monetary amount for or condition of pretrial release, normally set by a judge at the initial appearance. The purpose of bail is to ensure the return of the accused at subsequent proceedings. If the accused is unable to make bail, he or she is detained in jail. The Eighth Amendment provides that excessive bail shall not be required.

Bill of Rights - The first ten amendments to the U.S. Constitution.

Booking - Fingerprinting, photographing, and recording of personal information of a suspect in police custody.

Complaint - A sworn allegation made in writing to a court or judge that an individual is guilty of some designated (complained of) offense. This is often the first legal document filed regarding a criminal offense. The complaint can be "taken out" by the victim, the police officer, the district attorney, or another interested party. Although the complaint charges an offense, an indictment or information may be the formal charging document.

Courtroom Work Group - All the parties in the adversarial process who work together to settle cases with the least amount of effort and conflict.

Crime Control Model - A model of criminal justice that emphasizes the control of dangerous offenders and the protection of society. Its advocates call for harsh punishments, such as the death penalty, as a deterrent to crime.

Criminal Justice System - The agencies of government - police, courts, and corrections - responsible for apprehending, adjudicating, sanctioning, and treating criminal offenders.

Criminal Trial - A full-scale inquiry into the facts of the case before a judge, a jury, or both.

Determinate Sentences - Fixed terms of incarceration, such as 3 years' imprisonment. Determinate sentences are felt by many to be too restrictive for rehabilitative purposes; the advantage is that offenders know how much time they have to serve - that is, when they will be released.

Discretion - The use of personal decision making by those carrying out police, judicial, and sanctioning functions within the criminal justice system.

Disposition - For juvenile offenders, the equivalent of sentencing for adult offenders. The theory is that disposition is more rehabilitative than retributive. Possible dispositions may be to dismiss the case, release the youth to custody of his or her parents, place the offender on probation, or send him or her to a correctional institution. For adult defendants found guilty, sentencing usually involves a fine, probation, and/or incarceration.

Due Process Model - View that focuses on protecting the civil rights of those accused of crime.

Exclusionary Rule - The principle that prohibits using evidence illegally obtained in a trial. Based on the Fourth Amendment "right of the people to be secure in their persons, houses, papers, and effects, against unreasonable searches and seizures," the rule is not a bar to prosecution, as legally obtained evidence may be used in a trial.

Grand Jury - A group (usually consisting of twenty-three citizens) chosen to hear testimony in secret and to issue formal criminal accusations (indictments). It also serves an investigatory function.

Hands-Off Doctrine - The judicial policy of not interfering in the administrative affairs of a prison.

Hung Jury - A jury that cannot reach a decision in a criminal case. If a jury is hung, the prosecution can retry the case.

Incarceration - Confinement in jail or prison.

Indictment - A written accusation returned by a grand jury charging an individual with a specified crime, based on the prosecutor's presentation of probable cause.

Information - Like an indictment, a formal charging document. The prosecuting attorney makes out the information and files it in court. Probable cause is determined at the preliminary hearing, which, unlike grand jury proceedings, is public and attended by the accused and his or her attorney.

Interrogation - The questioning of a suspect in police custody.

Justice Model - A philosophy of corrections that stresses determinate sentences, abolition of parole, and the view that prisons are places of punishment and not rehabilitation.

Law of Criminal Procedure - Judicial proceedings that define and guarantee the rights of criminal defendants and control the various components of the criminal justice system.

Lineup - Witnesses may be brought in to view the suspect in a group of people with similar characteristics and asked to pick out the suspect.

Nonintervention Model - The view that arresting and labeling offenders does more harm than good, that youthful offenders in particular should be diverted into informal treatment programs, and that minor offenses should be decriminalized.

Plea Bargaining - The discussion between the defense counsel and the prosecution by which the accused agrees to plead guilty for certain considerations. The advantage to the defendant may be a reduction of the charges, a lenient sentence, or (in the case of multiple charges) dropped charges. The advantage to the prosecution is that a conviction is obtained without the time and expense of lengthy trial proceedings.

Preliminary Hearing - The step at which criminal charges initiated by an information are tested for probable cause; the prosecution presents enough evidence to establish probable cause - that is, a *prima facie* case. The hearing is public and may be attended by the accused and his or her attorney.

Presentencing Investigation - An investigation performed by a probation officer attached to a trial court after the conviction of a defendant. The report contains information about the defendant's background, education, previous employment, and family; his or her own statement concerning the offense; the person's prior criminal record; interviews with neighbors or acquaintances; and his or her mental and physical condition (that is, information that would not be made part of the record in the case of a guilty plea or that would be inadmissible as evidence at a trial but could be influential and important at the sentencing stage). After conviction, a judge sets a date for sentencing (usually 10 days to 2 weeks from the date of conviction), during which time the presentence report is made. The report is required in felony cases in federal courts and in many states, is optional with the judge in some states, and in others is mandatory before convicted offenders can be placed on probation. In the case of juvenile offenders. The presentence report is also known as a social history report.

Probable Cause - The evidentiary criterion necessary to sustain an arrest or the issuance of an arrest or search warrant; less than absolute certainty or "beyond a reasonable doubt" but greater than mere suspicion or hunch. A set of facts, information, circumstances, or conditions that would lead a reasonable person to believe that an offense was committed and that the accused committed that offense. An arrest made without probable cause may be susceptible to prosecution as an illegal arrest under false imprisonment statutes.

Probable Cause Hearing - A hearing to determine if there is sufficient evidence to warrant a trial; also called a preliminary hearing.

Recognizance - Pledge by the accused to return for trial, which may be accepted in lieu of bail.

Rehabilitation Model - View that sees criminals as victims of social injustice, poverty, and racism and suggests that appropriate treatment can change them into productive, law-abiding citizens.

Restorative Justice Model - View that emphasizes the promotion of a peaceful, just society through reconciliation and reintegration of the offender into society.

Right to Counsel - The right of a person accused of crime to have the assistance of a defense attorney in all criminal prosecutions.

Discussion Exercises

1. Although we have witnessed a decrease in the rates of many crimes in recent years, currently we are at an all-time high in the number of people under some form of correctional supervision. Have students discuss how this can be so. One obvious answer is that we have a wider variety of supervision options available to us today than in the past.

2. Discretion allows the various "gatekeepers" at each stage of the criminal justice system the power to determine who continues and who is diverted from the system. Ask students to identify these gatekeepers and discuss their decision making process. That is, what are the factors that impact their choice to move a case further in the system.

3. Out of the six models of justice presented in the chapter, which one do the students think offers the strongest framework and which one do they think offers the weakest? Have them explain why they have made these choices.

InfoTrac Assignment

GETTING STARTED: Search term words for subject guide: Due Process, Crime Control, Justice, Rehabilitation Model, Restorative Justice Model.

CRITICAL THINKING PROJECT: Using the search term "Due Process," find relevant articles.

Here are three articles:

Erickson, Kris. "Constitutional Law: Use of force by mental health workers violated due process." *Journal of Law, Medicine & Ethics.*

Fisher, Barry J. "Judicial Suicide or Constitutional Autonomy? A capital defendant's right to plead guilty." *Albany Law Review*.

Odeshoo, Jason R. "Truth or Dare? Terrorism and 'truth serum' in the post-9/11 world." *Stanford Law Review*.

Test Bank

Fill in the Blank

1. **Probable cause** is sufficient evidence that a crime has been committed and that the suspect committed the crime.
    (page number 495)

2. **Arrest** occurs when the police take a person into custody for allegedly committing a criminal act.
    (page number 495)

3. Misdemeanor charges issued by the prosecutor's office against the defendant are known as a **complaint**.
    (page number 495)

4. A **lineup** consists of witnesses that are brought in to pick out the suspect from a group of individuals.
    (page number 495)

5. **Booking** is when a person is taken to the police station to be fingerprinted, photographed, and to have personal information recorded.
    (page number 495)

6. The charging document filed by the prosecutor is called an **information**.
    (page number 495)

7. An **indictment** is the document issued by the grand jury when there is sufficient evidence for the accused to stand trial.
    (page number 495)

8. When defendants are asked to plead guilty as charged in return for consideration for leniency or mercy, they are offered a **plea bargain**.
    (page numbers 499-500)

9. **Probation** is a legal disposition that allows the convicted offender to remain in the community, subject to conditions imposed by court order under the supervision of an officer.
    (page number 500)

10. A **hung jury** is when a jury fails to reach a decision, thereby leaving the case unresolved.
    (page number 500)

11. **Parole** is a process whereby an inmate is selected for early release and serves the remainder of the sentence in the community under the supervision of an officer.
(page number 500)

12. The **criminal justice funnel** shows that cases are dismissed at many stages of the ~~~~~ process, and relatively few actually reach trial.
~~er 501)

13. The policy whereby U.S. courts exercised little control over the operations of criminal justice agencies is known as the **hands-off doctrine**.
(page number 502)

14. The **exclusionary rule** states that illegally seized evidence cannot be used at trial.
(page number 502)

15. **Due process** is where the rights of defendant are protected at all times by federal and state constitutional mandates, statutes, and case law.
(page number 504)

Multiple Choice

1. The agencies of government charged with law enforcement, adjudicating crime, and correcting criminal behavior are known as:
   a. due processes
   b. probation
   c. the sheriff's department
   d. the criminal justice system
   (Answer = d, page number 492)

2. The major component of the criminal justice system is:
   a. courts
   b. corrections
   c. law enforcement
   d. all of the above
   (Answer = d, page number 492)

3. The contemporary criminal justice system consists of _____ public agencies.
   a. 55
   b. 550
   c. 5,500
   d. 55,000
   (Answer = d, page number 492)

4. The justice system today employs approximately how many people?
   a. 100,000
   b. 1 million
   c. 2 million
   d. 10 million
   (Answer = c, page number 492)

5. How much does it cost to build a prison cell?
   a. $70,000
   b. $7,000
   c. $700
   d. $7
   (Answer = a, page number 492)

6. How many men and women are currently in the nation's jails and prisons?
   a. 500,000
   b. 1 million
   c. 1.5 million
   d. 2 million
   (Answer = d, page number 494)

7. Currently, almost _____ million people are under the control of the correctional system.
   a. 2
   b. 7
   c. 10
   d. 15
   (Answer = b, page number 494)

8. The initial contact an offender has with the justice system is usually with the:
   a. courts
   b. police
   c. congress
   d. prison
   (Answer = b, page number 495)

9. After a crime is recognized, police officers will gather facts, or evidence, to identify the perpetrator, justify an arrest, and bring the offender to trial. This is known as a(n):
   a. investigation
   b. arrest
   c. arraignment
   d. grand jury
   (Answer = a, page number 495)

10. When the police take a person into custody for allegedly committing a criminal act it is known as a(n):
    a. investigation
    b. arrest
    c. arraignment
    d. grand jury
    (Answer = b, page number 495)

11. Sufficient evidence that a crime has been committed by the suspect is known as:
    a. reasonable belief
    b. beyond a reasonable doubt
    c. fundamental fairness
    d. probable cause
    (Answer = d, page number 495)

12. Charges issued by the prosecutor's office against the defendant are known as a(n):
    a. complaint
    b. indictment
    c. information
    d. lineup
    (Answer = b, page number 495)

13. When witnesses are brought in to pick out the suspect from a group of individuals it is known as a:
    a. lineup
    b. backup
    c. drift
    d. social control
    (Answer = a, page number 495)

14. With sufficient evidence, the grand jury issues an:
    a. information
    b. arrest
    c. arraignment
    d. indictment
    (Answer = d, page number 495)

15. The charging document filed by the prosecutor is known as an:
    a. information
    b. arrest
    c. arraignment
    d. indictment
    (Answer = a, page number 495)

16. A group of citizens brought together to consider the case in a closed hearing in which only the prosecutor presents evidence is called a:
     a. grand jury
     b. petit jury
     c. probable cause hearing
     d. preliminary hearing
     (Answer = a, page number 495)

17. The philosophy where the state acts in the best interests of children in trouble is known as:
     a. parental control
     b. due process
     c. crime control model
     d. *parens patriae*
     (Answer = d, page number 496)

18. Juveniles who commit crimes are called:
     a. status offenders
     b. criminals
     c. delinquents
     d. adults
     (Answer = c, page number 496)

19. Juveniles who are incorrigible, truants, runaways, or unmanageable are called:
     a. criminals
     b. delinquents
     c. status offenders
     d. adults
     (Answer = c, page number 496)

20. The Supreme Court granted procedural and due process rights to juveniles in what case?
     a. *Gregg v. Georgia*
     b. *Furman v. Georgia*
     c. *Wilkins v. Missouri*
     d. *In Re Gault*
     (Answer = d, page number 496)

21. A hearing held to determine if there is sufficient evidence to warrant a trial is known as a:
     a. probable cause hearing
     b. preliminary hearing
     c. all of the above
     d. none of the above
     (Answer = c, page number 498)

22. When the defendant is brought before the court, told of formal charges, informed of Constitutional rights, has bail considered, and the trial date is set, this is known as:
   a. a grand jury hearing
   b. the arraignment
   c. a probable cause hearing
   d. a preliminary hearing
   (Answer = b, page number 498)

23. Money bond set by judicial authority to ensure the presence of suspects at trial while allowing them their freedom until that time is known as:
   a. jail
   b. probation
   c. parole
   d. bail
   (Answer = d, page number 499)

24. When defendants are asked to plead guilty as charged in return for consideration for leniency or mercy, this is known as:
   a. probation
   b. parole
   c. prison
   d. plea bargaining
   (Answer = d, page numbers 499-500)

25. When a jury fails to reach a decision, thereby leaving the case unresolved, this is known as a:
   a. hung jury
   b. grand jury
   c. petit jury
   d. all of the above
   (Answer = a, page number 500)

26. A sentence that a defendant receives after being found guilty at trial is called a(n):
   a. arraignment
   b. probable cause hearing
   c. exclusionary rule
   d. disposition
   (Answer = d, page number 500)

27. A legal disposition that allows the convicted offender to remain in the community, subject to conditions imposed by the court under supervision of an officer, is known as:
   a. prison
   b. jail
   c. parole
   d. probation
   (Answer = d, page number 500)

28. A process whereby an inmate is selected for early release and serves the remainder of the sentence in the community under the supervision of a officer is known as:
    a. probation
    b. parole
    c. incarceration
    d. arrest
    (Answer = b, page number 500)

29. The first 10 amendments of the U.S. Constitution which are guarantees of freedom are known as:
    a. The Exclusionary Rule
    b. The Bill of Rights
    c. The Declaration of Independence
    d. The Magna Carta
    (Answer = b, page number 502)

30. All evidence obtained by illegal searches and seizures is inadmissible in criminal trials according to the:
    a. exclusionary rule
    b. Bill of Rights
    c. Declaration of Independence
    d. grand jury
    (Answer = a, page number 502)

31. Which model states the overriding purpose of the justice system is to protect the public, deter criminal behavior, and incapacitate known criminals?
    a. nonintervention
    b. due process
    c. crime control
    d. restorative justice
    (Answer = c, page number 503)

32. A type of prison sentence in which the court has determined the exact length of imprisonment and parole supervision is fixed within statutory limits is called a(n):
    a. indeterminate sentence
    b. death sentence
    c. determinate sentence
    d. probation sentence
    (Answer = c, page number 504)

33. Which model argues that civil rights of the accused should be protected at all costs?
    a. crime control
    b. due process
    c. nonintervention
    d. restorative justice
    (Answer = b, page number 504)

34. Which model supports determinate sentencing?
    a. crime control
    b. due process
    c. justice
    d. rehabilitation
    (Answer = c, page number 504)

35. Which model adheres to the principles of individualized justice, treatment, and rehabilitation of offenders?
    a. nonintervention
    b. due process
    c. crime control
    d. restorative justice
    (Answer = b, page number 504)

36. Which model embraces the notion that given the proper care and treatment, criminals can be changed into law-abiding citizens?
    a. crime control
    b. due process
    c. justice
    d. rehabilitation
    (Answer = d, page number 506)

37. Which model calls for limiting government intrusion into people's lives?
    a. due process
    b. nonintervention
    c. restorative justice
    d. justice
    (Answer = b, page number 506)

38. The view that diversion programs are designed to remove offenders from the justice system when they actually maintain the offenders' involvement in the system is known as:
    a. determinate sentencing
    b. widening the net
    c. probable cause
    d. disposition
    (Answer = b, page number 507)

39. Which model maintains that the true purpose of the criminal justice system is to promote a peaceful, just society?
    a. crime control
    b. due process
    c. restorative justice
    d. rehabilitation
    (Answer = c, page number 507)

40. Currently, which model(s) seem(s) to be most supported by legislators and the general public?
   a. crime control
   b. justice
   c. restorative justice
   d. both a and b
   (Answer = d, page number 507)

True/False

1. Common criminal justice agencies have existed for over a thousand years.
   (Answer = false, page number 492)

2. The initial contact an offender has with the justice system is usually with the correctional agency.
   (Answer = false, page number 495)

3. After a crime is recognized, police officers will conduct an arrest to gather sufficient facts, or evidence, to identify the perpetrator, justify an arrest, and bring the offender to trial.
   (Answer = false, page number 495)

4. An arrest occurs when the police take a person into custody for allegedly committing a criminal act.
   (Answer = true, page number 495)

5. Arrests can be made at the scene of a crime or after a warrant is issued by a magistrate.
   (Answer = true, page number 495)

6. If sufficient evidence is gathered, the police will turn the case over to the judge's office.
   (Answer = false, page number 495)

7. Because it is a tremendous personal and financial burden, the Declaration of Independence mandates that before a person is forced to stand trial for a serious crime, the state must first prove there is at least reasonable belief that the accused committed the act.
   (Answer = false, page number 495)

8. Bail is a money bond, the amount of which is set by judicial authority.
   (Answer = true, page number 499)

9. After a criminal trial, a defendant who is found guilty as charged is sentenced by the presiding judge.
   (Answer = true, page number 500)

10. Offenders who are found not guilty and are formally sentenced come under the jurisdiction of correctional authorities.
    (Answer = false, page number 500)

11. At the end of the correctional sentence, the offender is released into the community.
    (Answer = true, page number 500)

12. Discretion marks each stage of the criminal justice system.
    (Answer = true, page number 500)

13. Celebrity cases do a good job reflecting one's experience in the criminal justice system.
    (Answer = false, page number 500)

14. It is estimated that 90% of all cases are resolved through plea bargaining.
    (Answer = true, page number 502)

15. Procedural laws control the actions of the agencies of justice and define the rights of criminal defendants.
    (Answer = true, page number 502)

Essay Questions

1. Trace the origin of criminal justice. Compare and contrast the early origins of American justice with today's era of justice.
    (page numbers 492-495)

2. Define and describe the criminal justice system. What are the various components and how do they interact with one another?
    (page numbers 492-500)

3. Trace the process of justice. Examine the various steps that a criminal defendant goes through as they are processed through the criminal justice system.
    (page numbers 495-500)

4. Explain the criminal justice funnel. Is this a realistic model of criminal justice in our society?
    (page numbers 500-501)

5. What is the role of the criminal courts? Which models of justice are being most used in our criminal courts?
    (page numbers 502-508)

Chapter Fifteen

Police and Law Enforcement

Summary

Chapter Fifteen examines police and the law enforcement system. Police history is traced from the London Police to the advent of professionalism. The different levels of law enforcement are introduced with the various police functions being detailed. How the police are changing with the advent of community-oriented policing and problem-oriented policing is discussed with the various rules of law that directly affect policing. Chapter Fifteen concludes with various issues in policing, such as discretion, female and minority officers, and violence.

Chapter Objectives

After reading this chapter the student should be able to:

- Be familiar with the history of American Policing
- Understand how reform movements created the ideal of police professionalism
- Recognize that there are law enforcement agencies on the federal, state, and local level
- Comment on the efforts to improve patrol and investigative effectiveness
- Discuss the changing role of police
- Be able to comment on how the courts have set limits on the extent of police interrogations, and search and seizure evidence
- Understand the police personality and its effect on performance and discretion
- Talk about how women and minority officers are changing police
- Become familiar with the issues surrounding police use of force

Chapter Overview

Introduction
History of Police
    The London Police
    Policing the American Colonies
    Early American Police Agencies
    Reform Movements
    The Advent of Professionalism
Law Enforcement Agencies Today

Federal Law Enforcement
County Law Enforcement
State Police
Metropolitan Police
Police Functions
Patrol Function
Investigation Function
Changing the Police Role
Community-Oriented Policing (COP)
Problem-Oriented Policing
Does Community Policing Work?
Police and the Rule of Law
Custodial Interrogation
Search and Seizure
Issues in Policing
Police Personality and Subculture
Discretion
Race, Culture, Gender, and Criminology: Racial Profiling
Minority and Female Police Officers
The Police and Violence
Summary

Chapter Outline

I. Introduction

    A. Police - gatekeepers of the criminal justice system.

        1. Initiate contact with law violators.

        2. Decide whether to formally arrest or settle informally.

        3. Racial profiling - research shows that minorities are more adversely affected than whites by police misconduct.

        4. Most visible members of the criminal justice system.

II. History of Police

    A. U.S. police agencies can be traced to early English society.

        1. Before Norman Conquest, no regular police force.

        2. Pledge system - every man was responsible for aiding his neighbors and protecting the settlement from thieves and marauders.

        3. Tithing - people grouped into a collective of 10 families.

        4. Hundred - 10 tithings.

        5. Constable - dealt with more serious breaches of the law.

        6. Shire reeve - forerunner of today's sheriff; appointed by the crown to supervise a certain territory and assure the local nobleman that order would be kept.

        7. Watch system - watchmen that protect cities and towns by patrolling at night and protecting against robberies, fires, and disturbances.

8. Justice of the Peace - created in 1326 to assist the shire reeve in controlling the county.
B. The London Police
   1. Sir Robert Peel, England's home secretary, in 1829 had Parliament pass an "Act for Improving the Police in and Near the Metropolis."
      a. Act established the first organized police in London.
   2. Composed of 1000 men, along military lines; a distinctive uniform.
   3. Led by 2 magistrates, later known as commissioner.
C. Policing the American Colonies
   1. Law enforcement paralleled the British model.
   2. County sheriff became the most important law enforcement agent.
      a. peacekeeping and crime fighting.
      b. collected taxes.
      c. supervised elections.
      d. reacted to citizen's complaints.
      e. investigated crimes that already occurred.
      f. paid by the fee system; given a fixed amount for every arrest made, subpoena served, or court appearance made.
   3. Town marshal policed cities.
      a. aided often unwillingly by constables, night watchmen, police justices, and city council members.
      b. offered rewards for the capture of felons.
   4. After revolution, larger cities had elected or appointed leaders.
      a. nightwatchmen - called leatherheads, because of their leather helmets, patrolled the streets calling the hour.
D. Early American Police Agencies
   1. 19th century - urban mob violence led to modern police departments.
   2. Boston - 1st formal police department in 1838.
   3. Politics dominated the departments.
   4. Mid-19th century - detective bureau set up in Boston police.
   5. Police in 19th century - incompetent, corrupt, and disliked.
E. Reform Movements
   1. Uniforms introduced in 1853 in New York.
   2. Late 1850's - precincts linked to central headquarters by telegraph.
   3. Call boxes - allowed patrol officers to communicate with commanders.
   4. Nonpolice functions abandoned after civil war.
   5. Efforts to prevent police corruption, but not very successful.
   6. Boston Police Strike of 1914:
      a. dissatisfaction with the status of police officers in society.
      b. police unionized, held a strike and lost public support.
      c. striking officers were fired and replaced.
      d. ended police unionism for decades.
   7. Wickersham Commission - created by President Herbert Hoover to study police issues on a national scale.
F. The Advent of Professionalism
   1. 1920's - August Vollmer, police chief of Berkeley, CA.

        a. instituted university training as part of development of police officers.

        b. helped develop School of Criminology at the University of California at Berkeley - the model for justice related programs around the country.

   2. Technological breakthroughs:

        a. communications - telegraph call boxes installed in 1867.

        b. transportation - bicycles - 1897; automobiles - 1910.

   3. 1960's - efforts to promote understanding between police and community.

        a. reduce police brutality.

        b. recognize the stresses of police work.

III. Law Enforcement Agencies Today

A. Today about 800,000 full-time law enforcement officers in the U.S., employed in almost 18,000 different agencies.

B. Federal Law Enforcement - about 50 different organizations.

   1. The Federal Bureau of Investigation

        a. 1870 - attorney general hired investigators to enforce the Mann Act (prohibits prostitution across state lines).

        b. 1908 - investigators became the Bureau of Investigation.

        c. 1930's - reorganized under J. Edgar Hoover into FBI.

        d. today, an investigative agency with jurisdiction over all matters in which the U.S. is or may be an interested party.

        e. jurisdiction limited to federal matters: espionage, sabotage, treason, civil rights violations, murder and assault of federal officers, mail fraud, robbery and burglary of federally insured banks, kidnapping, and interstate transportation of stolen vehicles and property.

        f. offers services to local law enforcement agencies.

        g. vast fingerprint file.

        h. sophisticated crime laboratory.

        i. FBI National Crime Information Center - computerized network to link local police departments by terminals.

        j. post 9/11, the FBI has shifted its priority to counterintelligence, counterterrorism, and cyber terrorism.

   2. Other Federal Agencies

        a. Drug Enforcement Administration (DEA) - investigate illegal drug use; conduct independent surveillance and enforcement to control the importation of narcotics.

        b. U.S. Marshals - court officers who implement federal court rulings, transport prisoners, and enforce court orders.

        c. Bureau of Alcohol, Tobacco, Firearms, and Explosives (ATF) - has jurisdiction over the sale and distribution of firearms, explosives, alcohol and tobacco products.

        d. Internal Revenue Service (IRS) - established 1862, enforces violations of income, excise, stamp and other tax laws.

Pursues gamblers, narcotics dealers, and other violators who do not report illegal financial gains as income.

3. Department of Homeland Security (DHS) - created after 9/11 by President George W. Bush.

    a. mission:

        i. prevent terrorist attacks within the U.S.

        ii. reduce America's vulnerability to terrorism.

        iii. minimize the damage and help recover from attacks that do occur.

    b. 4 main directorates:

        i. The Border and Transportation Security directorate.

        ii. The Emergency Preparedness and Response directorate.

        iii. The Science and Technology directorate.

        iv. The Information Analysis and Infrastructure Protection directorate.

C. County Law Enforcement

1. Independent agency whose senior officer, the sheriff, is usually elected.
2. Evolved from early English shire reeve.
3. Today, nearly 300,000 full-time employees; including 165,000 sworn.
4. Law enforcement services provided:

    a. routine patrol.

    b. respond to citizen calls.

    c. investigate crimes.

    d. keepers of the county jail.

    e. court attendants.

    f. executors of criminal and civil processes.

D. State Police

1. Texas Rangers - 1835 - considered the first state police force.
2. Connecticut and Pennsylvania lead state policing in 20th century.
3. State police agencies created from low regard of public for crime-fighting ability of local police and the increasing mobility of criminals.
4. Today about 56,000 full-time state police officers.
5. Major role:

    a. controlling traffic on the highway system.

    b. tracing stolen automobiles.

    c. aiding in disturbances.

    d. crowd control.

E. Metropolitan Police

1. Today, there are more than 13,000 local police departments nationwide with about 565,000 full-time employees, including 440,000 sworn personnel.
2. About 800 departments employ just 1 officer.
3. Larger, urban departments operate without specific administrative control from any higher governmental authority.

    a. common for mayor to control hiring and firing of police chief.

4. Duties include:
    a. law enforcement functions.
    b. order maintenance functions.
    c. service functions.

IV. Police Functions

A. Patrol Function
1. Involves police visible presence.
2. Purpose:
    a. deter crime.
    b. maintain order.
    c. enforce laws.
    d. aid in service functions.
3. Techniques:
    a. foot patrol - officer walk the area, or beat, assigned.
    b. aggressive preventive patrol - designed to deter crime.
4. Improving patrol:
    a. proactive policing.
    b. full enforcement/zero tolerance.
    c. targeting crimes.
    d. making arrests.
    e. adding patrol officers.

B. Investigation Function
1. Detective - established by the London Metropolitan Police in 1841.
    a. usually enter a case after it has been reported to police.
    b. use various investigatory techniques: mug shots and becoming familiar with the modus operandi of the offender.
    c. use sting type operations to solve some cases.
    d. morals or vice squads - specialize in victimless crimes such as prostitution or gambling.
2. Are Investigations Effective?
    a. Rand Corporation - 1975 study of 153 detective bureaus.
        i. found much of detectives' time was spent in nonproductive work.
        ii. that investigative expertise did little to help solve cases.
        iii. estimated that half of detectives could be removed without reducing clearance rates.

V. Changing the Police Role

A. Community-Oriented Policing (COP)
1. Wilson and Kelling article, "Broken Windows: The Police and Neighborhood Safety" called for a return to 19th century community policing.
    a. police should get out of their cars.
    b. elicit citizen cooperation.
    c. community preservation, public safety, and order maintenance should be primary focus, not crime fighting.

          d. foster a proactive role in the community rather than a reactive one.
      2. Implementing COP
          a. foot patrol implemented; little effect on crime, but improves citizen attitudes toward police.
          b. neighborhood watch, community newsletters, and other devices to bring the police and the community together.
      3. Community policing in action
          a. implemented in large cities, suburbs, and rural communities.
          b. some assign officers to neighborhoods, organize training programs for community leaders, and feature a bottom-up approach to dealing with community problems.
      4. Neighborhood policing
          a. policing must be flexible and adaptive.
          b. allocate resources to meet needs of various neighborhoods.
          c. neighborhood initiatives ideal way to fight crime.
          d. citizens provide information in crime investigations.
  B. Problem-Oriented Policing (POP) - an aggressive strategy of playing an active role in identifying particular community problems.
      1. Criminal acts/criminal places
          a. combating auto theft - use of "bait cars" parked in high-theft areas and are equipped with technology that alarms law enforcement when stolen.
          b. reducing violence - members of a gang tactical unit work with neighborhood groups to identify gang problems and then devise a solution.
          c. Operation Ceasefire - reduces youth homicide and youth firearm violence.
  C. Does Community Policing Work?
      1. Many have embraced community policing as revolutionary.
      2. Credited with reducing crime rates in large cities such as Boston and New York.
      3. Most professional and highly motivated will support COPS.
      4. Critics say return to old style of policing is negative.
      5. Difficult to retrain officers from their traditional roles.
      6. Some consider the roles of COPS in conflict with effective law enforcement.
      7. Some administrators consider law enforcement as their top priority; community service not necessarily a significant police role.
      8. Research indicates that COP programs improve community relations, upgrade police image, and reduce levels of community fear.

VI. Police and the Rule of Law
  A. Custodial Interrogation
      1. 5th Amendment guarantees people the right to be free from self-incrimination.

2. *Miranda v. Arizona* (1966) - Court created objective standards for questioning by police after defendant taken into custody.
3. Miranda warning - officers must inform of the 5th Amendment
    a. right to remain silent.
    b. if they make a statement, it can be used against them in court.
    c. right to call attorney and have attorney present at interrogation.
    d. if they cannot afford attorney, state will appoint one.
4. If Miranda is not issued, then interrogation cannot be admitted at trial.
5. The Miranda rule today:
    a. defendant's perjured testimony allows government to use illegal evidence to impeach testimony.
    b. witnesses are allowed even if their revealed identity was in violation of Miranda.
    c. Miranda only applies to attorneys; not priest or probation officers.
    d. inevitable discovery rule - information of evidence provided by suspect permissible if evidence would have been obtained anyway.
    e. public safety doctrine - admissible evidence can be obtained without Miranda if the information sought is needed for public safety.
    f. initial errors do not make subsequent statements inadmissible; just give the Miranda warning.
    g. suspects do not have to understand the outcomes of waiving their Miranda rights.
    h. mentally impaired defendants admissions can be admitted if police acted properly and defendant understood Miranda.
    i. attorney's request to see defendant does not affect the validity of the right to counsel.
    j. mentally ill schizophrenia people may voluntarily confess and waive their Miranda rights.
    k. once Miranda rights invoked, police cannot reinitiate interrogation.
    l. admitting a coerced confession to trial can result in overturning a conviction.
    m. ambiguous statements about attorneys is not protected under Miranda.
    n. failure to give a suspect a Miranda warning is not illegal unless the case becomes a criminal matter.
    o. a voluntary statement given in the absence of the warning can be used to obtain evidence that can be used at trial.
B. Search and Seizure
    1. Search warrant - judicial order, based on probable cause, allowing police officers to search for evidence in a particular place, seize that evidence and carry it away. Evidence seized with a valid warrant, can be used at trial.

2. Under certain circumstances search may be conducted without warrant:
   a. threshold inquiry (stop-and-frisk) - reasonable belief; frisking is limited to a pat down of the outer clothing for a weapon.
   b. search incident to an arrest - for safety, to preserve evidence, and prevent escape.
   c. automobile search - may be searched if believed to have been involved in a crime.
   d. motorist search - if danger is perceived, then officer can order drivers and passengers from car during routine traffic stop and conduct limited search.
   e. consent search - if people consent, they and their vehicle may be searched.
   f. plain view - contraband can be seized when it is in plain view.
   g. seizure of nonphysical evidence - such as conversation, police can seize if individuals had no reason to expect privacy.
   h. hot pursuit/exigency - during emergency situations.

VII. Issues in Policing
A. Police Personality and Subculture
   1. Thought to be authoritarian, suspicious, racist, hostile, insecure, conservative, cynical, secretive, and isolated.
   2. The Police Subculture
      a. William Westly argued that officers develop into cynics; learn to mistrust citizens.
      b. come to believe that people or out to break the law and harm officers.
      c. most officers ban together in clannishness, secrecy, and insulation from others in society.
B. Discretion - crucial force in all law enforcement decision-making.
   1. Environmental and community factors - community crime levels, informal rules, social climate, community attitudes, treatment facilities, alternatives.
   2. Departmental factors - departmental norms, peers, directives, supervisors.
   3. Situational factors - demeanor, crime scene, witness, backup.
   4. Legal factors - type of crime, seriousness of crime.
   5. Extralegal factors - income, race, gender.
   6. Limiting police discretion:
      a. police administrators have tried to establish guidelines for officer behavior.
      b. develop civilian review boards that monitor police behavior and investigate civilian behavior.
C. Minority and Female Police Officers
   1. Minority police officers
      a. first African American officer in Chicago in 1872.
      b. still underrepresented, but pressure to increase the numbers.

       c. Black officers suffer double marginality - deal with the expectation they will give members of their own race a break and experience overt racism from police colleagues.

       d. findings show that black officers are often tougher on black offenders to prove lack of bias.

  2. Female police officers

       a. first female officer in 1845 in New York; matrons restricted to handling females in custody.

       b. 1910 in Los Angeles, first woman to have title of police officer and full arrest powers.

       c. 1972 - Title VII of the Civil Rights Act - police departments began to hire females and assign regular patrol duties.

       d. how effective are female police officers?

          i. evaluations show them to be equal or superior to male officers.

          ii. likely to receive community support.

          iii. less likely to be charged with police misconduct.

          iv. have not received support from colleagues.

          v. struggling for acceptance.

          vi. common to be sexually harassed by coworkers.

  3. Black female police

       a. account for 2% of police officers.

       b. perceive significantly more racial discrimination than either other female or black male officers.

       c. little unity among female officers.

D. The Police and Violence

  1. How common is the use of force today?

       a. recent survey - of 43 million police-citizen interactions, 1% or 422,000 involved the use or threatened use of force.

       b. use of weapons is rare.

  2. Race and Force

       a. minorities more likely to perceive that police will hassle them.

       b. minorities more likely to know one mistreated by police.

  3. Deadly force - actions of a police officer that shoots and kills a suspect fleeing from arrest, assaulting a victim, or attacking the officer.

       a. estimates that police now kill 250 to 1,000 citizens each year.

       b. the following are related to police violence:

          i. exposure to threat and stress.

          ii. police workload.

          iii. firearm availability.

          iv. population type and density.

          v. race and class discrimination.

          vi. lack of proper training and preparation.

  4. Controlling force

       a. *Tennessee v. Garner* - 1985, Court banned the shooting of unarmed or nondangerous fleeing felons.

        b. developing administrative policies that limit the use of deadly force and contain armed offenders until trained backup teams arrive.
5. Killing police
    a. the police are killing fewer people.
    b. fewer police are being killed in the line of duty.
    c. 2000 - 51 law enforcement officers killed in the line of duty.
    d. about half of slain officers killed while making an arrest or conducting a traffic stop.
6. Nonlethal weapons:
    a. wood, rubber or polyurethane bullets.
    b. pepper spray and tasers.
    c. other nonlethal weapons are still in development
        i. guns that shoot nets.
        ii. guns that squirt sticky glue.
        iii. lights that temporarily blind a suspect.

VIII. Summary

Key Terms

Aggressive Preventive Patrol - A patrol technique designed to suppress crime before it occurs.

Blue Curtain Subculture - According to Westly, the secretive, insulated police culture that isolates the officer from the rest of society.

Bureau of Alcohol, Tobacco, Firearms, and Explosives (ATF) - Government agency that has jurisdiction over the sale and distribution of firearms, explosives, alcohol, and tobacco products.

Community-Oriented Policing (COP) - A police strategy that emphasizes fear reduction, community organization, and order maintenance rather than crime fighting.

Constable - The peacekeeper in early English towns. The constable organized citizens to protect his territory and supervised the night watch.

Deadly Force - The ability of the police to kill suspects if they resist arrest or present a danger to an officer or the community. The police cannot use deadly force against an unarmed fleeing felon.

Department of Homeland Security (DHS) - An agency of the federal government charged with preventing terrorist attacks within the United States, reducing America's vulnerability to terrorism, and minimizing the damage and aiding recovery from attacks that do occur.

Drug Enforcement Administration (DEA) - The federal agency that enforces federal drug control laws.

Federal Bureau of Investigation (FBI) - The arm of the U.S. Justice Department that investigates violations of federal law, gathers crime statistics, runs a comprehensive crime laboratory, and helps train local law enforcement officers.

Foot Patrols - Police patrols that take officers out of cars and put them on a walking beat to strengthen ties with the community.

Gatekeepers - The police, who initiate contact with law violators and decide whether to formally arrest them and start their journey through the criminal justice system, settle the issue informally (such as by issuing a warning), or simply take no action at all.

Inevitable Discovery Rule - A rule of law stating that evidence that almost assuredly would be independently discovered can be used in a court of law, even though it was obtained in violation of legal rules and practices.

Internal Revenue Service (IRS) - Government agency that enforces violations of income, excise, stamp, and other tax laws.

Justice of the Peace - Established in 1326 in England to assist the shire reeve in controlling the county, these justices eventually took on judicial functions in addition to being peacekeepers.

Miranda Warning - The result of two U.S. Supreme Court decisions (*Escobedo v. Illinois* [378 U.S. 478] and *Miranda v. Arizona* [384 U.S. 436]) that require police officers to inform individuals under arrest of their constitutional right to remain silent and to know that their statements can later be used against them in court, that they can have an attorney present to help them, and that the state will pay for an attorney if they cannot afford to hire one. Although aimed at protecting an individual during in-custody interrogation, the warning must also be given when the investigation shifts from the investigatory to the accusatory stage - that is, when suspicion begins to focus on an individual.

Modus Operandi (MO) - The working methods of particular offenders.

Morals Squad - Plainclothes police officers or detectives specializing in victimless crimes such as prostitution or gambling.

Mug Shots - Pictures of offenders that can be viewed by victims in an attempt to identify the perpetrator.

Pledge System - An early method of law enforcement that relied on self-help and mutual aid.

Problem-Oriented Policing (POP) - A style of police management that stresses proactive problem solving rather than reactive crime fighting.

Public Safety Doctrine - Evidence can be obtained without a Miranda warning if the information the police seek is needed to protect public safety.

Racial Profiling - Selecting suspects on the basis of their ethnic or racial background.

Reactive Policing - Police officers responding only to calls for help.

Reeve - In early England, the senior law enforcement figure in a county, the forerunner of today's sheriff.

Search Warrant - A judicial order, based on probable cause, allowing police officers to search for evidence in a particular place, seize that evidence and carry it away.

Sheriff - The chief law enforcement officer in a county.

Shire - Counties in England and much of Europe in the eleventh century.

State Police - A law enforcement agency with statewide jurisdiction; the major role of state police is controlling traffic on the highway system, tracing stolen automobiles, and aiding in disturbances and crowd control.

Sting - An undercover police operation in which police pose as criminals to trap law violators.

Tithing - During the Middle Ages, groups of about ten families who were responsible for maintaining order among themselves and dealing with disturbances, fines, wild animals, and so on.

U.S. Marshals - Court officers who help implement federal court rulings, transport prisoners, and enforce court orders.

Vice Squad - Police officers assigned to enforce morally tinged laws, such as those governing prostitution, gambling, and pornography.

Watch System - In medieval England, men organized in church parishes to guard against disturbances and breaches of the peace at night; they were under the direction of the local constable.

Wickersham Commission - Created in 1931 by President Herbert Hoover to investigate the state of the nation's police forces, a commission that found police training to be inadequate and the average officer incapable of effectively carrying out his duties.

Discussion Exercises

1. Have the class watch the 1973 movie, *Serpico*. After the movie, break the class up into discussion groups. Ask the groups to discuss such topics as the blue curtain subculture, ethics, Internal Affairs, and discretion.

2. Much of the discussion on police profiling in this chapter centers on studies that have examined this practice with black and Latino citizens. In light of today's terrorist concerns and military actions, to what extent is profiling an issue for citizens from the Middle East?

3. Students always express interest in the ability of police officers to stop and search their automobiles. Have students discuss the circumstances under which this occurred to them and then discuss the legal issues that made this an appropriate response for the officer.

InfoTrac Assignment

GETTING STARTED: Search term words for subject guide: London Police, Federal Law Enforcement, State Police, Patrol, Community-Oriented Policing, Custodial Interrogation, Searches, Seizures, Discretion.

CRITICAL THINKING PROJECT: Using the search term "Custodial Interrogation," find relevant articles.

Here are three articles:

Clymer, Steven D. "Are Police Free to Disregard Miranda?" *Yale Law Journal*.

Levenberg, Thomas O. "Fifth Amendment - Responding to Ambiguous Requests for Counsel during Custodial Interrogations." *Journal of Criminal Law and Criminology*.

Weisselberg, Charles D. "In the Stationhouse after Dickerson." *Michigan Law Review*.

Test Bank

Fill in the Blank

1. In the criminal justice system, the police are the most visible, have the most contact with the public, and would be considered **gatekeepers** to the system.
    (page number 514)

2. The **pledge system** operated during the Middle Ages where every man living in the villages scattered throughout the countryside was responsible for aiding his neighbors and protecting the settlement from thieves and marauders.
    (page number 514)

3. Supervised by the constable, the **watch system** was created to watch cities and towns.
    (page number 514)

4. The **justice of the peace** was created in 1326 to assist the shire reeve in controlling the county.
    (page number 514)

5. **Sir Robert Peel** established the first police force in London.
    (page number 515)

6. The **sheriff** was the most important law enforcement agent in colonial America.
    (page number 515)

7. Created by President Hoover, the **Wickersham Commission** identified many of the problems of policing.
    (page number 516)

8. **August Vollmer** instituted university training as part of police training at UC-Berkeley.
    (page number 517)

9. When police play an active role in the community, identify neighborhood problems and needs, and set a course of action for an effective response, this is known as **community-oriented policing**.
    (page number 524)

10. **Neighborhood policing** is policing designated for a specific neighborhood and done at that level rather than far away.
    (page number 525)

11. **Problem-oriented policing** is a new, aggressive strategy where police play an active role in first identifying particular community problems.
    (page number 525)

12. If the defendant is not given the **Miranda Warning** before the investigation, the evidence gained from the interrogation cannot be admitted at trial.
    (page number 527)

13. The **Fifth Amendment** guarantees people the right to be free from self-incrimination.
    (page number 527)

14. A **search warrant** is a judicial order, based on probable cause, allowing police officers to search for evidence in a particular place, seize the evidence, and carry it away.
    (page number 528)

15. **Deadly force** refers to the actions of a police officer who shoots and kills a suspect.
    (page number 538)

Multiple Choice

1. In the criminal justice system, the police are the most visible, have the most contact with the public, and are known as:
    a. detectives
    b. a vice squad
    c. gatekeepers
    d. a morals squad
    (Answer = c, page number 514)

2. One who might be considered the first real police officer who dealt with more serious breaches of the law is known as the:
    a. constable
    b. shire reeve
    c. justice of the peace
    d. watch system
    (Answer = a, page number 514)

3. People grouped into a collective of 10 families are known as a:
    a. watch system
    b. pledge system
    c. hundred
    d. tithing
    (Answer = d, page number 514)

4. Ten tithings were grouped into a:
    a. watch system
    b. pledge system
    c. tithing
    d. hundred
    (Answer = d, page number 514)

5. During the Middle Ages, every man living in the villages scattered throughout the countryside was responsible for aiding his neighbors and protecting the settlement from thieves and marauders. This was called the:
   a. watch system
   b. shire reeve system
   c. pledge system
   d. justice of the peace system
   (Answer = c, page number 514)

6. Created in 1326 to assist the shire reeve in controlling the county, this position was known as the:
   a. watch system
   b. pledge system
   c. shire
   d. justice of the peace
   (Answer = d, page number 514)

7. This group patrolled at night and was created to watch England's larger cities and towns.
   a. pledge system
   b. watchmen
   c. shire reeve
   d. justice of the peace
   (Answer = b, page number 514)

8. The forerunner of today's sheriff is known as the:
   a. justice of the peace
   b. watch system
   c. shire reeve
   d. pledge system
   (Answer = c, page number 514)

9. He established the first police force in London:
   a. Edwin Sutherland
   b. Travis Hirschi
   c. August Vollmer
   d. Sir Robert Peel
   (Answer = d, page number 515)

10. The most important law enforcement agent in colonial America was known as the:
   a. sheriff
   b. justice of the peace
   c. watch system
   d. pledge system
   (Answer = a, page number 515)

11. The nation's first formal police department was created in:
    a. New York
    b. Philadelphia
    c. Boston
    d. Miami
    (Answer = c, page number 515)

12. The commission created by President Hoover to study police issues on a national scale is known as the:
    a. Warren Commission
    b. Wickersham Commission
    c. Knapp Commission
    d. Mollen Commission
    (Answer = b, page number 516)

13. While serving as Police Chief of Berkeley, CA, he instituted university training as a part of police training:
    a. Sir Robert Peel
    b. August Vollmer
    c. Travis Hirschi
    d. Edwin Sutherland
    (Answer = b, page number 517)

14. Currently, there are about _____ full-time law enforcement officers in the U.S.
    a. 80,000
    b. 150,000
    c. 500,000
    d. 800,000
    (Answer = d, page number 517)

15. The federal government maintains about how many organizations involved in law enforcement?
    a. 100
    b. 200
    c. 50
    d. 10
    (Answer = c, page number 517)

16. Which Act prohibited prostitution across state lines?
    a. Miranda
    b. Wickersham
    c. Knapp
    d. Mann
    (Answer = d, page number 517)

17. Which division of the FBI is a computerized network linked to local police departments that provides ready information on stolen vehicles, wanted persons, stolen guns, and other crime related material?
     a. The Uniform Crime Report
     b. National Crime Information Center
     c. The Critical Incident Response Group
     d. The Child Abduction and Serial Killer Unit
     (Answer = b, page number 518)

18. Which of the following federal agencies has as its mission the enforcement of violations of income, excise, stamp, and other tax laws?
     a. DHS
     b. FBI
     c. IRS
     d. DEA
     (Answer = c, page number 518)

19. An area or beat that an officer walks is known as a(n):
     a. bike patrol
     b. foot patrol
     c. aggressive preventive patrol
     d. none of the above
     (Answer = b, page number 521)

20. The method of patrol designed to deter crime is known as the:
     a. foot patrol
     b. bike patrol
     c. community policing patrol
     d. aggressive preventive patrol
     (Answer = d, page number 521)

21. Photographs of offenders taken by law enforcement for victims to use in identifying offenders are known as:
     a. complaints
     b. mug shots
     c. search warrants
     d. arrest warrants
     (Answer = b, page number 522)

22. The working methods of particular criminals are known as their:
     a. modus operandi
     b. corpus delicti
     c. mens rae
     d. actus reus
     (Answer = a, page number 522)

23. An operation where police pose as fences with thieves interested in selling stolen merchandise is known as:
    a. selective enforcement
    b. a watch system
    c. the pledge system
    d. a sting
    (Answer = d, page number 523)

24. Detectives assigned to investigate crimes such as prostitution are known as the:
    a. vice squad
    b. morals squad.
    c. all of the above
    d. none of the above
    (Answer = c, page number 523)

25. The view that police should play an active role in the community, identify neighborhood problems and needs, and set a course of action for an effective response is called:
    a. neighborhood policing
    b. problem-oriented policing
    c. community-oriented policing
    d. the Knapp commission
    (Answer = c, page number 524)

26. Policing designated for a specific neighborhood and done at that level rather than far away is known as:
    a. neighborhood policing
    b. community-oriented policing
    c. problem-oriented policing
    d. the Knapp commission
    (Answer = a, page number 525)

27. A new, aggressive strategy where police play an active role in first identifying particular community problems is known as:
    a. community-oriented policing
    b. problem-oriented policing
    c. neighborhood policing
    d. the Knapp commission
    (Answer = b, page number 525)

28. Which Amendment guarantees people the right to be free from self-incrimination?
    a. 4th
    b. 5th
    c. 6th
    d. 8th
    (Answer = b, page number 527)

29. Information that is provided by the suspect and leads to the seizure of incriminating evidence is permissible if the evidence would have been obtained anyway by other means or sources. This is known as:
   a. the exclusionary rule
   b. fruits of the poisonous tree
   c. the Miranda warning
   d. the inevitable discovery rule
   (Answer = d, page number 528)

30. A judicial order, based on probable cause, allowing police officers to search for evidence in a particular place, seize that evidence, and carry it away is known as a(n):
   a. waiver
   b. search warrant
   c. arrest warrant
   d. evidence
   (Answer = b, page number 528)

31. Under what circumstances may a warrantless search be conducted?
   a. at the time of an arrest
   b. when contraband is in plain view
   c. when a person consents to the search
   d. all of the above
   (Answer = d, page number 529)

32. The code of silence among police officers is known as the:
   a. green grass
   b. red shoes
   c. blue curtain
   d. tan dungarees
   (Answer = c, page number 530)

33. The policy of police officers to concentrate on some crimes, but handle the majority of them in an informal manner, is known as:
   a. the pledge system
   b. selective enforcement
   c. a foot patrol
   d. aggressive preventive patrol
   (Answer = b, page number 531)

34. Expectations that Black police officers will give members of their own race a break and the experience of overt racism from police colleagues is known as:
   a. racial favorites
   b. racial profile
   c. double marginality
   d. racial marginality
   (Answer = c, page number 536)

35. Black females account for _____ of police officers
   a. 0%
   b. 2%
   c. 10%
   d. 15%
   (Answer = b, page number 537)

36. What percent of police-citizen interactions involve the use or threatened use of force?
   a. 1%
   b. 5%
   c. 10%
   d. 15%
   (Answer = a, page number 538)

37. The number of shooting incidents involving deadly force has been:
   a. increasing at an alarming rate
   b. increasing at a minor rate
   c. declining
   d. we are unable to tell
   (Answer = c, page number 538)

38. How many citizens are killed by police each year?
   a. 25-100
   b. 250-1,000
   c. 1,250-2,000
   d. 2,500
   (Answer = b, page number 538)

39. The actions of a police officer who shoots and kills a suspect whom is either fleeing from arrest, assaulting a victim, or attacking the officer is called:
   a. deadly force
   b. blue curtain
   c. crackdown
   d. search and seizure
   (Answer = a, page number 538)

40. Which of the following has not been associated with police violence?
   a. rural populations
   b. firearm availability
   c. police workload
   d. exposure to stress
   (Answer = a, page number 538)

True/False

1. The top priority of the FBI is to protect the U.S. from terrorist attacks.
   (Answer = true, page number 518)

2. The U.S. Marshals are court officers who help implement federal court rulings, transport prisoners, and enforce court orders.
   (Answer = true, page number 518)

3. The Drug Enforcement Administration administers immigration laws, deports illegal aliens, and naturalizes aliens lawfully present in the United States.
   (Answer = false, page number 518)

4. The Immigration and Naturalization Service investigates illegal drug use and carries out independent surveillance and enforcement activities to control the importation of narcotics.
   (Answer = false, page number 518)

5. The Bureau of Alcohol, Tobacco, Firearms, and Explosives has jurisdiction over the sales and distribution of firearms, explosives, alcohol, and tobacco products.
   (Answer = true, page number 518)

6. The Internal Revenue Service, established in 1862, enforces violations of income, excise, stamp, and other tax laws.
   (Answer = true, page number 518)

7. The Department of Homeland Security is mainly concerned with issues of terrorism.
   (Answer = true, page number 518)

8. The county police department is an independent agency whose senior officer, the sheriff, is usually elected.
   (Answer = true, page number 519)

9. The Texas Rangers, organized in 1835, are considered the first state police force.
   (Answer = true, page number 519)

10. The investigation stage entails police officers' visible presence on the streets and public places of their jurisdiction.
    (Answer = false, page number 522)

11. Investigators must often enter a case after it has been reported to police and attempt to accumulate enough evidence to identify the perpetrator.
    (Answer = true, page number 522)

12. Traditional policing models were reactive, responding to calls for help rather than attempting to prevent crimes before they occurred.
(Answer = true, page number 524)

13. The Fourth Amendment guarantees people the right to be free from self-incrimination.
(Answer = false, page number 527)

14. A search warrant is a judicial order, based on probable cause, which allows police officers to search for evidence in a particular place, seize that evidence, and carry it away.
(Answer = true, page number 528)

15. A warrantless search is valid if it is made incident to a lawful arrest.
(Answer = true, page number 529)

Essay Questions

1. Trace the history of law enforcement. Where did policing begin and with whom?
(page numbers 514-516)

2. What events cause the advent of professionalism in policing? Who would be considered directly responsible for introducing professionalism to policing?
(page number 516)

3. Define federal law enforcement. What are some of the various law enforcement organizations under the federal system?
(page numbers 517-519)

4. Compare and contrast county law enforcement with metropolitan police. What are the distinguishing characteristics of each? Which, if either, has more power and why?
(page numbers 519-520)

5. Compare and contrast community-oriented policing with problem-oriented policing. Which works best? Why?
(page numbers 523-527)

Chapter Sixteen

The Judicatory Process

Summary

Chapter Sixteen begins with a detailed explanation of the federal and state court structure. The actors in the judicatory process are examined and the pretrial procedures are explained. Plea-bargaining is discussed as well as the specifics of the criminal trial. Sentencing is distinguished from the criminal trial and Chapter Sixteen concludes with a discussion of the death penalty.

Chapter Objectives

After reading this chapter the student should be able to:

- Be familiar with the state and federal court structure
- Discuss the duties of a judge, defense counsel, and prosecutor
- Discuss the various pretrial procedures
- Discuss the plea bargaining process
- Be familiar with the process of the jury trial
- Review legal rights during trial
- Understand the various forms of sentencing used in the United States
- Know the difference between three strikes laws and truth in sentencing
- Discuss the sentencing process and outcomes and how people are sentenced
- Be familiar with arguments for and against the death penalty

Chapter Overview

Introduction
Court Structure
    State Courts
Policy and Practice in Criminology: Specialized Courts: Drugs and Mental Health
    Federal Courts
    Court Case Flow
Actors in the Judicatory Process
    Prosecutor
    Defense Attorney
The Criminological Enterprise: Ethical Issues in Criminal Defense
    Judge
Pretrial Procedures

Bail

Plea Bargaining

The Criminal Trial

Jury Selection

The Trial Process

Trials and the Rule of Law

Sentencing

Purposes of Sentencing

Sentencing Dispositions

Sentencing Structures

How People are Sentenced

Race, Culture, Gender, and Criminology: Race and Sentencing

The Death Penalty

The Death Penalty Debate

Comparative Criminology: The Death Penalty Abroad

Legality of the Death Penalty

Summary

Chapter Outline

I. **Introduction**

II. **Court Structure** - 16,000 courts in U.S. organized on the municipal, county, state, and federal levels.

A. State Courts

1. Lower courts - try misdemeanors; conduct preliminary processing of felony offenders.

2. Superior courts - try felony cases.

3. Appellate courts - review criminal procedure of trial court to determine whether offenders were treated fairly.

4. Superior appellate courts or state supreme courts - review lower court decisions.

B. Federal Courts

1. U.S. district courts - trial courts; have jurisdiction over cases involving violations of federal law.

2. Intermediate courts of appeal - hear appeals from U.S. District Court.

3. U.S. Supreme Court - highest federal appeal court; court of last resort for all cases in federal and state courts.

a. composed of nine members.

b. appointed for life by the President and approved by Congress.

c. court selects cases they want to hear.

i. selection by a writ of certiorari - requests a transcript of the case proceedings for review.

d. court decisions become precedent - must be honored by all lower courts.

i. these rulings are referred to as landmark decisions.

326

C. Court Case Flow
    1. Annually, about 100 million new cases brought to the courts.
    2. Cases brought to court are increasing although the crime rates are down.

III. Actors in the Judicatory Process

A. Prosecutors
    1. Represents the state in criminal matters before the court.
    2. State court prosecutors' offices employed about 79,000 attorneys, investigators and support staff.
    3. Types of prosecutors:
        a. federal - chief prosecuting officer is the U.S. Attorney General
            i. assistants are known as U.S. Attorneys - appointed by the President.
            ii. represent the government in federal district courts.
        b. state - district attorney, county attorney, prosecuting attorney, commonwealth attorney or state's attorney.
            i. typically elected officials.
        c. other staff attorneys and support personnel handle most criminal prosecution.
            i. work is often specialized into felonies, misdemeanors, trial, and appeal assignments.
    4. Prosecutorial discretion:
        a. the choice of acting on the information brought by the police or deciding not to file for an indictment.
        b. can attempt to prosecute and then drop the case - nolle prosequi.
        c. plea negotiations.
    5. Factors influencing decision making:
        a. characteristics of the crime.
        b. the criminal.
        c. the victim.
        d. offender's prior criminal record.
        e. victim cooperation.
        f. victim's attitude.
        g. the cost of prosecution to the criminal justice system.
        h. the possibility of undue harm to the suspect.
        i. the availability of alternative procedures.
        j. the availability of civil sanctions.
        k. the willingness of the suspect to cooperate with law enforcement authorities.
        l. case pressure.

B. Defense Attorneys - represent the accused in the criminal process.
    1. Public defender - salaried staff of full- or part-time attorneys that render indigent criminal defense services through a public or private nonprofit organization, or as direct government paid employees.

2. Assigned counsel - Appointment from a list of private bar members who accept cases on a judge-by-judge, court-by-court, or case-by-case basis.
3. Contract - nonsalaried private attorneys, bar associations, law firms, consortiums or groups of attorneys, or nonprofit corporations that contract with a funding source to provide court-appointed representation in a jurisdiction.
4. Conflicts of Defense
   a. officers of the court - obligated to uphold the integrity of the legal profession and to observe the requirements of the Code of Professional Responsibility of the American Bar Association in the defense of a client.
   b. defense advocate.
   c. clients who perjure themselves.
C. Judge - senior officer in a court of criminal law.
   1. During trial, judges rule on the appropriateness of conduct.
   2. Settle questions of evidence and procedure.
   3. Guide the questioning of witnesses.
   4. After trial, judges must instruct jury members on which evidence can be examined and which should be ignored.
   5. Formally charges the jury by instruction on the points of law.
   6. If jury trial is waived, judge must decide for complainant or defendant.
   7. If defendant is found guilty, judge decides sentence.
   8. Has considerable control over service agencies of the court, such as probation.
   9. Judicial selection:
      a. some states, the governor appoints judges.
      b. other states, judicial recommendations must be confirmed by another group like the state senate.
      c. popular election.
      d. Missouri Plan
         i. a judicial nominating commission to nominate candidates for the bench.
         ii. an elected official to make appointments from the list submitted by the commission.
         iii. subsequent nonpartisan, noncompetitive elections in which incumbent judges run on their records.
   10. Judicial overload:
      a. little or no formal training to be a judge.
      b. an overwhelming amount of work that has risen over the years.
      c. case pressure to move the cases.

IV. Pretrial Procedures
A. Criminal charge - a formal written document identifying the criminal activity, facts of the case, and the circumstances of the arrest.
   1. bill of indictment.
   2. information.

3. complaint.
B. Bail
    1. Money or security provided to the court to ensure the appearance of the defendant at trial.
        a. amount of bail set by magistrate.
        b. defendants denied or cannot afford bail or usually held in the county lockup or jail.
    2. Bail system dates back to English common law.
    3. In U.S. right to bail comes under the 8th Amendment of the Constitution.
    4. Bail today
        a. data indicates that most defendants (62%) made bail.
        b. estimated 38% held until the courts disposed of case.
    5. Making bail
        a. preventive detention - defendants who are detained because they cannot afford bail or the danger they present to the community.
        b. drug and public order offenders likely to be bailed.
        c. violent offenders more likely to be detained.
    6. The problems of bail
        a. penalizes the indigent offender who cannot pay the bond.
        b. state must pay for the detention of offender.
        c. increases punishment risk.
        d. bailing and bonding agents have been accused of unscrupulous practices such as bribing officials.
    7. Bail reform - began in 1961 to alleviate problems associated with bail.
        a. release on recognizance (ROR) - begun by the Vera Foundation in New York and proved to be successful.
        b. Federal Bail Reform Act of 1984 - made ROR an assumption unless the need for greater control can be shown in court.
        c. abuse by bail bonding agents have prompted some states to start a system of defendants posting 10% with the court. The full amount is required if defendant fails to show for court.
        d. encouraged the use of pretrial release.
        e. most defendants return for court.
        f. most bailees do not commit more crime while in the community.
    8. Preventive detention
        a. bailees may be responsible for 1.5 million serious crimes each year.
        b. person who has not been convicted of a crime is incarcerated for an extended period of time without the chance to participate in their own defense.
        c. *United States v. Salerno*, the Supreme Court upheld the Bail Reform Act's preventive detention because it is for public safety; it is not excessive, and it is does not have a punitive intent.

C. Plea Bargaining
    1. About 90% of felony defendants and 98% of misdemeanor defendants plea bargain to settle their case.
    2. Motivations for plea bargains:
        a. prosecution's strong case.
        b. to minimize sentence.
        c. avoid the harmful effects of a criminal conviction.
        d. to protect accomplices.
        e. defense attorney may seek to limit involvement in the case.
    3. Plea bargaining issues:
        a. costs of prosecution are reduced.
        b. efficiency of the courts is improved.
        c. prosecution can spend more time on cases of greater seriousness and importance.
        d. defendant may receive reduced sentence.
        e. encourages defendants to waive their constitutional right to trial.
        f. some feel it allows the defendant to best the system.
        g. raises the danger that an innocent person will be convicted.
        h. some feel it allows dangerous criminals to get off light.
        i. may undermine public confidence in the law.
    4. Control of plea bargaining
        a. doubtful it will be totally eliminated.
        b. efforts to convert plea bargaining into a visible, understandable and fair process.
        c. some states have abolished plea bargaining.

V. The Criminal Trial
  A. Jury selection - 1st stage in the trial process.
    1. Jurors selected randomly usually from voter registration lists with court jurisdiction.
    2. Venire - jury array or initial list of persons chosen capable of serving on the jury.
        a. court clerk randomly selects enough names to supply the required number of jurors.
    3. Usually, criminal trial jury consists of 12 persons, with 2 alternates.
    4. After jurors selected, the process of voir dire begins.
        a. jurors are questioned by both the prosecution and the defense to determine their appropriateness to sit on the jury.
        b. jurors with bias, relationship to defendant, or a formed opinion are replaced - challenge for cause.
        c. peremptory challenge - either side can excuse jurors for no particular reason.
            i. *Batson v. Kentucky*, the Court held that the use of peremptory challenges to dismiss all black jurors violated the defendant's right to equal protection of the law.

5. Impartial juries
   a. *Ham v. South Carolina* (1973) - Court held the defense counsel of an African American civil rights leader was entitled to question each juror on the issue of radical prejudice.
   b. *Turner v. Murray* - Court held that African American defendants accused of murdering whites are entitled to have jurors questioned about their racial bias.
   c. *Taylor v. Louisiana* - Court overturned the conviction of a man by an all-male jury because a Louisiana statute allowed women but not men to exempt themselves from jury duty.
B. The Trial Process - formal process conducted in a specific, orderly fashion in accordance with rules of criminal law, procedure, and evidence.
   1. Opening statements
      a. prosecution and defense address the jury and present their cases.
      b. describe what they will attempt to prove.
      c. describe the major facts of the case.
      d. introduce witnesses.
      e. defense emphasizes doubt about the guilt of the accused.
   2. The prosecution's case
      a. after opening statement, the state presents evidence through witnesses.
      b. direct examination - the prosecutor questions the witness to reveal the facts believed pertinent to the government case.
   3. Cross-examination - after prosecution's examination, the defense may question the prosecution's witness. (Same for the defense side of the trial.)
   4. The defense's case
      a. after prosecutor has presented all of its case, defense may ask for a directed verdict.
         i. judge directs the jury to acquit defendant, which ends the trial.
         ii. means prosecution did not present enough evidence to prove all crime elements.
         iii. if granted, trial ends; defendant is found not guilty.
         iv. if not granted, defense proceeds with trial.
      b. defense calls witnesses like the prosecution.
   5. Rebuttal
      a. after defense, prosecution may present rebuttal evidence.
         i. evidence that was not used during prosecution's presentation.
   6. Closing arguments
      a. attorneys review the facts and evidence of the case.
   7. Instructions to the Jury
      a. judge charges or instructs the jury on the principles of law to guide and control the decision making of the defendant's innocence or guilt.

        b. judge explains the level and burden of proof to find the
            defendant guilty.

8. Verdict
    a. jurors retire to deliberate on a verdict.
    b. in a criminal trial, verdict usually must be unanimous.
    c. if no verdict can be reached, trial may result in a hung jury.

9. Sentence
    a. if found not guilty, defendant is released.
    b. if convicted, judge may order a presentence investigation by
       probation department.
    c. in felony cases, judge sets a sentencing date.
    d. at sentencing, judge may consider other relevant evidence.
    e. criminal penalties include:
       i. fines
       ii. community supervision
       iii. incarceration
       iv. death penalty

10. Appeal
    a. after sentencing, defendants have a right to appeal.
    b. if appeal is granted, new trial is ordered.
    c. if appeal is sustained, offender serves the sentence imposed.

C. Trials and the Rule of Law

1. Right to a speedy and public trial
    a. 6th Amendment guarantees defendant the right to a speedy trial.
    b. accused is entitled to be tried within a reasonable period.
    c. defendant can waive the right to a speedy trial.
    d. Federal Speedy Trial Act of 1974 - mandates 30 days from
       arrest to indictment and 70 days from indictment to trial.

2. Right to a jury trial
    a. *Duncan v. Louisiana* - Court guaranteed the right to a jury trial.
    b. *Baldwin v. New York* - Court held that defendants are entitled to
       a jury trial if they face a prison sentence of more than 6
       months.
    c. *Williams v. Florida* - Court held that a 6 person jury fulfilled
       defendant's right to a trial by jury.

3. Right to be free from double jeopardy
    a. 5th Amendment provides no person "shall be subject for the
       same offense to be twice put in jeopardy of life or limb."
    b. however, a person tried in federal court can be tried in state
       court and vice versa.
    c. dual sovereignty doctrine - legal jurisdictions have the right to
       enforce their own laws and a single act can violate the laws
       of two separate jurisdictions.

4. Right to legal counsel
    a. 6th Amendment provides the right to be represented by an
       attorney in criminal trials.

b. most defendants are indigents.

c. *Powell v. Alabama* - Court held that an attorney was essential in capital cases where the defendant's life was at stake.

d. *Gideon v. Wainwright* - Court granted the absolute right to counsel in all felony cases.

e. *Argersinger v. Hamlin* - defendant's right to counsel was established in misdemeanor cases.

f. *Alabama v. Shelton* - defendant must have counsel if receives probation sentence in which a prison or jail term is suspended.

5. The right to be competent at trial

a. if defendant is mentally incompetent, trial must be postponed until treatment renders him or her able to participate in own defense.

b. *Riggins v. Nevada* - Court rules forced treatment does not violate due process rights if medically appropriate and essential for defendant's safety or safety of others.

6. Right to confront witnesses

a. *Maryland v. Craig* - Court ruled children can witness via closed-circuit television as long as defendant's rights are protected.

VI. Sentencing - imposition of a criminal penalty.

A. Purposes of Sentencing:

1. Deterrence.
2. Incapacitation.
3. Rehabilitation.
4. Desert/retribution.

B. Sentencing Dispositions:

1. Fines.
2. Probation.
3. Alternative or intermediate sanctions.
4. Incarceration.
5. Capital punishment.
6. Imposing the Sentence.

a. sentencing authority is exercised by the jury, an administrative body, a group of judges, or it may be mandated by statute.

b. sentencing is based on a variety of information available to the judge.

c. sometimes victim impact statements are allowed.

d. presentence investigation reports are often ordered by the judge.

i. prepared by the probation department.

ii. social and personal history as well as an evaluation of the defendant.

e. when accused is convicted of 2 or more charges, sentence must be issued on each charge.

      f. concurrent sentence - both sentences served at the same time, and imprisonment is completed after the longest time has been served.

      g. consecutive sentence - after completing one sentence, the other term of incarceration begins.

C. Sentencing Structures - according to the statutes of the jurisdiction in which the crime was committed.

  1. The indeterminate sentence - sentences with brief minimums and very long maximums, allowing parole boards to release when rehabilitated.

  2. The determinate sentence - fixed term issued by the judge that falls within the set statute.

  3. Structured sentencing - guidelines developed to control and structure the sentencing process and make it more "rational."

      a. based on the seriousness of the crime.

      b. based on the background of the offender.

  4. How are guidelines used?

      a. today 17 states use a type of structured sentencing.

      b. voluntary/advisory sentencing guidelines - guidelines used merely to suggest rather than mandate sentencing.

      c. presumptive guidelines - created by appointed sentencing commission, which determine an "ideal" sentence for a particular crime and offender.

  5. Configuring guidelines

      a. grid method.

  6. Future of structured sentencing

      a. research indicates judges diverge from guidelines.

      b. legislatures created loopholes in the guidelines.

      c. *Blakely v. Washington* - Court found sentencing guidelines were a violation of defendant's 6th Amendment rights because they allow a judge to consider aggravating factors that would enhance the sentence.

  7. Mandatory sentences

      a. require the incarceration of all offenders convicted of specific crimes.

      b. limits the judges' discretionary power.

      c. may supplement an indeterminate sentencing structure or is a feature of structured sentencing.

      d. some say they are overly restrictive.

  8. Truth in sentencing

      a. require offenders to serve a substantial portion of their prison sentences behind bars.

      b. parole eligibility and good time credits are limited.

      c. response to prison crowding.

      d. Violent Offender Incarceration and Truth-In-Sentencing Incentive Grants Program of the 1994 Crime Act:

          i. offered states funds to support the costs of longer sentences.
          ii. states must require convicted violent felony offenders to serve not less than 85% of their prison sentences.

9. Three strikes law
   a. life sentence for anyone convicted of a third offense.
   b. enables a judge to treat a third offense as a felony for purposes of applying the mandatory sentencing provisions.
   c. aimed at getting habitual offenders off the street.

D. How People Are Sentenced
1. Sentencing disparity
   a. common for people convicted of similar crimes to receive widely different sentences.
   b. few defendants actually serve their entire sentence.
   c. factors which influence sentencing:
      i. the severity of the offense.
      ii. offender's prior criminal record.
      iii. offender's use of violence.
      iv. offender's use of weapons.
      v. whether the crime was committed for money.
      vi. age, race, gender and economic status may also influence sentencing.

VII. The Death Penalty

A. In U.S. death penalty used in 38 states and the federal government with the approval of 75% of the population.
1. All but 4 states use lethal injection.
2. In 2003, 65 people were executed, 6 fewer than in 2002.

B. The Death Penalty Debate
1. Arguments for the death penalty:
   a. inherent in human nature.
   b. Bible describes methods of executing criminals.
   c. death penalty is in keeping with exacting the harshest penalty for the most severe crime.
   d. the only real threat available to deter crime.
   e. the ultimate incapacitation.
   f. cost effective.
   g. little racism; more whites are on death row.

2. Arguments against the death penalty:
   a. little deterrent effect.
   b. executions may increase the likelihood of murders being committed - referred to as the brutalization effect.
   c. capital punishment may be tarnished by racial, gender, ethnic, and other bias.
   d. it encourages criminals to escalate violent behavior.
   e. social vengeance by death is a primitive way of revenge.

        f. research indicates that many accept the death penalty, but
            believe it should be used rarely.
        g. it precludes any possibility of rehabilitation.
        h. death penalty is capricious; receiving death is similar to losing a
            lottery.
        i. punishment has never proven to be a deterrent.
        j. other nations have long abandoned the death penalty.
    C. Legality of the Death Penalty
        1. *Furman v. Georgia* - 1972 - Court held the discretionary imposition of
            the death penalty was cruel and unusual punishment under the 8th
            Amendment.
        2. *Gregg v. Georgia* - 1976 - Court found valid the Georgia statute that
            held a jury must find at least one "aggravating circumstance"
            before the death penalty can be imposed in murder cases.
        3. *Tison v. Arizona* - Court permitted executions of people who were
            major participants in a murder case and displayed reckless
            indifference to human life but did not actually kill anybody.
        4. *McCleskey v. Kemp* - Court upheld capital sentence of an African
            American man despite social science evidence that a black
            criminal who kills a white victim has a greater chance of receiving
            the death penalty.
        5. *Atkins v. Virginia* - Court rules that executions of mentally retarded
            criminals are "cruel and unusual punishments" prohibited by the
            8th Amendment.

VIII. Summary

Key Terms

Adversarial Process - The procedure used to determine truth in the adjudication of guilt
or innocence in which the defense (advocate for the accused) is pitted against the
prosecution (advocate for the state), with the judge acting as arbiter of the legal
rules. Under the adversarial system, the burden is on the state to prove the
charges beyond a reasonable doubt. This system of having the two parties
publicly debate has proved to be the most effective method of achieving the truth
regarding a set of circumstances. (Under the accusatory, or inquisitorial, system,
which is used in continental Europe, the charge is evidence of guilt that the
accused must disprove, and the judge takes an active part in the proceedings.)

Alternative Sanctions - The group of punishments falling between probation and prison;
"probation plus." Community-based sanctions, including house arrest and
intensive supervision, serve as alternatives to incarceration.

Assigned Counsel System - A list of private bar members who accept cases of indigent
criminals on a judge-by-judge, court-by-court, or case-by-case basis; this system
is used in less populated areas, where case flow is minimal and a full-time public
defender is not needed.

Bail - The monetary amount for or condition of pretrial release, normally set by a judge at the initial appearance. The purpose of bail is to ensure the return of the accused at subsequent proceedings. If the accused is unable to make bail, he or she is detained in jail. The Eighth Amendment provides that excessive bail shall not be required.

Bail Bonding Agent - A person whose business is providing bail to needy offenders, usually at an exorbitant rate of interest.

Bail Guidelines - Standard bail amounts set based on such factors as criminal history and the current charge.

Brutalization Effect - The belief that capital punishment creates an atmosphere of brutality that enhances rather than deters the level of violence in society. The death penalty reinforces the view that violence is an appropriate response to provocation.

Capital Punishment - The use of the death penalty to punish transgressors.

Complaint - A sworn allegation made in writing to a court or judge that an individual is guilty of some designated (complained of) offense. This is often the first legal document filed regarding a criminal offense. The complaint can be "taken out" by the victim, the police officer, the district attorney, or another interested party. Although the complaint charges an offense, an indictment or information may be the formal charging document.

Concurrent Sentence - Literally, running sentences together. Someone who is convicted of two or more charges must be sentenced on each charge. If the sentences are concurrent, they begin the same day and are completed after the longest term has been served.

Consecutive Sentence - Prison sentences for two or more criminal acts that are served one after the other.

Contract Attorney System - Providing counsel to indigent offenders by having attorneys under contract to the county handle all (or some) such cases.

Criminal Charge - A formal written document identifying the criminal activity, the facts of the case, and the circumstances of the arrest.

Cross-Examination - The process in which the defense and the prosecution interrogate witnesses during a trial.

Deposit Bail System - A system that allows defendants to post a percentage of their bond (usually 10 percent) with the court; the full amount is required only if the defendant fails to show for trial.

Determinate Sentences - Fixed terms of incarceration, such as 3 years' imprisonment. Determinant sentences are felt by many to be too restrictive for rehabilitative purposes; the advantage is that offenders know how much time they have to serve - that is, when they will be released.

Direct Examination - The questioning of one's own (prosecution or defense) witness during a trial.

Direct Verdict - The right of a judge to direct a jury to acquit a defendant because the state has not proven the elements of the crime or otherwise has not established guilt according to law.

Double Jeopardy - A defendant cannot be prosecuted by a jurisdiction more than once for a single offense.

Dual Sovereignty Doctrine - If a single act violates the laws of two states, the offender may be punished for each offense.

Federal Courts of Appeal - Court that hears appeals from the U.S. district courts.

Fine - A dollar amount usually exacted as punishment for a minor crime. Although fines are most commonly used in misdemeanors, they are also frequently employed in felonies where the offender has benefited financially.

Impact Statement - A victim's statement considered at a sentencing hearing.

Incarceration - Confinement in jail or prison.

Indeterminate Sentence - A term of incarceration with a stated minimum and maximum length, such as a sentence to prison for a period of from 3 to 10 years. The prisoner would be eligible for parole after the minimum sentence had been served. Based on the belief that sentences should fit the criminal, indeterminate sentences allow individualized sentences and provide for sentencing flexibility. Judges can set a high minimum to override the purpose of the indeterminate sentence.

Indictment - A written accusation returned by a grand jury charging an individual with a specified crime, based on the prosecutor's presentation of probable cause.

Information - Like an indictment, a formal charging document. The prosecuting attorney makes out the information and files it in court. Probable cause is determined at the preliminary hearing, which, unlike grand jury proceedings, is public and attended by the accused and his or her attorney.

Judge - The senior officer in a court of criminal law.

Jury Array - The initial list of persons chosen, which provides the state with a group of citizens potentially capable of serving on a jury; also called a venire.

Landmark Decision - A decision handed down by the Supreme Court that becomes the law of the land and serves as a precedent for similar legal cases.

Mandatory Prison Term - A statutory requirement that a certain penalty shall be set and carried out in all cases on conviction for a specified offense or series of offenses.

Missouri Plan - A way of picking judges through nonpartisan elections as a means of ensuring judicial performance standards.

Nolle Prosequi - The term used when a prosecutor decides to drop a case after a complaint has been formally made. Reasons for a *nolle prosequi* include insufficient evidence, reluctance of witnesses to testify, police error, and office policy.

Peremptory Challenge - The dismissal of a potential juror by either the prosecution or the defense for unexplained, discretionary reasons.

Plea Bargaining - The discussion between the defense counsel and the prosecution by which the accused agrees to plead guilty for certain considerations. The advantage to the defendant may be a reduction of the charges, a lenient sentence, or (in the case of multiple charges) dropped charges. The advantage to the prosecution is that a conviction is obtained without the time and expense of lengthy trial proceedings.

Precedent - A rule derived from previous judicial decisions and applied to future cases; the basis of common law.

Preventive Detention - The practice of holding dangerous suspects before trial without bail.

Probation - A sentence entailing the conditional release of a convicted offender into the community under the supervision of the court (in the form of a probation officer), subject to certain conditions for a specified time. The conditions are usually similar to those of parole. (Probation is a sentence, an alternative to incarceration; parole is administrative release from incarceration.) Violation of the conditions of probation may result in revocation of probation.

Prosecutor - Representative of the state (executive branch) in criminal proceedings; advocate for the state's case - the charge - in the adversary trial; for example, the attorney general of the United States, U.S. attorneys, attorneys general of the states, district attorneys, and police prosecutors. The prosecutor participates in investigations both before and after arrest, prepares legal documents, participates in obtaining arrest or search warrants, decides whether to charge a suspect and, if so, with which offense. The prosecutor argues the state's case at trial, advises the police, participates in plea negotiations, and makes sentencing recommendations.

Public Defender System - An attorney employed by the state whose job is to provide free legal counsel to indigent defendants.

Rebuttal Evidence - Evidence that was not used when the prosecution initially presented its case.

Recovery Agent - An individual hired by the bonding agent to track down a fugitive in order to recover the lost bond. These modern bounty hunters receive a share of the recovery, and unlike police, bounty hunters can enter a suspect's home without a warrant in most states; also called a skip tracer.

Redirect Examination - Questions asked by the prosecutor about information brought out during cross-examination.

Release on Recognizance (ROR) - A nonmonetary condition for the pretrial release of an accused individual; an alternative to monetary bail that is granted after the court determines that the accused has ties in the community, has no prior record of default, and is likely to appear at subsequent proceedings.

Removed for Cause - Removing a juror because he or she is biased, has prior knowledge about a case, or otherwise is unable to render a fair and impartial judgment in a case.

Sentencing Disparity - People convicted of similar criminal acts may receive widely different sentences.

Sentencing Guidelines - Guidelines to control and structure the sentencing process and make it more rational; the more serious the crime and the more extensive the offender's criminal background, the longer the prison term recommended by the guidelines.

Skip Tracer - An individual hired by the bonding agent to track down a fugitive in order to recover the lost bond. These modern bounty hunters receive a share of the recovery, and unlike police, bounty hunters can enter a suspect's home without a warrant in most states; also called a recovery agent.

Surety Bond - The 10 percent the defendant pays to the bonding agent, which serves as the bonding agent's commission.

Truth-In-Sentencing Laws - Laws that require offenders to serve a substantial portion of their prison sentence behind bars.

U.S. District Courts - Trial courts that have jurisdiction over cases involving violations of federal law, such as interstate transportation of stolen vehicles and racketeering.

U.S. Supreme Court - The court of last resort for all cases tried in the various federal and state courts.

Venire - The group called for jury duty from which jury panels are selected.

Voir Dire - The process in which a potential jury panel is questioned by the prosecution and the defense to select jurors who are unbiased and objective.

Writ of Certiorari - An order of a superior court requesting that the record of an inferior court (or administrative body) be brought forward for review or inspection.

Discussion Exercises

1. Have the students visit the local courts. Discuss their preconceived notions of court and their actual experience.

2. Divide the students into groups of 12. Provide each group with the same information concerning a criminal case. Ask the students to come to a consensus as to the guilt or innocence of the offender and an appropriate penalty that may be required. Then, ask the students to present their findings to the class and compare across the final decisions.

3. Divide the students into two groups. Have one develop an argument in support of the death penalty and have the other develop an argument against the death penalty. Discuss which side is able to make the stronger case. How does one's own position on this topic impact his or her evaluation of the debate?

InfoTrac Assignment

GETTING STARTED: Search term words for subject guide: State Courts, Federal Courts, Prosecutor, Defense Attorney, Judge, Bail, Plea Bargain, Jury, Death Penalty.

CRITICAL THINKING PROJECT: Using the search term "Death Penalty," find relevant articles.

Here are three articles:

Bedau, Hugo Adam. "Death's Dwindling Dominion: Public opinion is shifting against the death penalty. What will it take to abolish it?" *The American Prospect*.

De La Vega, Connie. "Going it Alone: The rest of the civilized world has abolished the death penalty. Will the United States follow suit?" *The American Prospect*.

Templeton, Jean M. "Shutting Down Death Row: Illinois' death-penalty reforms may presage a fairer criminal justice system." *The American Prospect*.

Fill in the Blank

1. A formal written criminal accusation given by a grand jury setting out the crimes for which the defendant is to stand trial is known as a **bill of indictment**.
    (page number 559)

2. The ***nolo contendere*** plea is equivalent to a guilty plea but cannot be used as evidence in subsequent cases.
    (page number 560)

3. **Arraignment** is the step at which the accused are read the charges against them, asked how they wish to plead, and advised of their rights.
    (page number 560)

4. **Bail** is money or some other security provided to the court to ensure the appearance of a defendant at trial.
    (page number 560)

5. **Preventive detention** is the practice of holding dangerous suspects before trial without bail.
    (page number 561)

6. Those who provide bail to indigent offenders, usually at high rates of interest, are known as **bail bonding agents**.
    (page number 562)

7. **Release on recognizance** is when the defendant is released on a promise to appear, without any requirement of money bond.
    (page number 563)

8. A **plea bargain** is the decision between the prosecutor and the defense attorney to have the defendant plead guilty in exchange for some concession.
    (page number 564)

9. **Venire** is the list of jurors called for jury duty from which jury panels are selected.
    (page number 566)

10. **Voir dire** is the process of jury selection by questioning the prospective panel members.
    (page number 566)

11. A **peremptory challenge** is when either the prosecutor or the defense can excuse jurors for no particular or undisclosed reason during the voir dire process.
    (page number 566)

12. **Direct examination** is initial questioning of a witness by the party who called the witness to obtain testimony regarding the case.
    (page number 567)

13. Questioning of a witness by the party that did not call the witness to obtain testimony regarding the case is known as **cross-examination**.
    (page number 567)

14. Secondary questioning of a witness by a party who called the witness to obtain testimony regarding the case is known as **redirect examination**.
    (page number 567)

15. A verdict in a case where the judge removes the decision from the jury by either telling them what to do or by actually making the decision is known as a **directed verdict**.
    (page number 567)

Multiple Choice

1. Trial courts of the federal court system are known as:
    a. state courts
    b. supreme courts
    c. federal courts of appeal
    d. U.S. District Courts
    (Answer = d, page number 550)

2. The courts that hear the first appeal in the federal system from the lower courts is known as:
    a. state courts
    b. supreme courts
    c. U.S. District Courts
    d. federal courts of appeal
    (Answer = d, page number 550)

3. The court of last resort for all cases tried in the various federal and state courts is known as the:
    a. state courts
    b. Supreme Court
    c. U.S. District Courts
    d. federal courts of appeal
    (Answer = b, page number 550)

4. An order issued by the Supreme Court when it decides to hear a case is known as a:
    a. warrant
    b. complaint
    c. writ of certiorari
    d. indictment
    (Answer = c, page number 550)

5. A decision by the Supreme Court that must be honored by all lower courts is known as a(n):
    a. prosecution
    b. indictment
    c. information
    d. precedent
    (Answer = d, page number 550)

6. A decision by the Supreme Court that becomes the law of the land and serves as a precedent for similar legal issues is known as a(n):
    a. prosecution
    b. indictment
    c. information
    d. landmark decision
    (Answer = d, page number 550)

7. The procedure used to determine truth in the adjudication of guilt or innocence in which the defense is pitted against the prosecution, with the judge acting as arbiter of the legal rules, is known as:
    a. an arraignment
    b. an indictment
    c. sentencing
    d. the adversarial process
    (Answer = d, page number 552)

8. They represent the state in criminal matters that come before the courts.
    a. judges
    b. juries
    c. prosecution
    d. public defenders
    (Answer = c, page number 552)

9. A salaried staff of full-time or part-time attorneys that render indigent criminal defense services through a public or private nonprofit organization, or as direct government paid employees are known as:
    a. public defenders
    b. prosecutors
    c. judges
    d. juries
    (Answer = a, page number 557)

10. Public defendant services provided mainly by local private attorneys appointed and paid by the court are known as:
    a. indigents
    b. judges
    c. bail bondsmen
    d. the assigned counsel system
    (Answer = d, page number 557)

11. The senior officer in a court of criminal law that rules on the appropriateness of conduct, settles questions of evidence and procedure, and guides the questioning of witnesses is known as the:
    a. prosecutor
    b. judge
    c. jury
    d. witness
    (Answer = b, page number 558)

12. A method of selecting judges with a three part approach is known as the:
    a. Missouri plan
    b. voir dire
    c. venire
    d. arraignment
    (Answer = a, page number 559)

13. A sworn written statement to a court by the police, the prosecutor, or an individual alleging that an individual has committed an offense and requesting indictment and prosecution is known as a(n):
    a. information
    b. indictment
    c. warrant
    d. complaint
    (Answer = d, page number 559)

14. The written accusation of the prosecutor setting out the charges against a defendant and used in place of the indictment in some jurisdictions is known as a(n):
    a. complaint
    b. information
    c. indictment
    d. warrant
    (Answer = b, page number 559)

15. A formal written criminal accusation given by a grand jury setting out the crimes for which the defendant is to stand trial is known as:
    a. information
    b. complaint
    c. bill of indictment
    d. warrant
    (Answer = c, page number 559)

16. Money provided to the court to ensure the appearance of the defendant at trial is the:
    a. voir dire
    b. information
    c. complaint
    d. bail
    (Answer = d, page number 560)

17. The step at which the accused are read the charges against them, asked how they wish to plead, and are advised of their rights is known as the:
    a. grand jury
    b. preliminary hearing
    c. first appearance
    d. arraignment
    (Answer = d, page number 560)

18. When defendants are detained because they cannot afford to make bail or because of the danger they present to the community, this is known as:
    a. direct examination
    b. preventive detention
    c. arraignment
    d. peremptory challenge
    (Answer = b, page number 561)

19. Those who provide bail to indigent offenders, usually at high rates of interest, are known as:
    a. bail bonding agents
    b. attorneys
    c. judges
    d. prosecutors
    (Answer = a, page number 562)

20. When the defendant is released on a promise to appear, without any requirement of money bond, it is known as:
    a. a peremptory challenge
    b. voir dire
    c. a deposit bail
    d. release on recognizance
    (Answer = d, page number 563)

21. When the defendant offers a percentage of the bail amount, such as 10%, with the court, this is known as:
    a. release on recognizance
    b. a deposit bail
    c. voir dire
    d. a peremptory challenge
    (Answer = b, page number 563)

22. The Federal Bail Reform Act of 1984 provides that federal offenders may be detained without bail under certain specifications. This is called:
    a. guideline sentences
    b. contextual discrimination
    c. bail guidelines
    d. an arraignment
    (Answer = c, page number 563)

23. The decision between the prosecutor and the defense attorney to have the defendant plead guilty in exchange for some concession is known as:
    a. plea bargaining
    b. voir dire
    c. venire
    d. cross-examination
    (Answer = a, page number 564)

24. A list of jurors called for jury duty from which jury panels are selected is known as:
    a. voir dire
    b. venire
    c. bail bondsmen
    d. the judge list
    (Answer = b, page number 566)

25. The process of jury selection by questioning the prospective panel members is known as:
    a. arraignment
    b. a probable cause hearing
    c. venire
    d. voir dire
    (Answer = d, page number 566)

26. The fact that either the prosecution or the defense can excuse jurors for no particular or undisclosed reason during the voir dire process is known as:
    a. a peremptory challenge
    b. a challenge for cause
    c. direct examination
    d. cross-examination
    (Answer = a, page number 566)

27. Initial questioning of a witness by the party who called the witness to obtain testimony regarding the case is known as:
    a. direct examination
    b. cross-examination
    c. redirect examination
    d. all of the above
    (Answer = a, page number 567)

28. Questioning of a witness by the party that did not call the witness to obtain testimony regarding the case is known as:
    a. direct examination
    b. cross-examination
    c. redirect examination
    d. all of the above
    (Answer = b, page number 567)

29. Secondary questioning of a witness by the party who called the witness to obtain testimony regarding the case is known as:
    a. direct examination
    b. cross-examination
    c. redirect examination
    d. all of the above
    (Answer = c, page number 567)

30. A verdict in a case where the judge removes the decision from the jury is called:
    a. a directed verdict
    b. redirect examination
    c. a bill of indictment
    d. a complaint
    (Answer = a, page number 567)

31. After the defense concludes its case, the government may present evidence to counteract the case of the defense. This is known as:
    a. hearsay evidence
    b. an indictment
    c. a rebuttal
    d. sentencing
    (Answer = c, page number 567)

32. The criminal sanction imposed by the court on a convicted defendant is known as:
    a. the indictment
    b. a rebuttal
    c. hearsay evidence
    d. sentencing
    (Answer = d, page number 568)

33. A statutory requirement that a certain penalty will be set and carried out is known as:
    a. a mandatory prison term
    b. a concurrent sentence
    c. a consecutive sentence
    d. a rebuttal
    (Answer = a, page number 571)

34. When both sentences are served at the same time, and the term of imprisonment is completed after the longest term has been served, this is known as a:
    a. consecutive sentence
    b. mandatory prison term
    c. rebuttal
    d. concurrent sentence
    (Answer = d, page number 571)

35. When a convicted offender completes one sentence before the other prison term begins, this is known as a:
    a. mandatory prison term
    b. rebuttal
    c. consecutive sentence
    d. concurrent sentence
    (Answer = c, page number 571)

36. A type of prison sentence where the exact length of imprisonment and parole supervision is fixed within statutory limits by a parole authority is called a(n):
    a. concurrent sentence
    b. consecutive sentence
    c. indeterminate sentence
    d. determinate sentence
    (Answer = c, page number 572)

37. A type of prison sentence where the exact length of imprisonment and parole supervision is fixed within statutory limits by the legislatures is called a(n):
    a. indeterminate sentence
    b. determinate sentence
    c. concurrent sentence
    d. consecutive sentence
    (Answer = b, page number 572)

38. _____ are based on the seriousness of the crime and the background of an offender. The more serious the crime and the more extensive the offender's criminal background, the longer the prison term recommended.
   a. Sentencing guidelines
   b. Determinate sentences
   c. Indeterminate sentences
   d. Concurrent sentences
   (Answer = a, page number 572)

39. When people convicted of similar criminal acts often receive widely different sentences, it is known as:
   a. guideline sentences
   b. sentencing disparity
   c. concurrent sentences
   d. consecutive sentences
   (Answer = b, page number 575)

40. Which Supreme Court case ruled that executions of mentally retarded criminals are "cruel and unusual punishments" prohibited by the Eighth Amendment?
   a. *Atkins v. Virginia*
   b. *Wilkins v. Missouri*
   c. *Furman v. Georgia*
   d. *Gregg v. Georgia*
   (Answer = a, page number 583)

True/False

1. The nation's 16,000 courts are organized on the municipal, county, state, and federal levels.
   (Answer = true, page number 550)

2. Most states employ a single tiered court structure.
   (Answer = false, page number 550)

3. A specialty court, Gun Court, has jurisdiction over the burgeoning number of cases involving substance abuse and trafficking.
   (Answer = false, page number 552)

4. The judge, the prosecutor, and the defense attorney are the key players in the adversarial process.
   (Answer = true, page number 552)

5. In the federal system, the chief prosecuting officer is the U.S. attorney general.
   (Answer = true, page number 553)

6. Federal prosecutors are semiprofessional, unpaid, contract workers.
    (Answer = false, page number 553)

7. Prosecutors maintain broad discretion in the exercise of their duties.
    (Answer = true, page number 554)

8. The discretion given to the prosecutor to decide to drop a case is known as *nolle prosequi.*
    (Answer = true, page number 554)

9. Characteristics of the crime, the criminal, and the victim are important influences on prosecutorial discretion.
    (Answer = true, page number 556)

10. The public defenders represent the state in criminal matters that come before the courts.
    (Answer = false, page number 557)

11. Judges have the easiest job when compared to that of prosecutors and public defenders.
    (Answer = false, page number 558)

12. Bail represents money or some other security provided to the court to ensure the appearance of the defendant at trial.
    (Answer = true, page number 560)

13. The bail system goes back to English common law.
    (Answer = true, page number 561)

14. Skip tracers can enter a suspect's house without a warrant in most states.
    (Answer = true, page number 562)

15. The brutalization effect proposes that executions actually decrease the likelihood of murders being committed.
    (Answer = false, page number 577)

Essay Questions

1. Compare and contrast federal and state courts. Differentiate some of the jurisdictional situations that may occur between the federal and state governments.
    (page numbers 550-552)

2. Describe the actors in the judicatory process. What are their roles? Who possesses power and over what aspects of the criminal procedure?
    (page numbers 552-559)

3. Define bail. What are the different types of bail available to a defendant? When is bail available and when is it not available to a defendant?
    (page numbers 560-564)

4. Describe plea-bargaining. What is the purpose of this practice and what are the benefits?
    (page numbers 564-565)

5. What is the jury selection process? What are the various methods that a prospective juror may be excused from a trial?
    (page numbers 565-566)

Chapter Seventeen

Corrections

Summary

Chapter Seventeen examines the corrections system of the criminal justice system. The chapter begins with the history of punishment and corrections from the Middle Ages to the modern era of today. The various types of punishment in the United States are explained and defined beginning with probation. The discussion continues with intermediate sanctions, jails, and prisons. Chapter Seventeen concludes with an explanation of parole and the parolee.

Chapter Objectives

After reading this chapter the student should be able to:

- Be familiar with the early history of punishment
- Describe the development of the prison as a means of punishment
- Describe the nature of probation and its various services
- Discuss the effectiveness of probation and the concept of revocation
- Be familiar with the various forms of alternative sanctions
- Know the purpose served by the jail, its problems, and what is being done to improve jail conditions
- Describe different types of correctional facilities and their level of security
- Understand the experience of living in prison
- Discuss correctional treatment and the nature of prison violence
- Show how the problems of parolees and inmate re-entry have influenced the correctional system

Chapter Overview

Introduction
History of Punishment and Corrections
      The Middle Ages
      Punishment in the Seventeenth and Eighteenth Centuries
      Corrections in the Late Eighteenth and Nineteenth Centuries
      Corrections in the Twentieth Century
      The Modern Era
      Contemporary Corrections
Probation
      Probationary Sentences

Chapter Outline

I. Introduction
II. History of Punishment and Corrections
   A. The Middle Ages
   1. Little law or governmental control existed (5th to 11th century A.D.).
   2. Offenses settled by blood feuds between families of injured parties.
   3. After 11th century, forfeiture of land and property were common punishment for lawbreakers.
   4. *Wergild* - payment to the injured party.

5. Corporal punishment - whipping or branding as a substitute penalty for a fine.
6. Wealthy could buy their way out of punishment while the poor were subject to execution and mutilation.
7. Punishment became gruesome and a public spectacle.

B. Punishment in the Seventeenth and Eighteenth Centuries
1. Population growth in England and France checked by warfare and internal disturbances.
2. Labor shortage due to warfare.
3. Punishment changed to meet demands of social conditions; instead of capital and corporal punishment, offenders were forced to labor.
   a. poor laws required poor, vagrants, and vagabonds to work in public or private enterprise.
   b. houses of correction developed to assign work details for petty offenders.
   c. galley slaves - offenders forced into sea duty; loathsome punishment.
   d. Vagrancy Act of 1597 - legalized deportation of offenders.
      i. transportation to colonies became a popular punishment.
      ii. supplied labor, was cheap, and was profitable for the government since owners paid for convict services.

C. Corrections in the Late Eighteenth and Nineteenth Centuries
1. Population in America increased, as did the gulf between poor workers and wealthy landowners.
2. Crime rate rose significantly leading to a return of physical punishment and the death penalty.
3. William Penn - Pennsylvania - led correctional reform.
   a. revised Pennsylvania's criminal code to forbid torture.
   b. penalties of imprisonment at hard labor, flogging, fines, and forfeiture of property were implemented.
   c. instituted house of corrections, similar to today's jail.
   d. in effect until Penn's death in 1718, when code reverted back to earlier emphasis on public punishment and harsh brutality.
4. 1776 - Penn's code readopted.
5. 1787 - Quaker, Dr. Benjamin Rush formed the Philadelphia Society for Alleviating the Miseries of Public Prisons.
   a. to bring humane and orderly treatment to the penal system.
   b. led to limiting the death penalty by the legislature to cases of treason, murder, rape, and arson.
6. 1790 - Quakers called for renovation of Prison system.
   a. Philadelphia's Walnut Street Jail:
      i. solitary confinement.
      ii. no right to work.
      iii. penitentiary house - quarters of Walnut Street Jail which housed solitary or separate cells.
   b. overcrowding undermined the solitary confinement.

7. The Auburn System - built in 1816 in New York.
    a. tier system - cells were built vertically on five floors of the structure.
    b. referred to as the congregate system - prisoners ate and worked in groups.
    c. 1819 - solitary cells constructed for unruly prisoners.
    d. three classes of inmates created:
        i. solitary confinement for prison discipline.
        ii. allowed labor as a form of recreation.
        iii. largest class worked and ate together in the day and in seclusion in the nights.
    e. philosophy - crime prevention through fear of punishment and silent confinement.
    f. total isolation abolished in 1823 due to high rates of mental breakdown, suicide, and self-mutilation.
    g. hard work and silence became foundation of Auburn system.
8. The New Pennsylvania System - 1818.
    a. single cell with no work and no classifications of inmates.
    b. called the Western Penitentiary - unusual architectural design.
        i. built in semicircle with cells along the circumference.
        ii. solitary confinement with an hour a day for exercise.
    c. supporters believed penitentiary to be a place to do penance.
        i. remove the sinner from society and allow prisoner isolation to reflect on evils of crime.
    d. depressed conditions; inmates treated harshly, routinely whipped or tortured.
        i. corporal punishment moved behind doors and became more savage.
9. Post-Civil War Developments - late 19th century like that of today.
    a. congregate system adopted in all states except Pennsylvania.
    b. prisons experienced overcrowding with the single cell principle often ignored
    c. prison industry developed:
        i. contract system - officials sold inmate labor to private businesses.
        ii. convict-lease system - state leased its prisoners to business for fixed annuals fee and gave up supervision and control.
        iii. state account system - prisoners produce goods in prison for state use.
    d. prison industry led to abuse of inmates.
    e. prisons manufactured clothes, shoes, boots, furniture, etc.
    f. 1880's - trade union opposition sparked restrictions on interstate commerce of prison goods and ended profitability.

  g. Z. R. Brockway - Warden of Elmira Reformatory in New York:
    i. advocated individualized treatment, indeterminate
      sentences, and parole.
    ii. program included elementary education for illiterates,
      designated library hours, lectures by college faculty,
      and vocational training shops.
D. Corrections in the Twentieth Century
  1. Mutual Welfare League leader T. M. Osborne advocated reform.
    a. proposed better treatment, end of harsh corporal punishment.
    b. creation of meaningful prison industry and education programs.
    c. prisoners should not be isolated from society.
  2. Opposition by conservative prison administrators and state officials.
    a. believed stern discipline needed to control dangerous inmates.
    b. solitary confinement in dark, bare cells was common.
  3. 1930's saw liberal reform:
    a. inmate suits changed from red and white stripe to gray.
    b. code of silence and lockstep shuffle ended.
    c. movies and radios appeared in prisons.
    d. visiting policies and mail privileges were liberalized.
    e. specialized prisons to treat different types of offenders.
    f. prison industry evolved.
      i. convict-lease system and forced inmate labor ended.
    g. severe discipline, harsh rules, and solitary confinement
      remained.
E. The Modern Era
  1. 1960 to 1980's - inmate litigation seeking greater rights and privileges.
    a. inmates received rights of freedom of religion, speech, medical
      care, due process, and proper living conditions.
  2. Since 1980's - prisoners' rights movement has slowed.
  3. Violence in correctional systems became national scandal.
    a. riots at New York's Attica Prison and New Mexico State
      Penitentiary.
  4. Failure of rehabilitation prompted many to reconsider incarceration.
  5. Inability of prison to reduce recidivism.
F. Contemporary Corrections
  1. Community-based programs:
    a. probation - supervision under control of the sentencing court.
    b. an array of intermediate sanctions.
  2. Secure confinement
    a. jail - house misdemeanants (and some felons) serving their
      sentence, as well as those awaiting trial not released on
      bail.
    b. parole - supervises prisoners given early release from their
      sentences.

III. Probation - suspension of the offender's sentence in return for the promise of good behavior in the community under the supervision of the probation department.

    A. Probationary Sentences

        1. May be granted by state and federal district courts and state superior (felony) courts.

        2. Accepted, widely used for adult felons, misdemeanants and juvenile delinquents.

    B. Probation Organizations

        1. About 2,000 adult probation agencies nationwide monitor more than 4 million adults under federal, state, or local probation.

        2. About 50% convicted of committing a felony.

    C. Probation Services

        1. Investigation - after conviction, probation department investigates offender's case submits presentence investigation to the sentencing judge.

        2. Treatment - if offender is sentenced to probation, the department assesses their personality and treatment needs - offender classification.

        3. Supervision - minimal risks will be given little supervision, perhaps a monthly visit or phone call.

            a. probationers are placed in treatment programs such as community mental health, substance abuse and family counseling clinics when available.

    D. Probation Rules and Revocation

        1. Probationers are given a set of rules to guide their behavior:

            a. maintaining steady employment.

            b. making restitution for loss or damage.

            c. cooperating with the probation officer.

            d. obeying all laws.

            e. meeting family responsibilities.

            f. individualized rules tailored to offender's specific needs.

        2. If rules are violated, probation may be revoked by the court and the person may begin serving their active sentence.

    E. Success of Probation

        1. Studies indicate that probation is not as successful as hoped.

            a. 60% of probationers successfully complete probation.

            b. most probation violations are for technical violations - violation of probation rules.

        2. Recidivism rate is lower for probationers than prison inmates.

IV. Intermediate Sanctions

    A. New form of corrections that falls between probation and incarceration.

        1. Alternative to incarceration.

        2. Punishments that are fair, equitable, and proportional.

        3. Likely candidates are convicted offenders who would be sent to prison, have a low risk of recidivating, and pose little threat to society.

B. Fines
    1. Monetary payments imposed on the offender as an intermediate punishment for criminal acts.
    2. Can be used alone or with other punishments.
    3. Often other monetary sanctions are added to fines, such as:
        a. court costs.
        b. public defender fees.
        c. probation and treatment fees.
        d. victim restitution.
        e. day fines - fines geared to an offender's net daily income in an effort to make them more equitable.

C. Forfeiture
    1. Financially based alternative sanction.
    2. The seizure of goods and instrumentality's related to the commission or outcome of a criminal act.
    3. Criminal forfeiture - targets criminal defendants and only follows a criminal conviction.
    4. Civil forfeiture - targets property used in a crime and does not require that formal criminal proceedings be initiated against a person or that they be proven guilty of a crime.
    5. Forfeiture evolved from the Middle Ages.
        a. forfeiture of an estate was a mandatory result of felony convictions.
        b. reintroduced to American law with the passage of the RICO and the Continuing Criminal Enterprises acts; allows the seizure of property derived from illegal enterprises.

D. Restitution
    1. Requires offender to pay the victim (monetary restitution) or serve the community (community service restitution).
    2. Offers convicted offenders a way to avoid jail, prison, or probation.
    3. Appears to benefit the victim, the offender, the criminal justice system, and society.
    4. Inexpensive, avoids stigma, and helps compensate crime victims.
    5. Most offenders successfully complete restitution and have low recidivism rate.

E. Split Sentencing and Shock Probation
    1. Alternative sanctions that allow judges to grant offenders community release only after they have sampled prison life.
    2. Split sentencing - jail term as condition of probation.
    3. Shock probation - resentencing an offender after a short prison stay.

F. Intensive Probation Supervision
    1. Involves small caseloads of 15 to 40 clients kept under close supervision by probation officers.
    2. Goals:
        a. diversion - keeping probationers from the overcrowded prisons.
        b. control - high-risk offenders kept under closer security.

c. reintegration - offenders can maintain community ties and be reoriented toward a more productive life while avoiding imprisonment.
3. Most have criteria as to eligibility:
  a. nature of the offense.
  b. offender's criminal background.
  c. some exclude violent offenders.
4. Failure rate is quite high, about 50%.
G. Home Confinement/Electronic Monitoring - house arrest or home detention.
  1. Requires convicted offenders to spend extended periods of time in their own homes as an alternative to incarceration.
  2. No data yet as to crime deterrence.
  3. Electronic monitoring device - offenders wear devices attached to their ankles, wrists, or necks that send signals back to the control office.
    a. if offender leaves designated area at unauthorized time, the signal is broken and failure recorded.
    b. other systems use a variety of technologies to monitor offender.
  4. Being hailed as one of the most important developments in correctional policy.
  5. Electronic monitoring works best on nonviolent offenders, drunk drivers.
H. Residential Community Corrections
  1. Nonsecure building that is not a part of a prison or jail and house pretrial and adjudicated adults.
  2. Residents depart for work, attend school, or participate in community correction activities and programs.
  3. Clients reestablish family and friendship ties.
  4. Shock of sudden reentry into society is reduced.
  5. Can provide intermediate sanctions as well as prerelease center for those about to be released from prison.
  6. Can be used as a halfway house.
I. Boot Camps/Shock Incarceration
  1. Typically involve youthful, first-time offenders.
  2. Feature military discipline and physical training.
  3. Short periods (90 to 180 days) of high-intensity exercise and work.
  4. Designed to promote responsibility and improve decision-making skills, build self-confidence, and teach socialization skills.
  5. Inmates treated with rough intensity by drillmasters.
  6. Results are mixed as to success rate.
J. Can Alternatives Work?
  1. Little evidence that alternatives prevent crime, reduce recidivism or work better than other programs.
  2. Other studies indicate that alternative sanctions have met their goal of providing correctional alternatives.

V. Jails
   A. Secure institution used to:
      1. Detain offenders before trial if they cannot afford or are not eligible for bail.
      2. House misdemeanants sentenced to terms of one year or less, as well as some nonserious felons.
   B. Originated in Europe in 16th century.
      1. Used to house those awaiting trial and punishment.
      2. Did not house sentenced criminals because punishment was fine, corporal punishment, or death.
   C. Walnut Street Jail - 1st modern jail - built 1790.
   D. Jail Populations
      1. Population steadily increasing; close to 700,000 people.
   E. Jail Conditions
      1. Jail conditions are marked by violence, overcrowding, deteriorated physical conditions, and lack of treatment efforts.
      2. New generation jails
         a. modern designs to improve effectiveness.
         b. officer is stationed in a "pod" to observe and relate to inmates.
         c. officer wears device with direct contact with central control.

VI. Prisons
   A. Federal Bureau of Prison and every state government maintain closed correctional facilities.
      1. Although crime rate has fallen for past decade, prison populations continue to rise; more felons sentenced to prison.
      2. Most rapid increases seen for violent offenders.
      3. As of January 1, 2004, 1,470,000 prisoners under federal and state jurisdiction.
   B. Types of Prisons
      1. Categorized according to level of security and inmate populations:
         a. maximum-security prisons - surrounded by high walls, have elaborate security measures, armed guards, and house potentially dangerous inmates.
         b. medium-security prisons - similar to maximum but usually contain less violent offenders.
         c. minimum-security prisons - operate without armed guards or walls; house the most trustworthy and least violent offenders.
      2. Super-maximum prisons
         a. found in more than 30 states.
         b. many subject inmates to nearly complete isolation and deprivation of sensory stimuli.
         c. considered the ultimate control mechanism for disruptive inmates.
      3. Farms and camps
         a. found primarily in the South and the West.

b. farms - inmates produce dairy products, grain, and vegetable crops used in state government facilities.

c. camps - forestry camp inmates maintain state parks, fight forest fires, and do reforestation work.

d. ranches - usually in the West, employ inmates in cattle raising and horse breeding.

e. road gangs repair roads and state highways.

4. Private prisons

    a. 1986 - U.S. Corrections Corporation opened 1st private state prison in Marion, Kentucky, a 300 bed minimum-security facility.

    b. as of 2004, privately operated facilities housed 95,522 inmates (5.7% of state and 12.6% of federal inmates).

    c. for-profit incarceration.

5. Legal issues

    a. concerns about a state supported entity that actually has more freedom to exert control that the state itself.

C. Prison Inmates: Male

1. Inmates are poor, young, with less than a high school education.

2. By 2010, inmates 51 and over will make up 33% of prison population.

3. Over 60% have been incarcerated before.

D. Living in Prison

1. Inmates are cut off from families, friends, and associates.

2. Inmates must deal with a lot of changes:

    a. fathers become depressed about children.

    b. families and friends have trouble visiting due to long distances.

    c. mail is censored and often destroyed.

    d. prison is a total institution regulating dress, work, sleep, and eating.

    e. losses include goods and services, heterosexual relationships, autonomy, security, and privacy.

    f. those who obey rules are offered, choice work, privileges and educational opportunities.

    g. those who break rules may be segregated, locked in their cells or put in solitary confinement (the hole).

    h. inmates must deal with sexual exploitation and violence.

    i. to avoid victimization, inmates must adapt to new lifestyle; some join gangs and cliques for protection.

    j. hustle - black market economy involving the sale of illegal commodities such as drugs, alcohol, weapons, and illegal food and supplies.

    k. inmates must deal with daily racial conflict.

    l. must deal with anxiety of release when parole nears.

3. Inmate society
    a. inmate subculture - unique social code; unwritten guidelines that express the values, attitudes, and types of behavior that the older inmates demand of younger inmates.
    b. prisonization process - inmate's assimilation into the prison culture through acceptance of its language, sexual code, and norms of behavior.
    c. importation model - inmate culture is affected by the values of newcomers.
4. The new inmate culture
    a. old inmate culture harmful due to values and norms insulated inmate from change efforts.
    b. old inmate culture created order and prevented violence.
    c. old inmate culture is dying or dead in most prisons.
    d. racial tension has created many divisions.
    e. predatory inmates victimize others without fear of retaliation.
    f. new inmate culture is one of danger and chaos.
    g. gangs forming and engaging in ever-increasing violent confrontations.
E. Prison Life: Females
    1. Make up 5-6% of adult prison population; increasing at a fast pace.
    2. Usually housed in minimum-security institutions more like college dorms.
    3. Women do not present the danger that men do in prison.
    4. Women deal with a lot of fear and violence.
    5. Many women undergo a process of socialization with danger and volatile situations.
    6. Often experience severe anxiety and anger due to separation from families.
        a. females may resort to self-destructive acts to cope with their problems.
        b. females are more likely to be treated with mood-altering drugs and placed in psychiatric care.
    7. Surrogate families develop in female prisons.
    8. Helping the female inmate:
        a. health care is an issue.
        b. many institutions have inadequate facilities to deal with pregnancy, HIV, and AIDS.
        c. Female inmates are still being trained vocationally for women's roles.
F. Correctional Treatment
    1. Over 90% participate in a program or activity after admission.
    2. Therapy and counseling - rely heavily on counseling and clinical therapy.

3. Therapeutic communities (TCs) - TC approach to substance abuse uses a psychosocial, experiential learning process that relies on positive peer pressure within a highly structured social environment.
4. Educational programs
    a. first treatment programs at the Walnut Street Jail were educational.
    b. today, most institutions provide some education.
5. Vocational rehabilitation
    a. most prisons operate numerous vocational training programs to help inmates develop skills for employment in society.
    b. work furlough programs in some prisons.
    c. prerelease and postrelease employment services in some prisons.
6. Private industry in prisons
    a. can take many forms; one is the free-venture program that hires inmates to work off prison grounds.
    b. attractive on paper, has used few inmates.
    c. increases employment opportunities on the outside.
7. Elderly inmates
    a. require healthcare, diets, and work and recreational opportunities that differ from the general population.
8. Inmate self-help
    a. inmates have organized self-help groups to prevent recidivism: Alcoholics Anonymous, Boy Scout Troops, racial and ethnic groups, and groups designed to help inmates find strength on the outside.
9. Does Rehabilitation Work?
    a. some question the effectiveness of rehabilitation.
    b. high-risk offenders are more likely to commit crimes after they have been placed in treatment programs.
    c. some view prisons as places of incapacitation and confinement; their purpose is punishment, not treatment.
    d. treatment more effective if matched with the needs of inmates.
G. Prison Violence
1. Jails and prisons have a climate of violence.
2. Causes of prison violence:
    a. inmates may suffer from personality disorders.
    b. prisons may convert people to violence by their inhumane conditions, overcrowding, depersonalization, and threats of rape.
    c. mismanagement, lack of strong security, and inadequate control by officials.
    d. changing prison population to younger, more violent inmates.

3. Prison riots
   a. causal factors include unnatural institutional environment, antisocial characteristics of inmates, inept management, inadequate facilities, etc.

H. Corrections and the Rule of Law
   1. Freedom of press and speech - courts ruled inmates retain freedom of speech and press unless it interferes with institutional freedom.
   2. Medical rights - inmates are entitled to proper medical attention.

I. Cruel and Unusual Punishment - many rulings by the Court as to cruel and unusual punishment violating the 8th Amendment.

VII. **Parole** - the planned release and community supervision of incarcerated offenders before the expiration of their prison sentences.

A. Discretionary Parole
   1. Some jurisdictions grant parole by a decision of a state parole board.
   2. Board meet offender, reviews the information, and decides whether or not to grant parole.
   3. Good time credits - reduce the minimum sentence and therefore hasten eligibility for parole.
   4. Considerations include inmate's offense, time served, evidence of adjustment, and opportunities on the outside.

B. Mandatory Parole
   1. States with determinate sentencing statutes do not use parole boards, but release inmates at the conclusion of their pre-determined sentence less accumulated good time.

C. The Parolee in the Community
   1. Offender supervised by trained parole officers to help readjust to the community.
   2. Parolees subject to strict standardized or personalized rules that guide their behavior and limit their activities.
   3. Parole can be revoked if offender commits another offense.

D. How Effective is Parole?
   1. Surveys indicate two-thirds of all released inmates are re-arrested within three years of leaving prison.
   2. Parolees who have a good employment record in the past and who maintain a job after release are least likely to recidivate.

VIII. **Summary**

Key Terms

Auburn System - The prison system developed in New York during the nineteenth century that stressed congregate working conditions.

Boot Camp - A short-term militaristic correctional facility in which inmates undergo intensive physical conditioning and discipline.

Z. R. Brockway - The warden at the Elmira Reformatory in New York, he advocated individualized treatment, indeterminate sentences, and parole. The reformatory program initiated by Brockway included elementary education for illiterates, designated library hours, lectures by local college faculty members, and a group of vocational training shops.

Capital Punishment - The use of the death penalty to punish transgressors.

Community Service Restitution - An alternative sanction that requires an offender to work in the community at such tasks as cleaning public parks or helping handicapped children in lieu of an incarceration sentence.

Congregate System - This prison system included congregate working conditions, the use of solitary confinement to punish unruly inmates, military regimentation, and discipline.

Contract System - A prison work system in which officials sell the labor of inmates to private businesses.

Convict-Lease System - The system used earlier in the century in which inmates were leased out to private industry to work.

Corporal Punishment - The use of physical chastisement, such as whipping or electroshock, to punish criminals.

Day Fines - Fines geared to the average daily income of the convicted offender in an effort to bring equity to the sentencing process.

Electronic Monitoring (EM) - Offenders wear devices attached to their ankles, wrists, or neck that send signals back to a control office; used to monitor home confinements.

Forfeiture - The seizure of personal property by the state as a civil or criminal penalty.

Free-Venture Programs - Privately run industries in a prison setting in which the inmates work for wages and the goods are sold for profit.

The Hole - Solitary confinement used as punishment for prisoners who flout prison rules.

Home Confinement (HC) - Convicted offenders must spend extended periods in their own homes as an alternative to incarceration; also called house arrest or home detention.

Importation Model - The view that the violent prison culture reflects the criminal culture of the outside world and is neither developed in nor unique to prisons.

Inmate Subculture - The loosely defined culture that pervades prisons and has its own norms, rules, and language.

Intensive Probation Supervision (IPS) - A type of intermediate sanction involving small probation caseloads and strict daily or weekly monitoring.

Intermediate Sanctions - An alternative to prison; these sanctions include fines, forfeiture, home confinement, electronic monitoring, intensive probation supervision, restitution, community corrections, and boot camp.

Jail - A place to detain people awaiting trial, hold drunks and disorderly individuals, and confine convicted misdemeanants serving sentences of less than one year.

Monetary Restitution - A sanction requiring that convicted offenders compensate crime victims by reimbursing them for out-of-pocket losses caused by the crime. Losses can include property damage, lost wages, and medical costs.

New Generation Jails - Jails that allow for continuous observation of residents. There are two types: direct and indirect supervision.

Offender Classification - If the offender is placed on probation, the department diagnoses his or her personality and treatment needs; offenders classified as minimal risks will be given little supervision, perhaps a monthly phone call or visit, whereas those classified as high risk will receive close supervision and intensive care and treatment.

Parole - The early release of a prisoner subject to conditions set by a parole board. Depending on the jurisdiction, inmates must serve a certain proportion of their sentences before becoming eligible for parole. If an inmate is granted parole, the conditions may require him or her to report regularly to a parole officer, refrain from criminal conduct, maintain and support his or her family, avoid contact with other convicted criminals, abstain from using alcohol and drugs, remain within the jurisdiction, and so on. Violations of the conditions of parole may result in revocation of parole, in which case the individual will be returned to prison. The concept behind parole is to allow the release of the offender to community supervision, where rehabilitation and readjustment will be facilitated.

Parole Grant Hearing - A meeting of the full parole board or a subcommittee that reviews information, may meet with the offender, and then decides whether the parole applicant has a reasonable chance of succeeding outside prison. Good time credits reduce the minimum sentence and hasten eligibility for parole. In making its decision, the board considers the inmate's offense, time served, evidence of adjustment, and opportunities on the outside.

Penitentiary - State or federally operated facility for the incarceration of felony offenders sentenced by the criminal courts; prison.

Poor Laws - Laws first appearing in England during the early seventeenth century that required that the poor, vagrants, and vagabonds be put to work in public or private enterprise under supervision of a state-appointed master.

Prison - A state or federal correctional institution for incarceration of felony offenders for terms of one year or more.

Prisonization Process - The inmate's assimilation into the prison culture through acceptance of its language, sexual code, and norms of behavior. Those who become the most prisonized will be the least likely to reform on the outside.

Residential Community Corrections (RCC) - A freestanding nonsecure building that is not part of a prison or jail and houses pretrial and adjudicated adults. The residents regularly depart to work, to attend school, and/or to participate in community corrections activities and programs.

Revocation - An administrative act performed by a parole authority that removes a person from parole or a judicial order by a court removing a person from parole or probation, in response to a violation on the part of the parolee or probationer.

Shock Incarceration (SI) - A short prison sentence served in boot camp-type facilities.

Shock Probation - A sentence in which offenders serve a short prison term to impress them with the pains of imprisonment before they begin probation.

Social Code - The unwritten guidelines that express the values, attitudes, and types of behavior older inmates demand of younger inmates. Passed on from one generation of inmates to another, the inmate social code represents the values of interpersonal relations within the prison.

Split Sentencing - A jail term is part of the sentence and is a condition of probation.

State Account System - Prisoners produce goods in prison for state use.

Super-Max Prison - An enhanced high-security facility that houses the most dangerous felons in almost total isolation. Also called ultra-max prison.

Surrogate Family - A common form of adaptation to prison employed by women, this group contains masculine and feminine figures acting as fathers and mothers; some even act as children and take on the role of either brother or sister. Formalized marriages and divorces may be conducted. Sometimes multiple roles are held by one inmate, so that a "sister" in one family may "marry" and become the "wife" in another.

Technical Violation - Revocation of parole because conditions set by correctional authorities have been violated.

Therapeutic Communities (TCs) - A treatment approach using a psychosocial, experiential learning process that relies on positive peer pressure within a highly structured social environment.

Walnut Street Jail - At this institution, most prisoners were placed in solitary cells, where they remained in isolation and did not have the right to work.

Discussion Exercises

1. Break the class up into groups. Assign to each group a correctional sanction. Have each group present to the class the positive and negative aspects of their correctional sanction. Then, cast votes as to which the group feels is most effective.

2. To some, probation is seen as merely a "slap on the wrist." Have the students discuss which criminal incidents are best served by probation and which are not.

3. Divide students into groups and have each investigate a different prison in your state (for example, maximum and minimum security facilities, male and female facilities, facilities for adults and juveniles, etc.). Then, have the students present their findings in class in order to demonstrate the range of facilities available.

InfoTrac Assignment

GETTING STARTED: Search term words for subject guide: Punishment, Corrections, Probation, Fines, Forfeiture, Restitution, Boot Camps, Jail, Prisoners, Parole.

CRITICAL THINKING PROJECT: Using the search term "Forfeiture," find relevant articles.

Here are three articles:

Edwards, Jim. "Prosecutors React to Knockdown of Forfeiture Spending: They stress the importance of stimulating prosecutions by reward." *New Jersey Law Journal*.

Naylor, R.T. "License to Loot? A critique of follow-the-money methods in crime control policy." *Social Justice*.

Shepard, Michael D. and Matthew D. Lee. "White Collar Crime and the Innocent Spouse." *American Journal of Family Law*.

Test Bank

Fill in the Blank

1. **Corporal punishment** includes such acts as whipping and branding.
    (page number 593)

2. Prisoner quarters that contained the solitary or separate cells are known as the **penitentiary house**.
    (page number 594)

3. A type of intermediate sanction involving small probation caseloads and strict monitoring is known as **intensive probation supervision**.
    (page number 601)

4. **Home confinement** requires convicted offenders to spend extended periods of time in their own homes as an alternative to incarceration.
    (page number 603)

5. A short-term military style correctional facility in which inmates undergo intensive physical conditioning and discipline are known as **boot camps**.
    (page number 605)

6. **Jails** detain people awaiting trial, hold drunks and disorderly individuals, and confine convicted misdemeanants serving sentences of less than one year.
    (page number 605)

7. **Prisons** are state and federally operated correctional facilities that receive felony offenders sentenced by the criminal courts.
    (page number 607)

8. A state or federal correctional institution for incarceration of felony offenders for terms of one year or more is known as a **prison**.
    (page number 607)

9. Solitary confinement of an inmate is also known as **the hole**.
    (page number 610)

10. The loosely defined culture in a prison that has its own set of norms, rules and language is known as the **inmate subculture**.
    (page number 611)

11. The values of interpersonal relations within the prison are known as the **social code**.
    (page number 611)

12. **Prisonization** is the assimilation into the prison culture that has its own set of behaviors and values.
(page number 611)

13. The **importation model** is the view that the violent prison culture reflects the criminal culture of the outside world.
(page number 611)

14. **Parole** is the early release of a prisoner from prison with conditions set by a correctional board.
(page number 620)

15. In states where discretionary parole is used, the release decision is made by a board that meets the convict, reviews the information, and makes the decision whether or not to grant parole. This is known as a **parole grant hearing**.
(page number 621)

Multiple Choice

1. During the Middle Ages, payment made by the offender to the victim was called:
   a. remuneration
   b. probation
   c. parole
   d. wergild
   (Answer = d, page number 592)

2. During the 18th century, this was a popular form of punishment which banished offenders to the American colonies as a source of labor.
   a. transportation
   b. prison
   c. parole
   d. probation
   (Answer = a, page number 593)

3. During the last part of the 18th century, there were how many types of crimes in England punishable by death?
   a. 3
   b. 350
   c. 35
   d. 3,500
   (Answer = b, page number 594)

4. Correctional reform in the United States was first instituted in Pennsylvania under the leadership of:
   a. George Washington
   b. Thomas Jefferson
   c. Richard Petty
   d. William Penn
   (Answer = d, page number 594)

5. Prisoner quarters that contain solitary or separate cells are known as:
   a. the hole
   b. the penitentiary house
   c. a jail
   d. a boot camp
   (Answer = b, page number 594)

6. During the Civil War era, prisons were major manufacturers of:
   a. clothes
   b. shoes
   c. boots
   d. all of the above
   (Answer = d, page number 595)

7. One of the worst prison riots in history occurred at:
   a. Attica Prison
   b. New Mexico State Penitentiary
   c. all of the above
   d. none of the above
   (Answer = c, page number 596)

8. Before probation can be revoked, the offender must:
   a. be given a hearing before a sentencing court
   b. be provided counsel if he or she requires legal assistance
   c. all of the above
   d. none of the above
   (Answer = c, page number 597)

9. How many agencies nationwide list adult probation as their major function?
   a. 200
   b. 2,000
   c. 200,000
   d. 2 million
   (Answer = b, page number 597)

10. As of 2003, approximately how many adults were under federal, state, or local probation?
    a. 4,000
    b. 40,000
    c. 4,000,000
    d. 400
    (Answer = c, page number 597)

11. What percentage of probationers are convicted of committing a felony?
    a. about 50%
    b. about 10%
    c. about 5%
    d. about 1%
    (Answer = a, page number 597)

12. What percentages of probationers are convicted of committing a misdemeanor?
    a. about 5%
    b. about 50%
    c. about 10%
    d. about 75%
    (Answer = b, page number 597)

13. What percentages of probationers successfully complete probation?
    a. 6%
    b. 10%
    c. 100%
    d. 60%
    (Answer = d, page number 599)

14. Revocation for violation of probation rules is known as:
    a. parole
    b. the importation model
    c. a technical violation
    d. a technicality
    (Answer = c, page number 599)

15. What percentage of eligible offenders successfully completes their restitution orders?
    a. 9%
    b. 90%
    c. 50%
    d. 8%
    (Answer = b, page number 601)

16. Under current federal practices, what percentage of all convicted federal offenders receive some sort of split sentence?
    a. 2%
    b. 5%
    c. 25%
    d. 52%
    (Answer = c, page number 601)

17. Intensive probation caseloads are usually what size?
    a. 5 to 10
    b. 5 to 20
    c. 20 to 40
    d. 15 to 40
    (Answer = d, page number 601)

18. What is the failure rate of intensive supervision probation cases?
    a. 10%
    b. 20%
    c. 40%
    d. 50%
    (Answer = d, page number 603)

19. The length of time offenders spend in boot camp is normally:
    a. 5 to 50 days
    b. 50 to 100 days
    c. 90 to 180 days
    d. 2 years
    (Answer = c, page number 605)

20. In 2004, how many people were incarcerated in jails across the U.S?
    a. 700,000
    b. 70,000
    c. 7,000
    d. 700
    (Answer = a, page number 606)

21. Jails being built today that use modern designs are referred to as:
    a. linear designs
    b. campus style
    c. intermittent surveillance
    d. new generation
    (Answer = d, page number 607)

22. A state or federal correctional institution for incarceration of felony offenders for terms of one year or more is known as a(n):
    a. prison
    b. jail
    c. boot camp
    d. Auburn system
    (Answer = a, page number 607)

23. As of 2004, how many prisoners were under federal or state jurisdiction?
    a. 10 million
    b. 5 million
    c. 1.5 million
    d. 1 million
    (Answer = c, page number 607)

24. Prisons that are surrounded by high walls, have elaborate security measures and armed guards are referred to as:
    a. minimum security
    b. medium security
    c. maximum security
    d. none of the above
    (Answer = c, page number 608)

25. Prisons that have less violent inmates, offer a variety of treatment and education programs, and resemble maximum security prisons are known as:
    a. medium security
    b. minimum security
    c. super maxi security
    d. none of the above
    (Answer = a, page number 608)

26. Prisons which operate without armed guards or walls and are usually constructed in compounds surrounded by chain links are known as:
    a. super maxi security
    b. maximum security
    c. medium security
    d. minimum security
    (Answer = d, page number 608)

27. Currently, the model for the super-max prison is located in:
    a. Raleigh, NC
    b. Las Cruces, NM
    c. Sacramento, CA
    d. Florence, CO
    (Answer = d, page number 608)

28. It is estimated that by the year 2010, _____ of the total prison population will be over 50 years of age.
    a. 25%
    b. 33%
    c. 50%
    d. 66%
    (Answer = b, page number 610)

29. What percentages of male inmates have been incarcerated before?
    a. 1%
    b. 6%
    c. 60%
    d. 100%
    (Answer = c, page number 610)

30. Solitary confinement of an inmate is commonly called:
    a. boot camp
    b. jail
    c. shock incarceration
    d. the hole
    (Answer = d, page number 610)

31. The loosely defined culture in a prison that has its own norms, rules, and language is known as:
    a. the inmate subculture
    b. the importation model
    c. parole
    d. segregation
    (Answer = a, page number 611)

32. The values of interpersonal relations within the prison are known as:
    a. the importation model
    b. parole
    c. segregation
    d. the social code
    (Answer = d, page number 611)

33. Assimilation into the prison culture that has its own set of behaviors is known as:
    a. the social code
    b. prisonization
    c. the importation code
    d. the parole grant hearing
    (Answer = b, page number 611)

34. The view that the violent prison culture reflects the criminal culture of the outside world is known as:
    a. the importation model
    b. the social code
    c. prisonization
    d. the parole grant hearing
    (Answer = a, page number 611)

35. Female inmates make up what percentage of the adult prison population?
    a. 5%
    b. 15%
    c. 20%
    d. 25%
    (Answer = a, page number 612)

36. The first prison treatment programs were:
    a. vocational
    b. educational
    c. religious
    d. counseling
    (Answer = b, page number 614)

37. Which of the following has not been associated with prison riots?
    a. environmental conditions
    b. conflict
    c. rising expectations
    d. all of the above have been associated with prison riots
    (Answer = d, page number 618)

38. Which of the following is not a recent gain in inmate rights?
    a. freedom of speech and press
    b. medical rights
    c. freedom from degrading treatment
    d. all of the above rights have been gained
    (Answer = d, page number 619)

39. The early release of a prisoner from prison with conditions set by a board is known as:
    a. the importation model
    b. the social code
    c. parole
    d. prisonization
    (Answer = c, page number 620)

40. In states where discretionary parole is used, the release decision is made by a board that meets the convict, reviews the information, and makes the decision whether or not to grant parole. This is known as:
   a. the importation model
   b. the parole grant hearing
   c. the social code
   d. prisonization
   (Answer = b, page number 621)

True/False

1. In ancient times, the most common state-administered punishment was banishment or exile.
   (Answer = true, page number 592)

2. In both ancient Greece and Rome, interpersonal violence, even murder, was viewed as a public matter.
   (Answer = false, page number 592)

3. Heavy government control existed during the early Middle Ages.
   (Answer = false, page number 592)

4. Poor laws developed in the early seventeenth century required that the poor, vagrants, and vagabonds be put to work in public or private enterprise.
   (Answer = true, page number 593)

5. Transportation to the colonies waned as a method of punishment with the increase in colonial population, the further development of the land, and the increasing importation of African slaves in the eighteenth century.
   (Answer = true, page number 593)

6. Between the American Revolution in 1776 and the first decades of the nineteenth century, the population of Europe and America decreased rapidly.
   (Answer = false, page number 593)

7. During the last part of the twentieth century, 350 types of crime in England were punishable by death.
   (Answer = false, page number 594)

8. Correctional reform in the United States was first instituted in Pennsylvania under the leadership of William Penn.
   (Answer = true, page number 594)

9. In the late 1700's, Pennsylvania took the radical step of establishing a prison that placed each inmate in a single cell with no work to do.
   (Answer = true, page number 594)

10. Although the congregate system eventually failed, it spread throughout the United States and many of its features are still used today.
   (Answer = false, page number 595)

11. Z.R. Brockway, warden at the Elmira Reformatory in New York, advocated individualized treatment, indeterminate sentences, and parole.
   (Answer = true, page number 595)

12. Between 1960 and 1980, a great deal of litigation was brought by inmates seeking greater rights and privileges.
   (Answer = true, page number 596)

13. Since 1980, the "prisoners' rights" movement has increased as judicial activism waned during the Reagan-Bush era.
   (Answer = false, page number 596)

14. Correctional treatment can be divided today into community-based programs and secure confinement.
   (Answer = true, page number 596)

15. Jails house misdemeanants (and some felons) serving their sentences, as well as felons and misdemeanants awaiting trial and not released on bail.
   (Answer = true, page number 605)

Essay Questions

1. Trace the history of punishment and corrections from the Middle Ages to our modern era. Which punishments were most effective?
   (page numbers 592-596)

2. Define probation. What are the various probation organizations and what types of services do they provide?
   (page numbers 596-599)

3. What are intermediate sanctions? Which intermediate sanctions are the most effective? Which intermediate sanctions are the least effective?
   (page numbers 599-605)

4. What is a jail? Describe the individuals who are incarcerated in our jails? What are the prerequisites for one being incarcerated in a jail?
   (page numbers 605-607)

5. Define prisons. What are the various types of prisons in the United States? Which types of inmates are sentenced to which classification of prison?
   (page numbers 607-613)

Appendix I

Research Paper Topics

PART ONE: CONCEPTS OF CRIME, LAW, AND CRIMINOLOGY

1. Assign each student a county in your state to profile on the basis of social, economic, and criminological factors. For the social picture the students may want to include such items as population size, rural versus urban area, rate of college graduates, divorce rate, etc. For the economic picture the students may want to include such items as percentage below poverty, average family income, percentage unemployed, rate of home ownership, etc. Census data are useful for the social and economic variables. Criminological factors, such as crime rates, arrest rates, number of officers, etc., can be obtained from your state crime information center. The focus of the written assignment, then, is to tie the various social and economic forces operating within the county to the levels and types of crimes identified.

2. There are thousands of agencies with the mission of providing services to victims of crime. Have your students complete an in-depth investigation into a specific agency at the local, state, or national level. The paper should include an historical look at the agency, provide statistics on the number and type of victims they assist, offer descriptions of the services provided, give an explanation of the philosophy of the agency, discuss funding sources, and provide information on the location of the agency. You may even want to include a personal interview with a representative of the agency.

PART TWO: THEORIES OF CRIME CAUSATION

1. Ask students to select a recent crime from a local newspaper. They can spend a short amount of time laying out the facts of the case or merely have them attach the article to their final paper. Then, they are to define and apply one theory that does a good job explaining this type of offense and one theory that does a bad job explaining this type of offense. They are to integrate facts from the article to support their argument. This paper works best if the student applies a specific theory, like Routine Activities Theory, rather than a more "umbrella" theory, like Social Disorganization Theories.

2. Each chapter in this section includes a discussion of public policy implications of the theories presented. Assign each student a theory for which they are to identify local, state, and national programs, policies, or laws that support its premise. A discussion of the theory, its policy implications, and its applications provide for the three parts to the paper.

PART THREE: CRIME TYPOLOGIES

1. Have each student select one type of crime. They should provide the legal definition for the offense, incidence rates at both the state and national levels, and clearance rates at both the state and national levels. To what extent does this crime in your state reflect nationwide trends?

2. Street crimes (violent and property), enterprise crimes, and public order crimes vary in definition, incidence level, and how society views them. Either have students compare and contrast across these three large crime classifications or have them select one crime from each of the three categories to use as a representative of that group of offenses. Students can then discuss how not all crimes are alike or viewed as such.

PART FOUR: THE CRIMINAL JUSTICE SYSTEM

1. There are hundreds of treatment and rehabilitation programs for offenders that have been utilized in the past or are currently in favor. Have students identify one such program and provide an analysis of it. Specific topics to be discussed include the type of offender the program targets, the history of the program, its breadth of use across various facilities, its level of success, the length of the program, the structure of the program, etc.

2. Students are always interested in the career opportunities available in the criminal justice system. This section discusses a wide range of professionals involved at various stages of the process. Assign students one of these professions to investigate and then report back to the class. Students should gather information on such topics as educational requirements, starting salary, opportunities for mobility, job description, skills required, contact information, job market status, working conditions, etc.

Appendix II

New to this Edition

- CriminologyNow™ is available for FREE when packaged with Siegel's Criminology, Ninth Edition. This web-based, intelligent study system helps students maximize their study time and helps instructors save time by providing a complete package of diagnostic quizzes, a Personalized Study Plan, integrated media elements—including an e-book and learning modules—and, an Instructor's Grade Book.

- A new Student Companion CD-ROM is packaged FREE with every new copy of the text. This valuable resource features CNN® video clips tied to chapter-opening vignettes and accompanied by critical thinking questions. Icons placed in the margins throughout the text point the student to chapter-related activities on the CD-ROM.

- New and expanded end-of-chapter pedagogy provides students with the tools they need to master and apply chapter concepts. Tools include: a chapter summary carefully correlated with chapter objectives; a scenario-based application, "Thinking Like a Criminologist"; new "Doing Research on the Web" with weblinks and InfoTrac® links; key terms; and "Critical Thinking Questions."

- Based on reviewer feedback, Chapters 1 and 2 have been streamlined and combined into a single new Chapter 1, "Crime, Criminology, and the Criminal Law," covering history, definitions of crime and criminology, and origins and basics of the criminal law.

- New chapter-opening vignettes feature fascinating, current cases that are each linked to CNN® video on the new Student Companion CD-ROM.

- New "Concept Summary" tables visually summarize key chapter concepts.

- A new "Comparative Criminology" box features comparative perspectives of international criminal law, crime, victimization, and punishment.

- Chapter 10, "Violent Crime," now provides more balanced coverage between the different types of violence. Topics discussed include sexual assault allegations at U.S. service academies, more on the USA PATRIOT Act, international comparative criminology, and expanded treatment of domestic terrorism.

- Chapter 12, "Enterprise Crime: White-Collar, Cyber Crime, and Organized Crime," includes expanded material on white-collar crime, and corporate and government crimes.

- This edition includes new coverage on key criminology topics such as analysis and critique of the UCR and NCVS, more extensive coverage of new methods of data collection (NIBRS), social policy issues related to developmental theories of criminology, and innovations in the criminal justice system such as mental health courts.

- This edition provides expanded coverage on key topics such as the victims rights movement, hate crimes, restorative justice, cyber-crime and identity theft, terrorism and Homeland Security, the USA PATRIOT Act, and the use of technology in crime fighting.

Tips for Integrating Thomson's
WebTutor™on WebCT into your Course

Feature	Description - Benefit
THOMSON PROVIDED CONTENT	
Summary Materials	Students will be able to view summary material tied directly to their course textbook. These can include, but are not limited to Chapter Outlines, Summaries, internet exercises, interactive games and PowerPoint presentations.
Multimedia Content	Our WebTutor Advantage products offer the added advantage of video clips, animations and/or simulations.
Quizzes	Allows students to practice what they have learned in the textbook. Quiz results are automatically entered into the WebCT gradebook. Students can take quizzes multiple times, or if the instructor prefers, they can limit the number of times, set a time limit, or specify a specific time when the quiz is available. These quizzes include content not found in the Instructors Testbank and can be edited by the instructor.
Flashcards	Flashcards allow students to review key terms from the textbook. Because students learn in many ways, flashcards (w/audio) allow students to hear the pronunciation of the term and in some cases, the definition. Flashcards are especially beneficial to the ESL or Learning Disabled student.
Web Links	Web links help keep the course current for the instructor and provide numerous opportunities for students to do additional research or project-based activities right on the web. Each WebTutor product comes pre-loaded with web links designed to enhance the course.
Discussion Topics	Threaded Discussion or Bulletin Board systems allow students and instructors to engage in a lively, on going discussion, anytime or anywhere. All Thomson WebTutor products come pre-loaded with suggested discussion topics. Of course, instructors and students can add their own.
PowerPoint Presentations	Many WebTutor products include PowerPoint presentations keyed to the textbook.
InfoTrac College edition	Students have access to InfoTrac College edition offering 24/7 access to millions of full-text articles from scholarly journals and popular periodicals. Students can search by keyword or subject. A must-have resource for any course that involves research.
COMMUNICATION TOOLS	
Integrated Calendar	An integrated calendar can serve as a syllabus tool for instructors and allows them to enter information and key dates for the course. A pop-up window will always notify students when NEW information is placed on the calendar. Instructors can also create a link that will take students directly to a content page (chapter summary, quiz, etc). Students (and instructors) can also use the compile feature to print all assignments for a selected date range. Private entries are also allowed.
e-mail	An integrated e-mail system automatically builds a directory for the course as students create accounts. Students are not required to have an external email account to use WebTutor.
Chat	Chat allows for real-time, synchronous communication with the class. There are many possible uses for chat including virtual office hours, group study sessions or projects, and guest speakers. All chat sessions are logged for the instructor to view - even if they are not an active participant.

Threaded Discussion or Bulletin Board	Threaded Discussion or Bulletin Board systems allow students and instructors to engage in a lively, on going discussion, anytime or anywhere. This tool has many applications including discussion of course topics, debates, or general discussions about course issues. Instructors can create private discussion forums, or allow students to post anonymously.
Whiteboard	A real-time tool that allows you to upload images or presentations for students to view. Instructors or students can draw to the whiteboard.
STUDENT MANAGEMENT TOOLS	
Progress Tracking	Instructors will receive reports on each student that allow them to identify students first and last login, a distribution of hits, percentage of content visited and a complete history of all pages visited. Instructors can use this tool to monitor students progress and identify problem areas in a timely manner.
Participation in Discussion	Instructors will receive information about students participation in the discussion area including the number of items read, the number of original postings and the number of follow up postings. In an online environment, this is a great tool for instructors to measure a student's participation in class.
Student Management - Gradebook	Allows instructors to view all students registered in the class and the results of their graded online quizzes and assignments.
Item Analysis	Allows instructor to get detailed item analysis of any quiz or survey item.
Page Tracking	Allows instructors to see which students have accessed pages of content (from a path) - both the number of times and the time spent. Using this information, instructors can identify where students are spending their time and which areas of the course either need work, or additional reinforcement in class.
Grader Management	Allows the instructor to add graders to the course who have access to quiz information for assistance with grading.
Course RESET	Allows instructors to reset portions of their course for easy transition from term to term without losing their customization. Instructors can reset the student database, e-mail, Bulletin Boards, grader database, chat logs, the calendar tool, and the page-tracking tool.
CUSTOMIZATION OPTIONS	
Look and feel	Instructors have complete control over the look and feel of their course - they can change screen colors, add text and images, counters and their school logo if they choose.
Syllabus Tool	Provides a template for instructors to create their course syllabus. Alternatively, can upload an existing syllabus from a Word, or HTML file.
Quizzes	All quizzes are fully editable. Instructors can also create their own quizzes, or banks of questions for additional study or exams. Randomized quizzes can be created by using the Question Set feature. Additionally quizzes can be set up to prompt students for a password or require that a student is accessing the quiz from a certain IP address.
Content	Instructors can edit, delete or hide any content provided in the WebTutor product. They can also add their own content as well as re-sequencing the way the current content is presented.
Selective Release of Content	Instructors can choose to release content based on certain criteria such as date or time, to a selected group of students, or based on the result of quiz scores.
Add additional WebCT tools	WebCT provides additional functionality for instructors wanting to take their course to the next level. Here are just a few: an assignment dropbox, student presentation areas or homepages, image libraries, audio and video files, and more.

HOSTING OPTIONS	
Locally Hosted *RECOMMENDED*	For schools that have WebCT, Thomson will provide the school with a content cartridge that they can install on their local server. Instructors and students also receive technical support from WebCT as well as the resources they have available on campus.
Centrally hosted	For schools that do not have WebCT 3.x or higher, we provide a hosted option (through WebCT). All centrally hosted courses include unlimited technical support directly from WebCT for both instructors and students.

For additional information, including Frequently Asked Questions, tours, and downloadable Instructor and Student guides, visit us at
http://webtutor.thomsonlearning.com

Tips for Integrating Thomson's
WebTutor™on Blackboard into your Course

Feature	Description - Benefit
THOMSON PROVIDED CONTENT	
Chapter Summary Materials	Students will be able to view summary material tied directly to their course textbook. These can include, but are not limited to Chapter Outlines, Summaries, internet exercises, interactive games and PowerPoint presentations.
Multimedia Content	Our WebTutor advantage products offer the added advantage of video clips, simulations and/or simulations.
Quizzes	Allow students to practice what they have learned in the textbook. Quiz results are automatically entered into the BB gradebook. Students can take quizzes multiple times, or if the instructor prefers, they can allow only one attempt, set a time limit, or specify a password for students to take a quiz. These quizzes include content not found in the instructor test bank and can be edited by the instructor.
Flashcards	Flashcards allow students to review key terms from the textbook. Because students learn in many ways, flashcards (w/audio) allow students to hear the pronunciation of the term and in some cases, the definition. Flashcards are especially beneficial to the ESL or Learning Disabled student.
Web Links	Web links help keep the course current for the instructor and provide numerous opportunities for students to do additional research or project-based activities right on the web. Each WebTutor product comes pre-loaded with web links designed to enhance the course.
Discussion Topics	Threaded Discussion or Bulletin Board systems allow students and instructors to engage in a lively, on going discussion, anytime or anywhere. All Thomson WebTutor products come pre-loaded with suggested discussion topics. Of course, instructors and students can add their own.
PowerPoint Presentations	Many WebTutor products include PowerPoint presentations keyed to the textbook.
InfoTrac College edition	Students have access to InfoTrac College edition offering 24/7 access to millions of articles from scholarly journals and popular periodicals. Students can search by keyword or subject. A must-have resource for any course that involves research.
Bb formatted Test banks	Instructors can request a Blackboard-formatted version of the ExamView testbank files for creation of their own quizzes and tests.
COMMUNICATION TOOLS	
Integrated Calendar	An integrated calendar provides the ability to view information at the institutional, course, and personal level.
Web Mail	Blackboard has third party software embedded in the product to seamlessly link to students existing email accounts.
Virtual Classroom	The Virtual Classroom allows for real-time, communication with the class and combines chat, whiteboard technology and a web browser into a synchronous learning tool. There are many possible uses for chat including virtual office hours, group study sessions or projects, and guest speakers. All chat sessions are logged for the instructor to view - even if they are not an active participant.
Threaded Discussion or Bulletin Board	Threaded Discussion or Bulletin Board systems allow students and instructors to engage in a lively, on going discussion, anytime or anywhere. This tool has many applications including discussion of course topics, debates, or general discussions about course issues. Instructors can create private discussion forums, or allow students to post anonymously. Instructors may assign a student moderator.

Group Pages	Group pages allow the instructor to create collaborative learning environment on-line for specific group of students. This is useful for group projects and presentations.
Announcements	An announcement feature allows instructors to post time sensitive information to their class.
STUDENT MANAGEMENT TOOLS	
Course Statistics	Instructors can generate reports on the class or an individual student showing when and how students are accessing their course. Instructors can use this tool to monitor students progress and identify problem areas in a timely manner.
Online Gradebook	Allows instructors to view all students registered in the class and the results of their graded online quizzes and assignments.
Item Analysis	Allows instructor to get detailed item analysis of any quiz or survey item.
Item Tracking	Allows instructor to gather tracking details by student or class on any content item within the course. Report shows number of hits, days and times visited, etc.
T.A or Grader Access	Allows instructor to add a level of access to Teaching assistants or graders for assistance with grading.
Recycle Course	Allows instructors to recycle their courses from term to term without losing their customization. Student rosters, Bulletin Boards, online gradebook, Virtual Classroom archives are reset in preparation for the next term.
CUSTOMIZATION OPTIONS	
Look and feel	Instructors have complete control over the look and feel of their course - they can change button names and colors, add text and images and their school logo if they choose.
Instructor Profile	Instructions can add a profile with contact information for themselves or other key resources such as teaching assistants.
Quizzes	All quizzes are fully editable. Instructors can also create their own quizzes, or pools of questions for additional study or exams. Using the pools feature, instructors can generate randomized quizzes.
Content	Instructors can edit, delete or hide any content provided in the WebTutor product. They can also add their own content as well as re-sequencing the way the current content is presented.
Add additional Blackboard tools	Blackboard provides additional functionality for instructors wanting to take their course to the next level. Here are just a few: a student/instructor dropbox and an Electronic Blackboard for notetaking.
HOSTING OPTIONS	
Locally Hosted - RECOMMENDED	For schools that have Blackboard 5.5 or higher, Thomson will provide the school with an access key so that they can download the content cartridge to their local server. Blackboard provides additional technical support to supplement resources available on campus.
Centrally hosted	For schools that do not have Blackboard 5.5, we provide a hosted option (through Blackboard). All centrally hosted courses include technical support directly from Blackboard.

For additional information, including Frequently Asked Questions, tours, and downloadable Instructor and Student guides, visit us at http://webtutor.thomsonlearning.com

INFOMARKS: MAKE YOUR MARK!

WHAT IS AN INFOMARK?

It's a single-click return ticket to any page, any result, any search from InfoTrac College Edition.

An InfoMark is a stable URL, linked to InfoTrac College Edition articles that you have selected. InfoMarks can be used like any other URL, but they're better because they're stable – they don't change. Using an InfoMark is like performing the search again whenever you follow the link – whether the result is a single article or a list of articles.

HOW DO INFOMARKS WORK?

If you can "copy and paste," you can use InfoMarks.

When you see the InfoMark icon--on a result page, its URL can be copied and pasted into your electronic document – web page, word processing document or e-mail. Once InfoMarks are incorporated into a document, the results are persistent (the URLs will not change) and are dynamic.

Even though the saved search is used at different times by different users, an InfoMark always functions like a brand new search. Each time a saved search is executed, it accesses the latest updated information. That means subsequent InfoMark searches might yield additional or more up-to-date information than the original search with less time and effort.

CAPABILITIES

InfoMarks are the perfect technology tool for creating:

- Virtual online readers
- Current awareness topic sites- links to periodical or newspaper sources
- Online/distance learning courses
- Bibliographies, reference lists
- Electronic journals and periodical directories
- Student assignments
- Hot topics

ADVANTAGES

- Select from over 15 million articles from more than 5,000 journals and periodicals
- Update article and search lists easily
- Articles are always full-text and include bibliographic information
- All articles can be viewed online, printed, or emailed
- Saves professors and students time
- Anyone with access to InfoTrac College Edition can use it
- No other online library database offers this functionality
- FREE!

www.infotrac-college.com

HOW TO USE INFOMARKS

There are 3 ways to utilize InfoMarks—in HTML documents, Word documents, and Email

HTML DOCUMENT

1. Open a new document in your HTML editor (Netscape Composer or FrontPage Express).
2. Open a new browser window and conduct your search in InfoTrac College Edition.
3. Highlight the URL of the results page or article that you would like to InfoMark.
4. Right click the URL and click Copy. Now, switch back to your HTML document.
5. In your document, type in text that describes the InfoMarked item.
6. Highlight the text and click on Insert, then on Link in the upper bar menu.
7. Click in the link box, then press the "Ctrl" and "V" keys simultaneously and click OK. This will paste the URL in the box.
8. Save your document.

WORD DOCUMENT

1. Open a new Word document.
2. Open a new browser window and conduct your search in InfoTrac College Edition.
3. Check items you want to add to your Marked List.
4. Click on Mark List on the right menu bar.
5. Highlight the URL, right click on it, and click Copy. Now, switch back to your Word document.
6. In your document, type in text that describes the InfoMarked item.
7. Highlight the text. Go to the upper bar menu and click on Insert, then on Hyperlink.
8. Click in the hyperlink box, then press the "Ctrl" and "V" keys simultaneously and click OK. This will paste the URL in the box.
9. Save your document.

EMAIL

1. Open a new email window.
2. Open a new browser window and conduct your search in InfoTrac College Edition.
3. Highlight the URL of the results page or article that you would like to InfoMark.
4. Right click the URL and click Copy. Now, switch back to your email window.
5. In the email window, press the "Ctrl" and "V" keys simultaneously. This will paste the URL into your email.
6. Send the email to the recipient. By clicking on the URL, they will be able to view the InfoMark.

TABLE OF CONTENTS

INTRODUCTION

InfoTrac College Edition, a complete Online Research and Learning Center, contains over 10 million full-text articles from nearly 5,000 scholarly and popular periodicals. Covering a broad spectrum of disciplines and topics, this online library is ideal for every type of research. *InfoTrac College Edition*'s articles are updated daily and include research dating back to 1980. In addition to the database, *InfoTrac College Edition* offers InfoWrite, a web-based training tool designed to help develop writing skills. InfoWrite assists students through difficult areas of research writing, such as choosing a topic, composing introductions and conclusions, and crediting sources.

24 Hours a Day

InfoTrac College Edition is accessible 24 hours-a-day, 7 days-a-week from any computer with Internet access. A free 4-month subscription to *InfoTrac College Edition* can be bundled with any Thomson text. Students will not only find an online library, but also online resources with information on financial aid, time management, and exam preparation.

Use it as Part of Your Course

InfoTrac College Edition also does something for you, the instructor. It gives you the flexibility to require outside readings without creating a separate printed reader, something students will appreciate. *InfoTrac College Edition* can be integrated into your course by using the articles to prepare lectures and assignments, or to ignite classroom discussions.

QUICK TIPS FOR THE CLASSROOM

InfoTrac College Edition is an excellent tool to introduce students to researching subjects. You can use it to prepare lectures and outside assignments or to build a reader from the database for your discipline. Students will appreciate the ease of online research, especially when writing papers, preparing class presentations, or researching a key topic. Below are some suggestions on how to incorporate *InfoTrac College Edition* in your classroom.

Writing Assignments
- Provide a topic to your students to research in *InfoTrac College Edition*. Instruct them to choose an article to write a thesis on and construct an outline for.
- Point students to *InfoTrac College Edition* as an excellent reference and information source when preparing their term papers.

Study Questions
- Prepare a list of study questions on a lecture topic and have the students research and answer them using *InfoTrac College Edition*.
- Many Thomson texts include end-of chapter questions. Have your students explore answers using the database.

Reading Assignments
- Select specific articles and assign them to your students for further reading.
- Utilizing the Critical Thinking section in InfoWrite, instruct students to choose an article and evaluate the facts and arguments in that article.

Classroom Activities
- Divide the classroom into groups and provide them with a topic to research and discuss for the next class. Have each group present their discoveries and summary of that topic.
- Set up classroom debates by providing a subject and assigning students to research a pro or con stance to discuss in class.

GETTING STARTED

Registration

Go to www.infotrac-college.com

Step 1

Click on **Register New Account**.

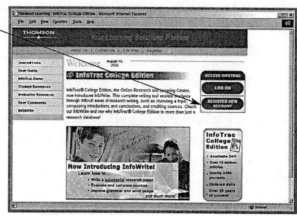

Step 2

Enter passcode and create a username.

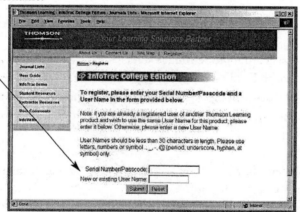

Step 3

Fill out the registration form completely to activate your account.

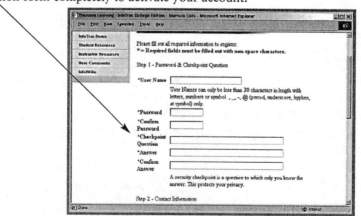

Note: After registration is complete, you will only need your <u>username and password</u> to logon.

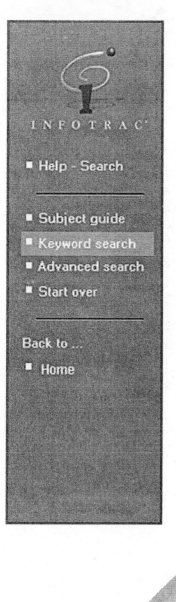

Features

1. The **Help-Search** button will assist you in your current search context.

2. The **Subject Guide** button allows you to search for topics.

3. The **Keyword Search** button allows you to match words in the article itself, not just in the controlled index terms.

4. The **Advanced Search** button allows you to select from the index to narrow your search for that particular term.

5. The **Start Over** button erases your current input and/or search results in the History section.

Subject Guide

Subject Guide allows you to do a broad search on a topic.

Step 1
Type in the term(s) you would like to search.

Step 2- Optional
You may refine your search by specifying dates, journals, and keywords.

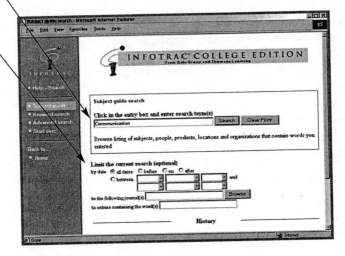

Step 3
A list of all the headings containing your specific topic along with the number of articles found within each heading will appear.

Click on **View** to go to the specific article(s).

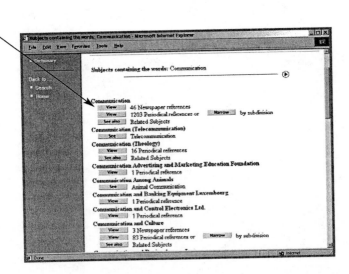

Narrow by Subdivision Results

If you would like to view subdivisions of your topic, click on **Narrow**.

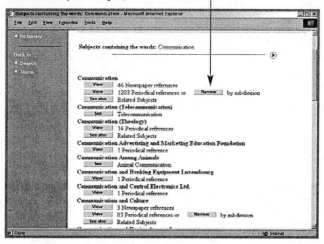

A list of subdivisions will appear. Click on the one that most pertains to your topic.

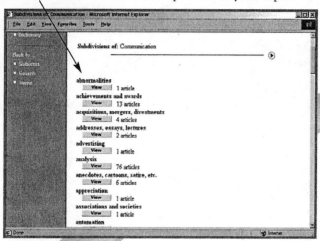

The articles will be listed in reverse chronological order. Click on the title to view.

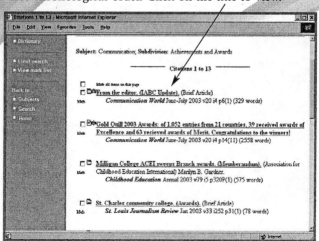

Keyword Search

The **Keyword Search** looks for the word(s) entered. It is more effective when looking for a specific topic, title, author name, or product.

Step 1
Type in the term(s) you would like to search.

Step 2- Optional
You can use logical operators (AND, OR, NOT) to create relationships between search terms.

Step 3- Optional
You may refine your search by specifying dates, journals, and keywords.

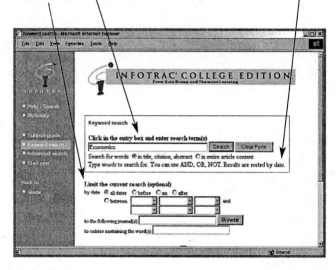

Step 4
The **Keyword Search** will give you a list of articles containing the terms searched. Results are listed in reverse chronological order.

Click on the title to view the full-text article.

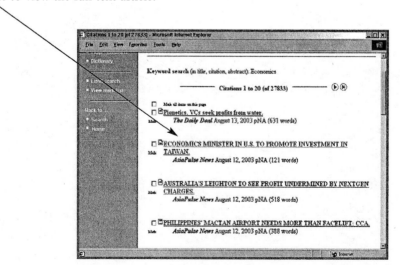

Advanced Search

The **Advanced Search** provides a variety of ways to search the database for articles.

Step 1
Select an index to search by.
What is an index? Each article is indexed by certain variables. These indices include the title, author, publication's name, where and when it was published (see the list on the next page).

Step 2
Type in the term(s) you would like to search.

Step 3- Optional
You may refine your search by specifying dates, journals, and keywords.

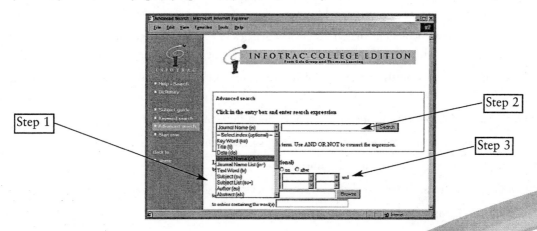

Example Search

If you want to find all the articles from the *Economist*, use the Advanced Search.

Step 1
Select the index **Journal Name** and type *Economist* in the **Search** field. Click **Search**.

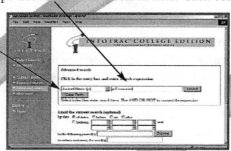

Step 2
Click on **View** to view a list of citations or **Modify** to change your search.

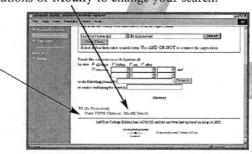

Indexes for Advanced Search

Abstract (ab): Includes words from article abstracts as well as from any author's abstracts.

Author (au): Authors are indexed in surname/given name order; for example, "nelan bruce w." It's best to search in surname-first order. Enter a surname and, optionally, a given name.

Date (da): The date the article was published.

Journal Name (jn): The name of the magazine or periodical.

Journal Name List (jn=): Provides a list of magazines or periodicals in which the search term appears.

Keyword (ke): Words in article titles and authors, as well as subjects, people, companies, products, vocations, events, etc., featured in articles.

Record Number (rn): A full record always includes a unique record number. If you note a record number, you can easily find the record again with the record number index.

Refereed (re): Experts in the same field as the writer review articles in the journal and ensure that the data and methodology has met a high standard. This is also knows as a peer reviewed.

Source (so): Lets you search for records by the type of source from which they're taken (e.g., magazine, journal, or newspapers).

Source List (so=): Lets you browse a list of subjects that contain the word or words you type.

Subject (su): Lets you search for references by the source types under which they are indexed.

Subject List (su=): Provides a list of references by source types.

Text Word (tx): Composed of all words from the body of articles.

Title (ti): The title index is composed of all words in the article.

Volume Number (vo): The volume of the magazine or periodical.

Using Wildcards in the Advanced Search

At times, you might want to find more than just exact matches to a search term. For instance, you might want to find both the singular and plural forms of a word or variant spellings. Wildcards let you broaden your searches to match a pattern.

InfoTrac provides three wildcards:

- An asterisk (*) stands for any number of characters, including none. For example pigment* matches "pigment," "pigments," "pigmentation," etc. The asterisk wildcard can also be used inside a word. For example, colo*r matches both "color" and "colour."
- A question mark (?) stands for exactly one character. Multiple question marks in a row stand for the same number of characters as there are question marks. For example, psych????y matches either "psychology" or "psychiatry", but not "psychotherapy."
- An exclamation point (!) stands for one or no characters. For example, analog!! matches "analog," "analogs" or "analogue" but not "analogous."

If you see a message about a search being invalid, you'll need to add at least one character before one of the wildcards.

Mark List

Clicking on the **Mark Box** allows you to select articles you would like to retrieve for later viewing. The **Mark Box** is available in two ways:

1. *While viewing the citation list.* You may select individual articles or you may select all the items on the page.

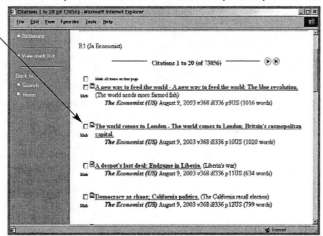

2. *While you are in article view.* Click on the **Mark Box** next to the article citation.

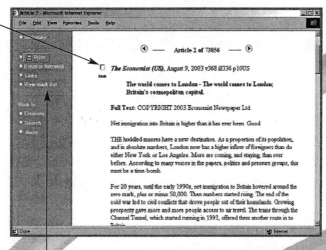

To view selected articles, click on **View Mark List.**

Limit Search

To focus a broad search, you may limit your search by date, journal, or keyword. There are two ways to limit a search:

1. *Limit a search that has already been performed.* To do this, click on **Limit Search** in the left navigation.

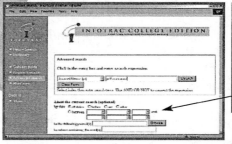

2. *Limit a current search.* To do this, fill out the **Limit Search** box below the search field.

Article Retrieval

There are three article retrieval options available:

- ◆ **Browser Print:** Print out the full text article
- ◆ **Acrobat Reader:** Review article as a PDF file
- ◆ **Email Delivery:** E-mail article to self or others

Click on **Print or Email** to view retrieval options.

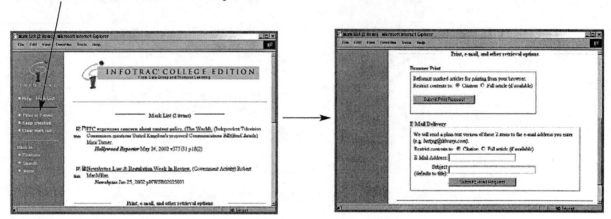

TROUBLESHOOTING & FREQUENTLY ASKED QUESTIONS

If you are experiencing any technical difficulties, you can send a form to Technical Support by clicking **Contact Us** on the *InfoTrac College Edition* homepage, or you can send an e-mail to support@thomsonlearning.com.

Q: *Are there any vowels in my passcode?*
A: There are no vowels in the passcode. If the letter appears to resemble a "U", it is actually the letter "V". If the letter appears to resemble like an "I", it is actually the number "1". If the letter appears to resemble like an "O", it is actually the number "0" (zero).

Q: *How far do the InfoTrac College Edition articles go back in time?*
A: *InfoTrac College Edition* dates back to 1980.

Q: *How often is the database updated?*
A: *InfoTrac College Edition* databases are updated every business day. Daily publications are indexed on a daily basis. Publications will vary by their frequency.

Q: *What if I lose or forget my username/password?*
A: E-mail tech support at the address above and they can help you within 24 hours on business days.

Q: *If I have a problem, what information do I need to provide in my message to InfoTrac College Edition customer service?*
A: Click on the Contact Us button on the welcome screen. You will be prompted for all necessary information.

Q: *How do I access the on-line help file?*
A: Each screen has context sensitive help. Just click on the help button.

QUICK START GUIDE FOR YOUR STUDENTS
The following pages may be duplicated and distributed to your students.

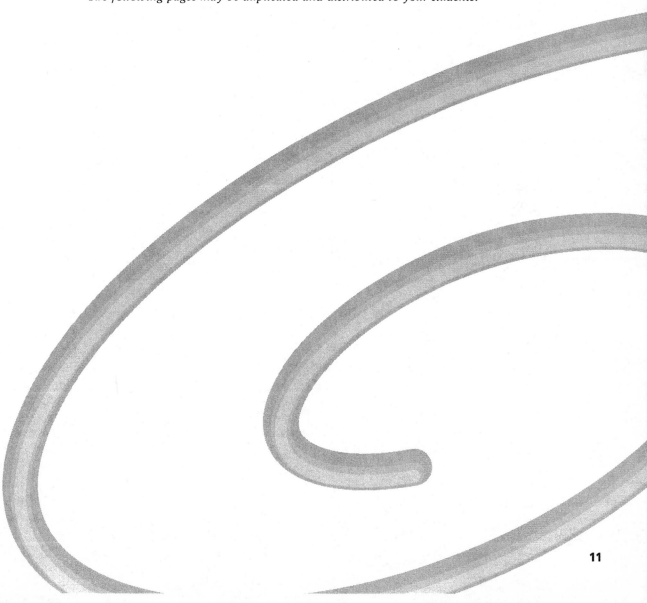

QUICK START GUIDE

InfoTrac College Edition, a complete Online Research and Learning Center, contains over 10 million full-text articles from nearly 5,000 scholarly and popular periodicals. Covering a broad spectrum of disciplines and topics, this online library is ideal for every type of research. *InfoTrac College Edition's* articles are updated daily and include research dating back to 1980. In addition to the database, *InfoTrac College Edition* offers InfoWrite, a web-based training tool designed to help develop writing skills. InfoWrite assists students through difficult areas of research writing, such as choosing a topic, composing introductions and conclusions, and crediting sources.

Registration

Step 1
Go to www.infotrac-college.com and click on **Register New Account**.

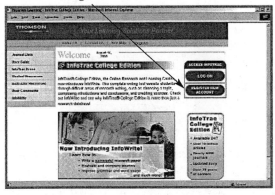

Step 2
Enter passcode and create a username.

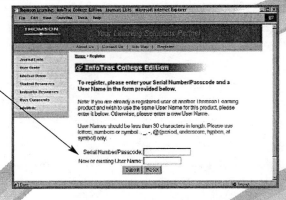

Step 3
Fill out the registration form completely to activate your account.

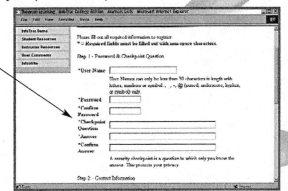

Note: After registration is complete, you will only need your <u>username and password</u> to logon.

USING INFOTRAC COLLEGE EDITION

There are three types of searches:

- · Subject Guide Search
- · Keyword Search
- · Advanced Search

Subject Guide Search

Step 1

Type in the term(s) you would like to search and click **Search**.

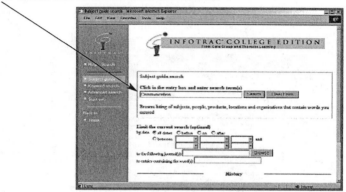

Step 2

After a list of results appear, select an article by clicking on the title. If your search words do not match the Subject Guide database, a list of similar and related subjects will appear. Simply select the subject that most closely matches your topic.

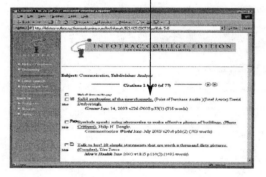 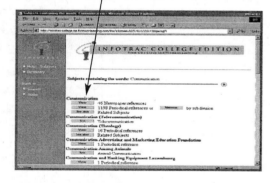

Step 4

A list containing bibliographic information for each article in your search to a maximum of 20 articles per page. To view an article, click on the citation.

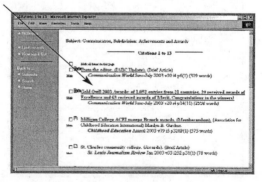

If the term(s) you typed in the **Subject Guide** cannot be found, it will automatically default to the **Keyword Search**.

Keyword Search

The **Keyword Search** looks for the word or words entered. It is more effective when looking for a specific topic, title, author, or product.

Search by **Keyword** just as you would by **Subject Guide**.

The search will return with a list of articles containing the keyword term(s). Results are listed from most recent to oldest publication date.

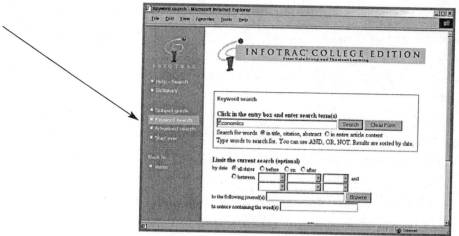

Advanced Search

With **Advanced Search**, a more specific search can be conducted.

Step 1

Select an index to search by. What is an index? Each article is indexed by certain variables. These indices include the title, author, publication's name, where and when it was published (see the list on the next page). Type your search criteria in the entry box to the right.

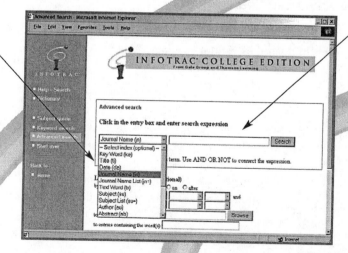

Step 2

If you want to search by multiple criterion, simply repeat the process with an operator between them.

- Logical operators(and/or/not) specify inclusive or exclusive relationships between search terms or result sets.
- Proximity operators (Wn, Nn) specify that two search terms must be within a specific distance (in words) of each other. Proximity operators work only with free text indexes such as keywords, abstracts, text, and titles.
- Range operators (since, before, etc.) specify upper bounds, lower bounds or both searches for numeric data. Numeric indexes include publication dates, number of employees and annual sales.

Indexes for Advanced Search

Abstract (ab): Includes words from article abstracts as well as from any author's abstracts.

Author (au): Authors are indexed in surname/given name order; for example, "nelan bruce w." It's best to search in surname-first order. Enter a surname and, optionally, a given name.

Date (da): The date the article was published.

Journal Name (jn): The name of the magazine or periodical.

Journal Name List (jn=): Provides a list of magazines or periodicals in which the search term appears.

Keyword (ke): Words in article titles and authors, as well as subjects, people, companies, products, vocations, events, etc., featured in articles.

Record Number (rn): A full record always includes a unique record number. If you note a record number, you can easily find the record again with the record number index.

Refereed (re): Experts in the same field as the writer review articles in the journal and ensure that the data and methodology has met a high standard. This is also knows as a peer reviewed.

Source (so): Lets you search for records by the type of source from which they're taken (e.g., magazine, journal, or newspapers).

Source List (so=): Lets you browse a list of subjects that contain the word or words you type.

Subject (su): Lets you search for references by the source types under which they are indexed.

Subject List (su=): Provides a list of references by source types.

Text Word (tx): Composed of all words from the body of articles.

Title (ti): The title index is composed of all words in the article.

Volume Number (vo): The volume of the magazine or periodical.

Using Wildcards in the Advanced Search

At times, you might want to find more than just exact matches to a search term. For instance, you might want to find both the singular and plural forms of a word or variant spellings. Wildcards let you broaden your searches to match a pattern.

InfoTrac provides three wildcards:

- An asterisk (*) stands for any number of characters, including none. For example pigment* matches "pigment," "pigments," "pigmentation," etc. The asterisk wildcard can also be used inside a word. For example, colo*r matches both "color" and "colour."
- A question mark (?) stands for exactly one character. Multiple question marks in a row stand for the same number of characters as there are question marks. For example, psych????y matches either "psychology" or "psychiatry", but not "psychotherapy."
- An exclamation point (!) stands for one or no characters. For example, analog!! matches "analog," "analogs" or "analogue" but not "analogous."

If you see a message about a search being invalid, you'll need to add at least one character before one of the wildcards.

Mark List

Clicking on the **Mark Box** allows you to select articles you would like to retrieve for later viewing. The **Mark Box** is available in two ways:

1. While viewing the citation list, you may select individual articles or you may select all the items on the page.

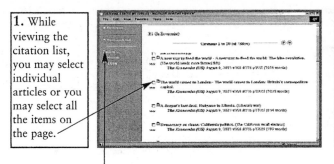

2. Check the **Mark Box** while you are in article view.

Click on **View Mark List** to view selected articles.

Limit Search

You may limit your search if you find yourself immersed in citations or of the citations are too general. Limit your search to dates, specific journals, and keywords. The **Limit Search** function is available in two ways:

1. *Limit a search that has already been performed.* To do this, click on **Limit Search** in the left navigation.

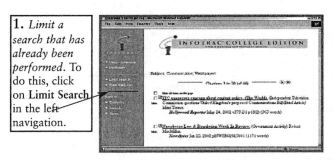

2. *Limit a current search.* To do this, fill out the **Limit Search** box below the search field.

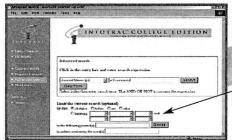

Article Retrieval

There are three article retrieval options available:

* **Browser Print:** Print out the full text article
* **Acrobat Reader:** Review article as a PDF file
* **Email Delivery:** E-mail article to self or others

Click on **Print or Email** on the left navigation bar while viewing citations.

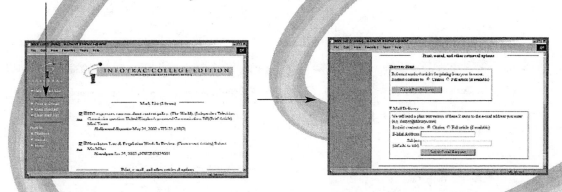

Chapter 1: Crime, Criminology, and the Criminal Law

Chapter Outline	Class Preparation and Lecture Tools	Student Mastery, Homework, and Tutorials
Chapter Resources	**Instructor's Manual** Chapter 1: Chapter Outline, Learning Objectives, Chapter Summary, Key Terms, Discussion Topics, Student Activities, and a **Test Bank**. **Multimedia Manager for Criminology: A Microsoft® PowerPoint® Tool** Lecture media tool with customizable PowerPoint® slides and images. **Transparency Masters for Criminology** Artwork from the main text that can be easily copied onto transparency acetates.	**Study Guide** Chapter 1: Chapter Outline, Learning Objectives, Key Terms, and Practice Tests containing multiple-choice, true/false, fill-in-the-blank, and essay questions. **Student Companion CD-ROM** Contains critical-thinking activities tied to the chapter-opening vignette, chapter-specific content and quizzing, and a **CNN®** **Video** clip on the Kobe Bryant case. **Book Companion Website** **http://cj.wadsworth.com/siegel_crim_9e** Outstanding study and review tools organized by chapter. **CriminologyNow™** **http://cj.wadsworth.com/siegel_crim_9e** A Web-based intelligent study system featuring diagnostic quizzes, a *Personalized Study Plan*, course management, and more. **Criminology: A Workbook Using MicroCase® ExploreIt® (with Software), Fifth Edition**
What Is Criminology? **A Brief History of Criminology**	**CourtTV Video** *Atlantic City Underground: American Babylon*	**InfoTrac® College Edition with InfoMarks™** *Keyword:* street youth and violence **Web Link** The work of Shaw and McKay: **www.csiss.org/classics/content/66**
What Criminologists Do: The Criminological Enterprise		**InfoTrac® College Edition with InfoMarks™** "Labeling and delinquency" **Web Link** Labeling theory overview: **http://home.comcast.net/~ddemelo/crime/labeling.html**
How Criminologists View Crime		**MicroCase® ExploreIt®** Chapter 1, "The Geography of Official Crime Rates"
Crime and the Criminal Law	**FFH Custom CJ Video** *Vol. 2: 21st Century Crime Fighting*	**Web Link** The Center for Restorative Justice & Peacemaking: **http://ssw.che.umn.edu/rjp/default.html**
Ethical Issues in Criminology		**Web Link** British Society of Criminology: Ethics: **http://www.britsoccrim.org/ethics.htm**

Testing and Assessment	Course Management
Test Bank (available in the **Instructor's Manual**) Chapter 1: Multiple-choice, true/false, fill-in-the-blank, and essay questions. The **Test Bank** is also available in **ExamView®** electronic format that can be customized to fit your needs. **ExamView**	**WebTutor™ Advantage on WebCT or Blackboard** **http://webtutor.thomsonlearning.com** An online course management system preloaded with text-specific content and resources.
Book Companion Website **http://cj.wadsworth.com/siegel_crim_9e** Assignable quiz questions: 15 multiple-choice, 5 true/false, and 5 essay questions.	**WebTutor™ Toolbox on WebCT or Blackboard** **http://webtutor.thomsonlearning.com** FREE online course management option.

Chapter 2: The Nature and Extent of Crime

Chapter Outline	Class Preparation and Lecture Tools	Student Mastery, Homework, and Tutorials
Chapter Resources	**Instructor's Manual** Chapter 2: Chapter Outline, Learning Objectives, Chapter Summary, Key Terms, Discussion Topics, Student Activities, and a **Test Bank.** **Multimedia Manager for Criminology: A Microsoft® PowerPoint® Tool** Lecture media tool with customizable PowerPoint® slides and images. **Transparency Masters for Criminology** Artwork from the main text that can be easily copied onto transparency acetates.	**Study Guide** Chapter 2: Chapter Outline, Learning Objectives, Key Terms, and Practice Tests containing multiple-choice, true/false, fill-in-the-blank, and essay questions. **Student Companion CD-ROM** Contains critical-thinking activities tied to the chapter-opening vignette, chapter-specific content and quizzing, and a **CNN®** **Video** clip on Eric Rudolph. **Book Companion Website** **http://cj.wadsworth.com/siegel_crim_9e** Outstanding study and review tools organized by chapter. **CriminologyNow™** **http://cj.wadsworth.com/siegel_crim_9e** A Web-based intelligent study system featuring diagnostic quizzes, a *Personalized Study Plan*, course management, and more. **Criminology: A Workbook Using MicroCase® ExplorIt® (with Software), Fifth Edition**
How Criminologists Study Crime		**Web Links** Princeton University Survey Research Center: **http://www.wws.princeton.edu/~psrc/.** The Bureau of Justice Statistics: **http://www.ojp.usdoj.gov/bjs/**
Measuring Crime Trends and Rates	**CNN® Today Video** *Criminology Vol. 7*, Segment 7: "Gun Crime"	**InfoTrac® College Edition with InfoMarks™** "Guns, Violent Crime, and Suicide in 21 Countries" **Web Links** NIBRS details: **http://www.ojp.usdoj.gov/bjs/nibrs.htm** Monitoring the Future website: **http://monitoringthefuture.org** **MicroCase® ExplorIt®** • Chapter 1, "The Geography of Official Crime Rates" • Chapter 3, "Self-Report Surveys"
Crime Trends	**FFH Video** *Thug Life in D.C.* (CLJ9049)	**InfoTrac® College Edition with InfoMarks™** • "Patterns of Substance Use in Milwaukee Gangs" • "Managing Crime in a Black Middle-Class Neighborhood" *Keyword:* crime trends **Web Link** Crime victimization data: **http://www.ojp.usdoj.gov/bjs/cvict.htm**
What the Future Holds	**FFH Video** *U.S.–Afghanistan Relations: Gaining Perspective* (FNN29393)	**InfoTrac® College Edition with InfoMarks™** *Keyword:* international crime
Crime Patterns	**CNN® Today Video** *Criminology Vol. 6*, Program 14: "Racial Profiling on the New Jersey Turnpike"	**InfoTrac® College Edition with InfoMarks™** "Making Guns Safer" *Keywords:* social class, sex differences

Testing and Assessment

Test Bank (available in the **Instructor's Manual**)

ExamView

Chapter 2: Multiple-choice, true/false, fill-in-the-blank, and essay questions. The **Test Bank** is also available in **ExamView®** electronic format that can be customized to fit your needs.

Book Companion Website
http://cj.wadsworth.com/siegel_crim_9e
Assignable quiz questions: 15 multiple-choice, 5 true/false, and 5 essay questions.

Course Management

WebTutor™ Advantage on WebCT or Blackboard WebTUTOR Advantage
http://webtutor.thomsonlearning.com
An online course management system preloaded with text-specific content and resources.

WebTutor™ Toolbox on WebCT or Blackboard WebTUTOR ToolBox
http://webtutor.thomsonlearning.com
FREE online course management option.

Chapter 3: Victims and Victimization

Chapter Outline	Class Preparation and Lecture Tools	Student Mastery, Homework, and Tutorials
Chapter Resources	**Instructor's Manual** Chapter 3: Chapter Outline, Learning Objectives, Chapter Summary, Key Terms, Discussion Topics, Student Activities, and a **Test Bank**. **Multimedia Manager for Criminology: A Microsoft® PowerPoint® Tool** Lecture media tool with customizable PowerPoint® slides and images. **Transparency Masters for Criminology** Artwork from the main text that can be easily copied onto transparency acetates.	**Study Guide** Chapter 3: Chapter Outline, Learning Objectives, Key Terms, and Practice Tests containing multiple-choice, true/false, fill-in-the-blank, and essay questions. **Student Companion CD-ROM** Contains critical-thinking activities tied to the chapter-opening vignette, chapter-specific content and quizzing, and a **CNN® Video** clip on the Giordano verdict. **Book Companion Website** http://cj.wadsworth.com/siegel_crim_9e Outstanding study and review tools organized by chapter. **CriminologyNow™** http://cj.wadsworth.com/siegel_crim_9e A Web-based intelligent study system featuring diagnostic quizzes, a *Personalized Study Plan*, course management, and more. **Criminology: A Workbook Using MicroCase® ExplorIt® (with Software), Fifth Edition**
Problems of Crime Victims	**CNN® Today Video** *Criminology Vol. 7*, Program 2: "Duct Tape Abuse," and Program 3: "A Daughter's Pain"	**InfoTrac® College Edition with InfoMarks™** • "Crime Victim Laws Sometimes Ignored" • Green, "Child Sexual Abuse" *Keyword:* crime victims **Web Link** National Center for Victims of Crime: http://www.ncvc.org/ncvc/Main.aspx
The Nature of Victimization	**A&E Video** *A Family Secret: The Death of Lisa Steinberg*	**InfoTrac® College Edition with InfoMarks™** "Violence Decreasing in U.S. High Schools" **MicroCase® ExplorIt®** Chapter 2, "Victimization Surveys"
Theories of Victimization	**CNN® Today Videos** • *Criminology Vol. 6*, Program 6: "Rape in Japan"	**InfoTrac® College Edition with InfoMarks™** "Human Agency, Capable Guardians, and Structural Constraints: A Lifestyle Approach to the Study of Violent Victimization" *Keywords:* date rape, acquaintance rape **Web Links** Crime victimization data: http://www.ojp.usdoj.gov/bjs/cvict.htm
Caring for the Victim	**FFH Videos** • *Glimmer of Hope* (CLJ8012) • *Healing the Heart: Forgive and Remember* (EFA10670)	**Web Links** Crime Victims Board of New York: http://www.cvb.state.ny.us/ Office for Victims of Crime (OVC): http://www.ojp.usdoj.gov/ovc/ National Organization for Victim Assistance: http://www.try-nova.org/

Testing and Assessment	Course Management
Test Bank (available in the **Instructor's Manual**) Chapter 3: Multiple-choice, true/false, fill-in-the-blank, and essay questions. The **Test Bank** is also available in **ExamView®** electronic format that can be customized to fit your needs.	**WebTutor™ Advantage on WebCT or Blackboard** http://webtutor.thomsonlearning.com An online course management system preloaded with text-specific content and resources.
Book Companion Website http://cj.wadsworth.com/siegel_crim_9e Assignable quiz questions: 15 multiple-choice, 5 true/false, and 5 essay questions.	**WebTutor™ Toolbox on WebCT or Blackboard** 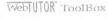 http://webtutor.thomsonlearning.com FREE online course management option.

Chapter 4: Choice Theories

Chapter Outline	Class Preparation and Lecture Tools	Student Mastery, Homework, and Tutorials
Chapter Resources	**Instructor's Manual** Chapter 4 Chapter Outline, Learning Objectives, Chapter Summary, Key Terms, Discussion Topics, Student Activities, and a **Test Bank.** **Multimedia Manager for Criminology: A Microsoft® PowerPoint® Tool** Lecture media tool with customizable PowerPoint® slides and images. **Transparency Masters for Criminology** Artwork from the main text that can be easily copied onto transparency acetates.	**Study Guide** Chapter 4: Chapter Outline, Learning Objectives, Key Terms, and Practice Tests containing multiple-choice, true/false, fill-in-the-blank, and essay questions. **Student Companion CD-ROM** Contains critical-thinking activities tied to the chapter-opening vignette, chapter-specific content and quizzing, and a **CNN®** **Video** clip called "Three Strikes Failure." **Book Companion Website** **http://cj.wadsworth.com/siegel_crim_9e** Outstanding study and review tools organized by chapter. **CriminologyNow™** **http://cj.wadsworth.com/siegel_crim_9e** A Web-based intelligent study system featuring diagnostic quizzes, a *Personalized Study Plan*, course management, and more. **Criminology: A Workbook Using MicroCase® ExplorIt® (with Software), Fifth Edition**
The Development of Rational Choice Theory	**CNN® Today Videos** • *Criminology Vol. 7*, Program 17: "SCOTUS Ruling"	**InfoTrac® College Edition with InfoMarks™** Bellamy, "Crime and Punishment" *Keywords*: correctional treatment **Web Links** Beccaria: **http://www.criminology.fsu.edu/ crimtheory/beccaria.htm** Bentham: **http://www.blupete.com/Literature/ Biographies/Philosophy/Bentham.htm**
The Concepts of Rational Choice		**Web Link** James Wilson, "Two Nations": **http://www.aei.org/boyer/jwilson.htm**
Is Crime Rational?		**InfoTrac® College Edition with InfoMarks™** Lichtenwald, "Drug Smuggling Behavior"
Eliminating Crime	**FFH Video** *The "Three Strikes" Law—The Legacy: Murder, Politics, and Prisons* (CLJ9126)	**InfoTrac® College Edition with InfoMarks™** "Civil Suits against Police Change Domestic Violence Response" *Keywords:* situational crime prevention, capital punishment, death penalty **Web Link** Prevention Through Environmental Design: **http://www.cpted.com.au/**
Public Policy Implications of Choice Theory		**MicroCase® ExplorIt®** • Chapter 5, "Fear of Crime" • Chapter 9, "Anomie, Routine Activities, and Robbery Rates"

Testing and Assessment	Course Management
Test Bank (available in the **Instructor's Manual**) Chapter 4: Multiple-choice, true/false, fill-in-the-blank, and essay questions. The **Test Bank** is also available in **ExamView®** electronic format that can be customized to fit your needs.	**WebTutor™ Advantage on WebCT or Blackboard** **http://webtutor.thomsonlearning.com** An online course management system preloaded with text-specific content and resources.
Book Companion Website **http://cj.wadsworth.com/siegel_crim_9e** Assignable quiz questions: 15 multiple-choice, 5 true/false, and 5 essay questions.	**WebTutor™ Toolbox on WebCT or Blackboard** **http://webtutor.thomsonlearning.com** FREE online course management option.

Resource Integration Guide

Chapter 5: Trait Theories

Chapter Outline	Class Preparation and Lecture Tools	Student Mastery, Homework, and Tutorials
Chapter Resources	**Instructor's Manual** Chapter 5: Chapter Outline, Learning Objectives, Chapter Summary, Key Terms, Discussion Topics, Student Activities, and a **Test Bank.** **Multimedia Manager for Criminology: A Microsoft® PowerPoint® Tool** Lecture media tool with customizable PowerPoint® slides and images. **Transparency Masters for Criminology** Artwork from the main text that can be easily copied onto transparency acetates.	**Study Guide** Chapter 5: Chapter Outline, Learning Objectives, Key Terms, and Practice Tests containing multiple-choice, true/false, fill-in-the-blank, and essay questions. **Student Companion CD-ROM** Contains critical-thinking activities tied to the chapter-opening vignette, chapter-specific content and quizzing, and a **CNN®** **Video** clip called "Killer Brain." **Book Companion Website** **http://cj.wadsworth.com/siegel_crim_9e** Outstanding study and review tools organized by chapter. **CriminologyNow™** Criminology ⊕ Now™ **http://cj.wadsworth.com/siegel_crim_9e** A Web-based intelligent study system featuring diagnostic quizzes, a *Personalized Study Plan*, course management, and more. **Criminology: A Workbook Using MicroCase® ExploreIt® (with Software), Fifth Edition**
Foundations of Trait Theory		**InfoTrac® College Edition with InfoMarks™** • Holton, "The New Synthesis?" • Bradley & Corwyn, "Socio-economic Status and Child Development" *Keyword:* sociobiology
Biosocial Trait Theories	**FFH Videos** • *Is Criminal Behavior Genetic?* (CLJ7339) • *Crime and Human Nature* (CLJ1327)	**InfoTrac® College Edition with InfoMarks™** • McGuffin & Neilson, "Behavior and Genes" • Caporael, "Evolutionary Psychology" *Keywords:* nutrition and behavior, testosterone and violence **Web Link** Diet and Crime: **http://news.bbc.co.uk/1/hi/health/2063117.stm**
Psychological Trait Theories	**FFH Video** *Mad or Bad? Psychologically Assessing Criminal Competence* (HPC30042)	**InfoTrac® College Edition with InfoMarks™** • "Facts about Fiction: In Defense of TV Violence" • "Who Us? Stop Blaming Kids and TV" **Web Links** Freud and his works: **http://users.rcn.com/brill/freudarc.html** The National Mental Health Association: **http://www.nmha.org/** Mental illness and crime: **http://www.karisable.com/crmh.htm** Bandura: **http://www.ship.edu/~cgboeree/bandura.html** IQ: **http://www.indiana.edu/~intell/**
Public Policy Implications of Trait Theory		**MicroCase® ExploreIt®** Chapter 7, "Social Psychological Processes: Bonds, Self-Control, and Deviant Associations"

Testing and Assessment	Course Management
Test Bank (available in the **Instructor's Manual**) Chapter 5: Multiple-choice, true/false, fill-in-the-blank, and essay questions. The **Test Bank** is also available in **ExamView®** electronic format that can be customized to fit your needs. 🔍**Exam**View	**WebTutor™ Advantage on WebCT or Blackboard** WebTUTOR Advantage **http://webtutor.thomsonlearning.com** An online course management system preloaded with text-specific content and resources.
Book Companion Website **http://cj.wadsworth.com/siegel_crim_9e** Assignable quiz questions: 15 multiple-choice, 5 true/false, and 5 essay questions.	**WebTutor™ Toolbox on WebCT or Blackboard** WebTUTOR ToolBox **http://webtutor.thomsonlearning.com** FREE online course management option.

Chapter 6: Social Structure Theories

Chapter Outline	Class Preparation and Lecture Tools	Student Mastery, Homework, and Tutorials
Chapter Resources	**Instructor's Manual** Chapter 6: Chapter Outline, Learning Objectives, Chapter Summary, Key Terms, Discussion Topics, Student Activities, and a **Test Bank.** **Multimedia Manager for Criminology: A Microsoft® PowerPoint® Tool** Lecture media tool with customizable PowerPoint® slides and images. **Transparency Masters for Criminology** Artwork from the main text that can be easily copied onto transparency acetates.	**Study Guide** Chapter 6: Chapter Outline, Learning Objectives, Key Terms, and Practice Tests containing multiple-choice, true/false, fill-in-the-blank, and essay questions. **Student Companion CD-ROM** Contains critical-thinking activities tied to the chapter-opening vignette, chapter-specific content and quizzing, and a **CNN®** Video clip on gun crime. **Book Companion Website** http://cj.wadsworth.com/siegel_crim_9e Outstanding study and review tools organized by chapter. **CriminologyNow™** http://cj.wadsworth.com/siegel_crim_9e A Web-based intelligent study system featuring diagnostic quizzes, a *Personalized Study Plan*, course management, and more. **Criminology: A Workbook Using MicroCase® ExplorIt® (with Software), Fifth Edition**
Socioeconomic Structure and Crime		**InfoTrac® College Edition with InfoMarks™** • "United States Poverty Studies and Poverty Measurement" • "Extent of Material Hardship and Poverty in the United States" *Keyword:* poverty and children **Web Link**–Child poverty: http://www.aecf.org/kidscount
Social Structure Theories		**Web Link**–Structural theory basics: http://www.crimetheory.com/Reading/further.htm
Social Disorganization Theories	**CNN® Today Video** *Criminology Vol. 7*, Program 8: "And Stay Out" **FFH Videos** • *Crackdown on Crime: Taking Back Our Neighborhoods* (CLJ5308) • *Street Crime: Community Efforts to Stop Crime* (EFA9374)	**InfoTrac® College Edition with InfoMarks™** "A Multilevel Contextual Model of Neighborhood Collective Efficacy" *Keyword:* housing rehabilitation **Web Link**–Collective efficacy and crime: http://www.wjh.harvard.edu/soc/faculty/sampson/1997.4.pdf **MicroCase® ExplorIt®** Chapter 8, "Social Disorganization & Property Crime"
Strain Theories	**FFH Video** *Jobs: A Way Out?* (BLV6317)	**InfoTrac® College Edition with InfoMarks™** • "Political Restraint of the Market and Levels of Criminal Homicide" • "Gender Differences in Strains Associated with Suicidal Behavior among Adolescents" *Keywords:* anomie, relative deprivation
Cultural Deviance Theories	**FFH Video**–*Teenagers and Gangs: A Lethal Combination* (EFA10787) **A&E Video**–*Gangbusters*	**InfoTrac® College Edition with InfoMarks™** "Cocaine, Kicks, and Strain: Patterns of Substance Use in Milwaukee Gangs"
Public Policy Implications of Social Structure Theory		**Web Link**–The Urban Institute's Justice Policy Center: http://www.urban.org/content/PolicyCenters/Justice/Overview.htm

Testing and Assessment

Test Bank (available in the **Instructor's Manual**)
Chapter 6: Multiple-choice, true/false, fill-in-the-blank, and essay questions. The **Test Bank** is also available in **ExamView®** electronic format that can be customized to fit your needs.

Book Companion Website
http://cj.wadsworth.com/siegel_crim_9e
Assignable quiz questions: 15 multiple-choice, 5 true/false, and 5 essay questions.

Course Management

WebTutor™ Advantage on WebCT or Blackboard
http://webtutor.thomsonlearning.com
An online course management system preloaded with text-specific content and resources.

WebTutor™ Toolbox on WebCT or Blackboard
http://webtutor.thomsonlearning.com
FREE online course management option.

Chapter 7: Social Process Theories

Chapter Outline	Class Preparation and Lecture Tools	Student Mastery, Homework, and Tutorials
Chapter Resources	**Instructor's Manual** Chapter 7: Chapter Outline, Learning Objectives, Chapter Summary, Key Terms, Discussion Topics, Student Activities, and a **Test Bank**. **Multimedia Manager for Criminology: A Microsoft® PowerPoint® Tool** Lecture media tool with customizable PowerPoint® slides and images. **Transparency Masters for Criminology** Artwork from the main text that can be easily copied onto transparency acetates.	**Study Guide** Chapter 7: Chapter Outline, Learning Objectives, Key Terms, and Practice Tests containing multiple-choice, true/false, fill-in-the-blank, and essay questions. **Student Companion CD-ROM** Contains critical-thinking activities tied to the chapter-opening vignette, chapter-specific content and quizzing, and a **CNN®** **Video** clip on sex offender registries. **Book Companion Website** http://cj.wadsworth.com/siegel_crim_9e Outstanding study and review tools organized by chapter. **CriminologyNow™** http://cj.wadsworth.com/siegel_crim_9e A Web-based intelligent study system featuring diagnostic quizzes, a *Personalized Study Plan*, course management, and more. **Criminology: A Workbook Using MicroCase® ExplorIt® (with Software), Fifth Edition**
Socialization and Crime	**FFH Videos** • *Brother of Mine: Youth Violence and Society* (CLJ8930) • *The Impact of Violence on Children* (CLJ5931)	**InfoTrac® College Edition with InfoMarks™** • "Effects of Remarriage following Divorce on the Academic Achievement of Children" • "Parenting and Adolescents' Accuracy in Perceiving Parental Values" • "Whatever Happened to Yesterday's Rebels? Longitudinal Effects of Youth Delinquency on Education and Employment" *Keyword:* parental deprivation **Web Link** Institute for Child and Family: **www.childpolicy.org/**
Social Learning Theory		**InfoTrac® College Edition with InfoMarks™** "Deviant Peer Affiliations, Crime, and Substance Use" *Keyword:* learning theory **MicroCase® ExplorIt®** Chapter 7, "Social Psychological Processes: Bonds, Self-Control, and Deviant Associations"
Social Control Theory	**FFH Video** *Catching Them Early* (FNN8586)	**Web Link** Hirschi's Work: **http://home.comcast.net/~ddemelo/crime/hirschi.html**
Social Reaction Theory		**InfoTrac® College Edition with InfoMarks™** "Gender, Reflected Appraisals, and Labeling"
Evaluating Social Process Theories		**InfoTrac® College Edition with InfoMarks™** "The Contribution of Self-Concept in the Etiology of Adolescent Delinquent"
Public Policy Implications of Social Process Theory		**InfoTrac® College Edition with InfoMarks™** *Keyword:* Head Start

Testing and Assessment	Course Management
Test Bank (available in the **Instructor's Manual**) Chapter 7: Multiple-choice, true/false, fill-in-the-blank, and essay questions. The **Test Bank** is also available in **ExamView®** electronic format that can be customized to fit your needs. **Book Companion Website** http://cj.wadsworth.com/siegel_crim_9e Assignable quiz questions: 15 multiple-choice, 5 true/false, and 5 essay questions.	**WebTutor™ Advantage on WebCT or Blackboard** http://webtutor.thomsonlearning.com An online course management system preloaded with text-specific content and resources. **WebTutor™ Toolbox on WebCT or Blackboard** http://webtutor.thomsonlearning.com FREE online course management option.

Chapter Outline	Class Preparation and Lecture Tools	Student Mastery, Homework, and Tutorials
Chapter Resources	**Instructor's Manual** Chapter 8: Chapter Outline, Learning Objectives, Chapter Summary, Key Terms, Discussion Topics, Student Activities, and a **Test Bank.** **Multimedia Manager for Criminology: A Microsoft® PowerPoint® Tool** Lecture media tool with customizable PowerPoint® slides and images. **Transparency Masters for Criminology** Artwork from the main text that can be easily copied onto transparency acetates.	**Study Guide** Chapter 8: Chapter Outline, Learning Objectives, Key Terms, and Practice Tests containing multiple-choice, true/false, fill-in-the-blank, and essay questions. **Student Companion CD-ROM** Contains critical-thinking activities tied to the chapter-opening vignette, chapter-specific content and quizzing, and a **CNN®** **Video** clip on political protestors. **Book Companion Website** **http://cj.wadsworth.com/siegel_crim_9e** Outstanding study and review tools organized by chapter. **CriminologyNow™** **http://cj.wadsworth.com/siegel_crim_9e** Criminology⊛Now™ A Web-based intelligent study system featuring diagnostic quizzes, a *Personalized Study Plan,* course management, and more.
Marxist Thought		**InfoTrac® College Edition with InfoMarks™** *Keyword:* Karl Marx **Web Link** Marx and his vision: **www.philosophypages.com/ph/marx.htm**
Developing a Conflict-Based Theory of Crime	**CNN® Today Video** **CNN** *Criminology Vol. 6,* Program 9: "Corporate Self-Reporting"	**Web Link** Ralf Dahrendorf: **globetrotter.berkeley.edu/Elberg/** **Dahrendorf/dahrendorf0.html**
Social Conflict Theory		**Web Link** William Chambliss: **http://www.gwu.edu/~soc/w_chambliss.html**
Critical Criminology		**InfoTrac® College Edition with InfoMarks™** • Taylor, "Crime and Social Criticism" • "Looking Back: Radical Criminology and Social Movements"
Contemporary Forms of Critical Theory	**FFH Video** *Domestic Violence: "Til Death Do Us Part"* (CLJ5796)	**InfoTrac® College Edition with InfoMarks™** • "Beyond Patriarchy? Theorizing Gender and Class" • "Who Rules Now? American Elites in the 1990s"
Public Policy Implications of Social Conflict Theory: Restorative Justice	**CNN® Today Video** **CNN** *Criminology Vol. 7,* Program 10: "Anti-War Protest"	**Web Link** Center for Restorative Justice and Peacemaking: **http://2ssw.che.umn.edu/rjp/**

Testing and Assessment	Course Management
Test Bank (available in the **Instructor's Manual**) **ExamView** Chapter 8 Multiple-choice, true/false, fill-in-the-blank, and essay questions. The **Test Bank** is also available in **ExamView®** electronic format that can be customized to fit your needs.	**WebTutor™ Advantage on WebCT or Blackboard** WebTUTOR™ Advantage **http://webtutor.thomsonlearning.com** An online course management system preloaded with text-specific content and resources.
Book Companion Website **http://cj.wadsworth.com/siegel_crim_9e** Assignable quiz questions: 15 multiple-choice, 5 true/false, and 5 essay questions.	**WebTutor™ Toolbox on WebCT or Blackboard** WebTUTOR™ ToolBox  **http://webtutor.thomsonlearning.com** FREE online course management option.

Chapter 9: Developmental Theories: Life Course and Latent Trait

Resource Integration Guide

Chapter Outline	Class Preparation and Lecture Tools	Student Mastery, Homework, and Tutorials
Chapter Resources	**Instructor's Manual** Chapter 9: Chapter Outline, Learning Objectives, Chapter Summary, Key Terms, Discussion Topics, Student Activities, and a **Test Bank**. **Multimedia Manager for Criminology: A Microsoft® PowerPoint® Tool** Lecture media tool with customizable PowerPoint® slides and images. **Transparency Masters for Criminology** Artwork from the main text that can be easily copied onto transparency acetates.	**Study Guide** Chapter 9: Chapter Outline, Learning Objectives, Key Terms, and Practice Tests containing multiple-choice, true/false, fill-in-the-blank, and essay questions. **Student Companion CD-ROM** Contains critical-thinking activities tied to the chapter-opening vignette, chapter-specific content and quizzing, and a **CNN® Video** clip called "Janklow Guilty." **Book Companion Website** **http://cj.wadsworth.com/siegel_crim_9e** Outstanding study and review tools organized by chapter. **CriminologyNow™** **http://cj.wadsworth.com/siegel_crim_9e** A Web-based intelligent study system featuring diagnostic quizzes, a *Personalized Study Plan*, course management, and more. Criminology Now™
The Life Course View		**InfoTrac® College Edition with InfoMarks™** "Masculine Somatotype and Hirsuteness as Determinants of Sexual Attractiveness to Women" *Keyword:* Terrie Moffitt
Theories of the Criminal Life Course		**InfoTrac® College Edition with InfoMarks™** "Crime in the Making: Pathways and Turning Points through Life" **Web Link** Farrington's work: **www.ncjrs.org/html/ojjdp/report_research_2000/findings.html**
Latent Trait View		**Web Link** Integrated Theories: **www.critcrim.org/critpapers/barak_integrative.htm**
Latent Trait Theories	**FFH Video** *Is Criminal Behavior Genetic?* (CLJ7339)	**InfoTrac® College Edition with InfoMarks™** "Criminal Behavior and Age: A Test of Three Provocative Hypotheses"
Evaluating Developmental Theories		**Web Link** Developmental pathways to crime: **http://www.ncjrs.org/pdffiles/165692.pdf**
Public Policy Implications of Developmental Theory		**InfoTrac® College Edition with InfoMarks™** "Family-Based Prevention of Offending: A Meta-Analysis"

Testing and Assessment	Course Management
Test Bank (available in the **Instructor's Manual**) Chapter 9: Multiple-choice, true/false, fill-in-the-blank, and essay questions. The **Test Bank** is also available in ExamView® electronic format that can be customized to fit your needs. **ExamView**	**WebTutor™ Advantage on WebCT or Blackboard** WebTUTOR Advantage **http://webtutor.thomsonlearning.com** An online course management system preloaded with text-specific content and resources.
Book Companion Website **http://cj.wadsworth.com/siegel_crim_9e** Assignable quiz questions: 15 multiple-choice, 5 true/false, and 5 essay questions.	**WebTutor™ Toolbox on WebCT or Blackboard** WebTUTOR ToolBox **http://webtutor.thomsonlearning.com** FREE online course management option.

Chapter Outline	Class Preparation and Lecture Tools	Student Mastery, Homework, and Tutorials
Chapter Resources	**Instructor's Manual** Chapter 10: Chapter Outline, Learning Objectives, Chapter Summary, Key Terms, Discussion Topics, Student Activities, and a **Test Bank.** **Multimedia Manager for Criminology: A Microsoft® PowerPoint® Tool** Lecture media tool with customizable PowerPoint® slides and images. **Transparency Masters for Criminology** Artwork from the main text that can be easily copied onto transparency acetates.	**Study Guide** Chapter 10: Chapter Outline, Learning Objectives, Key Terms, and Practice Tests containing multiple-choice, true/false, fill-in-the-blank, and essay questions. **Student Companion CD-ROM** Contains critical-thinking activities tied to the chapter-opening vignette, chapter-specific content and quizzing, and a **CNN®** **Video** clip on the D.C. Sniper trial. **Book Companion Website** http://cj.wadsworth.com/siegel_crim_9e Outstanding study and review tools organized by chapter. **CriminologyNow™** http://cj.wadsworth.com/siegel_crim_9e A Web-based intelligent study system featuring diagnostic quizzes, a *Personalized Study Plan,* course management, and more. **Criminology: A Workbook Using MicroCase® ExplorIt® (with Software), Fifth Edition**
The Causes of Violence	**CNN® Today Videos** • *Criminology Vol. 7,* Program 1: "Family Feud Turns Deadly" • *Criminology Vol. 6,* Program 3: "When Boys Find Guns"	**InfoTrac® College Edition with InfoMarks™** • "New Path for Aggressive Boys" • "New Horizons for the American West" *Keywords:* Freud, child abuse
Forcible Rape	**CNN® Today Videos** *Criminology Vol. 6,* Program 6: "Rape in Japan" **FFH Videos** • *Rape: The Ultimate Violation* (FNN10741) • *The Sex Offender Next Door* (EFA9226)	**InfoTrac® College Edition with InfoMarks™** "The Effects of Viewing R-Rated Movie Scenes that Objectify Women on Perceptions of Date Rape" *Keyword:* rape
Murder and Homicide	**CNN® Today Videos** • *Criminology Vol. 6,* Program 5: "Moms Who Kill" • *Criminology Vol. 6,* Program 8: "Green River Killings"	**InfoTrac® College Edition with InfoMarks™** "Serial Homicide: We Need to Explore behind the Stereotypes and Ask Why" **MicroCase® ExplorIt®** Chapter 11, "Violence and the Old West"
Assault and Battery	**FFH Video** *You Can't Beat a Woman* (CLJ8075)	**InfoTrac® College Edition with InfoMarks™** "Intimidation and Violence by Males in High School Athletics"
Robbery	**FFH Video** *Street Crime: Community Efforts to Stop Crime* (EFA9374)	**InfoTrac® College Edition with InfoMarks™** Koppen & Jansen, "The Road to the Robbery" **MicroCase® ExplorIt®** Chapter 9, "Anomie, Routine Activities and Robbery Rates"
Emerging Forms of Interpersonal Violence	**CNN® Today Videos** *Introduction to Criminal Justice Vol. 5,* Program 2: "Hate Crimes and 9/11"	**Web Link** FBI's hate crime data: www.fbi.gov/ucr/cius_01/01crime2.pdf
Terrorism	**CNN® Today Videos** *Introduction to Criminal Justice Vol. 5,* Program 3: "Most Wanted Terrorists"	**InfoTrac® College Edition with InfoMarks™** Betts, "Fixing Intelligence" *Keyword:* terrorism

Testing and Assessment	Course Management
Test Bank (available in the **Instructor's Manual**) Chapter 10: Multiple-choice, true/false, fill-in-the-blank, and essay questions. The **Test Bank** is also available in **ExamView®** electronic format that can be customized to fit your needs. **Book Companion Website** http://cj.wadsworth.com/siegel_crim_9e Assignable quiz questions: 15 multiple-choice, 5 true/false, and 5 essay questions.	**WebTutor™ Advantage on WebCT or Blackboard** http://webtutor.thomsonlearning.com An online course management system preloaded with text-specific content and resources. **WebTutor™ Toolbox on WebCT or Blackboard** http://webtutor.thomsonlearning.com FREE online course management option. 

Resource Integration Guide

Chapter 11: Property Crime

Chapter Outline	Class Preparation and Lecture Tools	Student Mastery, Homework, and Tutorials
Chapter Resources	**Instructor's Manual** Chapter 11: Chapter Outline, Learning Objectives, Chapter Summary, Key Terms, Discussion Topics, Student Activities, and a **Test Bank.** **Multimedia Manager for Criminology: A Microsoft® PowerPoint® Tool** Lecture media tool with customizable PowerPoint® slides and images. **Transparency Masters for Criminology** Artwork from the main text that can be easily copied onto transparency acetates.	**Study Guide** Chapter 11: Chapter Outline, Learning Objectives, Key Terms, and Practice Tests containing multiple-choice, true/false, fill-in-the-blank, and essay questions. **Student Companion CD-ROM** Contains critical-thinking activities tied to the chapter-opening vignette, chapter-specific content and quizzing, and a **CNN® Video** clip called "Ryder Sentenced." **Book Companion Website** **http://cj.wadsworth.com/siegel_crim_9e** Outstanding study and review tools organized by chapter. **CriminologyNow™** **http://cj.wadsworth.com/siegel_crim_9e** A Web-based intelligent study system featuring diagnostic quizzes, a *Personalized Study Plan,* course management, and more. **Criminology: A Workbook Using MicroCase® ExplorIt® (with Software), Fifth Edition**
Modern Thieves		**InfoTrac® College Edition with InfoMarks™** "Professional Crime: Change, Continuity, and the Enduring Myth of the Underworld"
Larceny/Theft		**InfoTrac® College Edition with InfoMarks™** "Bagging Profits Instead of Thieves" *Keywords:* credit card fraud, Lojack, confidence games **Web Links** Credit card theft: **http://www.ftc.gov/bcp/conline/pubs/credit/cards.htm** Auto theft prevention: **http://www.prevent-crime.com/auto-theft.html** **MicroCase® ExplorIt®** Chapter 6, "Motor Vehicle Theft"
Burglary	**FFH Video** *Crackdown on Crime: Taking Back Our Neighborhoods* (CLJ5308)	**InfoTrac® College Edition with InfoMarks™** *Keywords:* burglary, burglars **MicroCase® ExplorIt®** Chapter 8, "Social Disorganization and Property Crime"
Arson		**InfoTrac® College Edition with InfoMarks™** "Arson: A Review of the Psychiatric Literature" *Keyword:* arson

Testing and Assessment

Test Bank (available in the **Instructor's Manual**)
Chapter 11: Multiple-choice, true/false, fill-in-the-blank, and essay questions. The **Test Bank** is also available in **ExamView®** electronic format that can be customized to fit your needs.

ExamView

Book Companion Website
http://cj.wadsworth.com/siegel_crim_9e
Assignable quiz questions: 15 multiple-choice, 5 true/false, and 5 essay questions.

Course Management

WebTutor™ Advantage on WebCT or Blackboard
http://webtutor.thomsonlearning.com
An online course management system preloaded with text-specific content and resources.

WebTutor™ Toolbox on WebCT or Blackboard
http://webtutor.thomsonlearning.com
FREE online course management option.

Chapter 12: Enterprise Crime: White-Collar, Cyber, and Organized Crime

Chapter Outline	Class Preparation and Lecture Tools	Student Mastery, Homework, and Tutorials
Chapter Resources	**Instructor's Manual** Chapter 12: Chapter Outline, Learning Objectives, Chapter Summary, Key Terms, Discussion Topics, Student Activities, and a **Test Bank.** **Multimedia Manager for Criminology: A Microsoft® PowerPoint® Tool** Lecture media tool with customizable PowerPoint® slides and images. **Transparency Masters for Criminology** Artwork from the main text that can be easily copied onto transparency acetates.	**Study Guide** Chapter 12: Chapter Outline, Learning Objectives, Key Terms, and Practice Tests containing multiple-choice, true/false, fill-in-the-blank, and essay questions. **Student Companion CD-ROM** Contains critical-thinking activities tied to the chapter-opening vignette, chapter-specific content and quizzing, and a **CNN®** **Video** clip on the Martha Stewart sentence. **Book Companion Website** http://cj.wadsworth.com/siegel_crim_9e Outstanding study and review tools organized by chapter. **CriminologyNow™** http://cj.wadsworth.com/siegel_crim_9e Criminology ⊕ Now™ A Web-based intelligent study system featuring diagnostic quizzes, a *Personalized Study Plan*, course management, and more.
Enterprise Crime	**CNN® Today Video** *Criminology Vol. 7,* Program 9: "Corporate Self-Reporting" CNN	
White-Collar Crime	**CNN® Today Videos** • *Criminology Vol. 6,* Program 1: "Enron" CNN • *Criminology Vol. 7,* Program 13: "Martha Stewart"	**InfoTrac® College Edition with InfoMarks™** "Wide Disparity in White-Collar Sentences" *Keywords:* white collar crime, Enron, Worldcom, Tyco
Components of White-Collar Crime	**FFH Custom CJ Video** *Vol. 1: White Collar Crime*	**Web Link** FCPA: http://www.usdoj.gov/criminal/fraud/fcpa/dojdocb.htm
Causes of White-Collar Crime		**Web Link** White Collar Crime blog: http://lawprofessors.typepad.com/whitecollarcrime_blog/2004/11/sociological_or.html
White-Collar Law Enforcement Systems		**Web Link** National Whistleblower Center: http://www.whistleblowers.org
Cyber Crime	**CNN® Today Videos** • *Criminology Vol. 6,* Program 12: "Computer Forensics" CNN • *Criminology Vol. 7,* Program 11: "Internet Sex Death"	**InfoTrac® College Edition with InfoMarks™** • "Integrated Risk Management in the Internet Age" • Jacobson & Green, "Computer Crime" *Keyword:* learning theory
Internet Crime	**CNN® Today Video** *Introduction to Criminal Justice Vol. 5,* Programs 13–16: "Crime on the Internet"	**Web Link** Internet Fraud Complaint Center: http://www.ifccfbi.gov/index.asp
Computer Crime	**CourtTV Video** *Cybercrime* COURT TV	**InfoTrac® College Edition with InfoMarks™** Jacobson & Green, "Computer Crime"
Controlling Cyber Crime	**FFH Custom CJ Video** *Vol. 2: Cybercrime*	**Web Link** Computer Security Institute: http://www.gocsi.com/
Organized Crime	**A&E Videos** • *L.A. Mob* • *Vegas & the Mob* • *Crime Family*	**InfoTrac® College Edition with InfoMarks™** • "The Best Investigative Reporter You've Never Heard of" • O'Neal, "Russian Organized Crime" **Web Link** Organized Crime: organizedcrime.about.com

Testing and Assessment	Course Management
Test Bank (available in the **Instructor's Manual**) ExamView Chapter 12: Multiple-choice, true/false, fill-in-the-blank, and essay questions. The **Test Bank** is also available in **ExamView®** electronic format that can be customized to fit your needs.	**WebTutor™ Advantage on WebCT or Blackboard** WebTUTOR Advantage http://webtutor.thomsonlearning.com An online course management system preloaded with text-specific content and resources.
Book Companion Website http://cj.wadsworth.com/siegel_crim_9e Assignable quiz questions: 15 multiple-choice, 5 true/false, and 5 essay questions.	**WebTutor™ Toolbox on WebCT or Blackboard** WebTUTOR ToolBox http://webtutor.thomsonlearning.com FREE online course management option.

Resource Integration Guide

Chapter 13: Public Order Crime

Chapter Outline	Class Preparation and Lecture Tools	Student Mastery, Homework, and Tutorials
Chapter Resources	**Instructor's Manual** Chapter 13 Chapter Outline, Learning Objectives, Chapter Summary, Key Terms, Discussion Topics, Student Activities, and a **Test Bank.** **Multimedia Manager for Criminology: A Microsoft® PowerPoint® Tool** Lecture media tool with customizable PowerPoint® slides and images. **Transparency Masters for Criminology** Artwork from the main text that can be easily copied onto transparency acetates.	**Study Guide** Chapter13: Chapter Outline, Learning Objectives, Key Terms, and Practice Tests containing multiple-choice, true/false, fill-in-the-blank, and essay questions. **Student Companion CD-ROM** Contains critical-thinking activities tied to the chapter-opening vignette, chapter-specific content and quizzing, and a **CNN® Video** clip on the Gay Marriage Amendment. **Book Companion Website** http://cj.wadsworth.com/siegel_crim_9e Outstanding study and review tools organized by chapter. **CriminologyNow™** http://cj.wadsworth.com/siegel_crim_9e A Web-based intelligent study system featuring diagnostic quizzes, a *Personalized Study Plan*, course management, and more.
Law and Morality	**CNN® Today Video** *Criminology Vol. 7*, Program 14: "Gay Marriage in Canada"	**InfoTrac® College Edition with InfoMarks™** "'You Cannot Fix the Scarlet Letter on My Breast!': Women Reading, Writing, and Reshaping the Sexual Culture of Victorian America"
Homosexuality		**InfoTrac® College Edition with InfoMarks™** *Keywords:* homophobia, gay marriage
Paraphilias		**Web Link** More info on paraphilias http://cms.psychologytoday.com/conditions/paraphilias.html
Prostitution	**CNN® Today Videos** • Criminology Vol. 6, Program 10: "Child Prostitution" **CourtTV Video** *Crime Stories—Anatomy of a Crime: Sex for Sale*	**InfoTrac® College Edition with InfoMarks™** "Commercial Sexual Exploitation of Children: A Global Problem Requiring Global Action" **Web Link** International Sex Trade: web.amnesty.org/library/Index/ENGEUR700102004.
Pornography	**CNN® Today Video** *Introduction to Criminal Justice Vol. 6*, Program 16: "Child Pornography"	**InfoTrac® College Edition with InfoMarks™** "Filth in the Wrong People's Hands: Postcards and the Expansion of Pornography in Britain and the Atlantic World, 1880–1914" **Web Link** *Pope v. Illinois:* http://caselaw.lp.findlaw.com/scripts/getcase.pl?court=US&vol=
Substance Abuse	**FFH Video** *Drugs and Punishment: Are America's Drug Policies Fair?* (CLJ7519)	**Web Link** National Center on Addiction and Substance Abuse: http://www.casacolumbia.org

Testing and Assessment	Course Management
Test Bank (available in the **Instructor's Manual**) Chapter 13: Multiple-choice, true/false, fill-in-the-blank, and essay questions. The **Test Bank** is also available in **ExamView®** electronic format that can be customized to fit your needs.	**WebTutor™ Advantage on WebCT or Blackboard** http://webtutor.thomsonlearning.com An online course management system preloaded with text-specific content and resources.
Book Companion Website http://cj.wadsworth.com/siegel_crim_9e Assignable quiz questions: 15 multiple-choice, 5 true/false, and 5 essay questions.	**WebTutor™ Toolbox on WebCT or Blackboard** http://webtutor.thomsonlearning.com FREE online course management option.

Chapter 14: The Criminal Justice System

Chapter Outline	Class Preparation and Lecture Tools	Student Mastery, Homework, and Tutorials
Chapter Resources	**Instructor's Manual** Chapter 14: Chapter Outline, Learning Objectives, Chapter Summary, Key Terms, Discussion Topics, Student Activities, and a **Test Bank.** **Multimedia Manager for Criminology: A Microsoft® PowerPoint® Tool** Lecture media tool with customizable PowerPoint® slides and images. **Transparency Masters for Criminology** Artwork from the main text that can be easily copied onto transparency acetates.	**Study Guide** Chapter 14: Chapter Outline, Learning Objectives, Key Terms, and Practice Tests containing multiple-choice, true/false, fill-in-the-blank, and essay questions. **Student Companion CD-ROM** Contains critical-thinking activities tied to the chapter-opening vignette, chapter-specific content and quizzing, and a **CNN®** **Video** clip called "Early Release." **Book Companion Website** http://cj.wadsworth.com/siegel_crim_9e Outstanding study and review tools organized by chapter. **CriminologyNow™** http://cj.wadsworth.com/siegel_crim_9e A Web-based intelligent study system featuring diagnostic quizzes, a *Personalized Study Plan,* course management, and more.
Origins of the Criminal Justice System	**CNN® Today Videos** • *Criminology Vol. 6,* Program 11: "Sex Offenders Paroled," and Program 15: "Forensic Expert's Testimony in Question" • *Criminology Vol. 7,* Program 15: "Convicted Molester Paroled" **A&E Video** *Why O.J. Simpson Won*	**InfoTrac® College Edition with InfoMarks™** Dority, "The U.S. Criminal Injustice System" **Web Link** American Bar Foundation: http://www.abf-sociolegal.org/
What Is the Criminal Justice System?		**Web Link** Data on the Criminal Justice System: http://www.ojp.usdoj.gov/bjs/
The Process of Justice	**FFH Custom CJ Video** *Vol.1: The Court Process*	
Criminal Justice and the Rule of Law	**FFH Videos** • Amendments 5–8: *The Justice Amendments* (CLJ8104) • Amendment 4: *Unreasonable Search and Seizure* (CLJ8103)	**InfoTrac® College Edition with InfoMarks™** • Gardner, "Sixth Amendment Right to Counsel and Its Underlying Values" • Calabresi, "The Exclusionary Rule"
Concepts of Justice	**CNN® Today Video** *Criminology Vol. 6,* Program 16: "Moratorium on Executions" **CourtTV Video** *The System: Double Jeopardy*	**InfoTrac® College Edition with InfoMarks™** *Keyword:* due process **Web Link** National Center for Policy Analysis: http://www.ncpa.org/newdpd/index.php
Concepts of Justice Today		**Web Link** Perspectives on the Criminal Justice System: http://www.360degrees.org/

Testing and Assessment | Course Management

Test Bank (available in the **Instructor's Manual**)
Chapter 14: Multiple-choice, true/false, fill-in-the-blank, and essay questions. The **Test Bank** is also available in **ExamView®** electronic format that can be customized to fit your needs.

Book Companion Website
http://cj.wadsworth.com/siegel_crim_9e
Assignable quiz questions: 15 multiple-choice, 5 true/false, and 5 essay questions.

WebTutor™ Advantage on WebCT or Blackboard
http://webtutor.thomsonlearning.com
An online course management system preloaded with text-specific content and resources.

WebTutor™ Toolbox on WebCT or Blackboard
http://webtutor.thomsonlearning.com
FREE online course management option.

Resource Integration Guide

Chapter 15: Police and Law Enforcement

Chapter Outline	Class Preparation and Lecture Tools	Student Mastery, Homework, and Tutorials
Chapter Resources	**Instructor's Manual** Chapter 15: Chapter Outline, Learning Objectives, Chapter Summary, Key Terms, Discussion Topics, Student Activities, and a **Test Bank.** **Multimedia Manager for Criminology: A Microsoft® PowerPoint® Tool** Lecture media tool with customizable PowerPoint® slides and images. **Transparency Masters for Criminology** Artwork from the main text that can be easily copied onto transparency acetates.	**Study Guide** Chapter 15: Chapter Outline, Learning Objectives, Key Terms, and Practice Tests containing multiple-choice, true/false, fill-in-the-blank, and essay questions. **Student Companion CD-ROM** Contains critical-thinking activities tied to the chapter-opening vignette, chapter-specific content and quizzing, and a **CNN® Video** clip on Amber Alert. **Book Companion Website** http://cj.wadsworth.com/siegel_crim_9e Outstanding study and review tools organized by chapter. **CriminologyNow™** http://cj.wadsworth.com/siegel_crim_9e A Web-based intelligent study system featuring diagnostic quizzes, a *Personalized Study Plan,* course management, and more.
History of Police		**InfoTrac® College Edition with InfoMarks™** "The Demand for Order and the Birth of Modern Policing"
Law Enforcement Agencies Today	**FFH Video** *Crime Tech: New Tools for Law Enforcement* (EFA7958)	**Web Link** The Police Foundation: http://www.policefoundation.org
Police Functions	**FFH Video** *Protect and Serve? De-Policing in Urban Neighborhoods* (FNN29110)	**InfoTrac® College Edition with InfoMarks™** "A Medical Model for Community Policing" **Web Link** The "broken windows" concept: http://www.ncjrs.org/pdffiles1/nij/178259.pdf
Changing the Police Role	**FFH Video** *Beyond the Blue: Life as a Female Police Officer* (CLJ8572)	**Web Link** Community policing: http://www.policing.com
Police and the Rule of Law	**FFH Videos** • *Amendments 5-8: The Justice Amendments* (CLJ8104) • *Amendment 4: Unreasonable Search and Seizure* (CLJ8103)	**InfoTrac® College Edition with InfoMarks™** "Is *Miranda* Case Law Inconsistent? A Fifth Amendment Synthesis"
Issues in Policing	**CNN® Today Video** *Criminology Vol. 6,* Program 13: "Schwarz's Sentence Overturned" **CourtTV Videos** • *Florida v. Campbell—Driving While Black* • *California v. Powell*	**InfoTrac® College Edition with InfoMarks™** • "The Role of Race in Law Enforcement: Racial Profiling or Legitimate Use?" • "Police Officers' Judgments of Blame in Family Violence" *Keyword:* racial profiling **Web Link** Institute on Race and Justice: http://www.racialprofilinganalysis.neu.edu/

Testing and Assessment	Course Management
Test Bank (available in the **Instructor's Manual**) Chapter 15: Multiple-choice, true/false, fill-in-the-blank, and essay questions. The **Test Bank** is also available in **ExamView®** electronic format that can be customized to fit your needs. **Book Companion Website** http://cj.wadsworth.com/siegel_crim_9e Assignable quiz questions: 15 multiple-choice, 5 true/false, and 5 essay questions.	**WebTutor™ Advantage on WebCT or Blackboard** http://webtutor.thomsonlearning.com An online course management system preloaded with text-specific content and resources. **WebTutor™ Toolbox on WebCT or Blackboard** http://webtutor.thomsonlearning.com FREE online course management option.

Chapter 16: The Judicatory Process

Chapter Outline	Class Preparation and Lecture Tools	Student Mastery, Homework, and Tutorials
Chapter Resources	**Instructor's Manual** Chapter 16: Chapter Outline, Learning Objectives, Chapter Summary, Key Terms, Discussion Topics, Student Activities, and a **Test Bank.** **Multimedia Manager for Criminology: A Microsoft® PowerPoint® Tool** Lecture media tool with customizable PowerPoint® slides and images. **Transparency Masters for Criminology** Artwork from the main text that can be easily copied onto transparency acetates.	**Study Guide** Chapter 16: Chapter Outline, Learning Objectives, Key Terms, and Practice Tests containing multiple-choice, true/false, fill-in-the-blank, and essay questions. **Student Companion CD-ROM** Contains critical-thinking activities tied to the chapter-opening vignette, chapter-specific content and quizzing, and a **CNN® Video** clip on the Scott Peterson trial. **Book Companion Website** http://cj.wadsworth.com/siegel_crim_9e Outstanding study and review tools organized by chapter. **CriminologyNow™** http://cj.wadsworth.com/siegel_crim_9e A Web-based intelligent study system featuring diagnostic quizzes, a Personalized Study Plan, course management, and more.
Court Structure	**CNN® Today Video** *Introduction to Criminal Justice Vol. 5*, Program 18: "Prosecuting Child Pornography Cases" **FFH Video** *Order in the Court* (FNN11902)	**InfoTrac® College Edition with InfoMarks™** "State Judges for Sale" *Keyword:* David Westerfield **Web Link** National Center for State Courts: http://www.ncsc.dni.us
Actors in the Judicatory Process	**FFH Custom CJ Video** *Vol. 1, The Court Process* (0-534-52538-5)	**Web Link** Federal Judicial Center: http://air.fjc.gov/
Pretrial Procedures	**FFH Video** *Plea Bargains: Dealing for Justice* (CLJ4593)	**Web Link** Bounty hunters: http://www.bounty-hunter.net/home.htm
The Criminal Trial	**A&E Video** *It's Not My Fault: Strange Defenses* **FFH Video** *Evidence of Guilt: The Complexities of Jurisprudence* (EFA9244)	**InfoTrac® College Edition with InfoMarks™** "An Argument for Fairness and Against Self-Representation in the Criminal Justice System"
Sentencing	**CNN® Today Video** *Introduction to Criminal Justice Vol. 6*, Program 3: "Dog Maul Sentencing"	**InfoTrac® College Edition with InfoMarks™** logo) • "Three-Strikes Laws Proving More Show than Go" • "Are Three-Strikes Laws Handcuffing the Courts?"
The Death Penalty	**CNN® Today Video** *Criminology Vol. 7*, Program 16: "Death Sentence"	**InfoTrac® College Edition with InfoMarks™** • Vilbig, "Innocent on Death Row" • "A Dialogue of the Deaf? New International Attitudes and the Death Penalty in America"

Testing and Assessment	Course Management
Test Bank (available in the **Instructor's Manual**) Chapter 16: Multiple-choice, true/false, fill-in-the-blank, and essay questions. The **Test Bank** is also available in **ExamView®** electronic format that can be customized to fit your needs. **Book Companion Website** http://cj.wadsworth.com/siegel_crim_9e Assignable quiz questions: 15 multiple-choice, 5 true/false, and 5 essay questions.	**WebTutor™ Advantage on WebCT or Blackboard**  http://webtutor.thomsonlearning.com An online course management system preloaded with text-specific content and resources. **WebTutor™ Toolbox on WebCT or Blackboard** http://webtutor.thomsonlearning.com FREE online course management option.

Resource Integration Guide

Chapter 17: Corrections

Chapter Outline	Class Preparation and Lecture Tools	Student Mastery, Homework, and Tutorials
Chapter Resources	**Instructor's Manual** Chapter 17: Chapter Outline, Learning Objectives, Chapter Summary, Key Terms, Discussion Topics, Student Activities, and a **Test Bank.** **Multimedia Manager for Criminology: A Microsoft® PowerPoint® Tool** Lecture media tool with customizable PowerPoint® slides and images. **Transparency Masters for Criminology** Artwork from the main text that can be easily copied onto transparency acetates.	**Study Guide** Chapter17: Chapter Outline, Learning Objectives, Key Terms, and Practice Tests containing multiple-choice, true/false, fill-in-the-blank, and essay questions. **Student Companion CD-ROM** Contains critical-thinking activities tied to the chapter-opening vignette, chapter-specific content and quizzing, and a **CNN® Video** clip entitled "Life after Exoneration." **Book Companion Website** http://cj.wadsworth.com/siegel_crim_9e Outstanding study and review tools organized by chapter. **CriminologyNow™** http://cj.wadsworth.com/siegel_crim_9e A Web-based intelligent study system featuring diagnostic quizzes, a *Personalized Study Plan*, course management, and more.
History of Punishment and Corrections	**FFH Video** *Crimes and Punishment: A History* (CLJ6868)	**InfoTrac® College Edition with InfoMarks™** "Analysis: Prison Spending Outpaces Higher Education"
Probation		**InfoTrac® College Edition with InfoMarks™** "Spotlight on Probation in the Netherlands"
Intermediate Sanctions		**InfoTrac® College Edition with InfoMarks™** *Keywords:* alternative sanctions, community service restitution **Web Link** Day fine programs: **http://www.vera.org/publication_pdf/96_64.pdf**
Jails	**FFH Video** *The Second City: Inside the World's Largest Jail* (CLJ8699)	**Web Link** Jail Statistics: **http://www.ojp.usdoj.gov/bjs/jails.htm**
Prisons	**FFH Videos** • *Life Behind Bars* (EFA10167) • *Supermax, a Prison Within a Prison* (FNN9072)	**InfoTrac® College Edition with InfoMarks™** • "Cruel but Not Unusual: The Punishment of Women in U.S. Prisons" • "A History of Correctional Violence" *Keyword:* prison management companies
Parole	**FFH Video** *Parole Problems: Crime and Punishment* (EFA9175)	**Web Link** Federal Parole Board: **http://www.usdoj.gov/uspc**

Testing and Assessment	Course Management
Test Bank (available in the **Instructor's Manual**) **ExamView** Chapter 17: Multiple-choice, true/false, fill-in-the-blank, and essay questions. The **Test Bank** is also available in **ExamView®** electronic format that can be customized to fit your needs.	**WebTutor™ Advantage on WebCT or Blackboard** WebTUTOR Advantage http://webtutor.thomsonlearning.com An online course management system preloaded with text-specific content and resources.
Book Companion Website http://cj.wadsworth.com/siegel_crim_9e Assignable quiz questions: 15 multiple-choice, 5 true/false, and 5 essay questions.	**WebTutor™ Toolbox on WebCT or Blackboard** WebTUTOR ToolBox http://webtutor.thomsonlearning.com FREE online course management option.